CALIFORNIA NATIVE PLANTS
FOR THE GARDEN

CALIFORNIA NATIVE PLANTS
FOR THE GARDEN

Carol Bornstein, David Fross, Bart O'Brien

Cachuma Press
Los Olivos, California

Writers: Carol Bornstein, David Fross, Bart O'Brien
Editors: Marjorie Popper and John Evarts
Graphic Design, Production, and Proofreading: Katey O'Neill
Proofreading and Cartography: Sue Irwin
Printed in Singapore

Library of Congress Cataloging-in-Publication Data

Bornstein, Carol, 1953-
    California native plants for the garden / Carol Bornstein, David Fross, Bart O'Brien.-- 1st ed.
        p. cm.
    Includes bibliographical references.
    ISBN 0-9628505-8-6 -- ISBN 0-9628505-9-4
    1. Native plants for cultivation--California. 2. Native plant gardening--California. I.
Fross, David, 1946- II. O'Brien, Bart, 1956- III. Title.

SB439.24.C2B67 2005
635.9'51794--dc22

                                                                2005053148

Front cover: *Blue-eyed grass.* STEPHEN INGRAM
Back cover: *Sulfur buckwheat, Dr. Hurd manzanita, and other California natives.* STEPHEN INGRAM
Page i: *(clockwise from left) Douglas iris.* STEPHEN INGRAM; *Ashyleaf buckwheat.* STEPHEN INGRAM;
    Redwood sorrel. STEPHEN INGRAM; *Purple sage.* STEVE JUNAK
Page ii: *Spring display of California natives at the Santa Barbara Botanic Garden.* KAREN MUSCHENETZ
Page iii: *Island bush poppy.* DAN SONGSTER
Page iv (above): *Checkerbloom.* STEVE JUNAK
Page vi: *Matilija poppies.* KAREN MUSCHENETZ

CONTENTS

ACKNOWLEDGMENTS

It has been our pleasure to work with so many helpful and knowledgeable people in making *California Native Plants for the Garden* a reality.

Personal and professional thanks are wholeheartedly due to John Evarts and Marjorie Popper, our dedicated publishers and editors through thick and thin. It was John who first approached us with the idea of writing this book, to which we resoundingly agreed. Further thanks are due to Katey O'Neill for book design, production, and proofreading, and to Sue Irwin for proofreading and cartography.

We owe a special debt of gratitude to the reviewers of our manuscript, or portions thereof: Mary Carroll, Owen Dell, Greg Donovan, Stephen W. Edwards, Rainie Fross, Brett Hall, Judith Larner Lowry, Warren Roberts, Jennifer Scarano, Dan Songster, Jan Timbrook, Philip Van Soelen, and Ernie Wasson. This book has benefited immeasurably from their knowledge and efforts.

We wish to thank the following people for their insights, comments, and contributions which strengthened this book and made writing it easier: Randy Baldwin, Michael Barry, Michael Benedict, Jeff Bohn, Steve Boyd, Lilla and Peter Burgess, Betsy Clebsch, Betsy Collins, Cort Conley, Mike Curto, Joan DeFato, Lansing Duncan, Mike Evans, Olivier Filippi, Richard Fisher, Blair Fross, Tim Fross, Lorrae Fuentes, Clement Hamilton, Laurie Hannah, Dylan Hannon, Irene Holiman, Ginny Hunt, Susan Jett, Steve Junak, Robert Keeffe, Dave Kershaw, Sandra Landers, Patty Lindberg, Carol and John O'Brien, Ralph Philbrick, Roger Raiche, Leana Sims, M. Nevin Smith, Cliff Schmidt, Darcy and Paul Siegel, Roy Taylor, Matt Teel, Bernard Trainor, Richard Turner, and Walter Wisura.

Good photography always enhances gardening books and ours is no exception. We were fortunate to have so many talented photographers of California native plants and gardens involved in this project. Their photo credits are found with each caption.

We are deeply grateful to the many individuals who collectively create California native plant gardens (gardeners, growers, designers, contractors, and owners) for the wellspring of inspiration they so freely provided. Additional thanks go to the staff of Native Sons Nursery, Rancho Santa Ana Botanic Garden, and Santa Barbara Botanic Garden.

Finally, we remain indebted to those individuals who have written so eloquently and knowledgeably about California's native flora. Their words continue to move and enlighten us.

The Authors
August, 2005

DEDICATIONS

For my parents, Dara Emery, Ned Duke, and all my dear friends, plant-obsessed and otherwise.
Carol Bornstein

For Antoinetta DeFelice Ward.
David Fross

To Family: John and Carol, Terry and Randy, Shawn and Joan, Darcy and Paul, Ken and Marilyn, Otto and Notto, and Iggy. And to Gerda Isenberg for inspiration.
Bart O'Brien

*Pitkin Marsh lily, a rare subspecies of leopard lily, is the
centerpiece of a moist hillside garden in Lafayette.* STEPHEN INGRAM

INTRODUCTION

A fundamental question lies at the heart of any discussion of native plant cultivation. Why do we encourage and promote the use of native plants in our gardens and landscapes? The question is surely relevant in California, a state that encompasses unimaginable floristic riches but relies primarily on non-native species for most of its horticultural expression. Certainly there are compelling ecological, aesthetic, and functional reasons to support native plant use, and many gardeners are satisfied on these basic grounds. They remind us that California is blessed with thousands of plant species—many found nowhere else on Earth—which have evolved with, and in response to, our unique climates, soils, and fauna. Others are drawn to native plants for reasons that are relatively simple and more understated. Their interest is often rooted in a desire to reconnect with a plant community or develop a more coherent sense of place. It may be expressed by landscaping with species that bring the resinous fragrance of chaparral to a walkway, by planting in the backyard the same type of tree that shades a favorite wildland trail, or by growing a rare endemic that graces a nearby canyon. Whatever your reasons for planting natives, it is our hope that you find this book to be a thoughtful exploration of the pleasures, challenges, and rewards of gardening with California's remarkable flora.

California's native plant movement has a long and rich history. It is a story that involves individuals, groups, and institutions dedicated to the conservation, propagation, cultivation, and horticultural introduction of native species. Collectively, their work and research have encompassed every imaginable habitat and soil type in a state famous for its diversity. The names of teachers and mentors who influenced this body of knowledge are widely memorialized in the cultivar names given to California native plants, names like Theodore Payne, Lester Rowntree, Howard McMinn, Louis Edmunds, Marjorie Schmidt, Ken Taylor, James Roof, Gerda Isenberg, Percy Everett, Dara Emery, and Wayne Roderick. Of course, these innovators were joined by countless others who played a role in propelling the interest in natives: parents who encouraged young gardeners to experiment; botanists who coaxed students over the next hill to see a rare species; green-thumb enthusiasts who offered their neighbor a "new" plant to try.

The pioneers of native plant horticulture generated a wealth of information and new traditions in using the regional flora, yet most of our designed landscapes still feature plants from everywhere but California. With their peculiar amalgamation of plants from around the world, these generic landscapes offer little or no reference to place. They prevail in both private and public spaces in cities, suburbs, and rural towns. Indeed, for most Californians, native plants remain outside their daily experience, a vague veneer on the distant horizon.

This cottage garden in Los Angeles features a colorful blend of popular natives, including California poppy, elegant clarkia, deer grass, and lilac verbena. STEPHEN INGRAM

During the Gold Rush and the decades that followed, most of the settlers who came to California found a landscape and climate that were quite different from the well-watered places they had left behind. They were quick to interpret this new environment based on expectations and habits that they brought with them. Like elsewhere in the arid West, the success of their agricultural and industrial enterprises would ultimately require massive manipulation and control of the water supply through a complex system of dams, canals, concrete riverbeds, pipelines, and storage basins. Plants and seeds flowed in with the immigrants, and a foreign flora

Top: Various species of oaks and ceanothus are prominent in this 84-home neighborhood in Solvang that has been land-scaped with California natives. JOHN EVARTS
Bottom: The lush expanse of non-native grass at this ranch house is a fixture in California landscaping, while garden-worthy natives that grow nearby are excluded. SAXON HOLT

became part of the new cities. The nursery industry responded quickly to the demand, securing fan palms from the Mediterranean, rhododendrons from Asia, eucalyptus from Australia, and countless other exotic plants to match an exotic demand. A few raised their voices to protest these trends, but their concerns were no match for the appeal of water-loving turf and brilliant summer annuals that were beginning to fill the gardens, yards, and parkways of new homes and commercial centers. Compared to the rich greens, bright flowers, and bold textures of subtropical species, the natives must have seemed dull and gray. Moreover, the undeniable utilitarian success of exotic plants quickly overshad-owed the potential of California's flora. The demand by gardeners for novel plants also limited the interest in natives, although some of our showiest and best-known species, including Matilija poppy, coast redwood,

California poppy, and ceanothus, have for years been utilized here and in Europe, where they are renowned horticultural subjects. In recent decades, however, more California species have been making their way into our cultivated landscapes. And as they enter the main-stream, these plants challenge gardeners and designers to think in new ways about topics such as watering regimes, seasonal dormancy, and foliage color.

Several misconceptions about natives have stymied efforts to expand their use among landscapers, garden-ers, and nursery owners. The foremost fallacy is the notion that virtually all California natives do best with little or no water. It is true that much of our Mediterranean-climate flora is drought tolerant, an admirable characteristic that can be carried from the wild to the garden. Some plants, such as fremontias, even require a period of summer drought for any chance of success in California gardens. Most of the species included in this book are drought tolerant when planted in their natural range and perform beautifully without supplemental irrigation once established. Many, however, are flexible in the garden, and some will grow in traditionally watered gardens as if they had evolved there. Many others, such as white alder, south-ern maidenhair, or scarlet monkeyflower, require regu-lar irrigation to survive. Unfortunately, the emphasis on natives' drought tolerance and minimal maintenance requirements has tended to relegate them to drier, more marginal garden sites. They are repeatedly asked to shoulder the most difficult work in our landscapes while more favorable sites with generous water budgets and better soils are reserved for wide expanses of turf or yet another mix of exotic species.

Maintenance requirements are frequently neglected with native plant culture. Many have been grouped in a "low" or "no maintenance" category, a simplification that is often inaccurate. Such generalization is mislead-ing, since your site, budget, plant palette, and personal taste will determine the amount of care necessary in a particular garden or landscape. Some native plants are maintenance-free or nearly so, but most require regular, informed care to achieve a satisfactory appearance from one year to another. Pruning, monitoring insect popu-lations, replanting, weeding, and managing irrigation are as necessary with native plants as they are with any other group of cultivated plants.

The horticultural needs of most California native plants are similar to other groups of Mediterranean-climate plants. In fact, many gardeners are surprised to learn that the majority of natives are easily combined with the spectrum of exotic plants now found in our landscapes. There are exceptions, of course. A number of natives have exacting cultural requirements, such as those that cannot tolerate summer irrigation or absolutely require well-drained soil; these species will not survive

The deer grass and California buckeye in this Lafayette garden are examples of natives that are abundant in the wild and now increasingly used in horticulture. STEPHEN INGRAM

if their needs are ignored. For example, two of our most popular native genera, manzanita and ceanothus, are usually found in upland habitats with well-drained soils; gardeners often place them in heavy, poorly drained valley soils, predisposing the plants to difficulties or failure. Fortunately, there are many California plants that grow, even thrive, in conditions far different from those in their native habitats. They perform exceptionally well in an array of soils and climate zones.

Many of our native landscapes are seasonally dominated by muted tones of olive, gray, silver, and amber. An aesthetic shift is needed if we plan to invite these natives into our gardens. Compared to the often-vibrant greens of popular exotic species, these Mediterranean colors can be settling, even alluring. Moreover, some of our most attractive natives are dormant by midsummer. This is the time of year when the silvered silhouette of California buckeye, copper-brown seed heads of ashyleaf buckwheat, or the bleached stalks of foothill needlegrass add a distinctive beauty of their own. From this dormancy comes a seasonal elegance that is characteristic of all Mediterranean climates.

More than a century ago, native plant pioneer Theodore Payne began collecting wild species from the canyons and hillsides of southern California with the idea of using these plants in local gardens. A long legacy of advocacy has followed his lead and continues to this day. It is found in the research at botanic gardens, the educational work of organizations like the California Native Plant Society, the growth of websites featuring natives, and the publication of books like this. There are now thousands of native cultivars and species being grown in western gardens, and many previously hard-to-find plants are becoming available to gardeners. It is no longer uncommon to find rare and unusual plants at botanic garden sales or local native plant nurseries.

Natives offer a palette as diverse and varied as the people who have made California their home. These plants can provide aesthetic and habitat value, serve functional and conservation needs, or add an ethical or spiritual dimension to gardening. We have opportunities to renew and rediscover the native landscape in our gardens. It could be considered an act of regard. The principle requirement is patience. It begins with the simple act of planting and need not be grandiose: a California wild grape winding up an old chain-link fence or a small drift of deer grass in a shallow swale. Each gesture helps us to remember precisely who and where we are.

The Santa Barbara Botanic Garden, with its scenic meadow, was founded in 1926 in response to concern over the rapid disappearance of California's native flora. STEPHEN INGRAM

CHAPTER ONE

A SHORT HISTORY OF CALIFORNIA NATIVE PLANT HORTICULTURE

Caliornia's indigenous peoples have long had an intimate knowledge of native plants. This wisdom was gained through centuries of daily interaction with the surrounding flora and the utilization of common plants for every purpose imaginable, including food, medicine, shelter, fuel, fiber, dye, and ceremony. California Indians did not simply harvest plants; they actively managed many species to increase the quantity or improve the quality of desired products. Unfortunately, most immigrants who settled in California did not value or understand this knowledge, and much of it was lost through deliberate or inadvertent destruction of indigenous cultures and practices. California's tribes still use and manage native plants and vegetation, though on a greatly reduced scale.

Spanish missionaries and settlers brought the seeds of non-native horticultural and agricultural plants to California in the late 1700s and thus initiated the invasion of exotic species that continues to this day. They introduced a number of "classic" California garden plants, including figs, pomegranates, and olives. This period also witnessed the first deliberate introduction of ornamentals that have become widespread invasives, such as giant reedgrass and castor bean. At the same time, a number of weed species arrived, primarily in the coats of livestock, mixed with grain shipments, and within other accidental seed-carrying sources. Among these now ubiquitous plants were wild oats, mustards, brome grasses, and filaree. California native plants were probably cultivated at the missions, where many Native Americans lived and labored. A number of species, such as Matilija poppy, hollyleaf cherry, and California wild rose, may have been grown, although this is poorly documented.

California's early settlers largely ignored the horticultural potential of the native flora, but the novelty and astounding diversity of the state's plant life made a strong impression on some of the region's first explorers. Jean-Nicholas Collignon, a French scientist with the La Pérouse Expedition, was the first person to successfully collect and send California native plants to the Old World. Collignon gathered seeds and pressed plant specimens during La Pérouse's visit to the Spanish settlement of Monterey in September 1786. Collignon perished, along with the other members of the expedition,

following a shipwreck in 1788, but he had previously transferred some of his collections bound for France during stops at Macao and Kamchatka. Not long after his death, a seed from Collignon's samples produced the first plant originating from California—and all of western North America—to grow and bloom in the Jardin des Plantes in Paris, France. The species was sand verbena, and it was named and described in 1791 by the famous French naturalist Jean Baptiste Lamarck in his monumental *Encyclopedie Methodique, Botanique* and illustrated in *Tableau Encyclopedique.*

California Indians used native plant material for buildings like this partially constructed 'ap, a Chumash dwelling thatched with tule, at La Purisima Mission. DAVID FROSS

Other expeditions followed with increasing frequency, swelling the return flow of California plants and seeds to distant shores. Within a couple of generations, California species were being passionately sought out for horticultural purposes in Europe. Only 50 years after Collignon collected plants at Monterey, the first Old World cultivars of California native plants were selected and named. The earliest was Atrorubens currant, a selection named in 1837. It was derived from a species that ranges widely from California to British Columbia, and its exact geographic origin is unknown. The first cultivar of strictly California origin, Fastigiata Monterey cypress, was made in England a year later. The earliest known cultivar selected and named in California is *Ceanothus* 'Theodore Payne'. It dates from 1917 and has since been lost.

Top: The grasses beneath these valley oaks in the Santa Ynez Valley are a mixture of non-native species that arrived with Spanish settlers in the late 1700s. JOHN EVARTS
Middle: Exotic species that have become classic California garden plants were first introduced at settlements such as San Antonio Mission near Jolon. JOHN EVARTS
Bottom: California wild rose, such as this specimen growing at the Santa Barbara Botanic Garden, was probably among the few natives to be cultivated at California's Spanish missions. CAROL BORNSTEIN

By the early 20th century, a nexus of people and events that embraced California's Mediterranean climate and native flora was beginning to change statewide horticulture forever. Starting in the late 1890s and reaching a crescendo in the late 1920s, an influential group of forward-thinking Californians took it upon themselves to promote the beauty and appropriateness of native plants in gardens and landscapes. Their ideas, embodied in the Arts and Crafts movement that flourished in the first decades of the 1900s, celebrated local materials, craftsmanship, and a sense of place. Arts and Crafts ideals gave rise to architectural gems such as the Gamble House, the masterpiece of Charles and Henry Greene, and El Alisal, the idiosyncratic home of author Charles F. Lummis that he named after the immense California sycamore in his garden. During this same period, *plein-air* and impressionist painters were rediscovering the beauty of the state's natural landscapes, and thriving artists' colonies were established in Carmel, Laguna Beach, and elsewhere. William Wendt, John Gamble, Granville Redmond, and other artists depicted recognizable California species, such as poppy and coast live oak, in their signature California scenes. The stage was set for gardens to match these superlative examples of California art and architecture.

Two highly popular expositions featuring Mediterranean culture opened in 1915 and were a showcase for plants that, although not native, came

Theodore Payne buckwheat, seen in this private garden in Arroyo Grande, is one of several plants named in honor of the influential Los Angeles nurseryman. DAVID FROSS

Some California natives, such as this ceanothus at the Royal Horticultural Society's garden, Wisley, England, have long been used by European horticulturalists. BART O'BRIEN

from very similar climates. The Panama California International Exposition in San Diego's Balboa Park featured brilliant Spanish revival architecture complemented by a fusion of Mediterranean and tropical plantings; the Panama Pacific International Exposition in San Francisco's Marina District blended classical Mediterranean and Moorish architectural styles with a dynamic mixture of Mediterranean and standard landscape plants. During that same year, nurseryman Theodore Payne (1873-1963) was busy designing and planting the first public demonstration landscape of native plants. This five-acre garden in Exposition Park was adjacent to the Los Angeles County Museum, later renamed the Natural History Museum of Los Angeles County. Unfortunately, nothing remains of this key, influential garden. Theodore Payne operated his pioneering nursery from 1903 to 1962 and was a prominent voice for garden and landscape use of native plants until his death. A wild buckwheat, *Eriogonum parvifolium* var. *paynei,* and a lupine, *Lupinus paynei,* were named in his honor. Payne's visionary work is regarded as the touchstone of all California native plant horticulture. It is perpetuated by the Theodore Payne Foundation in Sun Valley, which was founded in 1960.

At the same time that native plant gardening began attracting a larger following, a handful of conservationists were raising concerns about the accelerating disappearance of California's wild flora as new cities, towns, and farms transformed the state's natural landscapes. In response to these intertwining issues, two large botanic gardens were created in the 1920s and dedicated exclusively to the conservation and promotion of California's native flora. Anna Dorinda Blaksley Bliss founded the Santa Barbara Botanic Garden in 1926 and Susanna Bixby Bryant established Rancho Santa Ana Botanic

Garden in 1927. (Originally, Rancho Santa Ana Botanic Garden was located in what is now Yorba Linda; it moved to Claremont in 1950.) Both gardens continue their advocacy and education efforts in conservation, research, and horticulture of California's flora.

Lester Rowntree (1879-1979) became the next widely known proponent of California's flora. She was a spirited and independent woman who chronicled her long, solo adventures through the wilds of California to gather seeds and search out unusual native plants. Two of her discoveries are still widely grown: *Sisyrinchium bellum* 'San Simeon' and *Ceanothus cuneatus* var. *rigidus* 'Snowball'. Rowntree captured the gardening public's imagination through her voluminous writings in newspapers and journals that were published in the United States and England. She also established a successful business selling seeds of native plants and authored two widely read gardening books, *Hardy Californians* (1936) and *Flowering Shrubs of California and Their Value to the Gardener* (1939).

In 1940 the Regional Parks Botanic Garden was established by the East Bay Regional Park District in Charles Lee Tilden Regional Park. Located in the Berkeley Hills, it became California's third exclusively native plant garden for the public. When the Regional

Queen Fabiola Ithuriel's spear (foreground) and Winifred Gilman sage border a pathway at Rancho Santa Ana Botanic Garden, founded in 1927. BART O'BRIEN

Top: The Regional Parks Botanic Garden, established in the 1940s in the Berkeley Hills, became the third public garden in the state dedicated exclusively to native plants. SAXON HOLT
Bottom: California native plants, including this stand of purple needlegrass, are prominently featured in the San Francisco Botanical Garden. SAXON HOLT

Parks Botanic Garden was threatened by a development scheme in 1965, the California Native Plant Society (CNPS) was founded to help save the site. Fortunately, CNPS's efforts were successful, and this nonprofit went on to become California's leading advocate for native plants. Today, CNPS continues to focus on education and the conservation and protection of California's native flora throughout the state.

During California's years of explosive growth and urbanization in the late 1940s through the early 1970s, interest in native plant horticulture persisted but did not thrive. Millions of people moved into the Golden State and very few of them had any experience with gardening in a Mediterranean climate. The promise of unending supplies of cheap water, coupled with the allure of lush lawns and exotic gardens that flourished and flowered year-round, pushed native plants to the fringes of gardens and public consciousness. During this period, only one book was published that championed California native plant horticulture: Lee Lenz's *Native Plants for California Gardens* (1956).

The record drought of the mid- to late-1970s was a wake-up call to many Californians. Public agencies, native plant enthusiasts, and others began to tout the water-conserving attributes of landscaping with the California flora. Within the space of five years, three influential publications were released that further stimulated the interest in native plant horticulture: The California Native Plant Society's *Native Plants—A Viable Option* (1977); Marjorie Schmidt's *Growing California Native Plants* (1980); and Lee Lenz and John Dourley's *California Native Trees and Shrubs for Garden and Environmental Use in Southern California and Adjacent Areas* (1981). An unfortunate legacy of this period was the belief that all California native plants were drought

tolerant and low maintenance. Some native plant advocates cautioned against such simplistic views, but much of the public soon began to equate native plant landscapes with no-water landscapes. As a result of this misperception, many homeowners were disappointed when their native plants failed to thrive in the absence of water or care. Native plant gardening is still burdened by such unrealistic expectations, but horticulturists are continually developing a more refined understanding of how these plants may perform in the garden.

Plant-happy Wayne Roderick (1920-2003) was among the most respected and knowledgeable native plant horticulturists of recent times. Wayne's extensive network of friends and colleagues, particularly those in

Jeffrey pine (foreground) and giant sequoia are seen here in the California Section of the University of California Botanical Garden, Berkeley, which is organized around plant communities. NATHAN SMITH

Top: Canyon Silver island snowflake, growing at the Santa Barbara Botanic Garden, is among the many new selections that should increase demand for California native plants in home gardens. STEPHEN INGRAM
Bottom: Renowned horticulturalist Wayne Roderick introduced many selections, such as Wayne's Dwarf blue-eyed grass shown here at Rancho Santa Ana Botanic Garden. BART O'BRIEN

western North America and Europe, enabled him to widely distribute the best of California's native plants to growers worldwide. Wayne's international standing was such that in 1992 he was the first non-British recipient of the prestigious Lyttel Trophy from the Alpine Garden Society in Great Britain. The fact that a number of California's native geophytes are now produced by the thousands by Dutch growers is but one small part of Wayne's enduring legacy. Three plant species were named in Wayne's honor: *Ceanothus roderickii, Erythronium purdyi* ssp. *roderickii,* and *Fritillaria roderickii.* Three of his numerous plant selections are included in the Plant Profiles section of this book: *Erigeron* 'W. R.'; *Garrya elliptica* 'Evie'; and *Heuchera micrantha* 'Martha Roderick'.

There are many important contributors currently working in the rapidly evolving field of native plant horticulture: gardeners, nursery people, designers, landscape contractors, restorationists, conservationists, farmers, and ranchers. New publications that extol

horticultural use and understanding of our flora, such as Judith Lowry's *Gardening With a Wild Heart* (1999), are reaching a wider, more receptive audience. An expanding number of native species and cultivars are coming into cultivation, and demand for them is increasing. More and more Californians are coming to appreciate the state's unique natural heritage, are rejoicing in a sense of place, and are realizing that conservation can begin in any home garden.

Coast redwood, the world's tallest tree, dominates this old-growth stand with lush understory vegetation at Prairie Creek Redwoods State Park. STEPHEN INGRAM

CHAPTER TWO

A LOOK AT CALIFORNIA PLANT LIFE

California's native flora is world famous for its splendor, variety, and high percentage of endemics. A number of its plants are best described by superlatives: coast redwood, the world's tallest living tree; giant sequoia, the world's most massive living tree; bristlecone pine, the world's oldest living conifer; and creosote bush, the world's oldest living shrub. With approximately 6300 native taxa, California claims the most diverse state flora in North America north of Mexico. Fully a third of California's native plants are found nowhere else. The state has also produced the largest number of native cultivars, now totaling over 6000, more than any other state in the union.

The feature most responsible for the unique California flora is the Mediterranean climate. This climate is characterized by long, warm, dry summers and relatively cool, moist winters. For the majority of California's Mediterranean plant life, "spring" commences with the autumn rains while "winter" is signaled by the dry summer months. California species are perfectly adapted to this cycle and cope with the warm-season drought in a variety of ways, ranging from summer dormancy to the capture of moisture from coastal fog. Four other areas of the world, all at similar latitudes, have a Mediterranean climate: the Mediterranean Basin, the Cape region of South Africa, central Chile, and southwestern Australia. Shrubs and trees from all the Mediterranean-climate regions tend to have small, leathery, evergreen leaves that are often aromatic. The presence of numerous annuals and bulbous species is another characteristic feature of these floras. Sadly, the world's Mediterranean-climate ecosystems are as threatened as rainforests, but the need to conserve them has yet to become a priority for the public, mass media, education community, or politicians.

The interactions between California's complex topography, geology, biota, and Mediterranean climate have created a truly specialized set of plants. This regional flora is so distinctive that it defines California's largest geographic unit, globally designated as the California Floristic Province. Such areas rarely conform to political boundaries, and the California Floristic Province is no exception. The southern edge of the province extends into northwestern Baja California, Mexico, while the northern boundary is less well-defined

and continues to be the subject of scholarly debate; some authorities extend the province into the southwestern corner of Oregon, while others draw the northern boundary at the Coast Ranges in Sonoma County, north of San Francisco Bay. For this book, we use the broader definition. The eastern boundary lies beyond California's tallest ranges, beginning at the arid, interior lands that comprise the Great Basin, Mojave Desert, and Sonoran Desert (known also within California as the Colorado Desert). The western boundary of the floristic province is the Pacific Ocean, although it includes coastal islands of California and Baja California.

A rich mosaic of plant communities is visible from this vista point on Highway 154 in Santa Barbara County and includes chaparral, grassland, and woodland. JOHN EVARTS

CALIFORNIA PLANT COMMUNITIES

In nature, groups of plants that are typically found growing together in similar environmental conditions are often characterized as a plant community. Knowledge about a species' natural habitat and the communities in which it occurs can help you successfully choose, combine, and care for plants in the designed landscape. Gardens modeled after a local plant community will have a high likelihood of success. Authorities define plant communities either broadly or narrowly. For this book, we use the broader definitions for common plant

Sources: Raven and Axelrod and Rancho Santa Ana Botanic Garden.

Above, left: California Floristic Province map. SUE IRWIN
Above: Toyon is abundant in this mature stand of chaparral in the Cleveland National Forest near Corona. BART O'BRIEN
Left: California's riparian woodlands, like this one along a placid stretch of the Santa Ynez River, are the natural habitat of many garden-worthy plants. JOHN EVARTS

communities in California. They are chaparral, coastal scrub, grassland, woodland, forest, alpine, desert scrub, and desert woodland.

California also has dozens of water-dependent plant communities, and they typically occur within one or more of the other communities described here. They range from those where moisture is relatively ephemeral, such as vernal pools, seasonal streams, and seeps, to

ones where it can be abundant, such as freshwater marshes, riparian woodlands, and desert oases. The complexity of these communities is difficult to neatly summarize, but the plants within them require the reliable presence of water at or near the surface—at least seasonally. In our gardens, plants from these moist habitats need ongoing access to water, as they rarely tolerate drought. California sycamore, white alder, Fremont cottonwood, creek dogwood, and giant chain fern are among the popular landscape plants that naturally grow in California's wetland environments.

Chaparral: The plant community that is perhaps most closely identified with our Mediterranean climate is chaparral. It is the primary source of California's bounty of garden shrubs, including mountain mahogany, toyon, summer holly, sugar bush, and the majority of manzanitas and ceanothus. Many chaparral plants are

characterized by thick, small, evergreen leaves and rigidly interwoven woody branches. They often form tall, dense stands of impenetrable vegetation. These drought-tolerant plants typically thrive in steep, hot, dry areas with shallow, well-drained, rocky soil and can be challenging to grow in gardens with heavy soils and frequent summer watering.

Coastal Scrub: Coastal scrub is dominated by showy, garden-worthy plants, such as sages, sagebrushes, and buckwheats. These plants often produce lush, larger leaves in the winter and tiny, gray-green leaves in the summer. Many species in this community are referred to as "subshrubs" since they are intermediate between woody shrubs and herbaceous perennials. Natural stands of these brittle plants are relatively low and are often easy to walk among. Coastal scrub is typically found in flatter, cooler coastal areas on soils that are either deeper or retain slightly less moisture than those that support chaparral.

Grassland: Native grassland communities in California are primarily composed of perennial bunchgrasses and sedges, liberally sprinkled with an array of annual and perennial wildflowers and numerous bulbs. Although no longer abundant, native grasslands, which include prairies and meadows, were once found from coastal bluffs to mountain valleys. Deer grass, checkerbloom,

Top: Coastal scrub, like this stand on Anacapa Island in Channel Islands National Park, is a plant community with a number of species used in home gardens. MARC SOLOMON
Bottom: The Santa Rosa Plateau Ecological Reserve in Riverside County includes rare remnants of native grassland that support perennial bunchgrasses, bulbs, and annuals. CAROL BORNSTEIN

blue-eyed grass, white mariposa lily, needlegrasses, sedges, lupines, and poppies are well-known grassland plants that provide stunning textures and colors in home gardens. However, gardeners wishing to model these attractive meadow-like settings will need to have a well-thought-out strategy for controlling weeds.

Top: This forest at Nelder Grove, Sierra National Forest, is dominated by giant sequoia and white fir and includes incense cedar, which is used in home gardens. BILL EVARTS
Bottom: California has a wide variety of oak-dominated woodlands, such as this blue oak woodland on Figueroa Mountain, Los Padres National Forest. JOHN EVARTS

Woodland: California is rich in woodland plant communities that are usually dominated by one or more species of oak or pine. In particular, the park-like oak woodlands of our foothills and mesas are among the most beloved natural plant communities in the state. Woodlands have a discontinuous overstory and are therefore distinguished from forests by numerous gaps in the canopy. As a result of these openings, woodlands have a varied pattern of sunlight and shade that creates a range of microhabitats for many plant and animal species. Their spatial diversity and rich plant palette are readily translated into beautiful gardens. Coast live oak, valley oak, California buckeye, coffeeberry, fuchsia-flowered gooseberry, hummingbird sage, creeping snowberry, western meadow rue, and currants are just a few of the many garden-friendly plants found in California's woodlands.

Forest: Forests have a nearly continuous canopy created by one or more types of trees. California's forest communities are divided into various categories, but for the purposes of this book, we have simply split them into two broad classes: mixed-evergreen forest and coniferous forest. Mixed-evergreen forest contains both coniferous and broad-leaved evergreen trees that retain leaves year-round, such as madrone and California bay, along with deciduous species, such as big-leaf maple and black oak. Coast redwood, incense cedar, various pines, and other cone-bearing trees dominate the canopy of coniferous forests. Plants inhabiting the understory of California's forests typically thrive where temperatures are cooler and moisture is more abundant. Forest plants

Top: Some excellent small-scale plants and selections for rock gardens grow in California's alpine plant communities, such as at Table Mountain, Inyo National Forest. STEPHEN INGRAM
Bottom: Desert woodland, shown here at Cima Dome in Mojave National Preserve, is the source of durable landscape plants for warm, inland gardens. STEPHEN INGRAM

Alpine: Alpine plant communities are found at and above tree line in California's higher mountain ranges. Alpine plants are notable for both their diminutive size and large showy flowers. Cliff-maids, alum roots, and penstemons are some of the genera represented in California's alpine flora. Many of these plants can be difficult to cultivate in low-elevation gardens, but some grow successfully in rock gardens or containers. Adaptable species from alpine plant communities combine well in rock gardens with other small-scale plants, such as dudleyas, coyote mints, or irises.

Desert Scrub and Desert Woodland: Although the deserts do not share California's Mediterranean climate and lie east and south of the California Floristic Province, they are the source of some excellent garden plants, especially for warm valleys and foothills. Desert scrub and desert woodland are two broad plant communities that occur in or along the edge of California's deserts. Desert scrub supports such distinctive species as Great Basin sagebrush, desert beargrass, apricot mallow, chuparosa, and Mojave yucca. Desert woodlands are home to desert willow, singleleaf pinyon, palo verde, and desert lavender.

are well adapted to deeper soils that often contain more organic material than those of chaparral or woodlands. California's forests offer a wealth of plants for shady gardens such as western mock orange, longleaf barberry, wild ginger, western sword fern, and redwood sorrel.

Spicebush, giant chain fern, and wild ginger make a pleasing combination in this Lafayette garden. STEPHEN INGRAM

CHAPTER THREE

DESIGNING A CALIFORNIA NATIVE GARDEN

Designing a garden with California's native flora is a rewarding experience that offers new opportunities and fresh perspectives. A broad array of plants is available to create beautiful landscapes in a variety of styles, ranging from naturalistic to highly formal. By using fundamental design principles, careful plant selection, and thoughtful maintenance, you can establish a garden that celebrates California's diverse flora, Mediterranean climate, and tradition of native plant horticulture.

Thematic elements in garden design are limitless and the most engaging appeal to all the senses. A landscape might be layered and diverse, reflecting a concern for wildlife, or it might be tightly disciplined and utilize few species, embracing a minimalist philosophy. Gardens are often a dynamic expression of our creativity, and they may take many forms. For example, they can be dramatic and feature bold color combinations, offer a collection of plants from a specific region, or help recreate a cherished setting from childhood memories. Whether daring and provocative or tranquil and introspective, all gardens benefit from classic design conventions—balance, contrast, focal points, and repetition—that help to provide unity and rhythm. These principles apply to native and non-native gardens alike.

From the earliest gardens of China and the Middle East to the present, landscape designs reflect one of two principal models. The first is based on an interpretation of orderly paradise and evolved from the walled gardens of Persia. The walls define and contain the garden and exclude the outside world. These gardens have distinctive geometric patterns and symmetrical balance and are often characterized as formal. The second model is based on idealized versions of natural landscapes and is typically considered informal. These gardens are constructed with asymmetrical grace and lack the geometric lines of formal gardens. Order is still imposed by the design but is closely aligned with a natural landscape.

With rare exceptions, gardens composed exclusively or primarily of native California plants have been informal or naturalistic in style. Landscape professionals and homeowners who use natives rarely build their designs around the concepts of symmetry, straight lines, and highly manicured plants. Yet the California flora is so diverse that it offers plants for every design possibility, including highly structured, formal landscapes.

Native plant horticulture combines both art and science, and only our imaginations limit the way native plants are used in gardens.

The vibrant colors of shrubby monkeyflower, lilac verbena, and coral bells are put to effective use among sandstone boulders in this Montecito landscape. STEPHEN INGRAM

Regardless of landscape style, California's mild weather allows for year-round gardening in most of the state. While ardent gardeners may relish this 12-month opportunity, others find it somewhat daunting. One way to create a seasonal respite from gardening is to design a landscape that mirrors the natural cycles of our Mediterranean climate. This approach acknowledges a quiet or dormant period in summer and early fall, when horticultural activities can wane. In such a garden, summer dormancy is a design element where dormant plants contribute dramatic shapes, colors, and textures that complement their evergreen companions. For example, the silvered, leafless branches of California buckeye offer striking form and color against a dark green background of coast live oak foliage. The bleached stalks and flowing textures of dry foothill needlegrass present a startling counterpoint to the burgundy trunks of manzanitas or glossy green leaves of many ceanothus. Pleasing contrasts like these add interest to the garden and help connect it to the natural patterns and rhythms of the California landscape.

If you find the subdued colors of seasonal dormancy too drab, you can introduce more vibrancy by creative

Flowing water, sitting areas, and outdoor alcoves are just some of the enticing elements in this multi-level landscape that features California natives in Lafayette. SAXON HOLT

plant selection and garden design. Begin by spicing up summer's earthy tones with late-blooming asters, goldenrods, and California fuchsias. The handsome bark of palo blanco or the bold foliage of incensio or Our Lord's candle will offset the drought-deciduous phase of a coastal scrub or chaparral garden. California's native flora offers foliage in shades of green as well as silvers, grays, blues, and whites, and by planting species that hold their leaves year-round you can enjoy these colors through all the seasons. The glossy, green leaves of Catalina cherry or the deep, leathery green of coffeeberry defy the dry seasons, as do the bold, glaucous leaves of white sage and chalk dudleya or the silvery-white, felted leaves of Canyon Silver island snowflake. You can also augment our natives by using horticulturally compatible species from other Mediterranean and dryland climate regions, such as lavenders, agaves, and alstroemerias.

SITE ANALYSIS

Garden design begins with an assessment of the opportunities and challenges of a given site and how they relate to the intended use of your landscape. A thoughtful analysis should examine broad regional climatic patterns as well as the intricate details of the immediate garden area, such as its topography, soil, and natural features. Taking photographs, making note of native plants in the neighborhood, checking prevailing wind patterns, and speaking with local gardeners are the kind of activities that greatly contribute to an effective site analysis. If there is no urgency to begin work on

Above: Surrounded by native shrubs in a Lafayette backyard, this golden-green patch of California fescue has been cut back as it heads into summer dormancy. SAXON HOLT
Left: Native evergreen shrubs, such as this coffeeberry at the Santa Barbara Botanic Garden, provide welcome greenery throughout the seasons. JOHN EVARTS

Top: David's Choice sandhill sagebrush (foreground) and Canyon Prince wild rye are good plants for gray foliage, seen here at Rancho Santa Ana Botanic Garden, Claremont.
STEPHEN INGRAM

Middle: Gardeners seeking yellow flowers in late summer or fall can try growing California goldenrod, like these at the Santa Barbara Botanic Garden.
STEPHEN INGRAM

Bottom: This Catalina California fuchsia in an Arroyo Grande garden is typical of cultivars of this species: durable, drought tolerant, and fall blooming.
DAVID FROSS

hills and mountains, known as an orographic effect, adds considerably to precipitation totals as elevation increases. Nearby landforms may influence air currents that control the penetration of coastal fog or exposure to Santa Ana winds. Coastal fog is a factor in some areas because it reduces evapotranspiration rates and adds critical amounts of summer moisture. Each climatic nuance can affect the success or failure of a particular plant or modify its sun or shade requirement.

Two important topographical characteristics of any site are the degree and direction of its slope. Soil drainage improves as slopes become steeper. This is significant because a number of native species require good drainage; many that perform poorly in heavy soil on level sites can be grown with confidence in the same soil if there is at least some modest slope to the land. Another benefit provided by sloping terrain comes from the natural tendency of cold air to flow to and collect in lower areas. Plants that cannot be grown in low-lying sites because of frost often succeed on slopes just above basins and valley floors. The direction of a slope, referred to as its aspect, influences a garden site for this simple reason: south-facing slopes receive far more solar energy than north-facing slopes. Consider the aspect of your site when selecting plants for the landscape.

Evaluating the natural features of a site provides opportunities to express local identity and regional character in the garden. Nearby plant communities, remnant native trees, or even small fragments of native vegetation offer design ideas and indications of a site's potential. Other features, such as natural drainages and rock outcrops, are elements to consider when enhancing the character of the site. As part of this process, detail the existing views and note the desirable scenes that invite framing as well as those that might require screening; this assessment should be done during the

Some pre-existing natural features of this site, such as large boulders and mature oaks, were carefully incorporated into the design of this Montecito landscape. STEPHEN INGRAM

the garden, study your site through a cycle of seasons. Whether starting with a vacant lot or renovating an existing landscape, these same practices apply.

Regional climatic information provides a basic framework from which to begin your site analysis, but knowledge of your local microclimate is a planning tool of equal or greater importance. Topography plays a key role in determining microclimates. For example, winter temperatures in a basin or valley can be significantly colder than in the adjacent foothills. Rainfall is also affected by topography, since the lifting of air masses by

Sun-loving sages and buckwheats are among the ecologically compatible plants from California and elsewhere in this Santa Barbara garden. CAROL BORNSTEIN

Sensible designs group plants together that have similar needs for water and sunlight, such as this vine maple and western sword fern in a Berkeley garden. SAXON HOLT

day and at night, so you can design a plan that blocks objectionable lights if necessary.

It is a good idea to have a laboratory test your irrigation water. Water quality may be a problem in areas of California that have excessive salt or mineral content in irrigation water. Some native plants are sensitive to water containing high levels of sodium, chloride, and boron, which often cause chlorosis and leaf burn. The University of California Cooperative Extension Office in your county can help identify regional problems and direct you to commercial laboratories for water-quality testing. If you plan to irrigate with gray or reclaimed water, be aware that they may have high concentrations of salts. This problem is often not immediately apparent, but will have a long-term negative effect on the plants that you are able to grow in the garden. The build-up of salts is a much greater issue for sites with heavy clay soils, as it is often impossible to leach salts from such soils.

When considering a site, be mindful of soil characteristics such as pH, depth, texture, and chemical composition. This information can be ascertained through a horticultural soil test. California's complex geology has resulted in a mosaic of rocks that have weathered into many classes of soils. Gardeners can encounter soil conditions ranging from heavy clay with an underlying hardpan to fast-draining sand in a stabilized dune. Such contrasting soil types may even occur in the same garden area. Some California soils have unique chemical properties that can limit your options. For example, "serpentine" soils, derived from serpentinite, California's state rock, are composed of iron and magnesium silicates and are very low in available nutrients, particularly calcium; these soils, primarily found in central and northern California, contain some of the state's rarest plant species but exclude many others.

PLANT SELECTION AND PLACEMENT

The natural habitat of a species can be a valuable guide to its horticultural requirements in the garden. Some familiarity with habitat types and plant communities will help you choose appropriate and compatible combinations of native plants. Ecological data is readily available for most California plants, while authoritative information regarding the origin of hybrids and cultivars can be more difficult to ascertain.

Grouping plants according to their horticultural needs informs the design process and helps create a manageable garden. This approach will reduce maintenance activities and insure a landscape filled with healthy vegetation. Species that prefer well-drained soils and full sun, such as fremontias, ceanothus, and manzanitas, can be planted together on an open, south-facing slope; moisture-loving plants, such as coast redwood, southern maidenhair, leopard lily, and scarlet monkey-flower, can be combined on a cool, north-facing bank. Some species have habitat needs that are more specialized. For example, island alum root, canyon

The sulfur buckwheat blossoms are eye-catching, but this Lafayette garden derives year-round interest from the foliage colors and textures of many plants. STEPHEN INGRAM

sunflower, California polypody, and a number of other perennials prefer dry, shady sites; plant them beneath oaks and other trees that are intolerant of summer moisture.

Consider foliage color and texture, along with plant shape and size, before thinking about flowers. Flowers are a more ephemeral element, and a garden is defined most of the year by plant structure, foliage color, and texture. Repetition of colors and textures helps to weave the garden into a logical whole; this is also achieved by using recurring forms. Shrubs and trees with similar shapes add a strong structural framework or foundation to the landscape.

Appropriate plant placement and spacing requires discipline. It is difficult to imagine that a coast live oak from a one-gallon container could shade a large portion of your garden in coming years. With maturity, the oak's spreading root system and canopy will have a pronounced effect on the surrounding environment. Both professionals and home gardeners make the mistake of providing inadequate space for plantings to reach their mature size, particularly groundcovers and hedges. As the plants grow, their natural form and health may be compromised by a lack of space, forcing gardeners to compensate by pruning. This results in excessive green waste. If open spaces between young plants are too stark for you,

These drifts of Point Sal sage and Santa Cruz Island buckwheat (behind) create a handsome border, even in summer, along a Montecito driveway. STEPHEN INGRAM

Southern maidenhair lines both sides of this walkway (with a giant chain fern on the right) and is a unifying element in this Berkeley side yard. STEPHEN INGRAM

Top: Native plants from California and other Mediterranean climates have been effectively combined in this Berkeley hillside landscape. STEPHEN INGRAM
Bottom: Manzanitas and Pacific wax myrtle create a pleasing backdrop for lavenders from the Mediterranean, which surround a mailbox in Lafayette. STEPHEN INGRAM

one option is to fill in the gaps with fast-growing, short-lived plants or annual wildflowers. These will eventually be overgrown by the other long-lived plants.

Landscapes are dynamic, and all gardens require periodic reevaluation, replacement planting, and design modifications. A variety of events, large and small, will precipitate such changes. For example, a previously sunny area, now shaded by a white alder, is replanted with shade-tolerant species; a one-gallon specimen replaces a large, mature fremontia blown over in a winter storm; or a ceanothus that grew larger than anticipated is pulled out to make room for its neighbors. Thoughtful design and planning are essential for success, but so is a willingness to respond to a garden's evolving character.

COMBINING CALIFORNIA NATIVES WITH PLANTS FROM OTHER REGIONS

Some gardeners believe that California native plants are so different, or so difficult to grow, they should be cultivated separately from non-natives. But such segregation is neither necessary nor warranted. Plants from California are grown in gardens around the world, where they thrive alongside other species that share their horticultural preferences. At home, California natives are easily combined with many plants from other parts of the globe, particularly those from the Mediterranean-climate regions: central Chile, southwestern Australia, the Cape region of South Africa, and the Mediterranean Basin. Some of the most familiar plants in our designed landscapes hail from these areas and make excellent partners with the native flora. A few popular examples are listed below.

- Chile: Chilean wine palm, puyas, alstroemerias, nasturtiums.
- Australia: eucalyptus, grevilleas, Australian tea tree, acacias, blue hibiscus, bottlebrushes, lilac vine,

kangaroo paws.
- South Africa: proteas, pincushions, geraniums, jade plant, aloes, numerous bulbs (freesia, gladiolus, watsonia, calla lily, clivia, baboon flower), many species in the sunflower family (gazania, blue marguerite, freeway daisy), agapanthus, iceplants, restios.
- Mediterranean Basin: Italian stone pine, Aleppo pine, olive, cork oak, strawberry tree, oleander, rockroses, many classic herbs (rosemary, lavender, thyme, oregano), bulbs (tulip, daffodil, crocus).

When designing a garden that includes native plants, you do not need to limit the plant palette to these Mediterranean partners alone. Water-thrifty plants from arid habitats, such as the Chihuahuan Desert or the steppes of Asia, are perfectly appropriate for gardens where minimal irrigation helps to define the design. For example, a desert theme might include

California natives can be paired with species from other regions, as with these desert bluebells and Huachuca agave (from the Southwest) in a Tucson garden. STEPHEN INGRAM

Above: Landscapes that include native plants will attract birds, such as this immature male Lesser Goldfinch perched in a Matilija poppy near Santa Ynez.
HUGH P. SMITH
Left: A pipevine swallowtail butterfly alights on a California Dutchman's pipe at a garden in Sebastopol.
PHILIP VAN SOELEN

California's desert willow, apricot mallow, and beavertail cactus with a host of agaves, cacti, and sages from Mexico. Alternatively, a cool, shady woodland of native spicebush, coral bells, and ferns would be a fitting environment for Japanese maples, camellias, and hellebores. Several other reliable standards in the California landscape include New Zealand flax, citrus, and Indian hawthorn from Asia, and jacaranda, bougainvillea, and trumpet vines from Brazil. All of these plants can complement California natives in a thoughtfully designed, aesthetically pleasing, and ecologically sensible garden. Some of these non-native plants can escape into and degrade adjacent wildlands in parts of California. Consult with your local CNPS chapter, botanic garden, cooperative extension office, or the California Invasive Plant Council for information pertinent to your area.

HABITAT GARDENS

Designing a habitat garden will have a special appeal to birders, butterfly lovers, and other naturalists who want to create an inviting environment for wildlife. A garden filled with native plants inevitably attracts birds and butterflies as well as beneficial insects, lizards, and other creatures. Native plants provide the key ingredients of food and shelter and in turn are pollinated and dispersed by wildlife. These landscapes can provide vital habitat for organisms whose natural homes have been diminished or fragmented due to human impacts.

Follow these basic guidelines in designing and maintaining a habitat garden:
- Ensure a steady source of food year-round by including a variety of plants that flower or fruit in each season.
- Create continuous layers of vegetation to attract species that occupy different niches.
- Leave some dead snags in trees as nesting or perching sites for raptors and small mammals. Create brush piles—away from structures—as shelter for small

mammals, birds, and insects.
- Supply water for drinking, bathing, and cooling.
- Resist the temptation to prune every spent flower. Let some ripen to provide nutritious seed.
- Restrict access of dogs and cats in the garden; they may chase and kill small mammals, lizards, birds, butterflies, and other wildlife.
- Avoid use of toxic chemicals that may upset food chains and harm all life forms.

PLANTING A MEADOW

Meadows offer an inventive alternative to the resource-intensive lawn, and they can be designed to suit most soil types in either sunny or partly shaded sites. Both aesthetic and functional, meadows can supply an ever-changing display of seasonal colors and textures. A meadow garden of California natives might feature a colorful carpet of seaside daisy, San Bruno Mountain golden aster, blue-eyed grass, Cape Mendocino reed-grass, and checkerbloom, or simply contain a blend of dune sedge and yarrow.

Top: Checkerbloom, California poppy, and Douglas iris bloom among bunchgrasses in this native plant meadow at the San Francisco Botanical Garden. SAXON HOLT
Bottom: Patience and weed control are needed to establish a meadow garden, such as this one in Solvang that includes penstemon, yarrow, and native grasses. STEPHEN INGRAM

Establishing a meadow garden requires patience, thoughtful planning, and appropriate care. Weed control is essential and best accomplished prior to planting. Options for planting are broadcasting seed, planting from containers, or a combination of the two. This choice is determined by your budget, plot size, time frame, availability of materials, and subsequent maintenance. It is critical that grasses have time to become established before wildflowers are added, as the latter can easily overwhelm the young grasses. Plant spacing, irrigation methods, and maintenance requirements will vary depending on the plant palette. Other than follow-up weeding, most meadows can be cared for with an annual pruning in late summer or fall, using a mower or string trimmer. Wait until some seeds have ripened before cutting to insure a new crop of wildflowers and grasses next year. A layer of organic mulch is useful for suppressing weeds and conserving soil moisture; however, it is not suitable when starting meadows from seed, as seeds require open soil with minimal or no cover, or a gravel mulch, for successful germination.

WILDFIRE AND GARDEN PLANNING

California's native vegetation has evolved in response to wildfire, and many species depend upon periodic burns for rejuvenation or reproduction. For more than a century, public agencies have endeavored to suppress wildland fires, and this policy has resulted in dangerously high levels of flammable vegetation in many areas. As our cities and towns continue to sprawl, an increasing number of Californians live in the urban-wildland interface where the threat of fire is particularly significant. Homeowners can begin to prepare for wildfire by replacing building materials that are invitations for disaster, such as wooden shingles, siding, and decks. In addition to appropriate home construction, they can take steps to increase the fire safety of their landscape.

There are conflicting opinions regarding which plants are fire-safe versus which are highly flammable. Some native plants, such as chamise, and exotics such as eucalyptus, have been identified as poor choices for home landscapes at the wildland's edge. Experts do agree that beneficial practices include removing dead branches, selectively thinning or "limbing-up" woody plants, and keeping vegetation away from the roof and eaves of any building in a high-fire area. Realize, however, that in a firestorm, everything will burn.

Prudent homeowners will want to follow these safety precautions in high-fire zones:

- Periodically reduce fuel loads by thinning trees and shrubs or heavily pruning species that can resprout from basal burls. Concentrate on removing dead and diseased wood as needed, at least annually.
- Cut back grasses and wildflowers as they brown, although you may want to leave some patches for seed harvesting, reseeding, or wildlife.
- Limit leaf litter and mulch layers to 4 inches in depth.
- Break up "fire ladders," especially near structures. These vertical columns of vegetation, from ground level to tree canopy, provide a continuous fuel supply that enables fire to spread rapidly throughout the landscape.
- Create firebreaks to prevent opportunities for fire to spread horizontally across large swaths of vegetation.
- Where appropriate, maintain a greenbelt of moisture-retentive, low-growing vegetation in a 30-foot-wide strip surrounding your home. Avoid denuding the landscape, however, as bare ground is more susceptible to erosion and reduces important wildlife habitat. Create a transition zone beyond the greenbelt by

Wildfires may be slowed by wide belts of well-hydrated, low-growing vegetation, such as this swath of Twin Peaks #2 coyote brush in La Honda. STEPHEN INGRAM

Top: Canyon Gray California sagebrush is an attractive groundcover that produces a minimum of green waste in this Montecito landscape. STEPHEN INGRAM
Bottom: Yankee Point ceanothus, non-native rockrose (bottom), and coast live oak are key elements in this water-conserving, low-maintenance landscape in Solvang. JOHN EVARTS

fragmenting dense native vegetation into smaller groups or establishing new plantings in distinct drifts.
• Keep vegetation adequately hydrated.

SUSTAINABLE, LOW-IMPACT DESIGN

A new era is burgeoning among Californians seeking ecological and innovative ways to garden. They support a concept known as "sustainable landscaping" where the goal is to consume minimal resources and create minimal waste, thereby helping to preserve natural ecosystems. Practitioners of sustainable, low-impact gardening are concerned about issues such as water supply, green waste, pesticides, and sources of landscape materials.

To design and maintain a sustainable, low-impact landscape, follow these guidelines:
• Select plants that fit the microclimates and spaces of the site, as these will thrive with less care.
• Create varied habitats that can attract and support beneficial wildlife.
• Use water and other limited resources in moderation.

• Compost green waste from pruning and weeding, and return it to appropriate sections of the garden as beneficial mulch or soil amendment.
• Avoid plants that are or have the potential to become invasive.
• Practice integrated pest management.
• Replace power equipment with hand tools.
• Make use of recycled, found, or local materials rather than products from afar.
• For hardscape features, consider alternative products such as pervious paving and rammed earth.
• Dispose of your construction waste responsibly.

With careful planning, these simple yet effective practices foster gardens that are both beautiful and harmonious with nature. Gardeners can indulge their creative talents while simultaneously championing stewardship of the natural world.

A hillside garden in Lafayette displays a diverse mix of natives, including woolly blue curls, shrubby monkeyflower, manzanitas, California fescue, and Calistoga yarrow. SAXON HOLT

CHAPTER FOUR

NATIVE PLANT CARE

After completing the creative and detailed process of designing a native plant landscape, you are ready for the next step: implementing your garden plan. This stage encompasses some of the most enjoyable gardening activities, including the purchase, installation, and care of plants. These are the actions that will bring your garden design to life.

The optimal time for planting most California natives is autumn, except in the mountains, high deserts, and other cold-winter areas of the state. Planting during this period—at the beginning of the rainy season—gives natives many months to establish root systems that will be much better prepared to survive California's long, warm, dry summers. Plants installed in fall also produce more new growth and flowers the following spring or summer than those that are planted later.

For the native plants of our Mediterranean climate, California's fall months are comparable to early spring in the rest of temperate North America. At this time soils are still warm but are not too hot for tender new roots. Capillary movement of water is upward, toward the soil surface. Nights are cool, promoting less shoot growth and more root growth, and days are also relatively cool, leading to less stress on new plantings. These cooler conditions are less favorable to many soil-borne pathogens that are apt to infect root systems that are broken or damaged during planting. California natives can be successfully planted outside this time period, but they will initially require much more care and attention. The exceptions to this general rule are those species that come from year-round moist environments, such as coast redwood, white alder, and giant chain fern. Although it is best to plant these water-loving species during fall and winter, you can be more flexible as to when you install them, but realize that they need adequate irrigation throughout their lives.

SITE PREPARATION AND SOIL MANAGEMENT

The celebrated diversity of California's native flora is due in part to the state's tremendously varied geology and geography. Some of our most reliable plants for horticulture, such as coast live oak, coffeeberry, and toyon, are widespread and found on a variety of soil types. Another group of natives is distinguished by its demand for well-drained soils and intolerance of water-logged situations. Plants that occupy steep slopes typical of chaparral plant communities fall into this category; proper site preparation and soil management can be crucial to their success in the garden. Still other species

This informal landscape in Montecito includes coffeeberry (foreground) and coast live oak, two of California's most adaptable plants for gardens. STEPHEN INGRAM

naturally occur only on soils that are characterized by a particular mix of nutrients and physical properties. Two examples are leather oak, which is restricted to serpentine soils, and saffron buckwheat, which is limited to volcanic outcrops. However, these two species, and many like them, can grow in soil types not found in their natural habitats and are easily cultivated in most home gardens.

If your goal is to create a landscape that is well adapted to your site, it is best to select plants that are compatible with your garden's soil conditions. Unless the soil has been significantly modified physically or chemically, such as by heavy compaction or over-fertilization, there is usually no need to add amendments; this once-routine practice is unnecessary in most cases. However, if your landscape plan includes natives that are highly incompatible with your soil, you will need to alter the soil structure. Plants that require excellent drainage often fail in heavy, slow-draining clay soil; plants that thrive in rich, moisture-retentive soils may not succeed in nutrient-poor, fast-draining sandy soil.

Top: Saffron buckwheat, growing over a retaining wall in Montecito, is an example of a plant from a specialized habitat that can thrive in home garden soils. STEPHEN INGRAM
Bottom: The plants in this mixed border at the Leaning Pine Arboretum, Cal Poly, San Luis Obispo benefit from the improved drainage of a raised bed. DAVID FROSS

One solution that works in both these cases is to amend the soil with organic matter; this adds nutrients and beneficial microorganisms and also improves soil structure. As organic matter becomes embedded in the pore spaces between large sand particles, it acts like a sponge and enhances the fertility and moisture-holding capacity of sandy soils. In heavy soils, it increases porosity and drainage by binding the fine clay particles together into larger aggregates.

When adding organic matter to the soil, work it into the entire garden area, not just the planting holes. A one-time application of organic matter will not provide long-term results since this material breaks down rapidly in our Mediterranean climate, leaving the parent soil with most of its original physical and chemical properties. To succeed with this technique requires an ongoing program of soil amending and mulching. If you are primarily cultivating chaparral or desert plants, use organic matter sparingly, if at all, since this can lead to excessively rich soil for species that are better adapted to the nutrient-poor soils of their native habitats.

For gardeners with heavy soils who wish to grow plants that require good drainage, consider mounding the native soil into berms. Mix gravel into the berm or mound if your plants need especially good drainage; sprinkle the soil surface with some of the gravelly substrate as well. Strive to create mounds that visually blend with the overall topography of the site—otherwise they will look contrived and unnatural. A few well-placed boulders can help create fast-draining pockets and add visual interest. Another approach is to build raised beds and amend the soil as desired. Before you create mounds, berms, or raised beds, it is a good idea to break up any shallow, preexisting hardpan layer.

When planting in adobe clay, it helps to premoisten the garden area to a workable consistency before the autumn rains begin. This gives you a chance to cultivate the soil when its moisture level is neither too dry nor too wet. Once rains have saturated a heavy soil, planting activity is inadvisable unless there has been an extended warm spell that has dried the ground. Cultivating wet clay soils promotes the formation of unworkable clods and simultaneously increases compaction.

Most garden soils, even in newly cultivated areas, will contain mycorrhizal fungi appropriate for the native plants that would naturally be found in the vicinity. Mycorrhizal fungi are beneficial organisms that inhabit roots of nearly all plants. These fungi assist their host plants with nutrient absorption from the soil. Some nurseries are inoculating their container-grown stock with these fungi, though the practice is not without controversy. On heavily graded sites where no topsoil remains, new gardens will almost certainly benefit from planting specimens that have been inoculated with mycorrhizal fungi. Another technique is to add these organisms directly to the soil when planting.

OBTAINING PLANTS AND SEEDS
Buying native plants is an adventure. It may require a bit of research because some California plants are not widely grown. Your quest for a particular plant will often lead to specialty nurseries and smaller growers. It may take time to obtain all of the plants that you want for your garden, as some natives are grown in small

Native plants not carried by retail nurseries are often found at specialty nurseries or plant sales, such as this fall sale at the Santa Barbara Botanic Garden. JOHN EVARTS

quantities and may only be available in one season of the year.

When buying seeds, it is a good idea to inquire about their freshness, since seed viability varies with species, age, and storage method. Always purchase your native plants and seeds from reputable nurseries and suppliers. Among other attributes, such businesses accurately label their plants, sell only properly permitted plants, pay royalties on patented and trademarked plants, and have a knowledgeable staff.

Collecting plants, seeds, divisions, or cuttings from public lands is illegal unless appropriate local, state, and federal permits are first obtained. A number of California's horticultural treasures are endangered in their wild habitats due to over-collecting, and numerous others may be pushed to the brink of extinction if illegal collecting activities are not stopped. Do not hesitate to ask vendors questions about their sources of native plants, especially when endangered, rare, or large specimens of slow-growing species are offered for sale.

When selecting plants at the nursery, keep in mind these guidelines:
- The plant with a balanced "root to shoot" ratio is the best buy. Do not automatically choose the largest or the smallest plant; the largest plant is likely older and root-bound (or it may have been over-fertilized), while the smaller plant may be too young and have a fragile rootball.
- Ask the sales staff if they will allow you to inspect the root system. The best plants will have numerous healthy white roots. (There are exceptions, such as barberries, which have yellow roots.) The roots should knit the rootball together but should not form a solid mass. Root inspection is not always possible, and it is not advisable for plants with fragile root systems, such as bush poppy, Matilija poppy, and some manzanitas.
- The lushest plant in the block may have received too much fertilizer and may not have a fully developed root system that is able to support all that foliage. Such plants are often prone to pests and diseases.
- Check the crown (where the stem meets the root) of the plant. For the majority of California native trees and shrubs, it is important that the crown is at, or slightly above, the soil level. If the crown is buried, the plant may be susceptible to crown rot. If the crown is too high, the plant may not be able to hold itself upright after it has been placed in the garden or a new container.
- Smell the soil at the drainage hole of the pot. Do not buy the plant if the soil has a foul stench; this indicates that the plant's root system is rotting.

PLANTING

Take extra time and care when setting a new plant in the ground, since poor planting techniques can compromise its success. The hole for each plant should be twice as wide as the size of the rootball. Avoid digging a hole that is perfectly round and smooth, as this can discourage root penetration into the surrounding soil. Make sure the rootball is moist before removing the plant from the container. Gently loosen the edges of any rootball that has formed a tight mat while in the nursery pot. Where gophers are a serious problem, consider enclosing the entire rootball with 1 inch or ½ inch aviary wire, leaving a small opening at the bottom. Fill in around the plant with the same soil you removed to make the hole, and gently tamp the soil to eliminate air pockets. Water thoroughly to settle the plant into the ground. When you are finished, the plant's crown should be less than 1 inch above the original ground level.

It is often necessary to create an irrigation basin after installing a new plant. This is particularly important if you plan to water by hand or when you are planting on a slope. To form the basin, mound the soil into a berm that surrounds the plant, and be sure the diameter of the basin is wider than the original hole. When the basin is filled with water, the water level should always be below the crown of the plant to prevent crown rot. Remove the berm before the rainy season because it will trap excess rainwater, which may cause crown or root rots.

Many gardeners will want to plant some of California's vibrant annuals and bulbs in their landscapes. These natives are not typically available in nursery pots, and they have their own particular requirements for successful planting, cultivation, and care. The Plant Profiles section of the book presents a diverse selection of California's native annuals and bulbs along with advice on how to grow them; annuals begin on page 200 and bulbs on page 210.

WATERING

Gardeners typically spend a good deal of time and money on site preparation and the selection, placement, and installation of plants. These are important, one-time events, but plant water needs are a concern throughout the life of your garden and ultimately require an equal or greater investment of resources. How you water will be the single most important ongoing factor influencing the success of your California native plant garden. Knowing the water requirements of your plants and monitoring the moisture in your soil are both essential parts of this process.

Among the enduring myths of native plant horticulture is that all California species, once established, can thrive without any irrigation. In reality, the water needs of California's flora are so varied as to form a broad continuum, ranging from plants that require regular watering to those that are drought tolerant. The water requirements for any given species in a designed

landscape are influenced by many factors, including the plant's age, its place of origin, and the microclimate of the garden. Some native plants normally require regular watering to survive wherever they are grown, such as Fremont cottonwood, white alder, creek dogwood, and most other riparian species. Many natives need moderate or regular water during summer when they are planted outside of their natural range. In inland southern California, for example, coast redwood, wild ginger, and seaside daisy must be irrigated in the dry months. A few natives require almost no supplemental water if they are planted in the fall, even though these drought-tolerant plants may need extra water during their first winter if there are long periods between rains. This group of plants, which is particularly susceptible to root rots, includes fremontias and many native penstemons.

Summer watering presents a challenge to native plant gardeners. Supplemental moisture in summer may be required to keep new plants alive or to help

These large coast redwoods in the Berkeley Hills would need substantial summer irrigation if they were located in a hot, dry area of the state. SAXON HOLT

Top: Fremontias, such as this specimen at the Santa Barbara Botanic Garden, die prematurely from fungal root or crown rots if watered in summer. KAREN MUSCHENETZ
Bottom: Western five-fingered fern, western sword fern, and wild ginger come from moist habitats and are appropriately grouped together in this Berkeley garden. STEPHEN INGRAM

some established plants look their best. There are, however, potential negative effects of summer irrigation, including the activation of a variety of soil-borne fungal pathogens that will cause root rots and crown rots. These fungal pathogens flourish in warm, moist environments—conditions that are alien to the majority of our native flora—and their activity in the garden can be devastating and quick. During the warm season, it is preferable to water on cloudy or slightly cooler days and early in the morning or in the evening. Always avoid mid-day overhead irrigation, as much of the water will evaporate before the plants absorb it. Experiment and choose what works best in your garden.

As a landscape of California native plants matures, it usually requires less water overall. Once the plants become established, you should irrigate deeply but infrequently. The goal is to promote deep rooting, so allow enough time for the water to thoroughly soak the soil. While light, frequent watering may be appropriate for seedlings, it is not recommended for older plants because it promotes shallow root systems that are less resistant to drought conditions and more susceptible to root-rot fungi. Since the watering needs of established plants differ from those of young plants, gardeners frequently ask the question: when is a plant considered established? The answer depends on a variety of factors, including soil types, watering regimes, age of the plant, fertilizers, and time of planting. As a general rule, consider a plant established when it has reached two to three times the size it was when planted or after it has been in the garden for two or three summers, or both.

There are a variety of strategies for efficient water use, and one of the most fundamental is known as hydrozoning. Under this approach, plants are grouped according to their water requirements. To be most effective, the use of hydrozoning should be considered at an early stage—ideally when you are designing your landscape. Some knowledge of the communities and natural habitats of your plants will also be valuable when hydrozoning. For example, beavertail cactus and coastal wood fern are drought tolerant in central California and theoretically can be placed in the same hydrozone, but they would be visually and ecologically incompatible because they are from radically different habitats. If your landscape design was determined by the horticultural needs of the plants, you have already effectively created hydrozones.

For many years drip irrigation has been a popular method for watering native plant gardens. It is easy to install, can be completely concealed under mulch, and directly irrigates plants through emitters that can be replaced or adjusted to control water volumes. Another option for watering your garden is micro-irrigation. This technique employs small spray heads that deliver water at a much-reduced rate when compared to standard

The fine spray produced by a micro-sprinkler is used to irrigate island alum root at a garden in Arcadia.
RICHARD FISHER

irrigation heads, yet applies more water than traditional drip irrigation. Micro-irrigation has the added advantage of allowing you to see what is being watered as soon as you turn the water on. It also moistens a larger soil area and thereby encourages more expansive root growth. You must, however, check to see that it is working properly—at least once a week for new plantings and once a month for established plantings. Be sure to install a filter at the beginning of your micro-irrigation and drip systems to prevent clogging of the spray heads and emitters. Standard, overhead spray watering is acceptable in some situations, particularly in the hot interior of southern California where dry, low-humidity conditions prevail. Due to numerous leaf spot and other fungal pathogens, standard overhead watering is often not recommended in cooler coastal zones of central or northern California unless it is accompanied by attentive management practices, such as careful timing of irrigation. Use caution on slopes where excessive run-off causes erosion; drip or micro-irrigation are better solutions in such circumstances.

When watering your native plants, always keep the following in mind:
- Check your soil. Never keep to a strict, automated schedule unless you have developed it through long, site-specific experience. All watering needs to be adjusted both seasonally and as plants mature.
- Do not water if the soil is already moist at root level. The soil surface will often appear to be dry even though the soil is adequately moist where the roots are growing.
- When in doubt, do not water—continue to carefully monitor the plant and soil until you are certain of its needs. It is much easier to add water to a plant than it is to dry out an over-watered specimen.
- Regularly check the moisture in the rootballs of newly installed plants and in the soil around them. Rootballs should be moist (not wet) to encourage the

roots to grow into the surrounding soil. Depending upon your garden's soil and the plant's container mix, it is possible for the soil to be damp or moist while the rootball is totally dry, especially in sites with heavy soils.

- If a plant is wilted, check the soil in the root zone. If the soil is dry, water. If the soil is moist, do not water, as this type of wilting often indicates that the plant suffers from root rot or has over-grown the capacity of its root system and needs to be cut back. Lush new growth will often wilt during the first warm spring days. If the plant perks back up in the late afternoon or evening, it is probably healthy. Such plants may require pinching or pruning as the hot weather intensifies.
- During droughts, it is imperative to water all your plants thoroughly during the normal rainy season, as this is when most species require water.
- After repeated cycles of watering and drying, some soils, particularly those with high clay content, will develop a thin dense crust that greatly impedes water penetration. Shallow cultivation of the soil on a regular basis or applying mulch will prevent this layer from forming and allows water to reach the root zone of the plants.

FERTILIZING

As a general rule, California natives thrive in nutrient-poor soils. You probably will not need to fertilize on a regular basis unless your soils are severely depleted or if a plant you are trying to grow only occurs naturally in soils with much higher fertility. Poor plant appearance and performance may signal that your soils are too low in nutrients. The best way to confirm this is to have your soil tested. Most tests will tell you what type of soil you have (sandy loam, adobe clay, etc.), its pH, organic content, and the amounts of key nutrients. For a more comprehensive assessment, you may also want the lab to conduct a tissue analysis on a sample collected from a poorly performing plant. These reports will invariably include recommendations for soil amendments and fertilizers geared to typical garden ornamentals or agricultural crops and not California natives, so you will need to adjust accordingly or consult a professional.

If you decide to add nutrients to your soil, the best time to fertilize most California natives is when the plants are actively growing, which is typically from late fall to spring. Some fertilizers remain active for long periods of time; therefore, plan accordingly to avoid over-fertilizing during the warm months of summer or when plants are dormant. Adding too much nitrogen can stimulate exuberant growth that is particularly susceptible to insects, diseases, and deer or rabbit browsing. In addition to being a waste of money, applying excess fertilizer can harm plants and pollute the environment by creating deleterious nutrient imbalances and contaminating water resources.

You can choose from a variety of organic and inorganic products to address any fertilization needs in your garden. Compost is a source of fertilizer for your garden that also improves soil structure. The occasional addition of compost is desirable for regularly irrigated parts of a garden and for many container-grown plants. Although compost is available at many retail garden centers, consider creating your own by recycling kitchen scraps, leaves, and other green waste.

MULCH

Horticulturists have extolled the virtues of mulch for decades, yet many California gardeners overlook this valuable resource. Mulch can significantly reduce moisture evaporation from the soil, thereby decreasing water demands and water bills. Mulch helps moderate soil temperature extremes, prevents formation of a soil crust, reduces dust levels, curbs erosion, and suppresses weeds. Since mulch is spread over the surface and not worked into the soil, it also provides a finished look to planted areas, especially when used to cover drip irrigation lines.

Leaf litter, wood chips, bark products, and other organic mulches add nutrients and improve soil structure as they decompose. As the mulch decomposes, it does the work for you. The nutrients also support biological activity in the soil. Organic mulch is particularly appropriate for woodland gardens, whose natural counterparts are characterized by a constantly replenished layer of decaying leaves and branches. Plan to apply organic mulch on an as-needed basis, since it can quickly decompose. Maintaining a two- to four-inch-deep layer is ideal. Be careful to keep the crown area of plants free of mulch, however. This zone is sensitive to crown rots caused by fungal and bacterial pathogens that are

Lilac verbena and Bee's Bliss sage flourish in a Montecito rock garden where the soil has not been amended with fertilizers. STEPHEN INGRAM

Woodchips have been spread as a mulch around a young San Diego sedge and other California natives in a newly installed garden in Solvang. STEPHEN INGRAM

Top: An assortment of dudleyas in a shallow container creates an attractive focal point near an entry to a courtyard in Montecito. CAROL BORNSTEIN
Bottom: Valentine shrubby monkeyflower hybrid at Rancho Santa Ana Botanic Garden in Claremont thrives in a container. BART O'BRIEN

favored by excessive moisture, especially during warm weather. Remember that organic mulch absorbs a certain amount of water before it percolates down to the soil below, so adjust your watering practices accordingly.

Inorganic mulch can be effective in many garden situations. For desert and rock gardens, a gravel or crushed-rock mulch makes sense aesthetically, ecologically, and horticulturally. This inorganic layer also helps retain moisture while trapping and holding warmth from the sun. In these more xeric gardens an organic mulch would be out of place, and it is also potentially harmful because it could retain more moisture and fertility than plants from dry habitats can tolerate.

CONTAINER GARDENING

Imagine a sculptural manzanita displayed in a large terra cotta pot in an open courtyard, a lush southern maidenhair tucked into a shady corner, or a cluster of dudleyas aligned along a sunlit stairway. These are a few examples of how native plants in containers can be a focal point or dramatic element in any garden or patio area. Many of the plants described in this book are noted as outstanding subjects for containers when provided with the proper conditions. By using containers, you can create the appropriate soil mix without going to the trouble and expense of amending the native soil extensively and repeatedly.

Most native plants growing in pots or other containers require porous, well-drained soil and ample watering. Even the most drought-tolerant shrub in a container may require regular watering, as it is not able to send its roots deep into the ground. Due to more frequent watering of potted specimens, nutrients are quickly leached from the soil; these nutrients need to be replenished to sustain plants and ensure their best performance.

The ideal time to fertilize container-grown native plants is from fall to spring, when the new growth emerges. Just as in open ground, a layer of organic or inorganic mulch will somewhat reduce evaporation and water needs for plants grown in containers and will correspondingly reduce fertilizer needs. The standard precaution to keep mulch away from the crown area should still be followed.

California native plants often produce extensive, fast-growing root systems, and even plants that appear to fit their container may need to be repotted or root-pruned. To root-prune, remove the specimen from its container, carefully slice off the outer half-inch of the rootball with a sharp knife or spade, and then repot the plant with fresh soil.

Always try to shield or insulate pots (especially black plastic) from direct hot sun; the pots can heat up to the point where sensitive young roots are killed, leading to the death or decline of the plants from subsequent fungal infection. You can protect potted specimens from searing heat by double potting. This entails placing a smaller pot in a larger container and filling the space between the containers with a coarse, porous material, such as gravel, pumice, lava rock, or perlite; fine-textured materials, such as sand or soil, will not work for this purpose, as plant roots will grow into them.

PRUNING BASICS

No matter what garden style you choose, California native plants—just like exotics—benefit from pruning for the purposes of rejuvenation, aesthetics, and health. Pruning may appear to be a mystifying or intimidating task, and there are entire reference books devoted to the subject. If you are a novice at pruning, work slowly at first and do not become discouraged by mistakes, as most plants are quite resilient. It is essential to have proper pruning tools that are clean, sharp, and well oiled. Perhaps the most valuable tools, however, are not those in your tool shed but the ones in your head. Train your eyes and take the time to observe the way plants respond to every season, both in the garden and in the wild. This will enable you to make thoughtful, informed pruning decisions. Under natural conditions California native plants are "pruned" by disturbances, such as animal browsing, fires, and storms, and some of our most useful pruning techniques mimic these processes. For example, lightly shearing toyon, Catalina cherry, or coffeeberry is analogous to animals browsing these plants' branch tips; cutting back a specimen of lemonade berry or California bay to ground level is similar to the effect of a fire. Regardless of how you prune, it is helpful to remember that your garden is a work of art, and pruning can be a way of expressing your creativity.

Rejuvenation: As plants mature, they often lose their ability to produce vigorous new growth. Over time, this may result in a specimen with reduced

flower and fruit production and a more open, less compact appearance. Periodic pruning can stimulate renewed vigor and is particularly helpful with older shrubs that may otherwise become leggy with age, such as toyon, western redbud, coyote brush, and mountain mahogany. In some cases the best way to rejuvenate is to cut the entire plant down to the ground in fall or winter, a technique known as coppicing or basal pruning. Although this method seems drastic, the result is comparable to the effect of fire, and the plant typically bounces back with amazing exuberance the following spring. California sunflower, Indian mallow, California fuchsias, and a variety of other subshrubs also benefit from this type of pruning. Since coppicing is not appropriate for some plants—including most manzanitas and ceanothus—consult the Plant Profiles section for more detailed advice on pruning a particular species.

Aesthetics: While some plants look good with little or no pruning, others benefit from seasonal grooming to remain attractive year after year. Removing faded flowers, broken branches, and pest-riddled or infested parts are standard practices that enhance a plant's aes-

Top: Hollyleaf cherry makes a fine choice for shearing and shaping into hedges, as exemplified by this garden entry to a home in Soquel. SUZANNE SCHETTLER
Bottom: The sinuous branching structure of this Howard McMinn manzanita at the Santa Barbara Botanic Garden has been revealed with careful pruning. JOHN EVARTS

This coast silk-tassel in an Arroyo Grande garden is vigorously resprouting after it was pruned to ground level using a technique known as coppicing. DAVID FROSS

thetic appeal. Some of our most common native shrubs become stunning focal points when they are pruned into small trees. Toyon, lemonade berry, mountain mahogany, and some taller ceanothus lend themselves to this treatment, which also creates additional planting space under the raised canopy. You can prune smaller shrubs to expose their inherent sculptural character. The trunk of Saint Catherine's lace becomes gnarled with age and its bark shreds; removing a branch here or there will reveal these attractive features. A manzanita's sinuous trunks and dark, smooth bark can be showcased with some careful pruning.

Plant Health: Preventative and corrective pruning play an important role in the health of your garden. Some plants develop crossing branches that rub each other, eventually creating a wound. You can avoid this by removing one of the limbs before there is a problem. Judicious pruning also helps keep certain insect and disease infestations in check. For example, thinning selected branches to increase light penetration and air circulation is an effective way to control powdery mildew. Plant injuries sustained by storm damage or animal browse may never heal properly, but corrective pruning can minimize the potential for long-term deformities and promote better healing. Crowding occurs when gardeners fill an area in the landscape with too many plants or when a specimen outgrows its space. To correct this situation, try pruning to reduce crowding; otherwise, your options are to remove specimens or replace large plants with smaller ones.

Pruning is essential in the control of mistletoe, a semiparasitic plant that can be a serious pest. In California several species of mistletoe attack white alder, California sycamore, flowering ash, Fremont cottonwood, oaks, pines, and other native plants. To curtail

The long-term structural and aesthetic integrity of this Fremont cottonwood in Ballard is threatened by these mistletoe clumps, which should be pruned off.
JOHN EVARTS

minor infestations of mistletoe, simply prune off any affected branches. When major limbs are infested, a more extensive treatment is recommended to preserve the structural and aesthetic integrity of the tree. In addition to pruning, paint the cut surface where the mistletoe stem was attached—carefully avoiding any surrounding tissue of the host plant—with Round-up® or ethephon, and then cover it with plastic for up to two years. This should kill any mistletoe that may have penetrated the vascular tissue of the host tree, although subsequent treatments are sometimes necessary.

WHEN TO PRUNE CALIFORNIA NATIVES

With a flora as diverse as California's, it should come as no surprise that the ideal time for pruning your native plants is variable. The following categories provide broad guidelines, and more specific information is given for each featured species in the Plant Profiles section that begins on page 40.

Winter-deciduous species (such as western redbud, creek dogwood, maples, and deciduous oaks): The best time to prune these plants is during their dormant period. With the leaves out of the way, it is much easier to see structural problems—such as crossing limbs—and to observe where removal of a specific branch will result in a more desirable shape.

Semi-evergreen species (such as Matilija poppy, shrubby monkeyflowers, goldenrods, irises, and sages): Depending upon the weather and your watering practices, these are species that begin to slow down and enter a resting period, usually in late summer to early winter. You can prune semi-evergreen plants when growth ceases completely—which may not always occur—or be guided by their appearance. Although some of our most beautiful native plants fall into this category, they do have a "down" time when they may look tired and bedraggled. The leaves of some species, such as California sagebrush and canyon sunflower, shrivel up and hang onto the stems during the dry season, creating a shaggy-dog appearance. Other species, including sages and shrubby monkeyflowers, may retain only modest tufts of green leaves at the branch tips while dropping most other leaves to reveal naked lower stems. Whether you choose to prune these plants at this time of year is a matter of perspective; one person's scruffy native, begging to be groomed, is another's harbinger of our subtle seasonal changes and a desirable emblem of the naturalistic garden.

Evergreen herbaceous perennials and shrubs (such as coast aster, lilac verbena, coffeeberry, toyon, coyote brush, ceanothus, and manzanitas): For shaping, the best time to prune plants in this category is right after they flower, unless fruits are desired for their wildlife or ornamental value. For rejuvenation, prune them in the fall.

Long-blooming plants (such as bush poppy, island

snapdragon, and penstemons): A fair number of California natives fit this description and reward us with multiple waves of flowers when an occasional summer irrigation is provided, especially in cooler regions. By pruning after the primary bloom cycle is over, you can stimulate a secondary flush of blossoms that is more vigorous than might naturally occur. The

Top: Late summer to early winter is a good time to prune or pinch back semi-evergreen natives, such as this hummingbird sage in a La Honda garden. STEPHEN INGRAM
Bottom: Hedges of Tecate cypress provide privacy at a Ballard residence; this durable conifer can be sheared at most times of the year. JOHN EVARTS

degree of pruning is species-dependent, and you may need to experiment to find what works best at your site. Gardeners in hotter areas may also extend blooming periods with summer watering, but the added moisture increases the risk of losing plants to root rot.

PEST AND DISEASE CONTROL

Every garden is occasionally afflicted by pest and disease problems, even those that are carefully planned and well maintained. Native California plants have their share of host-specific as well as non-specific pests, and many of these are discussed in the individual plant descriptions in the Plant Profiles section. The good news is that native plants also attract birds, beneficial insects, frogs, toads, lizards, and other natural enemies of many garden pests. These creatures help maintain a healthy balance in the landscape by keeping pests in check.

The concept of integrated pest management, or IPM, continues to gain favor among home gardeners, nursery growers, and farmers. IPM is a multi-pronged approach that aims to reduce pests and diseases in an environmentally responsible manner, using chemical controls as a last resort. Long-term control of a problem is possible through monitoring pest and disease populations, employing a combination of horticultural, biological, and chemical methods, and evaluating the effectiveness of each treatment. The goal in most cases is not complete elimination of pests and diseases but rather to

One goal of integrated pest management is to target a pest without harming beneficial organisms, such as the spider that spun the web in this Ballard garden. JOHN EVARTS

The young leaves and shoots of this California sycamore in Solvang are afflicted by sycamore anthracnose, a fungus that is common during wet springs. JOHN EVARTS

keep their levels acceptably low. Remember that poorly sited or highly susceptible plants will continue to have problems regardless of your control methods.

The first step in IPM is to assess the problem, seeking professional help if necessary. Next determine whether there is sufficient damage to warrant treatment, realizing that each situation is unique and that your tolerance level will vary depending upon the impacts of the infestation. Then develop a plan of action. This could mean modifying site conditions and your horticultural practices to benefit the afflicted plants. For example, powdery mildew on sages or roses may be an indication of too much shade or humidity, or poor air circulation. Removing affected foliage and pruning adjacent plants to increase sunlight on the infected plants may solve the problem. If gophers have invaded your garden, a combination of trapping, installing barriers, and building barn owl nesting boxes should help reduce these troublesome creatures.

Occasionally, a pest is so rampant that chemical controls are indicated. Always try the least-toxic, environmentally safe products first, such as insecticidal soaps, baking soda, and horticultural oils. Whenever you use a chemical product, be sure to follow the instructions carefully and protect yourself, pets, non-target plants, and beneficial insects. Let your neighbors know before applying any chemicals that might affect them or their pets, and dispose of excess materials and containers responsibly.

Some organic products and biological controls do have side effects. For example, sulfur spray can be an effective control for powdery mildew, but if applied to sensitive plants or when midday temperatures exceed 90°F, plant tissues will be damaged. *Bacillus thuringiensis*, a bacteria used to kill harmful caterpillars, such as cabbage loopers, armyworms, and cutworms, is a non-specific biological control. Caterpillars of desirable species of moths and butterflies that ingest plants sprayed with this product may also be killed.

Regardless of your treatment plan, evaluate the results. There is a good chance you will face similar problems again, and keeping records of what worked will guide your future pest-management efforts. It is helpful to remember that a healthy garden is teeming with life. Beneficial predators are continually seeking food sources, including a variety of plant pests, but these natural allies will pass your garden by if it is devoid of all insects. Sometimes it is easier to simply remove an afflicted plant than fuss with elaborate controls that may have other undesirable impacts. Many pests and diseases are often more of a visual nuisance than a serious concern. If you modify your aesthetic standards, you may find that tolerating some pest and disease problems is preferable to using harsh chemicals to control them.

WEED MANAGEMENT

Weeds are defined as plants that are out of place. In California they are primarily exotic intruders, such as bindweed, cape ivy, pampas grass, and many species of European annual grasses. Weeds compete with ornamental plants for water, nutrients, sunlight, and space; they also can harbor pests and diseases. These are good reasons to strive for a weed-free garden, although this goal is not always feasible. At times the scope of a weed problem reaches overwhelming levels, especially in long-neglected landscapes.

In some situations our native plants can become serious weeds. California poppies can choke out young, slow-growing shrubs. Point Saint George aster, strawberries, and a few other native groundcovers may overpower adjacent plantings. Due to its bitter-tasting foliage, Douglas iris thrives in heavily grazed coastal pastureland, where it is categorized as a noxious weed. Yellow bush lupine has escaped from its natural range of Ventura to Sonoma counties and is out-competing

Flowering plumes of pampas grass line a road at Stinson Beach; this species is emblematic of introduced plants that are now regarded as invasive weeds. RUSSELL BEATTY

A few California natives can be aggressive and "weedy" in gardens, such as the beach strawberry on the bank to the right of this Berkeley walkway. STEPHEN INGRAM

A deep layer of coarse mulch from a municipal green waste program is used to help suppress weeds at this young roadside planting of natives in Ballard. JOHN EVARTS

the indigenous coastal plants along the coast of Mendocino and Humboldt counties. The now ubiquitous pop weed is a relatively recent native addition to the weed flora of gardens throughout the California Floristic Province. Some of our native plants have even become unwelcome pests in other Mediterranean-climate regions of the world. Just as some species of eucalyptus and brooms are invasive exotics in California, our beautiful state flower, California poppy, is a pest in Spain, Portugal, Italy, Chile, and Australia.

As with other pest problems, you can apply IPM to develop a weed-management strategy that makes sense for your situation and budget. Many gardeners successfully control weeds by hand-pulling, mowing, mulching, and other labor-intensive techniques. Herbicides offer another approach to weed removal that may be cost-effective. However, other methods of weed management should always be considered first before resorting to chemicals that may have harmful side effects for people, plants, and animals.

Prior to planting in cleared sites, weed control can be achieved by one of three recommended methods: presprouting, soil solarization, or smothering. When using presprouting, the target area is irrigated to germinate weed seeds in the soil; after they emerge they can be hoed off or killed by some other mechanical means such as tilling. Repeat the process to help eliminate any unsprouted seeds that were brought closer to the soil surface during the first round. For soil solarization, first remove existing weeds; moisten, till, and grade the site, and then securely place a thin layer of clear plastic over the soil. The high temperatures that develop under the plastic will kill most weed seeds near the surface of the soil as well as some harmful pathogens and nematodes.

This technique is most effective in sites that are warm and sunny for four to eight consecutive weeks. Smothering weeds with black plastic, cardboard, or several layers of newspaper is also possible. These materials should be left in place for at least one growing season and preferably longer to control tenacious weeds.

If you decide herbicides are appropriate for treating your weed problems, there are two basic types of products: preemergent and postemergent herbicides. Preemergent herbicides are used to inhibit germination or to kill seedlings and are applied before the seeds sprout. They have varying degrees of residual effect in the soil. Postemergent herbicides are designed to control actively growing weeds. In addition to standard, commercial products, there are natural, less environmentally hazardous herbicides available. In all cases read and follow the manufacturer's directions and safely dispose of all containers.

ENVIRONMENTAL ISSUES

As more Californians grow native plants in their gardens and landscapes, it is natural that the following question would arise: Do these horticultural trends and activities pose any unintended threats to the health of wild and designed landscapes in California? The answer to that question is yes.

The act of propagating and growing plants for use in gardens, landscapes, restoration projects, and other purposes can have unforeseen consequences. All cuttings, seeds, and divisions can carry one or more viruses, fungal pathogens, or other diseases that can infect their wild relatives. Similarly, the soil mix in a container may harbor any number of pathogens that could affect other plants. Some of our native geophytes are particularly sensitive to virus infection. California's native lilies, for example, are especially susceptible to tobacco mosaic virus. Vigorously growing plants frequently do not show symptoms of this virus, but stressed plants will show the characteristic splotchy pattern in their foliage. *Phytophthora* and other root-rot pathogens are readily spread by contaminated soils in nursery containers. The fungal pathogen *Botryosphaeria dothidea,* responsible for branch dieback in giant sequoia, manzanitas, madrones, silk-tassels, and many other native plants, can be readily transported in the live tissue of container-grown plants.

Collecting seed or other propagules is, in effect, a method of artificial rather than natural selection. Often, the seeds that are easiest to collect by hand are the ones gathered. That means a collection may not include seeds that are the first and last to ripen and disperse, or those seeds from parts of the plant that are hard to reach. The selection process is further influenced by growing these seeds under conditions that will favor individuals that germinate quickly and respond best to the nursery environment. The seedlings are then exposed to watering and fertilizing regimes, soil mixes, pest control, and sun and shade patterns that differ from their natural habitat. The end result is a group of plants that have been selected to grow under nursery conditions. Such plants are likely to be better adapted to gardens than they are to natural environments. Therefore, these plants are not necessarily the best or most representative specimens to use in restoration, habitat creation, and other conservation projects.

Genetic contamination of gene pools of native plant populations is a vital issue, especially for rare or endangered species. The primary area of concern is the contamination of wild populations by plants in nearby gardens, landscapes, and agricultural plantings. This problem may be characterized by the inadvertent introduction of potentially damaging genetic material due to ongoing pollination between wild and horticultural plantings of native species and their close relatives. There are many documented cases of such interactions between different populations of the same species as well as examples of hybridization between native plant species and their relatives. For example, the deliberate introduction of Saint Catherine's lace of Santa Catalina Island to the Stanton Ranch garden on Santa Cruz Island has resulted in unexpected consequences to the genetic integrity of the Santa Cruz Island buckwheat. Beginning in 1971, hybrids between these two species were noted near the ranch, and by 1980 they had spread considerably farther to the south and west. Today, there is an ongoing effort to remove Saint Catherine's lace and its hybrids from Santa Cruz Island.

Ultimately, the best option for continued survival of California's treasured native flora is to protect large tracts of land from development and other intrusive

California sycamore, long used in parkways such as this one in Goleta, is hybridizing with plantings of the non-native London plane tree. STEPHEN INGRAM

human activities. Within these protected areas, it is important that humans not suppress fires, floods, and other natural disturbances with which the plants have evolved. There will also need to be active management of threats to the biologic integrity of such ecosystems, which may require eliminating invasive exotic species and containing populations of herbivores whose numbers have soared in the absence of predators. Even those few native species that have become problematic in the wild due to human-caused disturbances and introductions may require aggressive control.

The environmental issues raised here can help you make informed decisions when using California native plants in the garden. Although serious, these concerns are minor when compared to the joys and adventures of cultivating native plants. These introductory chapters, and the Plant Profiles section that follows, provide compelling reasons to give natives a much greater presence—indeed, a place of honor—in our gardens and landscapes.

PLANT PROFILES

The Plant Profiles section contains detailed horticultural information about a wide array of California native plants for the garden. Instead of attempting to be encyclopedic in our coverage, we have selected those plants that represent the best our flora has to offer to gardeners in the Mediterranean-climate regions of California. The Plant Profiles include more than 200 featured plants as well as another 300 species, cultivars, and hybrids that are more briefly described. The primary criteria used in determining which plants to include were reliability, availability, aesthetic value, and resistance to insect and pest problems. The majority of the featured plants met all of these criteria.

The Plant Profiles are arranged in alphabetical order by scientific (Latin) name. The first part of the Plant Profiles includes all plant types except for annuals and bulbs, which are grouped separately in their own sections at the end of the Profiles. The Index to Common and Scientific Plant Names, beginning on page 260, will help you locate a plant if you know its common name or its scientific name. If you are seeking a plant for a particular landscape need or one that possesses a certain characteristic, consult the lists in Recommended Plant Selections, beginning on page 216.

At the start of each profile, you will find a valuable summary of the plant's horticultural requirements and distribution. Our definitions and explanations of the terminology used in the summary information for the featured plants are given below.

Plant Type
The following standard terms are used to describe the featured plant: Tree, Shrub, Subshrub, Perennial, Grass, Fern, Succulent, Vine, Annual, and Bulb.

White sage, woolly blue curls, and a host of other native plants create a bold color palette at this private garden in Los Altos. SAXON HOLT

Geographic Zones

Coastal: (*Sunset* zones 15 to 17 and 22 to 24). Cool ocean air is a major influence on both summer and winter temperatures. Examples: San Diego, Los Angeles, Santa Barbara, San Luis Obispo, Berkeley, San Francisco, and Eureka.

Intermediate Valleys: (*Sunset* zones 14, 20, and 21). Valleys open to moderate ocean influence. Examples: San Gabriel, Santa Ynez, King City, Hollister, and Santa Rosa.

Interior Valleys: (*Sunset* zones 7, 18, and 19). Foothills and valleys without significant ocean influence. Coast and Peninsular ranges typically block any consistent maritime influence. Examples: Hemet, Riverside, Ontario, San Fernando, Simi Valley, Paso Robles, Covelo, and Grass Valley.

Central Valley: (*Sunset* zones 8, 9, and 14). Interior valleys without ocean influence. Examples: Bakersfield, Fresno, Sacramento, and Redding.

The pairing of California poppy with De La Mina verbena is a simple combination that yields a stunning result at the Santa Barbara Botanic Garden. JOHN EVARTS

Deserts: (*Sunset* zones 1A, 10, 11, and 13). Desert areas of California. Examples: El Centro, Indio, Twentynine Palms, Bishop, and Alturas.

The "high desert" comprises the Mojave Desert and Great Basin areas of the state (*Sunset* zones 1A, 10, and 11), and the "low desert" embraces the Sonoran Desert area within California (*Sunset* zone 13), also regionally known as the Colorado Desert.

High Mountains: (*Sunset* zones 1 to 3). Yellow pine forest belt and higher. (Elevation for this zone varies with latitude and local conditions and typically begins between 3000 and 6000 feet.) Examples: Lake Arrowhead, Big Bear, Mammoth Lakes, South Lake Tahoe, and Truckee.

Light

Sun: Full sun.
Partial shade: Filtered light or shade for part of the day.
Shade: No direct sun.

Soil

Adaptable: A plant that will tolerate a range of soil types.
Heavy: A soil with a relatively high proportion of clay, typically poorly drained unless moderated by slope.
Well-drained: Soils that drain well after water application. Some soils, such as rocky or sandy types, drain well based on their respective physical characteristics. Others, such as clay and silt-clay types, are normally poorly drained on level ground but may be considered well drained on slopes.

Water

The suggested water requirements in the summary text refer to established plants. Water needs vary considerably in California's diverse climates, and our categories are offered as a broad guideline to warm-season needs. Once established, very few of the species listed in the Plant Profiles require supplemental irrigation during the rainy season except during exceptionally dry years. Plants grown within their natural range usually require less supplemental irrigation.

Regular water: Every 3 to 7 days.
Moderate water: Every 10 to 14 days.
Occasional water: Every 3 to 4 weeks.
Infrequent water: Every 4 to 6 weeks.
Drought tolerant: Plants survive on rainfall once established except during periods of prolonged winter drought.

Natural Habitat and Range

Typical environment and plant community the plant occupies in the wild and its natural geographic distribution. (For more information about plant communities, see page 11.)

Abutilon palmeri
INDIAN MALLOW
Mallow Family (Malvaceae)

Plant Type: Semi-evergreen to evergreen subshrub.
Geographic Zones: All except frost-prone valleys, high mountains, and high deserts.
Light: Sun to partial shade.
Soil: Adaptable.
Water: Infrequent along the coast, occasional in interior climates.
Natural Habitat and Range: Dry rocky slopes, canyons, and washes in desert scrub below 2500 feet; Peninsular Ranges and southeast through the deserts of Arizona, New Mexico, and northern Mexico.

Indian mallow flower and fruits, Cataviña, Baja California.
BART O'BRIEN

Indian mallow in bloom, Leaning Pine Arboretum, Cal Poly, San Luis Obispo. CAROL BORNSTEIN

Indian mallow belongs to a genus of evergreen shrubs with festive blossoms that has long been a garden favorite in the frost-free portions of southern California. Also known as "flowering maples," these shrubs are tropical in origin. Their broad leaves and large, lantern-like flowers reflect adaptations to more mesic environments than those found in most of California. And yet, Indian mallow grows in one of the driest corners of the state and is as colorful as any of the commonly available non-native mallows found in garden centers.

Indian mallow is a sprawling shrub 3 to 5 feet tall with an equal spread. The olive gray leaves are heart shaped, 4 to 7 inches wide, and covered with soft, downy hairs. Production of luminous orange to gold flowers begins in spring and summer and continues through the year in the warmer portions of the state. The flowers are held in clusters on wiry stems and stand in bold contrast against the gray leaves. Indian mallow's decorative fruits may yield a generous supply of garden seedlings.

The gray felted foliage of Indian mallow goes well with other gray-, silver- or blue-leaved plants, such as Idaho fescue and Cleveland sage. It also serves as a foil for the dark green foliage and blue flowers of ceanothus. The broad, hairy leaves provide contrast for fine-textured species, including lilac verbena and Black Diamond chamise. Gardeners also use Indian mallow in a container or plant it along foundations. When frequently watered it tends to have a gray-green hue, whereas a specimen in a dry garden is silver gray.

Indian mallow attracts a variety of insects and should be checked frequently to avoid heavy infestations. Aphids, whitefly, and scale are particularly common, but are easily treated with horticultural soaps and oils. Pinching and pruning will improve the shape and appearance of older plants, and removing spent flowers lengthens the flowering period. Plants are damaged when temperatures fall below 25°F and will not survive frequent frosts.

Acer macrophyllum
BIG-LEAF MAPLE
Maple Family (Aceraceae)

Plant Type: Deciduous tree.
Geographic Zones: All except high mountains and deserts.
Light: Sun to partial shade.
Soil: Adaptable; well-drained preferred.
Water: Occasional to regular.
Natural Habitat and Range: Primarily in riparian woodland in southern California and additionally scattered in upland forests farther north. Found below 5000 feet, from San Diego County to British Columbia.

California's big-leaf maple makes an impressive addition to landscapes that can accommodate its size. Similar in stature to the maples of the eastern United

Top: Big-leaf maple tree in cultivation, private garden, Oakland. STEPHEN INGRAM
Bottom: Big-leaf maple, new leaves and flowers, Descanso Gardens, La Cañada. SAXON HOLT

States, it grows 30 to 100 feet tall and has a rounded silhouette. Its rapid growth rate and considerable size make it suitable for large gardens and parks. It is an excellent shade tree and creates a wonderful habitat for understory plants.

Big-leaf maple is named for the size of its leaves, which are the biggest of all the maples and measure up to 12 inches across. When they first appear, the leaves are burgundy in color. As they grow, the deeply lobed, coarsely toothed leaves become medium green. In fall, the leaves turn pale to bright yellow where winters are mild and golden to orange-yellow in colder regions.

Ornamental greenish yellow flowers emerge with the spring leaves and hang in fragrant 4- to 6-inch-long pendent racemes. The seedpods, called samaras, are briefly tinged pinkish red and add a colorful note before they turn brown. They remain on the tree in winter, adding movement to the stiff architecture of the rigid gray branches. Squirrels and chipmunks relish the seeds of big-leaf maple, and the tree's overall size and structure create valuable shelter for wildlife.

Young big-leaf maples appreciate moisture, but older trees are moderately drought tolerant and may develop woody surface roots. Although resistant to oak root fungus, big-leaf maples are highly susceptible to verticillium wilt, especially in hotter areas and when grown in heavy soils with poor drainage. Make pruning cuts to remove dead or crossing branches when the trees are dormant.

Other Species: Vine maple *(Acer circinatum)* is a shrub or small tree with red twigs, brilliant fall color, and showy red samaras. This slow-growing upright or reclining native rivals Japanese maple in beauty and is well suited to small gardens, becoming 4 to 20 feet tall. Vine maple is found naturally in shaded areas below 5000 feet in the forests of northern California to British Columbia. It does well in the cooler northern parts of the state where conditions resemble its native habitat. Vine maple is an ideal partner for coast redwood and giant chain fern in a woodland garden. It also provides accent in a Japanese-style planting or when placed in large containers.

Achillea millefolium
YARROW
Sunflower Family (Asteraceae)

Plant Type: Semi-evergreen herbaceous perennial.
Geographic Zones: All except deserts.
Light: Sun to partial shade.
Soil: Adaptable.
Water: Occasional to moderate.
Natural Habitat and Range: Many plant communities, especially grasslands below 11,000 feet; common throughout California, except deserts.

Yarrow is a variable perennial with a very broad distribution. It inhabits most temperate regions of the Northern Hemisphere, and many of the colorful yarrows found commonly in garden centers were collected and bred from European stock. California's yarrows, which grow in the southern portion of this extensive range, offer additional selections with considerable garden merit.

Island Pink yarrow, Santa Barbara Botanic Garden. STEPHEN INGRAM

The narrow feather-like leaves of yarrow are aromatic, finely divided, and soft to the touch. Plants vary in height from a few inches to as much as a foot, and foliage color ranges from dark green to silver gray. In late spring and summer, stiff flowering stems rise 6 inches to 3 feet high and bear small white to pink flowers in tight, 3- to 5-inch-wide flattened heads. The flower heads turn

Calistoga yarrow in bloom, private garden, Arroyo Grande.
DAVID FROSS

Cultivars: 'Calistoga' features billowing silver gray foliage with brilliant clean white flowers on 1-foot-high stalks. Its foliage color alone is enough to recommend it, and it is not as aggressive as some selections. 'Island Pink' from Santa Cruz Island (also known as "pink island form") has a vigorous habit with bright green foliage and rose pink flowers that fade to pale pink.

Adenostoma fasciculatum
CHAMISE
Rose Family (Rosaceae)

Plant Type: Evergreen shrub.
Geographic Zones: All except high mountains and deserts.
Light: Sun.
Soil: Adaptable, except alkaline.
Water: Drought tolerant.
Natural Habitat and Range: Chaparral below 5000 feet; Sierra Nevada foothills and Coast Ranges, from Mendocino County south to northwestern Baja California.

Prostrate chamise, Rancho Santa Ana Botanic Garden, Claremont. BART O'BRIEN

dusty brown as the seeds mature and persist into winter unless removed. Plants spread by rhizomes, forming small, dense colonies.

Yarrow requires only a sunny site and modest water for success in most California gardens. In a perennial border, it offers bright spring and summer flowers that serve well in both fresh and dried arrangements. Yarrow is often seeded as a groundcover or used as part of a hydroseeding mix to stabilize slopes. It makes a suitable turf substitute because it will tolerate light foot traffic and regular mowing; however, the stems and foliage will stain clothing. Mixed with other perennials, such as purple needle grass, dune sedge, or blue-eyed grass, it can form the foundation of a meadow garden. Yarrow also makes a good addition to a habitat garden; its foliage provides winter forage for birds, particularly juncos, sparrows, and towhees, and its spring flowers attract butterflies and bees.

Yarrow is a tough and robust plant that needs little maintenance, but it can spread aggressively in favorable sites. Deadheading will lengthen the flowering season, and use of a string trimmer will control particularly vigorous drifts. Dividing older plants or fertilizing every few years in the cool season will enhance vigor and flowering. Occasional summer water will improve the appearance of plants in areas away from the immediate coast. Aphid infestations can be troublesome, and rabbits, caterpillars, and birds that feed on the foliage may reduce the plant to a small tuft.

Chamise is the quintessential plant defining the majority of California's chaparral communities. Also known as greasewood, a name that comes from its high flammability, chamise resprouts vigorously from its basal burl after a fire or severe pruning. This long-lived shrub is useful in many garden situations because it is extremely heat and drought tolerant and its wide-spreading roots control erosion.

All forms of chamise have evergreen, needle-like, dark green leaves that are produced in tight bunches along the rigid stems. Terminal 1- to 3-inch-long clusters of small white flowers appear profusely in late spring and early summer. Flowers are short-lived but progress through a series of brown colors, from rust to chocolate. Chamise grows from 6 to 15 feet tall and is equally wide.

The fine-textured foliage and moderate size of chamise makes it an excellent candidate for background and slope plantings in gardens that are secure from fire danger. In garden conditions, as in the wild, chamise has few, if any, serious pests or diseases.

Though chamise itself is rarely grown in gardens, there are several selections that have potential. Plants known as prostrate chamise (*Adenostoma fasciculatum* var. *prostratum*) are natural choices for use as groundcovers. These mounding plants may be expected to grow 1 to 3 feet tall and should spread 6 to 8 feet across. California horticulturists utilize a number of rarely named clones from this plant, all of which originated on California's Channel Islands. Light pinching and pruning of the center of these plants will keep them shorter.

Cultivars: 'Black Diamond' produces thick, dense, upright growth and is slow growing. It may be used as a replacement for dwarf conifers in hot dry climates. 'Black Diamond' requires regular light pruning to keep it small and compact.

Other Species: Redshanks (*Adenostoma sparsifolium*) is similar to, but more attractive than, chamise. Its needle-like leaves are longer and brighter green. Their larger size and even distribution creates a puffy or cloud-like appearance. Redshanks grows to be a large shrub, or if pruned, it makes an attractive multi-trunked tree from 10 to 25 feet tall and equally wide. The long, shredded, ribbon-like strips of red-brown bark that clothe its trunks and branches give redshanks its common name. Large, frothy terminal clusters of tiny white flowers appear from mid- to late summer. Redshanks prefers well-drained soils. It performs poorly when grown in heavy clay.

Adiantum capillus-veneris
SOUTHERN MAIDENHAIR
Brake Fern Family (Pteridaceae)

Plant Type: Evergreen to deciduous fern.
Geographic Zones: All except high mountains.
Light: Partial shade to shade.
Soil: Adaptable; well-drained and lime-rich preferred.
Water: Moderate to regular.
Natural Habitat and Range: Found near seeps and springs on streambanks and canyon walls below 7500 feet; southern portions of North America to Central and South America.

Southern maidenhair appears delicate and fragile, but it is actually quite tough and durable. In California this common, widespread fern often grows in dramatic

Top: Southern maidenhair, Santa Barbara Botanic Garden.
STEPHEN INGRAM
Bottom: Western five-fingered fern, private garden, Berkeley.
BART O'BRIEN

colonies that hang on moist ledges and cliffs of shaded canyons or form cascading drifts along rocky seeps. In the garden this fern's dark wiry stems, airy green leaflets, and languid habit evoke images of natural grotto-like environments.

The arching fronds of southern maidenhair rise on purple-black stems from slender rhizomes, which have tiny russet-colored scales. Each frond is finely divided into fan-shaped leaflets held on a lax or pendent, thread-like stalk. In late spring or summer a brown or amber membranous fold (know as the indusium) forms on the underside of the margins of the leaflets.

Southern maidenhair lends elegance to container plantings, hanging baskets, and raised entry beds. It combines well with leopard lily, island alum root, and western azalea to create a shady border along the north side of a building, and it is effective massed in the understory of moisture-loving trees. Once established, southern maidenhair is amazingly resilient and requires only regular water, well-drained soils, and a shady site.

In cold climates it is fully winter dormant. Periodically remove old fronds to maintain its best appearance.

Other Species: Western five-fingered fern *(Adiantum aleuticum)* is also found in moist, shady environments. This fern forms small colonies of stout, scaly rhizomes that bear wiry black stems up to 2½ feet tall. Its leaves are divided into flat, tapered segments and are held like arched fingers. Five-fingered fern fills the same garden niche as southern maidenhair but is a better choice for use in northern California. Try it in containers or as part of a shaded rock garden. Native Americans have long used five-fingered fern's black stems in basketry.

Aesculus californica
CALIFORNIA BUCKEYE
Buckeye Family (Hippocastanaceae)

Plant Type: Deciduous tree.
Geographic Zones: All except high mountains and deserts.
Light: Sun.
Soil: Adaptable.
Water: Drought tolerant to regular.
Natural Habitat and Range: Woodlands mostly away from the coast and below 4000 feet; Siskiyou and Shasta counties south to Los Angeles and Kern counties.

California buckeye flowers and leaves, Santa Barbara Botanic Garden. STEPHEN INGRAM

California buckeye trunks, Leaning Pine Arboretum, Cal Poly, San Luis Obispo. DAVID FROSS

Few trees exhibit such a nuanced response to the varied microclimates of our state as California buckeye. This tree responds to heat or drought stress by dropping its leaves—this can happen as early as May or as late as October, depending upon environmental and site factors. California buckeye still provides year-round beauty to the garden; drought avoidance leads to the loss of the attractive foliage and flowers but reveals the handsome, thick-stemmed silhouette and silvery smooth bark.

The moist, warming weather of early spring sees California buckeye's brown buds burst forth in an exclamation of bright, apple green foliage. Shortly thereafter, production of the rapidly unfolding, palmately compound leaves stops, and all resources are focused on the numerous terminal bottlebrush-like flower clusters. The 4- to 12-inch-long inflorescences are white (rarely pink) and are composed of scores of five-petaled flowers with spidery anthers. The heavy round fruits ripen in late fall and split to reveal shiny, 1- to 3-inch-wide chestnut-brown seeds—the inspiration for the common name, buckeye.

One of our showiest flowering trees, California buckeye has numerous garden uses. It may be grown as a single- or multi-trunked tree or as a large shrub. Its deciduous rounded outline provides both complement and counterpoint to such evergreens as coast live oak, foothill pine, and California bay. A single California buckeye makes a handsome specimen tree, while several may form a large informal hedge. This tree is an excellent choice to shade the south or west side of a home. Used in front of a large blank wall, its sculptural form and structure is readily appreciated. Many plants, such as coyote brush, wire grass, seaside daisy, beach strawberry, Douglas iris, island snapdragon, and blue witches, grow well beneath California buckeye. Mature specimens may reach heights of 15 to 45 feet and typically spread wider.

California buckeye has no serious pest or disease problems, but the large brown seeds are poisonous to humans and most other mammals. The pollen and nectar of California buckeye are poisonous to European honeybees.

Agave shawii
SHAW AGAVE
Agave Family (Agavaceae)

Plant Type: Evergreen succulent.
Geographic Zones: All except frost-prone valleys, mountains, and high deserts.
Light: Sun to partial shade.
Soil: Adaptable, except poorly drained.
Water: Drought tolerant.
Natural Habitat and Range: Coastal scrub and chaparral below 1500 feet; southwestern edge of San Diego County south to Baja California.

Not for the cautious or timid, Shaw agave's sculptural rosettes of dark green, spiny, succulent leaves inspire bold use. Potted specimens are strikingly architectural, while a drift planted beneath a large picture window dramatically frames the base of the view—as long as you leave room for the 7- to 12-foot-tall flowering stems.

Each flower stalk of Shaw agave is crowned by a panicle of broad flat-topped clusters with dozens of golden to reddish erect tubular flowers that hummingbirds find irresistible. After blooming, the up to 3-foot-tall rosette dies and must be completely removed. Fortunately, the type of Shaw agave that naturally occurs in California forms new rosettes at the base of the plant before it blooms. Over the course of many years, a single plant may create a dense colony.

In the wild, Shaw agave grows with a wide variety of drought-tolerant species. This easily grown agave is not only at home in desert-like gardens; it also emboldens gardens with a southern California flair that include species such as Munz sage, Baja littleleaf rose, California buckwheat, California sagebrush, Catalina perfume, Tecate cypress, and chalk dudleya.

Sharp red-brown spines limit the use of Shaw agave in gardens and landscapes. Do not plan on using Shaw agave near paths or where children or pets may

Shaw agave in a dense colony, Santa Barbara Botanic Garden.
STEPHEN INGRAM

come in contact with them. The spiny rosettes are difficult to weed around, so it behooves the gardener to eliminate noxious perennial weeds (Bermuda grass, oxalis, etc.) prior to planting. A 2- to 3-inch-deep gravel mulch around the plants assists subsequent weed control efforts.

Other Species: Desert agave *(Agave deserti)* and Utah agave *(Agave utahensis)* require the heat and dryness found in their desert homelands and do not thrive in cool or coastal gardens. Both are spectacular, but formidable, container specimens. Desert agave has 2-foot-tall by 2-foot-wide rosettes of chalky blue-gray leaves that have small, black marginal spines and long, sharp, black needle-like tips. Desert agave prefers well-drained soils and is drought tolerant, even when young. Utah agave has smaller rosettes (1½-foot-tall by 1-foot-wide) and is much more variable across its range. Its thick leaves are usually olive to blue-green and have corky-white zigzag marginal spines and long white terminal spines that may reach 2 to 5 inches in length. Its spines are sharp and much more brittle than those of other native agaves. Utah agave requires good drainage and occasional summer watering.

White alder in a lawn planting, private garden, Newport Beach. DAVID FROSS

Alnus rhombifolia
WHITE ALDER
Birch Family (Betulaceae)

Plant Type: Deciduous tree.
Geographic Zones: All except deserts.
Light: Sun to partial shade.
Soil: Adaptable; moisture-retentive preferred.
Water: Regular.
Natural Habitat and Range: Along rivers, streams, and seeps in riparian woodlands below 7500 feet; Peninsular Ranges north to British Columbia and east to Idaho, excluding the Central Valley and the Modoc Plateau.

White alder, private garden, South Pasadena.
BARBARA EISENSTEIN

White alder is a broadleaved tree that is frequently used in urban and suburban landscapes. This fast-growing, heat-tolerant, moisture-loving tree does well as a lawn specimen or planted in groves. In hot, dry areas white alder creates a cool, forested effect as long as ample moisture is provided. Even in winter, white alder's straight, pole-like trunk and tiered branching cast an appealing shadow that is especially effective against the wall of a building. Its ash gray bark creates an interesting contrast, particularly when viewed against a dark background.

A mature white alder has a rounded crown and may reach up to 90 feet in height, although 40 to 60 feet is typical. Catkins form in late winter or early spring, usually on leafless stems; their chartreuse-brown color adds ephemeral interest. The finely toothed leaves are apple green when they emerge and turn dark green as they age. Small cone-like fruits persist into winter after dropping thin, winged seeds that are consumed by many seed-eating birds, including pine siskins and goldfinches. In warmer winters some trees may retain a portion of their leaves until spring.

Tent caterpillars, alder borers, and mistletoe present challenges to both alder species (see red alder below) and require attention. BT *(Bacillus thuringiensis)* effectively controls tent caterpillars, proper cultural care prevents serious infestations of alder borers, and removing infected branches manages mistletoe. Thoughtful placement of alders and deep watering are the best ways to avoid competition from their invasive, water-seeking roots. Like many other fast-growing trees, alders are weak-wooded and short-lived.

Other Species: Red alder *(Alnus rubra)* is found near rivers and streams along the immediate coast from central California to Alaska. It is similar to white alder but has larger leaves with a rolled margin; a rusty-colored down covers the lower leaf surface briefly in spring. Red alder is a reliable species for coastal gardens and tolerates brackish water.

Aquilegia formosa
WESTERN COLUMBINE
Buttercup Family (Ranunculaceae)

Plant Type: Semi-evergreen to evergreen perennial.
Geographic Zones: All.
Light: Sun to shade.
Soil: Adaptable; heavy and rich preferred.
Water: Moderate to regular.
Natural Habitat and Range: Moist places in woodlands below 9000 feet; California Floristic Province to Alaska, Montana, Utah, and Nevada.

Above: Western columbine, Rancho Santa Ana Botanic Garden, Claremont. BART O'BRIEN
Right: Western columbine, Inyo National Forest, near Tom's Place. STEPHEN INGRAM

hybridize, so if species purity is important, grow only a single species or strain.

The blue-green, deeply divided leaves of western columbine are evocative of maidenhair ferns, and although they tolerate low light, plants situated in deep shade seldom bloom. Western columbine is a beautiful companion for other partial-shade-loving plants, including Leatherleaf coffeeberry, giant chain fern, island alum root, Douglas iris, hummingbird sage, and currants.

Pests include mealybugs, red spider mites, and leaf miners. Mealybugs cluster at the leaf bases in the crown of older plants. Red spider mites form small loose webs on leaves and between leaflets of drought-stressed plants, and their feeding causes the leaves to have a finely stippled appearance. Leaf miners regularly appear on western columbine, but the damage they cause generally does not warrant any action.

Arbutus menziesii
MADRONE
Heath Family (Ericaceae)

Plant Type: Evergreen tree.
Geographic Zones: All except high mountains and deserts.
Light: Sun to partial shade.
Soil: Well-drained; acidic to neutral.
Water: Drought tolerant to occasional.
Natural Habitat and Range: Mixed-evergreen forests and occasional in chaparral below 5000 feet; California Floristic Province, excluding northwestern Baja California, and north to British Columbia.

Columbines are widely grown and appreciated for their brightly colored flowers, rosettes of delicately divided leaves, and ability to attract hummingbirds. Western columbine displays all these attributes. Its nodding flowers are composed of five funnel-like yellow petals and five red spurs that are filled with rich sugary nectar. Hummingbirds visit columbine flowers to drink the nectar; while feeding, they brush against and spread pollen from the stamens, thereby pollinating the plant.

Western columbine grows easily in most gardens. It requires ample water to thrive, but generally will not survive in soggy or waterlogged soils. Healthy, vigorous plants may reach 2 to 4 feet in height and are 1 to 2 feet across. Individual plants are not long-lived; a 2- to 3-year life span is average. To attract goldfinches and other seed-eating birds, allow some of western columbine's seedheads to mature; this will also ensure a future crop of seedlings in the garden. Columbines readily

Madrone in a private garden, Solvang. JOHN EVARTS

Madrone leaves and berries, private garden, Woodside.
BART O'BRIEN

Madrones are always eye-catchers. They stand out with a thin and stately elegance while reaching for sunlight in the woodlands and forests of northern California. They also grace cool north-facing ravines amidst southern California chaparral, where they hunker down with short stocky trunks and broad basal burls.

Madrone offers much to California gardeners. Its sensuously smooth red bark and nodding, white, honey-scented flowers are reminiscent of its close relatives, the manzanitas. However, madrones nearly always attain tree-like proportions (most manzanitas do not), and their flower clusters are three to four times larger than those of any manzanita. Madrone's large, lustrous, dark green, leathery leaves are pale whitish green below and have finely serrated margins. Madrone's round, fleshy, ½-inch fruits are red, orange, or yellow and ripen in late fall to early winter. The fruits remain showy for a month or more before birds devour them or holiday decorators harvest them and string them like popcorn and cranberries.

Madrone is a long-lived tree but is notoriously difficult to establish. A young madrone requires careful tending for several years. Death during this critical period most frequently stems from improper watering; either too much or too little. The tree may also fall victim to poor water quality or fungal diseases. When attempting to grow madrone outside of its native haunts, it is essential to start with a small (gallon-sized) plant. Larger specimens may be available, but they often fail to thrive. Never place a containerized madrone in direct sun for even short periods of time as its sensitive root system will almost invariably scorch and become a conduit for numerous soil- and water-borne fungal pathogens that kill the plant. Some nurseries apply fungicides to counterbalance these organisms, but this means that the plant may go through a difficult period of adjustment in your garden.

Mature madrones are susceptible to branch dieback from the fungus *Botryosphaeria dothidea,* and there is no known cure for this fungal pathogen. Madrones may also be afflicted by a variety of insect pests, although a single pest does not predominate. Keeping your madrone healthy and vigorous is the best way to prevent pest problems. Older madrones are an ongoing source of organic debris from the shedding of small branches, bark, leaves, flowers, and fruits. Most gardeners consider the required cleanup a small price to pay for the year-round beauty and character of a madrone.

Arctostaphylos species
MANZANITAS
Heath Family (Ericaceae)

Plant Type: Evergreen shrubs.
Geographic Zones: Unless specified, plants listed below may be expected to perform well in all zones other than high mountains and deserts.
Light: Sun, although several tolerate partial shade.
Soil: Individual species and cultivars vary, but nearly all plants listed here prefer or require well-drained, acid to neutral soils. In general, manzanitas will not tolerate alkaline soils.
Water: Drought tolerant to occasional. Plants must have adequate water while new growth is tender.
Natural Habitat and Range: These are classic chaparral plants, yet members of this diverse genus can be found from coastal bluffs to high mountain summits below 10,000 feet. Manzanitas grow in North America, especially California, and into Central America, as well as in Eurasia.

Sentinel manzanita blossoms, Rancho Santa Ana Botanic Garden, Claremont. KAREN MUSCHENETZ

Sentinel manzanita pruned to reveal its handsome bark, private garden, Solvang. JOHN EVARTS

There are manzanitas to suit nearly every landscape purpose, from carpeting groundcovers to small specimen trees. Few are adapted to all gardens, but those chosen few are among the most valuable additions to California gardens. With over 90 different kinds of manzanitas found in the wild and an additional 140 named cultivars, the gardener may be confronted with a bewildering array of choices. To this day, botanists are still hard at work defining the boundaries between manzanita species, subspecies, varieties, and hybrids, making it difficult for gardeners and horticulturists to place the most up-to-date names on some of these plants.

In nature, the majority of manzanitas have highly localized natural distributions. Many species are restricted to a particular geological formation or soil type. Often, these plants are so well adapted to these unusual substrates that they are the dominant vegetation—these areas are called manzanita barrens. If you are fortunate enough to live in one of these areas (there are many), you are much more likely to be successful cultivating the manzanita species native to your area than any of the others listed here. However, it is usually much more difficult to find them for sale.

Manzanitas are treasured for their dramatic form and structure; clean evergreen foliage; fragrant winter blossoms; clusters of small apple-like fruits; and magnificent smooth, sculpted, red-toned bark. A few manzanitas have shaggy or fibrous bark instead of the characteristic smooth bark. The bark of smooth-skinned manzanitas peels once a year—in late spring or early summer—to allow for expanding growth. This peeling signals the end of the growing season and the beginning of summer dormancy. At roughly this same time, manzanitas produce dormant (nascent) flower buds. If these structures are removed by pinching or pruning,

they will not be replaced until the following year, and you will have lost the year's flowers. These small, claw-like terminal buds remain in place through summer and fall until winter rains and cooler temperatures trigger flowering—seemingly overnight.

The characteristic, intricately branched growth habit of manzanitas is the result of their flowers. Whenever a manzanita flowers, the flower terminates the growth of the branch. One to several vegetative shoots develop below the cluster of flowers, but none of them continues along the same path as the shoot that bloomed. The resulting pattern of crooked twists and turns gives manzanitas their unique beauty and grace.

Young stems and newly expanding foliage are often richly colored in tones of red, copper, or bronze. The rigidly erect leaves of most manzanitas are models of adaptation to heat and drought. The great California native plantswoman, Lester Rowntree, observed this peculiar leaf arrangement and noted that it appeared as if the leaves were listening for something.

Many manzanita species bloom in winter and into spring, but the earliest flowering manzanitas (particularly Refugio manzanita) often begin to bloom in late September and October. The fall-blooming manzanitas are an important nectar source for both resident and migrating hummingbirds, since few other natives are flowering at that time. Native and European bees are the primary pollinators of manzanitas, and the honey they produce from the nectar of manzanita flowers is quite tasty. People who take the time to closely observe these blossoms are richly rewarded by their intense honey-like fragrance and their nodding bunches of thick, waxy, white to pink, urn-shaped flowers. Flower color can change considerably on the same plant from year to year, though the reason for this variability is not known.

The common name, manzanita, is Spanish for "little apple," a reference to the shape and appearance of the fruits, which can be quite showy. Some manzanita fruits are as bright red as holly berries, but most are green with a blush of red or bronze before aging to cinnamon brown. Many animals—including bears, coyotes, foxes, raccoons, gray squirrels, and quails—eat manzanita fruits.

Manzanita fruit, Rancho Santa Ana Botanic Garden, Claremont. DAN SONGSTER

Top: Howard McMinn manzanita in a naturalistic landscape, private garden, Ballard. JOHN EVARTS
Bottom: Howard McMinn manzanita sheared to a low, dense hedge, private garden, Lafayette. RON LUTSKO

Manzanita seeds are notoriously difficult to germinate, so seed-grown plants are rarely available. Nearly all commercial propagation of manzanitas is by cuttings, which helps to explain the profusion of cultivars in this genus—they are often the individuals that were the easiest to grow from cuttings.

Many manzanitas may prove difficult to grow when there is competition with the roots of established trees and shrubs. Manzanitas prefer good air circulation, and such conditions are especially important to those plants growing near the coast or in other humid environments where they are often attacked by leaf spot diseases.

Manzanitas have several problems that are nearly unique to their genus. One of these, Manzanita branch dieback, is a common ailment afflicting manzanitas almost throughout California. This problem is caused by the fungal pathogen *Botryosphaeria dothidea,* and there is no known cure. The fungal spores typically germinate and enter into the plant's tissues through wounds or intercellular cracks that occur as the flower buds rapidly expand and bloom in the moist winter and early spring months. Affected branches die back,

and the dead leaves may remain on the stems for many months. Removal of dead branches helps the aesthetic appearance of the plant but will not eliminate the fungus, which often extends a few inches to a foot or more into seemingly healthy live tissue. Pruning of infected plants is best accomplished during the summer months, when the pruning cuts dry and heal quickly. Always sterilize your pruners between each pruning cut to avoid spreading this pathogen. Be doubly sure to sterilize your equipment when you've finished working on a specimen and before you prune another plant. This fungal pathogen can also infect a wide array of other native plants, including coast redwood, California bay, coast silk-tassel, madrone, and incense cedar.

Alternaria leaf spot is a fungal pathogen that is rarely seen in hot interior climates but is pervasive in cool coastal environments. Leaves on affected plants develop perfectly round circles of black, grayish, or brownish dead tissue that are ¼ to ½ inch across. Frequently, there is a reddish appearance to the dying leading edge of leaf tissue, and leaves drop prematurely. *Alternaria* leaf spot is rarely fatal, except when it afflicts senescent plants or those species that are not adapted to cool coastal conditions. Clean up fallen leaves and avoid overhead irrigation to alleviate this condition in cool, humid gardens. Some fungicides have been successfully used to combat this pathogen.

Bright red swollen galls along the edges of young, tender leaves are sometimes mistaken for flowers or fruits. These galls are produced by manzanita leaf fold aphids *(Tamalia coweni),* which live inside the gall. Not long after the aphids leave their gall home, the gall tissue dies and turns dark brown or black. A short time later, the entire leaf dies and is shed. Manzanita species with smooth (non-hairy) leaves are more susceptible to this problem. Manzanita leaf gall is most commonly seen in plants that are producing succulent new growth out of season (in gardens, this is typically caused by giving the plants too much water). Don't worry about this pest—there isn't much you can do about it other than to remove the affected leaves if you find them offensive and change the way you water your plants next year.

The larval stage of the Pacific flatheaded borer *(Chrysobothris mali)* can kill or severely mutilate low-growing manzanitas by tunneling through their branches. This beetle grub is frequently a major concern to apple growers and other orchardists. Dead branches are the first sign that borers have infested your plants. A closer inspection reveals a sawdust-like material by a small hole or break in the branch. The clincher is the presence of lozenge-shaped tunnels in the dead branch. The white grub looks like a fat letter "T", as it has an enormous head and a small, narrow body. The tiny adult beetle is seen from April to August. The female beetle lays her eggs on bark that has been damaged by sunscald and pruning. There are no environmentally safe products available for controlling this pest.

Large tree-like manzanita shrubs
(reliably over 10 feet tall)

The smooth, muscular trunks and sinewy branches of tree-like manzanitas make them instantly recognizable and passionately sought-after garden subjects. These stately giants of the manzanita world may reach 15 to 25 feet in height and width in cultivation, but don't bank on those dimensions, as these are highly individualistic plants. Plan for a 10- to 12-foot-tall and -wide specimen and count your green thumbs if the plant grows larger. Two tree-like manzanitas warrant special mention here: Parry manzanita (*Arctostaphylos manzanita*) and bigberry manzanita (*Arctostaphylos glauca*). You can easily think of these two widespread species as northern and southern equivalents. Parry manzanita hales from a diversity of habitats—grasslands, woodlands, and chaparrals—from Mount Diablo north to Humboldt and Shasta counties; bigberry manzanita is found in chaparral environments from Mount Diablo south to northwestern Baja California. Both species embody the manzanita gestalt—evergreen leathery leaves, large terminal clusters of white to pale pink flowers, and smooth, rich, red-brown bark. Each is best grown as a specimen, except in the largest gardens where they may be employed as stunning informal hedges and screens.

Parry manzanita foliage color varies considerably from whitish, to blue-green, olive green, or dark green. It thrives in a wide array of garden conditions in central and northern California and is better than most manzanitas when it comes to tolerating richer and heavier soils and occasional summer irrigation. There are a number of cultivars of Parry manzanita; the most popular are 'Byrd Hill', 'Dr. Hurd', and 'Saint Helena'. Parry manzanita does best in gardens away from the immediate coast in the Coast Ranges, Central Valley,

Bigberry manzanita shading a bench, Santa Barbara Botanic Garden. JOHN EVARTS

Dr. Hurd manzanita in a private garden, Solvang.
JOHN EVARTS

and Sierra Nevada foothills. It will not tolerate desert or high mountain conditions, and its performance in southern California is uneven. In southern California, the most successful long-lived plants typically grow in heavier soils. For a memorable planting combine Parry manzanita, redberry, Hooker manzanita, California fescue, Ed Gedling whorled lupine, and mules ears.

The foliage of bigberry manzanita is a study in gray. The leaves vary in color from blue-gray to white-gray. A well-grown specimen is the center of attention in any garden it graces. Dry, well-drained chaparral slopes and the margins of our southern deserts are the natural haunts of this species. As one might logically expect from its common name, this plant has the largest fruit—up to ½ inch across—of all the manzanitas. The fruit is thin-skinned, quite sticky, and covers a hard, stone-like seed. Bigberry manzanita often performs unreliably when grown in rich or heavy soils, coastal conditions, and high-mountain and desert gardens. It seems much more comfortable in interior and southern California gardens with well-drained soils, where it revels in heat and summer dryness—even in the mountains at the western edges of the Mojave and Colorado deserts. Bigberry manzanita's stunning features combine well with an array of interior species: singleleaf pinyon pine, California fremontia, Our Lord's candle, sages, and beargrasses.

Medium to large manzanita shrubs
(from 3 or 4 to 10 feet tall)

Most manzanitas fall into this shrub category, and gardeners will find they have a phenomenal number of choices when they seek a manzanita in this size range. This group exemplifies the intricate branching pattern and dense foliage often associated with manzanitas. These plants are superb specimens in dry gardens and landscapes, particularly those that feature rocks and boulders.

Many native plant gardeners favor Louis Edmunds manzanita (*Arctostaphylos bakeri* 'Louis Edmunds'), and fortunately nearly everyone can grow and enjoy it. This choice manzanita features a unique, dark purple-mahogany bark on its elegant trunk and branches. The sage gray leaves are perfect foils for the numerous clusters of clear pink flowers. Louis Edmunds manzanita has a distinctively upright growth habit to 10 feet tall. It is best used as a focal point in the garden, but it is equally well employed as an informal screen with toyon and sugar bush or in a background planting with Matilija poppy, groundcover forms of ceanothus, and native sages.

The renowned Howard McMinn manzanita (*Arctostaphylos* 'Howard McMinn') is, without a doubt, everyone's manzanita. It tolerates average garden conditions that are supposed to be anathema to most California native plants: regular summer watering, overhead watering, heavy clay soils, and regular pruning and shearing. Through it all, Howard McMinn manzanita grows with abandon. Though it prefers full sun, it tolerates partial shade better than most other shrubby manzanitas. It is not only one of our most dependable natives in the garden, it is also an especially handsome shrub—winning a rare award of merit from the California Horticultural Society in 1956. The glossy green smooth leaves completely cover the underlying branch structure of young plants. Plants naturally open up as they age and reveal the striking, twisted branching habit associated with manzanitas. This free-flowering shrub is one of the last manzanitas to bloom in spring and features white to pale pink blossoms. Howard McMinn manzanita readily accepts pruning and can be kept to a height of 5 to 6 feet with an equal to slightly greater spread. Early garden writers thought this manzanita would top out at 3 feet, and it is humorous to follow the ever-increasing height estimates for this plant through the garden literature. Mature specimens can easily reach 8 feet in height and spread up to 15 feet wide. Gardeners use it in mid-size informal hedges, as espaliers, as a specimen shrub, and even as topiary. Massed plantings are especially effective. The clean, fine-textured foliage of Howard McMinn manzanita combines or contrasts with nearly any plant; an excellent pairing places it near Saint Catherine's lace. Contrary to most published information, Howard McMinn manzanita is of hybrid origin.

The natural distribution of Pajaro manzanita (*Arctostaphylos pajaroensis*) is centered about the small Monterey County town of Prunedale. This rare species has received considerable horticultural attention in recent years due to its attractive flowers, variable foliage, and differing plant sizes and habits. Flower color ranges from pure white to the darkest pink manzanita flowers known. The leaves are similarly variable

Top: Louis Edmunds manzanita pruned up at its base, private garden, Solvang. DAVID FROSS
Bottom: Howard McMinn manzanita above a retaining wall, private garden, Lafayette. STEPHEN INGRAM

and include specimens with slate blue, gray, gray-green, or dark green foliage. In addition, Pajaro manzanita often displays dark coppery new growth. Plants thrive best in gardens with well-drained soils, as this species is especially intolerant of heavy clay soils. Pajaro manzanita typically has a reddish gray fibrous bark, though some specimens do develop smooth trunks with age.

In the wild, the rare Refugio manzanita (*Arctostaphylos refugioensis*) is restricted to sandstone substrates around Refugio Pass in Santa Barbara County. As is typical for manzanitas, the species is quite variable. The new growth can be extremely colorful, from bright orange-red to red, though many plants

Pajaro manzanita's attractive flowers, private garden, Sebastopol. PHILIP VAN SOELEN

Sunset manzanita and non-native Japanese silver grass, private garden, San Luis Obispo. DAVID FROSS

apparently lose this trait in cultivation. The size of the branched flower clusters is also highly variable and is normally quite generous, measuring from 2 to 6 inches across. The base of each broad leaf is lobed, and the leaves clasp the stems. Refugio manzanita is often fast growing in gardens and may top out from 6 to 12 feet high and have a similar spread. These plants are typically multi-trunked and may resemble small trees.

Sentinel manzanita (*Arctostaphylos* 'Sentinel') is a close relative of Howard McMinn manzanita, and both share the same wide tolerance of garden conditions. 'Sentinel', however, has a much different garden persona; it has a distinctly upright growth habit and quickly reaches a mature height of 6 to 8 feet and spreads from 4 to 10 feet wide. 'Sentinel' shows more of its branching structure and rich red-brown bark at an earlier age than 'Howard McMinn'. Leaves are dark green with a dull, grayish cast. The liberally produced flowers are generally pink but may appear white in some years. With its neutral foliage, 'Sentinel' is the perfect foil for more colorful plants, such as Carmel creeper ceanothus with its shiny green leaves, island snapdragon, California fuchsias, and California's brightly colored annual wildflowers. 'Sentinel' harmonizes well with numerous natives, including California sagebrush, island bush poppy, sages, and buckwheats.

Growers introduced Sunset manzanita (*Arctostaphylos* 'Sunset') to commemorate *Sunset* magazine's 75th anniversary. Many thought this shrub would be a passing fad because it soon dropped out of nursery production throughout the state and was drifting into obscurity. Then a strange thing happened. Unlike the majority of manzanitas, this one lived nearly everywhere it had been planted. Gardeners, growers, landscapers, and designers discovered that 'Sunset' was a manzanita that did perform. This realization saved it from oblivion and brought it to the attention of a much wider audience. 'Sunset' is not a typical manzanita; it has rough bark, ¾-inch-long flower clusters, and dense foliage that conceals its branch structure. It offers pleasing, medium green foliage and bright copper-colored spring growth. The individual leaves are roughly triangular in shape. Sunset manzanita tolerates light pruning

and stays dense with age, which makes it an ideal choice for use as a large formal or informal hedge. Mature plants typically reach 5 to 8 feet high and spread wider. This plant grows rapidly when it is well sited.

Low manzanita shrubs and groundcovers (from 4 inches to 3 to 4 feet tall)

While this category includes an enormous number of manzanitas in the wild, precious few grow well throughout the geographic range of California gardens. The following deserve consideration.

Edmunds manzanita (*Arctostaphylos edmundsii*) is quite rare in nature, as it is only found on a few coastal bluffs and hillsides from south of Carmel to Big Sur. This highly variable species has contributed a number of excellent named cultivars. The species and its cultivars are nearly carefree in gardens (only Howard McMinn manzanita offers better garden tolerance). They tolerate heavy soils, partial shade, above average summer irrigation, and are not as particular as other manzanitas in their requirement for good drainage. However, plants are sometimes damaged or killed during periodic severe freezes in more inland gardens.

Bert Johnson manzanita (*Arctostaphylos edmundsii* var. *parvifolia* 'Bert Johnson') and Carmel Sur manzanita (*Arctostaphylos edmundsii* 'Carmel Sur') are two of the best-performing cultivars derived from Edmunds manzanita. These two cultivars could not be more different. 'Bert Johnson' produces a profusion of conch shell pink to white flowers and has a dense, mounding growth habit, tiny dark green leaves, and bronzy new foliage. This choice manzanita fits well in a refined garden, though it is equally at home in a rugged rock garden. Mature shrubs of 'Bert Johnson' reach 1 to 3 feet tall and 4 to 6 feet wide. It rarely requires pinching or pruning.

'Carmel Sur' is a manzanita that almost never blooms. This vigorous clone is widely grown and appreciated for its tolerance to garden conditions and its low,

Top: Carmel Sur manzanita along a walkway, private garden, Montecito. STEPHEN INGRAM
Bottom: Monterey Carpet manzanita close-up, Santa Barbara Botanic Garden. STEPHEN INGRAM

tailored growth habit. New foliage in spring is bright and shiny green. The leaves densely clothe the prostrate stems that hug the ground. When planting 'Carmel Sur' as a groundcover, place the individuals 4 to 5 feet apart. Established plantings smother most annual weeds. Mature plants may reach 1 to 2 feet tall and 6 feet wide.

Hooker manzanita (*Arctostaphylos hookeri*) is a rare species from the northern half of the Monterey Bay area, where it grows on sandstone generally within sight of the Pacific Ocean. In the wild this manzanita forms dense mounds of foliage from 2 to 8 feet in height and spreads from 3 to 15 feet wide. Virtually all of the cultivars that have been made to date from this species were selected for use as groundcovers. The most carefree and dependable of these is Monterey Carpet manzanita (*Arctostaphylos hookeri* 'Monterey Carpet'). The name is misleading, as plants of this clone tend to mound up almost as quickly as they spread out. The leaves are a deep olive gray-green, and the young stems are dark red-purple. Contrary to most manzanitas, the individual leaves of 'Monterey Carpet' are coarsely and irregularly serrated. This clone is frequently slow to

establish, but it has a long and impressive record of reliable performance in gardens throughout low elevation, non-desert portions of California.

John Dourley manzanita (*Arctostaphylos* 'John Dourley') is the chameleon of the smaller manzanita selections, seasonally displaying an abundance of deep pink blossoms, coppery new growth, red-burnished fruits, and slate gray foliage. This vigorous, easily grown plant has a mounding growth habit and may eventually reach up to 4 feet tall and 6 feet wide. California's native sages and buckwheats are excellent companions for this outstanding cultivar.

Pacific Mist manzanita (*Arctostaphylos* 'Pacific Mist') grows dependably throughout much of California. The color of its 2- to 3-inch-long, narrow, pointed leaves varies depending on its location. The generally gray-green leaves are grayer in hotter interior gardens and greener in cooler coastal gardens or when grown in partial shade. The dark red stems do not branch freely, and young plants can appear sparse for a year or two unless they are pinched or lightly pruned. Within three to five years, the intertwined snake-like branches may form a dense weed-smothering groundcover. The leading ends of the branches are always turned upward, giving massed plantings a soft, irregular edge. 'Pacific Mist' is an excellent groundcover selection for larger spaces and gentle slopes. Mature plants may reach 2 to 3 feet tall and spread from 6 to 15 feet wide. Its small clusters of pure white flowers are produced only rarely. 'Pacific Mist' may be effectively combined with many native sages (including 'Allen Chickering' and 'Winifred Gilman'), Montara California sagebrush, and taller manzanitas.

Sandmat manzanita (*Arctostaphylos pumila*) occurs naturally only on stabilized coastal dunes near Monterey, where it forms large low-growing colonies

Pacific Mist manzanita used as a groundcover, with California poppy, private garden, La Honda. STEPHEN INGRAM

that spread by rooting branchlets. Despite its highly restricted natural distribution, it has proven to be one of the easiest and most adaptable manzanitas in the garden. Sandmat manzanita tolerates heavy soils in both coastal and inland gardens. It also thrives with or without summer irrigation. Unlike most manzanitas, this species readily tolerates light shade, though it does prefer full sun even in inland gardens. The small, spatulate convex leaves are covered with short, fine white hairs that give the plant an olive green to sage green appearance. Flowers are almost always pure white and are produced in tiny terminal clusters. In garden conditions, expect sandmat manzanita to reach 1 to 3 feet in height and to spread 3 to 6 feet wide. Sandmat manzanita is currently difficult to find in nurseries because it grows poorly in containers.

Kinnikinnick (*Arctostaphylos uva-ursi*) is the most widespread of all manzanitas, naturally occurring throughout the northern Polar Regions around the world and extending south to the summits of at least two Guatemalan volcanoes (though it has yet to be found anywhere in Mexico). In California, it is found along the immediate coast from Del Norte County

Emerald Carpet manzanita spilling over a retaining wall, private garden, Lafayette. STEPHEN INGRAM

Above: Sandmat manzanita, San Francisco Botanical Garden.
DAVID FROSS
Left: Kinnikinnick close-up, private garden, Berkeley.
STEPHEN INGRAM

south to the Big Sur area of Monterey County and in a few widely isolated populations in the Sierra Nevada. There are numerous cultivars of kinnikinnick of California origin, but nearly all are difficult to grow beyond their native humid, cool, coastal or high-mountain habitats. The search for widely adaptable cultivars continues to this day, but without much success. The two oldest and most commonly encountered cultivars are Point Reyes kinnikinnick (*Arctostaphylos uva-ursi* 'Point Reyes') and Radiant kinnikinnick (*Arctostaphylos uva-ursi* 'Radiant'), though neither are exceptional performers when grown in hot or inland gardens. 'Point Reyes' tolerates more heat and drought. It has thick, dark green, rounded leaves and trailing to arching snake-like branches. 'Radiant' is a fast, vigorous grower with thinner, brighter green, oblong leaves and a ground-hugging growth habit. Kinnikinnick greatly benefits when peat moss is used to acidify the soil if the plant is grown outside its native range. It may require regular applications of a foliar nitrogen fertilizer if the leaves turn yellow. In cool coastal gardens with acidic soil, kinnikinnick becomes a pleasing groundcover, growing from 4 to 18 inches tall and 6 to 12 feet wide. Newly planted kinnikinnicks benefit from light pinching shortly after they bloom in winter. Young vigorous plantings are most satisfactory, as older plantings frequently assume a patchy appearance and do not smother weeds. Emerald Carpet manzanita (*Arctostaphylos* 'Emerald Carpet') is a naturally occurring hybrid of *Arctostaphylos uva-ursi* and *A. nummularia* that was collected from the immediate coast of Mendocino County. Emerald Carpet manzanita is a prostrate groundcover that has shiny dark green leaves, reddish stems, and tiny clusters of pure white flowers. Similar to its kinnikinnick parent, it requires an acid soil and rapidly becomes chlorotic when the soil is not to its liking.

Aristida purpurea var. purpurea
PURPLE THREE-AWN
Grass Family (Poaceae)

Plant Type: Semi-evergreen to deciduous, warm-season perennial grass.
Geographic Zones: All except high mountains.
Light: Sun.
Soil: Adaptable.
Water: Drought tolerant to occasional.
Natural Habitat and Range: Rocky or sandy soils on slopes in many plant communities below 6000 feet; in southern California and extending to the Great Plains and northern Mexico.

Purple three-awn in a massed planting, private garden, near San Luis Obispo. DAVID FROSS

Purple three-awn during spring, Santa Barbara Botanic Garden. STEPHEN INGRAM

Purple three-awn is distinctive among California bunchgrasses for its color and year-round beauty. Regardless of the season, this fine-textured grass consistently looks good, whether flushed with maroon or bleached to light straw. Although modest in size, purple three-awn adds drama to a meadow garden or perennial border when planted in large drifts. It can also command center stage in a decorative pot or serve as a foil for cacti in a succulent garden.

The color of the inflorescence distinguishes purple three-awn. Throughout most of the year in warm coastal locations, but less so elsewhere, a continual stream of eggplant-colored, slightly nodding flower stalks rise above the tufted clump of narrow, light green leaves. As its common name implies, it has clusters of three thread-like awns, which are 1 to 3 inches long.

Purple three-awn requires nothing more than sunny, dry conditions and occasional pruning. In coastal gardens this bunchgrass grows perpetually, so deciding when to prune is a bit of a challenge. If you

want to encourage more flowering stalks, cut purple three-awn down to the crown whenever too many old, faded stalks accumulate. If you prune before the flowers mature, however, you sacrifice one of the most appealing features of this grass; only mature flower stalks sport the puffy bottlebrush-like awns that capture light so beautifully. The drying awns do get caught in animal fur, so gardeners with pets should take this factor into consideration. Purple three-awn may self-sow in favorable situations. If you prefer to contain this bunchgrass, remove the maturing flower stalks before they ripen.

Aristolochia californica
CALIFORNIA DUTCHMAN'S PIPE
Pipevine Family (Aristolochiaceae)

Plant Type: Deciduous vine.
Geographic Zones: All except high mountains and deserts.
Light: Sun to shade.
Soil: Adaptable.
Water: Drought tolerant to moderate.
Natural Habitat and Range: Along streambanks and in woodlands below 1500 feet; foothills of the northern Sierra Nevada and Coast Ranges from the Santa Lucia Mountains to the Oregon border.

California Dutchman's pipe receives its name from its odd flowers, which dangle from naked stems. These bulbous, U-shaped, 1½-inch-long flowers are formed by fused sepals and resemble a fanciful Dutchman's pipe.

California Dutchman's pipe, private garden, Berkeley.
BART O'BRIEN

Artemisia californica
CALIFORNIA SAGEBRUSH
Sunflower Family (Asteraceae)

Plant Type: Evergreen subshrub.
Geographic Zones: All except high mountains and deserts.
Light: Sun.
Soil: Adaptable, except poorly drained.
Water: Drought tolerant to occasional.
Natural Habitat and Range: Coastal scrub and chaparral below 2500 feet; Mendocino County south to northwestern Baja California.

Canyon Gray California sagebrush, Santa Barbara Botanic Garden. STEPHEN INGRAM

Their coloration is as unusual as their shape; each body is pale green with long burgundy veins, and the open mouth has purple-brown lips and a dusky throat. Appearing in winter and spring, the flowers' color and often-foul odor attract fungus gnats that act as pollinators.

California Dutchman's pipe is a rhizomatous vine. Its dull brown, rope-like stems grow to 12 feet in length and can wind and curl through the branches of nearby shrubs and trees. Its fuzzy, heart-shaped leaves are mint green when young. They grow 3 to 6 inches long and maintain a fresh, pale green appearance throughout summer and early fall. The beguiling flowers can be viewed in detail when the vine grows near a garden bench or among shrubs at the edge of a path.

Try planting this vine as a small-scale groundcover under oaks or with coffeeberry, spicebush, and pink-flowering currant. In California habitat gardens, it not only provides cover, but also is a larval food source of the pipevine swallowtail butterfly *(Battus philenor).* Although slow growing initially, once established, California Dutchman's pipe knits shrubs and trees together into loose thickets. Some gardeners use this robust and durable vine to cover a trellis or chain-link fence. In favorable sites it can be aggressive and may require pruning.

California sagebrush is the quintessential component of the coastal scrub community. With its characteristic pungent aroma, California sagebrush announces its presence to the nose first and to the eye second. What attracts the eye is its soft, fine-textured foliage.

This plant moves through two distinct phases each year. During the cool rainy months of the year, California sagebrush produces large, finely divided gray-green leaves that make the plant appear lush and soft. These winter leaves are shed in late spring or early summer and are replaced by much smaller and sparser

Mugwort at the base of a hillside, private garden, Oakland.
STEPHEN INGRAM

silver gray foliage that reveals the plant's twiggy structure. Towards the end of summer or in fall, California sagebrush produces its terminal wands of inconspicuous gray-yellow flowers. These late-season flowers provide a critical supply of pollen, nectar, and seeds for a wide array of insects, birds, and small mammals. Copious amounts of tiny seeds are scattered just in time to germinate with the late fall and winter rains. An abundance of volunteers may result, but unwanted seedlings are easily removed.

California sagebrush typically plays a subordinate role in the garden, with the exception of the cultivars listed below, and gardeners often use it to fill in around other plants, even temporarily. The appearance of established older plants is greatly enhanced by hard pruning in the late fall or early winter, after they have bloomed but before new lush growth emerges.

Cultivars: Canyon Gray California sagebrush (*Artemisia californica* 'Canyon Gray') and Montara California sagebrush (*Artemisia californica* 'Montara') differ from typical California sagebrush due to their groundcover habit. Canyon Gray California sagebrush forms a prostrate mat of foliage and flower stems that reaches about 1 foot tall and spreads to at least 10 feet. If left unpruned, the center of the plant slowly mounds up to at least 3 feet tall and may open up with age. To keep it flat, remove upright to arching growth in the plant's center as soon as it appears. Montara California sagebrush produces pleasing mounds of foliage about 2 feet tall and 3 to 5 feet wide; flowers appear on short terminal stems. Both of these groundcovers are effectively used in massed plantings and as foils for the green foliage of coyote brush, coffeeberry, and many of the manzanitas.

Other Species: Great Basin sagebrush (*Artemisia tridentata*) is widely grown and appreciated for its fragrant, silver to gray foliage. This low-maintenance woody shrub is well suited to full sun, well-drained soils, and hot, dry climates. It reaches 5 to 8 feet tall and has an equal spread; it tolerates much colder temperatures than other sagebrushes listed here. To enhance its appearance, prune the dead flower stalks in late fall. Mugwort (*Artemisia douglasiana*) is a good choice for use in informal, lush green riparian gardens, as its coarsely serrated leaves, which are dark green above and silvery beneath, provide contrast. Plants spread by underground rhizomes, and the erect stems of regularly watered plants may reach heights up to 6 feet. Mugwort tolerates more shade and heavier soils than other sagebrushes. Cut it to the ground in late fall or early winter to remove aging stems and open the way for new spring growth.

Artemisia pycnocephala 'David's Choice'
DAVID'S CHOICE SANDHILL SAGEBRUSH
Sunflower Family (Asteraceae)

Plant Type: Evergreen shrub.
Geographic Zones: All except Central Valley, high mountains, and deserts.
Light: Sun to partial shade.
Soil: Adaptable; well-drained preferred.
Water: Drought tolerant to occasional.
Natural Habitat and Range: Sandhill sagebrush is found in coastal sage below 600 feet; along the immediate coast from Monterey County to southwestern Oregon. This selection is from the Point Reyes headlands, Marin County.

David's Choice sandhill sagebrush is one of the most widely grown and appreciated California native plants. This outstanding cultivar performs well in many

David's Choice sandhill sagebrush and chalk dudleya, Leaning Pine Arboretum, Cal Poly, San Luis Obispo. DAVID FROSS

garden situations: in mixed borders, along path edges, as a small-scale groundcover, among rocks and boulders, and in containers. Its small size, adaptability, and low-maintenance requirements also explain its popularity.

The soft silvery mounds of David's Choice sandhill sagebrush may grow 6 inches tall and up to 2 feet wide. The finely cut blue-green to silver gray leaves are densely clothed with soft white hairs. Some gardeners feel that the 6- to 12-inch-long flower stalks detract from the gently undulating mounds of foliage and remove them as they emerge. Others leave the stalks and cut them back as they dry in the early fall months. For an especially pleasing combination, grow David's Choice sandhill sagebrush with Aulon beach strawberry and Douglas iris.

Sandhill sagebrush (*Artemisia pycnocephala*), from which this cultivar is derived, is often short-lived. It grows to 2½ feet tall with a slightly wider spread. In gardens, sandhill sagebrush requires grooming and pinching. It thrives in coastal gardens, but in hot inland gardens it often dies during periods of summer heat. A combination of sandhill sagebrush and Santa Ana Cardinal or Susanna coral bells makes a stunning display.

Asarum caudatum
WILD GINGER
Pipevine Family (Aristolochiaceae)

Plant Type: Evergreen herbaceous perennial.
Geographic Zones: All except Central Valley, high mountains, and deserts.
Light: Partial shade to shade.
Soil: Adaptable; humus-rich and acidic preferred.
Water: Occasional to regular.
Natural Habitat and Range: Moist sites in forests, from sea level to 5000 feet; Santa Cruz County north to British Columbia.

Wild ginger is one of the few California natives that evokes images of a lush, tropical environment. In its natural habitat, this low-spreading groundcover blankets the soil of coast redwood and mixed-evergreen forests. Gardeners prize wild ginger for its prostrate habit and its glossy, heart-shaped leaf blades, which measure 2 to 4 inches long and up to 7 inches wide. The verdant leaves hide unusual-looking late winter or spring flowers, which are pollinated by fungus gnats. Each flower is a deep maroon-colored cup of three sepals, which flare at the top then gradually taper to a point.

Wild ginger is an ideal companion for island alum root, redwood sorrel, coast redwood, western azalea, and ferns. It is at home in both formal gardens and naturalistic plantings. In southern California, it must be

Wild ginger leaves and flower, Santa Barbara Botanic Garden.
STEPHEN INGRAM

given summer water and fares better in coastal gardens than hot, inland areas. In coastal northern California, it will grow in full sun if given regular irrigation. Water quality is important, as both alkaline and salt-laden waters damage the plant. The leaves of wild ginger droop and appear dull when the plant is not watered sufficiently, but it bounces back quickly when water is replenished.

To achieve a dense groundcover quickly, divide wild ginger's rhizomes in fall or winter and include a few rooted nodes in each piece you replant. Try growing wild ginger in a large pot if you want luxuriant foliage but don't want to supply all the water a groundcover needs. Add one of the large-leaved coral bells or Pacific reedgrass as vertical accents. Although it is not closely related to the ginger that is grown for culinary use, wild ginger does indeed have a spicy, pungent scent when crushed. Some Native American tribes use the plant for medicinal purposes and make a refreshing tea from its roots.

Asclepias speciosa
SHOWY MILKWEED
Milkweed Family (Asclepidaceae)

Plant Type: Deciduous herbaceous perennial.
Geographic Zones: All except high mountains and deserts.
Light: Sun.
Soil: Adaptable; heavy preferred.
Water: Drought tolerant to occasional.
Natural Habitat and Range: Open areas in many plant communities below 6000 feet; North Coast Ranges and Sierra Nevada to central Canada and western Texas.

The English treat showy milkweed as a garden aristocrat, but surprisingly, it is rarely grown here in its

Showy milkweed in full bloom, Rancho Santa Ana Botanic Garden, Claremont. BART O'BRIEN

California's milkweeds make an important contribution to any habitat garden. They attract a diverse array of insects and are especially vital to the perpetuation of monarch butterflies. Adult monarch butterflies reap nectar from milkweeds and a variety of plants, but their larvae feed only on the foliage, stems, and flower buds of plants in the milkweed genus, which contain toxins that many animals avoid. Monarch butterfly larvae are immune to these toxic substances, and their consumption of milkweeds affords them some protection from predation. Milkweeds also host many colorful insects, such as golden aphids, red milkweed beetles, blue milkweed beetles, large milkweed bugs, and tarantula hawk wasps. In nearly all cases, these insects do little or no serious damage to your milkweed plants.

Narrow-leaved milkweed with monarch butterfly larvae, private garden, Santa Ynez. MARY JANE WEST-DELGADO

native land. It performs well in most gardens, but it is not a good choice for a tailored or formal landscape because it spreads easily via underground stems. To showcase its attributes, plant it in mixed borders, grassland gardens, or habitat gardens. Showy milkweed is particularly effective when combined with masses of our larger grasses, such as Canyon Prince wild rye, deer grass, or needlegrasses.

This long-lived plant has bold, softly hairy gray foliage, stiffly erect stems, and numerous 3-inch-wide balls of carnation-scented, star-shaped pinkish flowers. Showy milkweed's flowering stems range in height from 2 to 4 feet. It develops large inflated seed pods that mature in late fall. The wind disperses showy milkweed's numerous chocolate brown seeds, which are topped by white, parachute-like structures.

California's milkweeds evolved from species acclimated to a tropical climate, and their long period of winter dormancy serves to protect their tender new growth from cold weather. Vigorous new shoots often do not emerge until April or early May. Some gardeners leave the prior year's attractive dried flower stalks until this new growth appears; if the stalks are removed, mark the location of the dormant plants so that cultivation, weed control, and other garden activities will not inadvertently destroy or damage them.

Other Species: Narrow-leaved milkweed *(Asclepias fascicularis)* is the most favored larval monarch host in California. It may not be appropriate for small gardens, as it can spread aggressively.

Aster chilensis
COAST ASTER
Sunflower Family (Asteraceae)

Plant Type: Evergreen herbaceous perennial.
Geographic Zones: All except high mountains and deserts.
Light: Sun to partial shade.
Soil: Adaptable.
Water: Drought tolerant to occasional.
Natural Habitat and Range: Meadows, open slopes, clearings, salt marshes, and coastal bluffs in many plant communites below 4500 feet; Santa Barbara County to British Columbia.

Asters have long provided fall color as a bridge to the emerging textures and colors of the winter landscape.

Point Saint George aster, private garden, Arroyo Grande.
DAVID FROSS

Bright, festive blossoms characterize the genus, and garden centers sell a bewildering number of choices. Coast aster has a coarser texture and paler flowers than many of the more commonly available exotic species, but it is more durable and better suited to an informal garden.

The growth habit of coast aster varies; it can sprawl or send erect branched stems to a height of 3 feet. Its lance-shaped leaves range in color from glossy green to dull olive. Colorful, daisy-like flowers form in terminal or lateral heads. Each is a compound flower with blue, lavender, or white petals (ray flowers) that surround a cluster of numerous yellow disk flowers. In autumn, after the petals drop, tawny, bristle-like fruits form on the stiff stems.

Coast aster enhances meadow gardens and mixed borders, where it combines well with other perennials and grasses, such as yarrow, Idaho fescue, and seaside daisy. It is effective on a large scale when planted with Grey Dawn wild rye or dune sedge as a component of a natural meadow. This vigorous perennial spreads via rhizomes and colonizes easily. Use it to help stabilize slopes and banks or as an understory plant.

Diseases or pests seldom trouble coast aster, although mildew can be a problem in warm, humid weather. Aphids will occasionally damage lush spring growth, and you may need to protect young plants from rabbits and ground squirrels. Prune coast aster after it flowers to freshen its appearance.

Cultivars: *Aster chilensis* 'Point Saint George' forms a groundcover 4 to 6 inches tall. From summer to late fall, it yields pale violet flowers on short stalks held just above the dense foliage. This aster will quickly colonize large areas and should be sited with care. It tolerates modest foot traffic and can be mowed on occasion to maintain a tight, turf-like appearance.

Atriplex lentiformis ssp. *breweri*
QUAIL BUSH
Goosefoot Family (Chenopodiaceae)

Plant Type: Semi-evergreen shrub.
Geographic Zones: All except high mountains.
Light: Sun.
Soil: Adaptable.
Water: Drought tolerant to occasional.
Natural Habitat and Range: Saline places in coastal scrub, edges of coastal salt marsh, and grasslands below 2000 feet; Channel Islands; Orange County north to San Francisco Bay and inland to the western Central Valley.

Quail bush has many desirable qualities that first impressions might not reveal. Gardeners can rely on this tough shrub when they need a plant for difficult sites. Quail bush tolerates salt spray and adapts to saline soils. It also provides habitat value and fire-resistant foliage.

This subspecies is the coastal form of quail bush. It becomes a sizable shrub, growing 4 to 10 feet in height and often considerably wider. The bluish gray to silvery leaves measure 1 to 2 inches long and ½ to 2 inches wide. The tiny, creamy white flowers are held in terminal clusters and emerge in late summer or fall. They draw attention by their sheer numbers and rapidly turn a light tan that contrasts pleasingly with the gray foliage.

Quail bush, as its common name suggests, is an excellent plant for habitat gardens. Quails, sparrows, and small mammals use it for cover and eat the seeds. In addition, quail bush makes a fine hedge or windbreak in areas exposed to salt spray or where soils are alkaline and/or saline. It also helps curb erosion on steep slopes.

Prune quail bush lightly in winter to remove spent flowers, promote a bushy character, and control size.

Quail bush during fall, Santa Barbara Botanic Garden.
JOHN EVARTS

A more aggressive pruning every 5 to 7 years will remove old wood, rejuvenate the plant, and ensure continued fire resistance. Quail bush can be sheared into a formal hedge if desired. This requires more frequent pruning and results in fewer flowers. Monthly summer irrigation benefits coastal plantings and is essential to plants in hotter inland areas. Pests and diseases are insignificant.

Baccharis pilularis
COYOTE BRUSH
Sunflower Family (Asteraceae)

Plant Type: Evergreen shrub.
Geographic Zones: All except high mountains and deserts.
Light: Sun.
Soil: Adaptable.
Water: Drought tolerant to occasional.
Natural Habitat and Range: Dunes and bluffs, dry slopes, and open woods in chaparral and coastal scrub communities below 2500 feet; northwestern Baja California to the Oregon coast.

Coyote brush can evoke a curious range of responses from gardeners. Many recognize its merits in the landscape and praise coyote brush (also known as coyote bush) for its hardiness and reliability. Some, like Judith Lowry, author of *Gardening with a Wild Heart*, find in this humble shrub a deeper connection to the California landscape; these admirers even belong to a playful and loose affiliation called Friends of the Coyote Bush. Still others regard this "coyote" as a weed and cannot imagine using it in their gardens.

Like many wide-ranging species, coyote brush's growth habit varies considerably. On windswept headlands it is commonly a prostrate shrub with a dense, congested habit, while in open fields it typically has a more spreading, erect form and can reach 8 feet in height. Its thick, resinous, green or olive green leaves measure up to ¾ inch long and have coarsely serrated teeth. Fall-blooming male or female flowers are borne on separate plants and cover the stems with an abundance of cream-colored rayless flowers. The male flowers are quickly shed, but debris from the female plants' fluffy fruits can be a nuisance. Most horticultural selections are male for this reason.

Even though it is well known as a tough and drought-tolerant species, coyote brush's garden performance will improve greatly with moderate summer watering and occasional pruning. Prune coyote brush into a tight hedge, leave it in a natural condition as an informal screen, or even shear it as topiary. Coppicing will freshen both upright and groundcover forms.

Twin Peaks #2 coyote brush (both sides of path) and Pigeon Point coyote brush (bright green, low-spreading plant in lower right foreground), private garden, La Honda. STEPHEN INGRAM

Pruning is best accomplished in late winter before the flush of spring growth begins.

Coyote brush adds significant value in the habitat garden. It is frequently used in restoration projects because it spreads rapidly and quickly provides food and cover for a variety of birds, mammals, and insects. Some birds, like wrentits and white-crowned sparrows, may spend their entire lives among stands of coyote brush.

Coyote brush is prone to attacks by mites, leafhoppers, lace bugs, white fly, and occasionally flathead borers. Each requires treatment and can compromise the aesthetics of the planting. Coppicing will effectively break the cycle of heavy infestations, but in some cases removing infected plants is required. Vigorous, healthy plants suffer fewer infestations, and regular maintenance can help keep insects to a manageable level.

Cultivars: Two male selections of coyote brush are commonly grown in the nursery trade and are sometimes incorrectly labeled. 'Twin Peaks #2' is a spreading cultivar to 3 feet tall and 8 feet wide. Its bright green leaves are held tightly along the stems. It grows as a dense, mounding form that eventually becomes a sizeable shrub with age. 'Pigeon Point' is a smaller shrub with larger, bright green leaves. It has a lax, undulating habit and grows to 2 feet tall and 8 feet wide. Both selections can be sheared or even mowed as a lawn alternative. Some local agencies include them on lists for use in fire-prone regions because they demonstrate fire resistance as long as they are watered and pruned consistently to remove bulk and maintain a low form.

Berberis species
BARBERRIES
Barberry Family (Berberidaceae)

Plant taxonomists have long struggled to find the appropriate genus for this group of useful ornamental shrubs. Collectively, they were first classified as *Berberis,* then they were listed as *Mahonia;* more recently, the editors of *The Jepson Manual* have returned the California species to *Berberis.* Most gardeners disregard the taxonomic detail of the controversy and focus on barberries' salient features, such as their brilliant yellow flowers, colorful waxy berries, and dark red winter leaves. These attributes ensure that barberries, no matter how they are categorized, will contribute year-round beauty to the garden.

The California species are evergreen shrubs of varying size and share a number of common features. All have pinnately compound leaves that range in color from matte gray to polished forest green. Sharp teeth line the margins of each stiff leaflet. Compound spikes 1 to 6 inches long bear pale or luminous yellow flowers in spring.

Top: Longleaf barberry in fall, Regional Parks Botanic Garden, Berkeley. SAXON HOLT
Bottom: Golden Abundance barberry with blossoms, Rancho Santa Ana Botanic Garden, Claremont. BART O'BRIEN

The small, grape-like fruits attract both birds and mammals and can be blue, shiny red, purple, or black.

Barberries grow in a variety of California habitats, from exposed, dry slopes of Mojave Desert ranges to moist, shaded forests of the Siskiyou Mountains. Consequently, their use and garden tolerances can vary widely with the species, but all are durable, disease-resistant landscape plants. They can be slow to establish and many new plantings don't begin to grow until firmly rooted. Most are drought tolerant but species from woodland communities are better suited to gardens that receive some summer water.

Maintenance requirements are minimal. Occasional pruning to shape or remove selected canes is recommended, but be careful not to remove next season's flower buds. Cutting a plant to the ground in fall or winter encourages fresh new growth and helps to control cabbage looper caterpillars, which may disfigure and skeletonize the plant's foliage. A timely application of BT *(Bacillus thuringiensis)* will also control caterpillars.

Berberis aquifolium
OREGON GRAPE

Plant Type: Evergreen shrub.
Geographic Zones: All except high mountains and deserts.
Light: Sun to shade.
Soil: Adaptable.
Water: Infrequent to occasional.
Natural Habitat and Range: Dry, open, and wooded slopes in forests below 7000 feet; California Floristic Province to British Columbia and Idaho.

Compacta Oregon grape with coffeeberry hedge, private garden, San Luis Obispo. DAVID FROSS

Oregon grape is the most frequently grown of the barberries. An erect shrub 3 to 7 feet tall, it spreads slowly by thick rhizomes to form dense clumps. The leaves have three to nine leaflets with glossy dark green surfaces and spined margins. Fresh spring growth is often bronze-colored, and a few reddish older leaves are usually present all year. The foliage may darken to purple or maroon in areas subject to cold winter temperatures, especially if plants are exposed to full sun. The sweetly scented spring flowers are held in dense 1- to 3-inch-long clusters near the tips of the stems. Dark blue autumn berries have a powdered appearance and make a tasty jelly. Some indigenous people use the roots for medicinal purposes and to create yellow dyes.

This shrub grows well in most California gardens. Resistant to oak root fungus and other root rots, it is a good choice for sites prone to these diseases. Oregon grape tolerates many soil conditions, and western gardeners have used it for years in foundation plantings, low screens, barriers, and hedges. Although it accepts most exposures, Oregon grape fares better in partial shade when it is grown in warmer interior climates. The dense foliage, spring flowers, and succulent berries make a valuable contribution to any habitat garden. Control its height and form with light pruning, or cut older plants to the ground to encourage fresh growth.

Cultivars: Compacta Oregon grape (*Berberis aquifolium* 'Compacta') is a dwarf selection that grows 1 to 3 feet tall and has a clumping habit. It spreads slowly by rhizomes but will eventually form low drifts. Spring growth is copper-colored and glossy. Mature leaves are flat green and lack the glossy character of the species. Although not a heavy flowering selection, 'Compacta' makes a good groundcover or low barrier in median strips. When taller stems rise above the foliage, remove them to maintain an even appearance.

Other Species: Creeping barberry *(Berberis aquifolium* var. *repens)* is found in the mountains of western North America, typically in the understory of coniferous forests. It spreads by creeping rhizomes to form small, open drifts 1 to 2 feet tall. The 4- to 8-inch-long leaves are divided into broad blue-green to green leaflets with spined edges like a holly leaf. Winter foliage is often richly colored, ranging from rose to burgundy. Flowers form in late spring, followed by blue berries. Creeping barberry will require patience, but with time it develops into a durable, small-scale groundcover.

Berberis nervosa
LONGLEAF BARBERRY

Plant Type: Evergreen shrub.
Geographic Zones: All except high mountains and deserts.
Light: Sun to shade.
Soil: Adaptable.
Water: Occasional to regular.
Natural Habitat and Range: Shaded slopes in woodlands and forests below 6000 feet; Northern California to British Columbia.

Longleaf barberry beneath coast redwood, Regional Parks Botanic Garden, Berkeley. SAXON HOLT

Longleaf barberry grows in small, stiff-branched colonies to a height of 3 feet and spreads slowly by rhizomes. Its 12- to 18-inch-long leathery green leaves become wine-colored in cool winter climates. They are divided into 9 to 19 egg-shaped leaflets that have bristle-like teeth. Upright 2- to 6-inch-long terminal spikes with fragrant yellow flowers form in spring. In autumn, the flowers yield elongated bunches of blue berries that have a frosted appearance. Longleaf barberry grows well in dry or moist shady conditions. Plant it as a groundcover or mix it with other woodland species.

Berberis nevinii
NEVIN BARBERRY

Plant Type: Evergreen shrub.
Geographic Zones: All except high mountains.
Light: Sun to partial shade.
Soil: Adaptable.
Water: Drought tolerant to occasional.
Natural Habitat and Range: Gravelly slopes and sandy washes in coastal scrub, chaparral, and woodlands below 2000 feet; San Diego County to Los Angeles County.

Nevin barberry behind Bee's Bliss sage, Leaning Pine Arboretum, Cal Poly, San Luis Obispo. THOMAS ELTZROTH

Nevin barberry with ripening fruits, Santa Barbara Botanic Garden. CAROL BORNSTEIN

Nevin barberry is a rare endemic that has been extirpated from much of its restricted original range and is now federally listed as an endangered species. It has rigid, multi-branched, upright stems and attains 6 to 12 feet in height and width. Nevin barberry has compound 3-inch-long leaves that are divided into three to five pointed leaflets, each with sharp, toothed spines. Young leaves open with a distinctive chartreuse-gray color and mature to a flat blue-green. Nevin barberry blooms generously in the spring. Its fragrant flowers, held in loose 1- to 2-inch-long axillary clusters, cover the foliage in a mantle of yellow-gold. Translucent red to orange berries follow in summer and seldom persist, as western bluebirds and other animals quickly eat them after they ripen.

This adaptable shrub fares well in most California gardens. Plant it alone as a specimen or en masse to create a hedge. Nevin barberry's foliage combines well with a wide palette of colors, and the spiny leaves make an intimidating barrier. It will endure non-irrigated gardens but is fresher with some supplemental water in the summer months. Little pruning is required, although it can withstand heavy shearing. Coppicing rejuvenates older specimens.

Berberis pinnata
CALIFORNIA BARBERRY

Plant Type: Evergreen shrub.
Geographic Zones: All except high mountains and deserts.
Light: Sun to shade.
Soil: Adaptable.
Water: Drought tolerant to occasional.
Natural Habitat and Range: Rocky slopes and coastal bluffs in coastal scrub, chaparral, woodlands, and forests below 4000 feet; northwestern Baja California to Oregon.

Top: California barberry with clusters of autumn berries, Santa Barbara Botanic Garden. STEVE JUNAK
Bottom: Golden Abundance barberry in full flower, Rancho Santa Ana Botanic Garden, Claremont. BART O'BRIEN

California barberry looks like Oregon grape, but its leaves have crinkled or wavy edges and are more sharply divided. Most plants will reach 4 to 8 feet tall, and slowly creeping runners allow it to form dense drifts over time. In spring, its brightly colored new growth has bronze, copper, and reddish hues. California barberry's upright stems bear 1- to 2-inch-long clusters of yellow flowers, which are later followed by dark blue autumn berries. Its landscape uses are similar to Oregon grape.

Cultivars: *Berberis* 'Golden Abundance' is a vigorous hybrid selection that grows up to 8 feet tall and 6 to 12 feet wide. It spreads by rhizomes and eventually creates a dense thicket of rigid stems. The glossy green leaves of 'Golden Abundance' are divided into thick, spined leaflets that have a reddish midrib. In spring, abundant clusters of yellow flowers are massed on terminal shoots; purple-blue berries follow in fall. 'Golden Abundance' prefers full sun and infrequent water except

in hot interior climates where afternoon shade and occasional water produce more appealing specimens.

Two similar selections, *Berberis* 'Ken Hartman' and *Berberis* 'Skylark', are thought to be selections of *Berberis pinnata* or hybrids resulting from a cross between *Berberis pinnata* and another species. Both are handsome shrubs growing to 8 feet tall, and each features brilliant new growth: 'Ken Hartman' has copper colors and crinkled leaf surfaces, while 'Skylark' has reddish bronze new growth. They both bear typical yellow flowers and blue-black berries with a waxy, frost-like blush.

Bothriochloa barbinodis
SILVER BEARDGRASS
Grass Family (Poaceae)

Plant Type: Deciduous to semi-evergreen, warm-season perennial grass.
Geographic Zones: All except northern coastal, high mountains, and deserts.
Light: Sun.
Soil: Adaptable.
Water: Drought tolerant to occasional.
Natural Habitat and Range: Dry slopes, mesas, and gravelly sites in coastal scrub and deserts below 4000 feet; southern California to Oklahoma, Texas, and Mexico.

Silver beardgrass is one of California's most attractive bunchgrasses. Its silky plumose inflorescences resemble those of the exotic pampas grass, but this smaller native grass has none of pampas grass's dreaded invasive properties. Silver beardgrass would surely have greater popularity—especially among grass lovers—were it not for its tendency to look straggly while in nursery containers.

Silver beardgrass backlit by afternoon sun, Santa Barbara Botanic Garden. CAROL BORNSTEIN

When in bloom silver beardgrass ranges from 2 to 4 feet tall and 1 to 2 feet across. The slightly hairy leaves are often tinged with orange, red, or purple when the new growth emerges or in response to cold temperatures during autumn and winter. For much of the year, 3- to 4-inch-long silvery or creamy white panicles top the wiry, cane-like stems that resemble thin bamboo stalks. These initially slender inflorescences become feathery with age, and their soft, sensuous texture invites stroking. Few other native grasses are as dramatic in bloom, especially when backlight from the sun exposes the thousands of silky hairs on its cone-shaped inflorescences.

The somewhat lanky, upright habit of silver beardgrass limits its use in gardens. For maximum impact, plant several together in an undulating swath, preferably with a dark backdrop to accentuate the plumose inflorescences. Silver beardgrass adds a vertical element to a meadow garden or perennial border. It also can help stabilize slopes. Although it is drought tolerant in coastal gardens, it prefers supplemental water in inland gardens. It produces seedlings under favorable conditions, but they are rarely problematic. Rejuvenate plants by cutting them back after flowering in fall or early winter or when they become too floppy. Silver beardgrass has no known pest problems.

Bouteloua species
GRAMA GRASSES
Grass Family (Poaceae)

Plant Type: Semi-evergreen to deciduous, warm-season perennial grasses.
Geographic Zones: All except northern coastal.
Light: Sun.
Soil: Adaptable.
Water: Drought tolerant to occasional.
Natural Habitat and Range: Dry rocky slopes and gravelly drainages in desert scrub, woodlands, and coniferous forests; Peninsular Ranges, desert mountains to southern Canada, eastern United States, and South America.

The genus *Bouteloua* contains many species that are important forage grasses in North America. These grasses have evolved under a regime of frequent grazing by large mammals. They make good candidates for turf because they can withstand moderate foot traffic and regular mowing. Not only utilitarian, the two warm-season species of *Bouteloua* described here are also delightful ornamental grasses.

Side-oats grama *(B. curtipendula)* is an erect, ½- to 3-foot-tall tufted grass. Some forms produce short rhizomes. During cool temperatures the narrow,

Blue grama in a meadow planting, private garden, Santa Barbara. CAROL BORNSTEIN

flat, bluish green leaf blades of this bunchgrass are typically flushed with rose or maroon. Side-oats grama gained its common name from the one-sided arrangement of its pendulous, purplish spikes. These wiry stalks begin blooming in late spring, and close inspection reveals flowers with bright orange anthers. Its inflorescences age to a light sand color before they shatter.

Extremely drought tolerant, side-oats grama is easy to cultivate as long as it is not overwatered or shaded. Use it as a strong vertical accent in dry borders and rock or meadow gardens. The flower spikes are effective in both fresh and dried arrangements. Side-oats grama has no known pest problems.

Blue grama *(B. gracilis)* shares similar cultural requirements and garden applications with side-oats grama. The tufted, slowly spreading clumps of this dainty bunchgrass are 4 to 16 inches tall. When in bloom, plants may reach 2 feet in height. The thin leaf blades are sage green or slightly bluish. In spring and summer, blue grama produces its charming, shiny umber inflorescences. The straight, toothbrush-like spikes are held perpendicular to the stalk and curl gracefully as they fade to a straw color.

The delicate appearance of blue grama is misleading. This tough grass tolerates foot traffic and a wide range of growing conditions. It has become a popular drought-tolerant turf throughout the Great Plains and Southwest. Blue grama does particularly well in high-desert areas. In coastal California blue grama retains some green foliage in winter; in inland gardens it goes dormant and turns a light tan color. Mow it monthly in summer to a height of 2 or 3 inches, or leave it unmowed for a natural meadow look. This durable bunchgrass is pretty enough to use alone in rock gardens, to edge the front of a dry border, or as a focal point in a rustic pot.

Brahea edulis
GUADALUPE ISLAND FAN PALM
Palm Family (Arecaceae)

Plant Type: Evergreen tree.
Geographic Zones: All except frost-prone valleys, mountains, and high deserts.
Light: Sun.
Soil: Well-drained.
Water: Drought tolerant to moderate.
Natural Habitat and Range: Steep rocky slopes in island woodland below 2700 feet; Guadalupe Island, Baja California.

Guadalupe Island fan palms line an avenue in The Huntington Library and Botanical Gardens, San Marino. BART O'BRIEN

About 250 miles west of Baja California is remote Guadalupe Island, the southernmost outpost of the California Floristic Province. Guadalupe Island fan palm is an unexpected endemic of this desolate island. It shares its home with many horticulturally desirable rare plants as well as other more familiar California native plants, such as island snapdragon, Monterey pine, island oak, and California sagebrush.

Guadalupe Island fan palm grows slowly and may eventually reach a height of 30 feet. Its palm fronds are self-pruning and have stalks 4 to 6 feet long that carry equally long, rounded, shiny green leaves with deeply cut edges. Its dark brown trunks are conspicuously ringed by old leaf scars. Arching to pendulous inflorescences up to 10 feet long carry innumerable, tiny, creamy white flowers. The scientific name *edulis* refers to the black, round, 1 to 1½ inch fruits that are edible and reportedly range in taste from prunes to poor-quality dates.

Guadalupe Island fan palm is an excellent choice for southern California gardens and should be more widely grown. This pest- and disease-free palm grows effectively as a specimen, in colonnades, or in small groves. Combine it with Guadalupe Island rock daisy, Canyon Silver island snowflake, Saint Catherine's lace, island snapdragon, and Montara California sagebrush for a green and gray foliage delight.

Other Species: Blue fan palm (*Brahea armata*) grows in palm oases in Baja California at the southern fringe of the California Floristic Province. In the wild, it is a frequent companion of California fan palm. Its silver blue leaves and enormous arching inflorescences—up to 25 feet long—are spectacular. Unfortunately, this palm is usually expensive to purchase and grows extremely slowly. Young plants make striking container specimens.

Calamagrostis foliosa
CAPE MENDOCINO REEDGRASS
Grass Family (Poaceae)

Plant Type: Semi-evergreen, cool-season perennial grass.
Geographic Zones: All except interior valleys, high mountains, and deserts.
Light: Sun to partial shade.
Soil: Adaptable.
Water: Moderate to occasional.
Natural Habitat and Range: Rocky places, headlands, and bluffs in coastal scrub below 4000 feet; Mendocino, Humboldt, and Del Norte counties.

Growing Cape Mendocino reedgrass gives gardeners an opportunity to enjoy both a rare and beautiful grass. This delightful species has blue-green leaves that are often highlighted with purple streaks. In spring, flower spikes arch above the leaves in tight, silver heads; they open silver green, then turn tawny as seeds develop in the summer.

Cape Mendocino reedgrass forms a loose, 1- by 2-foot-wide mound. It combines well with blue-eyed grass, seaside daisy, checkerbloom, dune sedge, and Canyon Prince wild rye in meadow plantings. Use it at the front of a perennial border, or plant it repeatedly through a garden as a unifying element. When included in slope plantings, its bent flower spikes create an attractive cascading pattern.

Cape Mendocino reedgrass with ripe seed heads, private garden, Lafayette. STEPHEN INGRAM

Cape Mendocino reedgrass fares best in central or northern California coastal gardens that receive moderate moisture. In southern California or warmer interior sites, it will require some shade and additional water to prosper. This grass tolerates wind and salt spray, which makes it an excellent choice for coastal cliffs and bluffs. Similar to other cool-season grasses, Cape Mendocino reedgrass will exhibit some summer dormancy but seldom loses its blue-green color. The seed heads shatter after they mature, and the spent heads fall away. Remove the thatch that develops on specimens by running a steel rake vigorously through the tufts. Plants usually become senescent after three to seven years if they are not divided or replaced with fresh material. Unlike many grasses, it does not respond well to shearing. Cape Mendocino reedgrass is free of diseases and pests.

Other Species: Pacific reedgrass (*Calamagrostis nutkaensis*) is a coarse-textured perennial with arching green leaves that grow to 3 feet high from a basal crown. The narrow, 1- to 2-foot-long flower spikes of this cool-season grass rise above the foliage in spring. It is found in moist areas in open grasslands, on north-facing slopes, and in swales along the coast from San Luis Obispo County to Alaska. Pacific reedgrass adapts to sun or shade in coastal gardens but prefers partial shade in interior plantings. Pair it with Douglas iris, snowberry, and coral bells in a more shaded site or with coffeeberry, spicebush, and pink-flowering currant in a sunny location.

Calliandra eriophylla
FAIRY DUSTER
Pea Family (Fabaceae)

Plant Type: Semi-evergreen to deciduous shrub.
Geographic Zones: All except northern coastal, high mountains, and high deserts.
Light: Sun.
Soil: Adaptable; non-alkaline and well-drained preferred.
Water: Drought tolerant to infrequent.
Natural Habitat and Range: Washes and alluvial fans in desert scrub below 5000 feet; Colorado Desert to Arizona, Texas, and northern Mexico.

Several large, primarily tropical genera are each represented in the California flora by a single species. Desert lavender, chuparosa, California Dutchman's pipe, and fairy duster all fall into this category. These token species often bear exotic-looking flowers, and fairy duster is no exception. It displays delightful puffs of colorful blossoms from late winter to early summer.

Fairy duster is a sturdy yet fine-textured shrub that typically grows 1 to 3 feet tall and 3 to 4 feet across at maturity. The pinnately compound blue-green to gray-green leaves are tiny and slightly pubescent. The flowers are actually masses of inch-long stamens (*calliandra* is Greek for beautiful stamen) that form light to deep pink starbursts of color. The attractive, 2-inch-long seedpods are flattened and have red margins and a silky coat of short hairs that catch the sun's rays.

Despite its desert origins, fairy duster grows surprisingly well in warmer coastal environments. Vigorous plants will bloom for several months and may supply a crop of volunteer seedlings. Fairy duster requires no maintenance and is not bothered by insects or diseases.

In its natural habitat fairy duster is valued as a forage plant and for its ability to control erosion, as it spreads by rhizomes. In the garden it works well alone as an accent, massed as a small-scale groundcover, or punctuating the edges of a dry streambed. Try

Fairy duster displays its numerous beautiful stamens, Rancho Santa Ana Botanic Garden, Claremont. SAXON HOLT

using fairy duster in combination with cacti and other succulents, where its delicate texture lends a softening effect, or place it next to a path in order to appreciate its wispy flowers up close. For an especially fine presentation, plant it in a red-glazed high-fired pot.

Calocedrus decurrens
INCENSE CEDAR
Cypress Family (Cupressaceae)

Plant Type: Evergreen tree.
Geographic Zones: All except deserts.
Light: Sun.
Soil: Adaptable; non-alkaline and well-drained preferred.
Water: Infrequent to occasional.
Natural Habitat and Range: Coniferous forests and woodlands from 2000 to 8000 feet; in many California mountain ranges, north to Oregon and south to the mountains of northwestern Baja California.

Incense cedar trees claim many admirers, including John Muir who observed: "In its prime, the whole tree

Incense cedar, close-up of foliage and open cones, private garden, Mount Shasta. THOMAS ELTZROTH

is thatched with them (leaves), so that they shed off rain and snow like a roof, making fine mansions for storm-bound birds and mountaineers." Indeed, many birds use these trees for shelter and food; chickadees harvest scale insects from the thin bark of young trees, and raptors nest in the elbowed limbs of mature trees. Although not quite a "mansion" by most standards, this tree makes a stately addition to many California landscapes.

Incense cedar grows slowly at first, but in favorable sites it adds 2 to 3 feet in height per year once established. In the wild it can top out at 150 feet; in the garden it usually reaches 50 to 80 feet. Young trees grown in full sun display a classic pyramidal form and have broad, forest green sprays of flattened, scale-like leaves. Both the wood and foliage emit an appealing spicy fragrance. Narrow furrows crease its thick, cinnamon red bark near the base of the trunk. Male cones shed dusty yellow pollen around the time of the winter solstice. When the narrow, 1-inch-long female cones open in late summer, they resemble ducks' bills.

The wood of this important western timber tree is used to fabricate shingles and cedar chests and is the source of most North American pencils. Incense cedar tolerates heat and air pollution more reliably than many other conifers, requires little pruning, and makes a good specimen tree, large screen, or street tree. It is disease and pest free, with the exception of squirrels that occasionally damage young branches and developing cones.

Calycanthus occidentalis
SPICEBUSH
Sweet-Shrub Family (Calycanthaceae)

Plant Type: Deciduous shrub.
Geographic Zones: All except high mountains and low deserts.
Light: Sun to partial shade.
Soil: Adaptable.
Water: Occasional to regular.
Natural Habitat and Range: Moist places along streams, lakes, seeps, and ponds in woodlands and forests below 4000 feet; North Coast Ranges, southern Cascade Range, and foothills of the Sierra Nevada.

Incense cedar shades a storefront in Los Olivos.
JOHN EVARTS

Top: *Spicebush with coral bells (foreground), Leaning Pine Arboretum, Cal Poly, San Luis Obispo.* THOMAS ELTZROTH
Bottom: *Close-up of spicebush flower, Santa Barbara Botanic Garden.* CAROL BORNSTEIN

Spicebush's fragrant flowers and leaves give this deciduous shrub its common name. The flowers appear in late spring and continue to bloom well into summer with an exotic spicy fragrance suggestive of a wine cellar. Bright green spring foliage, luminous pale golden autumn leaves, and decorative woody fruits that persist into winter contribute to spicebush's year-round aesthetic value.

This round, 5- to 8-foot-tall shrub has 3- to 6-inch-long and 1- to 3-inch-wide leaves. The foliage is aromatic when crushed, and its glossy green color contrasts with the slate brown stems. Spicebush's solitary maroon flowers measure 1 to 2 inches in diameter and are reminiscent of small water lilies.

With its lush foliage, spicebush combines well with foothill sedge, western meadow rue, Douglas iris, and giant chain fern in shaded corners or among trees in a woodland garden. It serves equally well in a sunny border

with coffeeberry and deer grass. Use it to cover or soften a wall, as an informal hedge bordering lawns, or along creeks and perennial streams as a component of a riparian planting. Once established, it is fast growing and will begin to spread by layering and rhizomes, eventually forming a thicket that helps control erosion on shaded slopes and provides cover for wildlife. Spicebush may require containment to keep it from spreading. Pruning is seldom necessary, although it can be shaped, hedged, or even trained into a small multi-trunked tree. Spicebush is resistant to oak root fungus and is insect and disease free.

Calystegia macrostegia ssp. macrostegia 'Anacapa Pink'
ANACAPA PINK CALIFORNIA MORNING GLORY
Morning Glory Family (Convolvulaceae)

Plant Type: Evergreen vine.
Geographic Zones: All except frost-prone valleys, mountains, and deserts.
Light: Sun.
Soil: Adaptable.
Water: Infrequent to moderate.
Natural Habitat and Range: Coastal scrub and chaparral below 1600 feet; from Monterey County south to Guadalupe Island and northwestern Baja California. This selection is from Anacapa Island.

Anacapa Pink California morning glory is one of the state's few native vines. It climbs by twining its bright green pliable stems around anything it finds, such as wires, cables, posts, boulders, pots, and other plants. This vigorous vine appears to engulf small houses when it is grown in favorable sites along the southern California coast— so consider yourself warned. In such gardens this plant may become a pest, but when planted further north or inland it is easier to control.

Anacapa Pink California morning glory has a long flowering season, and its lush, bright green leaves remain attractive throughout the

Anacapa Pink California morning glory growing on a fence, Rancho Santa Ana Botanic Garden, Claremont. BART O'BRIEN

year. It was selected for its pink, 3-inch-wide funnel-shaped flowers that have creamy white centers. The typical form of California morning glory *(Calystegia macrostegia)* found in the wild has uniform creamy white flowers and is rarely grown.

Plant this vine to cover a chain-link fence or a bland building. You may display it on a gazebo or other garden structure as long as you are prepared to keep it in check. An adventurous gardener may experiment with using Anacapa Pink California morning glory as a rambunctious groundcover.

To manage this vine's exuberant growth, promptly remove volunteer seedlings. Plants will grow back quickly if they are pruned or thinned back to green stems, while those cut back to older woody stems may not resprout. Prune in late winter after the possibility of a killing frost has passed, and clean out the dead material beneath the actively growing leaves and stems periodically.

Carex species
SEDGES
Sedge Family (Cyperaceae)

Plant Type: Deciduous to evergreen perennials.
Geographic Zones: Varies by species.
Light: Sun to shade.
Soil: Adaptable; moisture-retentive preferred.
Water: Infrequent to regular.
Natural Habitat and Range: Marshes, meadows, streambanks, and gravelly slopes in coastal scrub, woodlands, and forests below 13,500 feet; throughout California.

Dune sedge forms a meadow in front of a screen of mixed natives, private garden, San Luis Obispo. DAVID FROSS

The California flora offers a sedge for practically every imaginable garden situation. Sedges grow in a

Foothill sedge in a pot next to silver shield (from Australia), private garden, Arroyo Grande. DAVID FROSS

wide array of natural habitats, from wind-blown coastal dunes and dry serpentine outcrops to moist alpine meadows and dense riparian thickets. The increasing garden interest in grasses and grass-like plants has led to a corresponding interest in our native sedges. Although relatively new to California gardens, a number of *Carex* species have become quite popular and demonstrate the landscape potential of this genus.

More than 125 species of sedges are native to California. Most are a rich shade of green, and they range in size from a few inches to 6 feet tall. Their tiny flowers come in many hues, including cream, lime green, pale gold, russet, and black and are held above the leaves in dense spikelets. Fruits are earthen-colored and may persist, further darkening with age.

Sedges are a genus of moisture-loving plants—many species are semiaquatic—but most are tolerant of periodic dry conditions. They are extremely versatile and can fill an array of garden and landscape niches. Planted en masse, they can serve as a lawn alternative. They work equally well in garden sites that transition from dry to wet conditions. These perennials either form clumps or spread by runners. Combine the running forms with California goldenrod and coast aster for slope or bank stabilization, or plant them in the dry shade found under oaks. Grow clumping forms in woodland gardens, or mix them with other herbaceous companions like island alum root, western meadow rue, and native lilies in a shady urban breezeway.

Maintenance of sedges varies by species. Most respond well to occasional shearing, with the exception of San Diego sedge. Removing seed heads will often improve their appearance. Disease and pest free, sedges offer solutions to many problematic garden situations and are particularly effective in areas with heavy, poorly drained soils.

California meadow sedge *(Carex pansa)* and dune sedge *(Carex praegracilis)* are remarkably similar species.

They both spread by runners and are useful as groundcovers, lawn substitutes, and bank stabilizers. They also mix well with robust perennials in a meadow garden. These two species have dark green foliage with a tousled appearance. Over time they will form a solid vegetative carpet that can handle substantial foot traffic. They can serve as a lawn if they are managed

San Diego sedge in a drought-tolerant landscape, private garden, Solvang. JOHN EVARTS

with regular irrigation and traditional turf practices. If regularly watered but left unmowed they will grow to 12 inches tall with a floppy habit. They make good groundcovers in drainage basins because they will tolerate both winter inundation and summer drought. Both species are summer dormant and turn a buff color if they receive no irrigation or subsurface moisture. They may spread rapidly in lighter sandy soils but are easily controlled with an edging shovel or root barrier.

Mountain sedge *(Carex subfusca)* is a vigorous, aggressive species with short rootstocks that spread quickly in seasonally wet areas. It forms a dense green cover 12 to 18 inches high with an arching, upright appearance. Like other creeping sedges, mountain sedge can be utilized in either sun or shade as a groundcover, along watercourses, or in the dry shade of oaks. Withholding water will keep it from spreading, but plants left dry in the summer will become beige-colored and dormant.

San Diego sedge *(Carex spissa)* is a dramatic clump-forming species that can reach 6 feet tall. Its stout, pallid blue-gray blades are thick and have a deep midrib and sharply toothed edges that are capable of cutting unsuspecting hands. In spring, miniature cattail-like flower spikes add a striking counterpoint to the colorful foliage and handsome fountain-like form. Use San Diego sedge for contrast in moist, shady areas dominated by greens, as a specimen in a dry seasonal stream, or in a container to highlight its dramatic form. Unlike other sedges, San Diego sedge does not respond well to shearing and is best groomed with a steel rake.

Foothill sedge *(Carex tumulicola)* forms dense green tufts to 2 feet tall and spreads slowly with age. Tough, durable, and drought tolerant, this sedge has a more refined appearance when it is grown in the shade, as flowering is reduced and it retains a clean, glossy

green appearance year-round. In full sun foothill sedge takes on a rougher appearance; it seeds heavily and often develops a tawny cast in warmer climates. Use foothill sedge massed as a groundcover, in a woodland garden, for erosion control, or spilling gracefully over the edge of a decorative container. (Many of the plants grown in the California nursery trade as *Carex tumulicola* have been identified as *Carex divulsa,* gray sedge, a species that is native from Europe and North Africa east to Central Asia. Check with suppliers to ensure plants are true to name.)

Carpenteria californica
BUSH ANEMONE
Mock Orange Family (Philadelphaceae)

Plant Type: Evergreen shrub.
Geographic Zones: All except high mountains and deserts.
Light: Sun to shade.
Soil: Adaptable.
Water: Infrequent to occasional.
Natural Habitat and Range: Dry slopes and ridges in woodlands and forests from 1500 to 4000 feet; Sierra Nevada foothills between the San Joaquin and Kings rivers.

Many of California's best-known plant species have highly restricted ranges and are threatened or endangered

Bush anemone in full bloom, private garden, Norfolk, England. DAVID FROSS

Bush anemone, close-up of flower, Rancho Santa Ana Botanic Garden, Claremont. MARC SOLOMON

in their native habitat. Bush anemone is one of these "narrow" endemics, and planting this species in your garden allows you to celebrate a rare plant while also enjoying what some would argue is one of our showiest flowering shrubs.

Bush anemone is an evergreen shrub 5 to 12 feet tall with an open, uneven form. Its upright stems rise from a multi-branched crown and display peeling bark that is ivory and tan. The leathery, lanceolate leaves are opposite, 2 to 5 inches long, and have a dark green, polished appearance. Rolled margins hide the fine hairs that whiten the undersides. Lightly fragrant camellia-like flowers form in terminal clusters on green- to rose-colored stems. They open into flat, white flowers 2 to 3 inches wide with central clusters of bright yellow stamens.

Featured as a specimen, bush anemone's brilliant white flowers can light up a shady corner. When combined with coffeeberry, spicebush, and oaks it can help build the foundation of a woodland garden. Try using it as a foil to the soft gray textures of a coastal scrub garden, massed along a wall for a dramatic spring display, or as part of a white-flowered garden. It grows well in both coastal and interior climates, but its appearance is improved in warmer sites if it receives protection from the afternoon sun. Removal of persistent older leaves, which have a rolled, droopy appearance, and the addition of supplemental summer water will help maintain a fresher, more appealing form. Cut back the top ⅓ to ½ of bush anemone's stems after it flowers to improve its lax, open habit. Large woody plants can be sheared or coppiced to encourage fresh new growth.

Monitor bush anemone for ants, aphids, and scale as they can disfigure plants and produce secondary problems with sooty mold. Various fungal diseases commonly referred to as leaf spots occasionally present difficulties in gardens with overhead irrigation and poor air circulation.

Cultivars: Bush anemone's long history in cultivation—specimens were grown in England as early as 1880—has produced a number of named selections, but only one, 'Elizabeth', is consistently available in California. It has a compact form and produces a profuse display of 2-inch-wide flowers with as many as 20 flowers per cluster.

Ceanothus species
CEANOTHUS
Buckthorn Family (Rhamnaceae)

Plant Type: Evergreen and deciduous shrubs.
Geographic Zones: Varies by species.
Light: Sun to partial shade.
Soil: Adaptable; well-drained preferred.
Water: Drought tolerant to occasional.
Natural Habitat and Range: Dry ridges and slopes in coastal scrub, chaparral, open woodlands, and forests below 10,000 feet; across North America from southern Canada to Guatemala.

Wheeler Canyon ceanothus provides nectar for a swallowtail butterfly, private garden, Santa Ynez. MARY JANE WEST-DELGADO

California's Mediterranean climate supports approximately 60 species and varieties of ceanothus. Members of this widespread genus are found throughout the state. They grow in some of California's harshest habitats, ranging from wind-buffeted coastal headlands to dry, exposed slopes at the edge of the Mojave Desert. Ceanothus come in numerous forms from prostrate mats to small trees, and many have brilliant blue flowers. The large number of ceanothus selections found in California gardens emanates from the extraordinary diversity this genus exhibits in the wild.

Snow Flurry ceanothus in full bloom, Leaning Pine Arboretum, Cal Poly, San Luis Obispo. THOMAS ELTZROTH

Cultivation of ceanothus species for horticultural purposes began in Europe as early as 1713. Plants in this genus are known by a number of common names, including wild-lilac, mountain-lilac, California-lilac, blue blossom, buckbrush, and ceanothus. (The genus name ceanothus, when used in a common reference, applies to both singular and plural usage.) The Royal Horticultural Society of England has granted 13 Awards of Merit to species and selections of the genus. There are over 75 species and cultivars available in California garden centers, and new selections appear each year from botanic gardens and native nurseries.

California's ceanothus are evergreen with the exception of two rarely grown species. The foliage comes in many sizes and shapes and varies from broad, smooth, elliptic 3-inch-long leaves to narrow, rolled 3/16-inch-long leaves. Leaf arrangement can be opposite or alternate, and leaf colors range across a spectrum of green, from black-green to yellow-green and from muddy shades of olive to sparkling jade green.

Small flowers massed in densely arranged lateral or terminal inflorescences produce the spectacular spring displays for which ceanothus is known. Many species have a strong, sweet smell in bloom, and some emit a resinous fragrance from the foliage. Inflorescence shape and size are as variable as the leaves and range from tight button-like clusters to compound 6- to 12-inch-long panicles. Flower colors follow the diverse nature of the genus; they can be white, blue, purple, or rarely, pink. But it is the intoxicating array of blue flower colors to choose from that continues to draw gardeners to the genus. There seems to be a ceanothus for every shade and hue of blue imaginable, including denim, aqua, china, sky, Persian, navy, violet, Medici, slate, and madder blue. These colors can be vivid and radiant or chalky and flat. The bracts on the budding inflorescences are often a different color than the open flowers and add a bicolor sequence to the floral display. Flowering times differ by species, with blooms typically appearing from midwinter to early summer. The rounded, three-lobed fruits change color—from ruby to maroon to burgundy—as they ripen. The mature capsules split in the heat of early summer and project the small seeds forcefully.

A species of ceanothus will perform best in a garden where conditions match or approach those found where it grows in the wild. Most California ceanothus grow in areas that experience an extended summer drought. They tolerate a range of soil types but often are located on steep slopes in well-drained soils with low or marginal fertility. Nitrogen-fixing bacteria—found in nodules on their wide-spreading roots—aid in their adaptation to these dry, nutrient-poor conditions. Considering the natural habitat of the genus, it is not surprising that most California species will endure long periods of drought, are intolerant of wet summer environments, and require little or no fertilization.

The primary requirements for garden success with ceanothus are a well-drained soil and a light watering

Ray Hartman ceanothus espalier, private garden, Napa. RON LUTSKO

hand. Numerous fungal organisms (water molds and rots, such as *Fusarium* sp., *Phytophthora* sp., and *Rhizoctonia* sp.) attack plants in poorly drained soils. These organisms can also present difficulties if cultural practices include frequent summer irrigation. Judiciously applied summer water is acceptable for established

Ray Hartman ceanothus pruned to form a small tree, private garden, Solvang. STEPHEN INGRAM

plantings and will improve the appearance of most selections, but allow soils to dry between waterings.

Ceanothus will follow a similar pattern of growth and flowering in most gardens. During the first few years after planting, they undergo rapid growth and flower moderately. A period of slower growth generally follows, accompanied by exceedingly heavy flower production. After 7 to 12 years of growth, plants continue to bloom but with fewer flowers; inflorescence size also decreases in many cultivars. At this point, plants will usually begin to develop a more open and woody character. This process occurs earlier with some species and cultivars.

Many gardeners complain that ceanothus are short-lived landscape plants. This reputation is largely undeserved as in many cases early mortality is the result of improper site selection. Poorly drained soils combined with frequent summer irrigation will kill most ceanothus in a few years. Some species and cultivars, such as Hearst ceanothus and Dark Star ceanothus, are shorter-lived than others. Island ceanothus and Carmel ceanothus, however, can live for as many as 25 years in a garden setting. Most of the California species (and resulting cultivars) have evolved in fire-active plant communities, such as chaparral and coastal scrub. These communities are subject to periodic fires that remove senescent stands, activate the dormant seed bank, and cover the charred earth with fresh young seedlings. In their native habitat many species lose vigor and decline after 15 to 20 years, based on an evolved

adaptation to fire. The natural process of fire renews the older stands in a rhythmic cycle that might have a 10-, 25-, or 50-year cadence.

Ceanothus serve many useful landscape and garden functions. Larger-growing selections attain up to 10 feet of height in a few years and can provide a quick screen or grow to be handsome freestanding specimens. With careful pruning they can be trained as small trees or sheared as a formal hedge. With meticulous attention they may even be espaliered on walls or fences. Medium-sized shrubs make good screens, and with so many selections to choose from, you can extend the flowering season from midwinter into summer. Gardeners also find many uses for low-growing ceanothus: as groundcovers in the dappled shade of a woodland garden, to cover a sunny south-facing slope, or as rock garden specimens. With labor-intensive pruning, low-growing ceanothus can even be shaped into small hedges or trained up a trellis. In the last 20 years, horticulturists have added many new and promising groundcover selections.

Annual pruning of new growth, although not essential, will maintain a smaller, more compact form and improve the appearance of most species. For best results, prune immediately after flowering and only back to the new year's flush of growth. If you make these cuts later in the year, you may inadvertently remove next year's flowers. Most plants respond to the removal of spent flowers and fruit with a tidier form and enhanced vigor. To develop an arborescent character with taller-growing species, begin training them early and cut out interior dead wood as plants age to create a cleaner look. Ceanothus will tolerate shearing for hedges and to create a formal effect, but avoid heavy cuts into woody tissue that can lead to stem and branch dieback.

Ceanothus make valuable contributions to any habitat garden by providing food and cover. Birds feed on the insect populations found on ceanothus, and

Yankee Point ceanothus as a low hedge behind non-native pachysandra, private garden, Montecito. STEPHEN INGRAM

quails, rabbits, chipmunks, and ground squirrels consume its small hard seeds. Bees, both native and domestic, and other pollinating insects frequent the plants in bloom. Several species of butterflies and moths use ceanothus as larval food, including Ceanothus silk moth, California tortoiseshell, California hairstreak, and artful dusky wing skipper. Some farm operations plant windrows of ceanothus around their plots to lure beneficial predatory insects as part of integrated pest management programs.

A number of insects damage ceanothus. Feeding by large populations of aphids, mealybugs, scales, and white flies can disfigure plants, while gall formation caused by the stem gall moth *(Periploca ceanothiella)* can distort stems and flowers. Some portions of the state are relatively free of stem gall moths; in other areas, they are so prevalent it is prudent to avoid the use of the moth's preferred hosts—larger-leaved species such as blue blossom ceanothus and Carmel creeper ceanothus. Environmentally friendly controls of this pest are not available, but close monitoring of irrigation and fertilization to prevent off-season (summer/fall) flushes of growth will help prevent serious damage.

Boring insects, especially the sycamore borer *(Synanthedon resplendens)* and the Pacific flatheaded borer *(Chrysobothris mali),* can potentially cause serious problems for ceanothus. They bore into the main trunk or larger branches and create shallow, irregular mines or tunnels just under the bark. The area above these burrows is dark-colored and often has sap exuding from the wound. Left untreated, borers will usually kill infected plants. Unfortunately, there are no environmentally safe methods of treatment available. Early detection and applications of pesticides will moderate the problem. Like the stem gall moths, borers have a regional distribution pattern; they are problematic in some areas and uncommon in others.

Insects are not the only animals that consume ceanothus. Deer browse heavily on young plants. Large-leaved species and cultivars are particularly susceptible to damage from deer and will require protective cages for at least the first few years. Ceanothus with foliage that has spiny margins and a thick, leathery texture are less likely to attract deer, but all newly planted ceanothus are vulnerable. Deer are not likely to kill established plants, but they will browse lightly, even on older plants, when other food is scarce. You may also need to protect young plants from mice, rabbits, and wood rats.

Selected species and cultivars for California gardens

Ceanothus species hybridize frequently, both in the garden and in the wild. Most ceanothus cultivars available for use in the garden were derived from garden hybrids, or they were selected from a wild population and reproduced clonally to perpetuate a unique trait or quality. With a few exceptions, the species are more commonly grown for restoration purposes, while the cultivars are used in gardens.

Large shrubs

Island ceanothus *(Ceanothus arboreus)* is a mounding shrub or small tree that can attain 20 feet in height. It is found on rocky slopes and exposed ridgelines in forests, woodlands, and chaparral on Santa Catalina, Santa Cruz, and Santa Rosa islands. Its broad, oval leaves grow up to 3 inches long and have emerald green surfaces and felted white undersides that contrast boldly against the smooth, gray bark of the trunk and stems. Flowers held in branched clusters 3 to 5 inches long range in color from slate blue to washed denim. Island ceanothus lives longer and grows best in coastal gardens but also performs well in interior gardens, especially if it receives protection from afternoon sun. It is tolerant of heavier soils and can easily be trained into a small tree. 'Cliff Schmidt' is a graceful fountain-like selection that reaches 20 feet tall. It produces abundant powder blue flowers in spring and a second lighter crop of flowers in fall.

Ceanothus 'Gentian Plume' displays stunning gentian blue flowers throughout spring. The flowers are borne on branched 8- to 14-inch-long clusters that are held above the dark green, glossy 2½-inch-long leaves. This fast-growing shrub can reach 6 to 8 feet in height in its first year and eventually may become 20 feet tall and equally wide. Without training, 'Gentian Plume' becomes leggy, and young plants require pruning and pinching to achieve a desirable form. Place several together as a quick screen or to create a dramatic splash of blue. Durable and garden tolerant, 'Gentian Plume' is suitable for use in both coastal and interior gardens.

Gentian Plume ceanothus in a foundation planting, private garden, Carpinteria. CAROL BORNSTEIN

Snow Flurry ceanothus brightens a trail in the Santa Barbara Botanic Garden. CAROL BORNSTEIN

Above: Ray Hartman and Yankee Point ceanothus with non-native rockrose, private garden, Solvang.
STEPHEN INGRAM
Left: Ray Hartman ceanothus blossoms, Rancho Santa Ana Botanic Garden, Claremont.
BART O'BRIEN

Ceanothus 'Ray Hartman' is, with good reason, the best known and most commonly grown of the bigger ceanothus hybrids. A striking selection, its large, glistening green leaves combine the best characteristics of its parents—island ceanothus and Carmel creeper ceanothus. 'Ray Hartman' can attain 18 feet in height and width in three to five years and makes a good quick screen or, if pruned, a small tree. Its prominent rose-colored buds open to display profuse clusters of sky blue flowers. 'Ray Hartman' grows reliably in both interior and coastal sites.

Ceanothus 'Sierra Blue' is known for its vivid, dark masses of violet blue flowers, which hang from its stems in 8-inch-long clusters. This open, free-formed shrub reaches 15 feet or more in height and width. It is fast growing and has polished, 1- to 2-inch-long leaves. 'Sierra Blue' prefers full sun, and plants grown in shady conditions tend to have sparse foliage. Pruning will improve its form, and it makes an excellent choice for southern California coastal and interior gardens.

Blue blossom ceanothus (*Ceanothus thyrsiflorus*) is found in chaparral and woodland communities of the outer Coast Ranges from Santa Barbara County to southern Oregon. It usually grows as an erect shrub to 25 feet tall and wide, but some plants are low growing or form mounds. Its elliptic, 1- to 2-inch-long leaves have a shiny green surface. Flower color varies, but most plants produce rich blue flowers in cylindrical, 1- to 3-inch-long clusters in mid- to late spring. Selections of blue blossom ceanothus perform best in coastal gardens, but they can succeed in interior sites as well. One of these selections, *Ceanothus thyrsiflorus* 'Snow Flurry', features glossy green leaves and fresh white flowers that fade to dusty white. Mature 'Snow Flurry' specimens are massive and can reach 18 feet high with a spread of 25 feet or more. Diligent pruning will control this fast-growing, garden-tolerant cultivar.

Medium-sized shrubs

Ceanothus 'Concha' flowers heavily, beginning in late winter, and produces 1½-inch-long clusters of luminous cobalt blue flowers. Its dark, narrow, 1-inch-long leaves have a warty surface that glints appealingly in the sun, and its graceful, arching branches form a

Concha ceanothus with spring bloom, Rancho Santa Ana Botanic Garden, Claremont. BART O'BRIEN

Dark Star ceanothus by a stairway in a private garden, Oakland. BART O'BRIEN

Julia Phelps ceanothus in the Royal Horticultural Society's garden, Wisley, England. DAVID FROSS

dense, 6-to 8-foot-tall mound. This commonly grown cultivar has rose-colored buds and is one of the most adaptable dark-flowered ceanothus selections available.

Ceanothus 'Dark Star' provides stunning spring floral displays, which is why it is among the most popular native shrubs planted in California. The masses of bottle-shaped clusters it produces have brilliant cobalt blue flowers. The arching branches are densely covered with ⅜-inch-long deeply veined leaves that are vivid dark green to almost black. 'Dark Star' is fast growing and quickly reaches a height of 6 feet with a 6- to 10-foot spread. It is most suited to coastal sites and may be short-lived in interior gardens. 'Dark Star' is sensitive to water molds in poorly drained soils.

Ceanothus 'Far Horizons' has clear blue flowers that consistently bloom early. They appear in distinctive button-like clusters that contrast with the plant's small, dark green leaves. Its arching and spreading branches can reach 5 to 7 feet high and 6 to 10 feet wide. 'Far Horizons' performs best in coastal gardens, but you can also grow it in interior gardens if you provide partial shade and judicious summer water.

Ceanothus griseus 'Louis Edmunds' is a selection that attains massive width and only medium height. It spreads 12 to 20 feet wide and can reach 6 feet tall. Its 3-inch-long clusters of chicory blue flowers persist longer than those of many other selections. Its folded, dark green glossy leaves measure about 2 inches long. Gardeners find 'Louis Edmunds' to be a reliable performer and use it to cover large hillsides or prune it as an informal hedge.

Ceanothus 'Julia Phelps' shares many traits with *Ceanothus* 'Dark Star'. Both flower abundantly and are short-lived selections that fare poorly in inland gardens and heavy soils. Their leaves are so similar that it is difficult to distinguish between them when the plants are still in containers. Compared to 'Dark Star', 'Julia Phelps' grows taller, to 8 feet, and spreads wider, to 12 feet or more. It produces indigo blue flowers in 1-inch-long clusters.

Ceanothus cuneatus var. *rigidus* 'Snowball' is one of the earliest-blooming ceanothus cultivars, providing a splash of winter color as early as January. This shrub displays tight, spherical, ¾-inch-wide flower clusters that have an amber cast before the clear white flowers open. 'Snowball' forms mounds 4 to 6 feet tall and 6 to 10 feet wide, and its stiffly arching branches are covered with thick, leathery, olive green, ¼-inch-long leaves. Plant it with other drought-tolerant shrubs on dry, sunny slopes.

Ceanothus 'Skylark' is a good choice for gardens lacking space. It has a compact, dome-like form and smaller size and reaches about 4 feet high with a 6 foot spread. Its curled, dark green, 2-inch-long leaves have a thick, resinous texture, and its cerulean blue flowers bloom from late spring to early summer, which is later than most ceanothus. Lightly prune spent flowers to improve this shrub's appearance, as 'Skylark' tends to hold old inflorescence stalks longer than other selections.

Centennial ceanothus in a poolside landscape, private garden, Montecito. STEPHEN INGRAM

Groundcovers and lower-growing shrubs

Ceanothus 'Centennial' is a low, spreading selection with creeping stems 8 to 12 inches high. Its small round leaves have a wavy, polished green surface that sparkles in the sun. The cobalt blue flowers are concentrated in tight clusters shaped like marbles; when viewed against the green foliage they glisten almost like water. Along the coast, 'Centennial' is at its best in full sun, but it requires some shade in interior sites.

Point Reyes ceanothus (*Ceanothus gloriosus*) is an endemic from the coastal bluffs and dunes of Marin, Sonoma, and Mendocino counties, where it grows in coastal scrub and pine forest. Its distinctively toothed leaves have a leathery texture and a dark green sheen on their surface. Point Reyes ceanothus is typically low growing or creeping and usually reaches less than 5 feet in height; it may spread much wider, requiring pruning in smaller gardens. Lavender blue to blue (rarely white) flowers are produced in small, short-stalked clusters from early to midspring. Point Reyes ceanothus is best used in coastal gardens, but it will tolerate interior conditions if some shade and additional water are provided. The cultivar 'Anchor Bay', a dense, garden-tolerant selection with slightly darker flowers, grows to 3 feet

high with a 6-foot spread. It performs admirably in both coastal and interior portions of California. Gardeners consider 'Anchor Bay' to be one of the best groundcover selections available. 'Heart's Desire' is a spreading selection to 12 inches high with bronze green leaves and pale blue flowers. Although not a heavily flowering cultivar, it is an excellent groundcover choice for coastal

Anchor Bay ceanothus flowers, Santa Barbara Botanic Garden. STEPHEN INGRAM

gardens and has demonstrated promise in interior sites with partial shade.

Carmel ceanothus (*Ceanothus griseus*) is the most commonly planted ceanothus species in California.

Top: Yankee Point ceanothus used as a border along a sidewalk, private garden, Solvang. JOHN EVARTS
Bottom: Diamond Heights ceanothus growing over a concrete wall, private garden, Arroyo Grande. DAVID FROSS

Hearst ceanothus covering a slope in a private garden, Montecito. STEPHEN INGRAM

It grows naturally along the coast from Santa Barbara to Mendocino counties in a variety of habitats, including dunes, exposed bluffs and headlands, and steep canyon slopes. Plants range in height from 1 to 15 feet and feature glossy, dark green, 1- to 2-inch-long ovate to elliptic leaves. Flower colors vary from dark shades of indigo to denim blue. Most of the selections made from Carmel ceanothus are durable and garden tolerant when used in coastal sites. Away from the coast they require supplemental summer water and are often short-lived. A number of groundcover selections have been made from Carmel creeper ceanothus (Ceanothus griseus var. horizontalis). Plants grown under this name in the nursery trade are variable, but most are large-leaved with pale blue flowers, reach 3 to 5 feet high, and spread to 12 feet. They can be pruned to maintain a lower aspect by removing upright and arching branches, and they make excellent groundcovers in seaside gardens exposed to strong prevailing winds and salt spray. 'Yankee Point' is a low-growing selection that has smaller leaves than typical selections derived from the variety horizontalis. It will grow to 3 feet high with an 8- to 15-foot spread, but when crowded it can reach 5 to 8 feet in height. Long favored by the California landscape trade for its durable character and tolerance of both interior and coastal conditions, 'Yankee Point' has become a ubiquitous feature in the suburban landscape. 'Diamond Heights' is a variegated selection from a landscape planting in San Francisco. Its leaves have a marbled, lime gold margin and often feature a narrow splash of dark green in the center. Flowers on the 2-inch-long panicles are a peculiar dull blue when viewed against the strong chartreuse-colored foliage. Although 'Diamond Heights' does not bloom heavily, some gardeners find the color combination objectionable and remove the flower buds before they open. It is slower growing than typical selections from Ceanothus griseus and has a creeping habit, attaining 12 inches in height and 4 to 6 feet in width. Shade tolerant even in coastal sites, it is best with partial shade in interior gardens to prevent bleaching of the leaves. 'Diamond Heights' is an excellent choice for shady borders and combines well with blue-eyed grass, coffeeberry, and foothill sedge. Its vibrant foliage brightens the ground beneath native oaks.

Hearst ceanothus (Ceanothus hearstiorum) is a rare species found on the hills above Arroyo de la Cruz near Hearst Castle in San Luis Obispo County. A young

Joyce Coulter ceanothus planted between a lawn and patio, private garden, Montecito. STEPHEN INGRAM

Frosty Dawn ceanothus grows in a gravel mulch, Rancho Santa Ana Botanic Garden, Claremont. STEPHEN INGRAM

plant forms a unique star-shaped pattern as it grows, eventually becoming a prostrate mat 6 to 12 inches high with a 6- to 12-foot-wide spread. The narrow ¾-inch-long green leaves have a crinkled texture and a reflective surface. Powdery blue flowers appear in 1-inch-long clusters throughout early spring. This often short-lived ceanothus prefers coastal gardens but will tolerate interior sites if given shade and supplemental summer water.

Ceanothus 'Joyce Coulter' is a low, spreading hybrid that is a particularly garden- and water-tolerant groundcover. This selection grows 2 to 5 feet tall with trailing branches that can spread 12 feet or more. The elliptic, 1-inch-long leaves have a textured green surface. Sky blue flowers are produced for many weeks in 3- to 5-inch-long heads. Prune 'Joyce Coulter' as a hedge, or plant it so it can spill over walls. To cover broad banks, use it along with Ken Taylor fremontia and Bee's Bliss sage. In interior sites, supply supplemental summer water.

Maritime ceanothus *(Ceanothus maritimus)* is a rare endemic found growing in association with Hearst ceanothus on the coastal bluffs and hills surrounding the Arroyo de la Cruz drainage in San Luis Obispo County. Both creeping and mounding forms exist in the wild. Leathery, olive green leaves with white undersides clothe maritime ceanothus's rigid stems, and flowers ranging in color from white to indigo begin blooming relatively early—in late January or early February. Plant maritime ceanothus as a small-scale groundcover, as an accent in a dry border, or as a highlight in a rock garden. It is a slow-growing and long-lived species that will do well in both coastal and interior sites. In warmer inland gardens it may benefit from partial shade. Maritime ceanothus adapts to many soil types;

it will even grow in heavy soils as long as they are adequately drained. Popular selections include 'Frosty Dawn', which has dark, smoky blue flowers and a dense, spreading habit to 12 inches high; 'Popcorn', which features fluffy white flowers and a mounding habit to 2 feet high; and 'Point Sierra', which has ash green, cotoneaster-like foliage and wisteria blue flowers.

A previously recognized variety of blue blossom ceanothus *(Ceanothus thrysiflorus* var. *repens* 'Taylor's Blue') is still grown under the variety *repens* name but is no longer recognized by taxonomists as a distinct variety. Nomenclature notwithstanding, this selection is horticulturally distinct and develops into a 3-foot-high mound with arching branches that spread 10 to 15 feet wide. 'Taylor's Blue' features 2- to 3-inch-long cylindrical clusters of light blue flowers that bloom for an extended period. Prune the branch tips to control its growth, and use it in front of other shrubs or on slopes and banks as a groundcover. 'Taylor's Blue' is a remarkably garden-tolerant selection and will grow in interior valleys if protection from the afternoon sun is provided.

Cercidium floridum
PALO VERDE
Pea Family (Fabaceae)

Plant Type: Deciduous tree.
Geographic Zones: Central to southern intermediate and interior valleys and low desert.
Light: Sun.
Soil: Adaptable; well-drained preferred.
Water: Drought tolerant.
Natural Habitat and Range: Washes and sandy areas in desert woodland below 1200 feet; California's Colorado Desert to Arizona and northern Mexico.

Palo verde in a desert-themed private garden, Walnut Creek.
RUSSELL BEATTY

Palo verde in a desert wash, Anza-Borrego Desert State Park.
BILL EVARTS

Palo verde is an excellent small- to medium-sized tree for hot California climates. Its Spanish name translates to "green stick," which is appropriate since this desert native quickly sheds its tiny leaves and remains leafless much of the year, revealing the rich yellow-green trunk and branches. Due to the strictures imposed by the harsh desert environment, this is a tree that lives for springtime. The sight of a palo verde tree in full bloom in this season is not soon forgotten. The thousands of fragrant, golden yellow flowers tend to open all at once, attracting numerous insects, including many species of bees. The tree produces leaves, flowers, and seedpods over the course of a few brief weeks before drifting into a prolonged dormant period that reigns over the rest of the year. Don't for a minute think that a dormant palo verde is dull or uninviting. Palo verde trees are perfect to garden under because of the light shade cast by their leafless branches. When these trees are carefully watered during the hot summer months, they may respond by producing additional leaves and flowers.

Fast growing when young, palo verde may eventually reach up to 30 feet tall. It requires judicious pruning to form a canopy that one can walk under; otherwise expect a relatively short main trunk and a dense thicket of branches. Some specimens are spiny and others are nearly spineless. Palo verde is typically pest and disease free, but termites may attack it.

Cultivars: A most unusual three-way hybrid between the two California species, palo verde and littleleaf palo verde (*Cercidium microphyllum*), and Mexican palo verde (*Parkinsonia aculeata*) combines the best traits of the three. This plant is called Desert Museum palo verde (×*Parkinsidium* 'Desert Museum') and is propagated by grafting or by cuttings. Mature plants have a wide-spreading, rounded crown that may reach 30 feet tall and 30 to 40 feet wide. These plants also have green trunks and branches and cast a pleasant garden-friendly shade. Fortunately, it has no spines. If the tree is watered occasionally in the summer months, it produces waves of ½-inch-wide yellow blooms from spring to fall.

Cercis occidentalis
WESTERN REDBUD
Pea Family (Fabaceae)

Plant Type: Deciduous shrub or small tree.
Geographic Zones: All except cool northern coastal, high mountains, and low desert.
Light: Sun to partial shade.
Soil: Adaptable; well-drained preferred.
Water: Drought tolerant to occasional.
Natural Habitat and Range: Dry slopes and canyons, streambanks in many plant communities below 4500 feet; inner North Coast and Klamath ranges; Sierra Nevada, Cascade and Peninsular ranges, and east to Texas.

Above: Western redbud on the slope of a drainage swale with native and non-native shrubs, private garden, Solvang. DAVID FROSS
Left: Western redbud seedpods, Ballard.
JOHN EVARTS

Western redbud is truly a four-season plant that deserves its reputation as one of our state's most beautiful spring-flowering natives. This multi-trunked tree or shrub reaches 6 to 20 feet tall and is among the few woody plants native to California that gardeners can select as a patio tree.

The large, rounded leaves of western redbud have heart-shaped bases and are notched at the tip. Initially apple green, thin, and delicate, the leaves develop a leathery texture as they age to bluish green. Magenta to rosy pink (rarely white) blossoms, which resemble pea flowers, begin to bloom in late winter or early spring. They line the naked, silvery gray branches and are soon accompanied by young leaves. Scattered flowers may also appear in late summer and fall. Plants grown in full sun and with winter chilling produce more abundant flowers. Its conspicuous flattened seedpods measure 1½ to 3½-inches long; during the year they change in color from lime green to eggplant purple before drying to a dark brown or charcoal gray. If the sight or sound of these natural wind chimes annoys you, remove them with a few gentle swats of a badminton racket. In colder areas, western redbud may brighten the landscape with a fall color display of yellow or red leaves.

Western redbud responds well to pruning, and an annual thinning of the oldest trunks keeps it in robust condition. Alternatively, cutting the entire clump to the ground can rejuvenate an unpruned plant. Several California tribes use this technique to encourage the production of straight new stems, which are prized for basketry. Western redbud is easy to cultivate and has no pest problems. Although it is resistant to oak root fungus, avoid overwatering it in heavy soils.

Western redbud makes a fine accent in a perennial border or woodland garden. Its blossoms are splendid when paired with any of the blue ceanothus, native irises, or coral bells; the maroon to purple phase of its mature pods complements the soft pinks of red-flowered buckwheat, alkali sacaton, and summer-blooming clarkias.

Cercocarpus betuloides
MOUNTAIN MAHOGANY
Rose Family (Rosaceae)

Plant Type: Evergreen shrub or small tree.
Geographic Zones: All except deserts.
Light: Sun to partial shade.
Soil: Adaptable.
Water: Drought tolerant to occasional.
Natural Habitat and Range: Dry rocky areas on slopes in chaparral and woodlands below 6000 feet; in most California mountain ranges of the California Floristic Province.

California's native flora offers a rich selection of shrubs with rounded growth habits. But when gardeners need more upright shrubs for narrow planting areas and side yards, their choices are relatively limited. One

Mountain mahogany along a path, kept low by pruning, Santa Barbara Botanic Garden. SAXON HOLT

of our best plants for this landscape niche is mountain mahogany. Its rigid, silver-barked trunks carry short branches of small, deeply pleated, dark green leaves. It grows 10 to 15 feet tall but can easily be kept pruned to 6 feet wide or less. Although its flowers are not particularly showy, they produce feather-like seeds that decorate the plant. Atop each seed is a 1- to 2-inch-long curled plume that is covered with stiff white hairs. Mountain mahogany reaches its pinnacle of beauty during this seed-bearing period and appears to glitter when backlit by the sun.

Mountain mahogany typically branches from the base, though some individuals form rhizomatous spreading colonies. The only care this fast-growing plant occasionally needs is a thinning of unwanted trunks or branches; cut them back to the ground to promote a fresh and light appearance. This shrub may be coppiced and makes an excellent choice for a screen or hedge. With judicious fall pruning, mountain mahogany can be trained into a multi-trunked small tree.

Other Species: Santa Catalina Island mountain mahogany *(Cercocarpus traskiae)* is an outstanding small tree for gardens, patios, and courtyards. In the wild this endangered species is restricted to a single canyon on Santa Catalina Island where eight plants survive. Fortunately, it is in cultivation on the mainland and is occasionally offered for sale. This long-lived plant typically produces multiple silver gray trunks and reaches from 12 to 20 feet tall with an equal to slightly wider spread. The cupped leaves are dark green above and are densely covered with soft whitish hairs beneath. Its small flowers and long-tailed seeds are similar to those of mountain mahogany.

Chilopsis linearis
DESERT WILLOW
Trumpet Vine Family (Bignoniaceae)

Plant Type: Deciduous tree.
Geographic Zones: All except immediate coast and high mountains.
Light: Sun.
Soil: All except for cold, heavy, wet soils.
Water: Drought tolerant to moderate when established, but blooms more heavily with occasional deep summer watering.
Natural Habitat and Range: Desert washes and drainages in desert woodland below 5000 feet; California deserts to southwestern Utah, western Texas, and Mexico.

Desert willow grown as a small, multi-trunked tree, private garden, Bishop. STEPHEN INGRAM

Desert willow is simply the best summer-blooming large shrub or small tree that California has to offer. Its common name may conjure up images of a lush-leaved, water-guzzling plant that thrives only in an arid climate. In reality, however, desert willow is one of the most adaptable and easily grown of California's native

Desert willow's showy blossoms are plentiful, Anza-Borrego Desert State Park. JOHN EVARTS

plants. Sun and heat—the more the better—and occasional deep irrigation are the only ingredients desert willow requires to produce refreshing dappled shade and beautiful blossoms throughout the warmest months of the year. Desert willow is dormant from late fall through midspring (with one semi-evergreen exception listed below), making it an excellent choice for providing maximum winter sunshine to homes, patios, and gardens.

Desert willow has narrow, willow-like leaves that range in color from gray-green to rich dark green. Its young stems are often nearly black, while the older branches and trunks are a rough-textured taupe. The 1- to 3-inch-long flowers are produced in showy terminal clusters and are extremely variable in color. They may be white, pink, lavender, or burgundy, but nearly all have a contrasting pattern of lines and dots in the throat and all are attractive to hummingbirds. Its brown, bean-like seedpods age to ashy gray and are carried through the winter months.

This plant is fast growing and may reach 12 to 20 feet in height with an equal spread. It requires minimal pruning when grown as a large shrub or as an informal multi-trunked tree. To create a more formal, tree-like appearance, remove basal water sprouts when they emerge. Structural pruning is best accomplished when the plant is leafless. Desert willow is pest and disease free, but it may be subject to root rot if grown in saturated soils where winter temperatures are cold. Jojoba,

Indian mallow, Louis Hamilton apricot mallow, desert lavender, and beavertail cactus make good companions for desert willow.

Cultivars: There are several distinctive named selections. 'Bubba' has wide, dark green leaves and dark violet flowers. 'Burgundy Lace' offers gray-green leaves and uniformly dark wine red flowers. 'Lois Adams' has green leaves and crepe-textured violet flowers that produce few, if any, fruits. 'Mesquite Valley Pink' is a selection with green leaves and uniformly pink flowers. 'Regal' has gray-green leaves and large bicolored flowers that are pale lilac above rich purple, and 'Warren Jones' sports semi-evergreen gray-green leaves and especially large pale pink flowers.

Chitalpas (✕*Chitalpa taskentensis*), hybrids between desert willow and the non-native common catalpa tree *(Catalpa bignonioides),* are increasingly seen in gardens and landscapes throughout California and the Southwest. Compared to desert willow, these hybrids are much bigger trees, have larger, pale green leaves, and produce more blooms. Two clones, which are 20- to 30-foot-tall trees, are available. 'Morning Cloud' displays pure white flowers that have dark purple lines in the throat, and 'Pink Dawn' has pale pink flowers with a creamy throat. These hybrids are well adapted to hot interior climates. They are subject to mildew and do not flower prolifically when grown near the coast or in cool climates. Chitalpas are susceptible to verticillium wilt and should not be grown where this organism is present.

Clematis lasiantha
CHAPARRAL CLEMATIS
Buttercup Family (Ranunculaceae)

Plant Type: Woody deciduous vine.
Geographic Zones: All except high mountains and deserts.
Light: Sun to partial shade.
Soil: Adaptable; well-drained preferred.
Water: Drought tolerant to occasional.
Natural Habitat and Range: Slopes and canyons in chaparral and woodlands below 6000 feet; Sierra Nevada foothills and coastal mountains from Trinity and Shasta counties south to northwestern Baja California.

Chaparral clematis is like the phases of the moon, waxing and waning through the seasons. As it weaves its leaf petioles through the nearest tree or shrub, we hardly notice it until the flowers burst into bloom, often covering the supporting host plant in creamy white. Then things quiet down until, months later, the fluffy fruits ripen and we are reminded again of its presence.

Chaparral clematis displays flowers with many stamens, Santa Barbara Botanic Garden. STEVE JUNAK

The vining stems of chaparral clematis are capable of climbing up to 18 feet high. The long-petioled, pinnately compound leaves consist of three to five coarsely toothed, medium green leaflets. In spring, the ¼-inch-wide flower buds appear, looking quite similar to old-fashioned silk buttons. The greenish white sepals turn white as they unfold, exposing a profusion of long white stamens. Numerous silky-haired fruits ripen from these 1-inch-wide blossoms and hang like gossamer balls from the woody stems, providing as much decorative value as the flowers. Some gardeners find them objectionable as they darken to dirty grayish white and persist before disintegrating. A few light swats with a badminton racket will dislodge them handily.

Chaparral clematis is an undemanding vine in the garden. Let it cover a dark wall or fence, or better still, allow it to weave through and decorate nearby shrubs or trees. Flowering is more abundant on plants grown in sunny locations and can be enhanced by shortening each branch tip in early winter. Older vines develop an impressively thick, rope-like character. Insect or disease problems are insignificant.

Other Species: Virgin's bower *(Clematis ligusticifolia)* typically occurs in wetter sites and flowers somewhat later in the summer than chaparral clematis. The flowers are borne in larger clusters, but the sepals are shorter and there are fewer stamens. It usually has five to seven leaflets. Its range extends north into British Columbia, east to the Rocky Mountains, and south into northwestern Mexico.

Comarostaphylis diversifolia
SUMMER HOLLY
Heath Family (Ericaceae)

Plant Type: Evergreen shrub or small tree.
Geographic Zones: All except high mountains and deserts.
Light: Sun to partial shade.
Soil: Adaptable; well-drained preferred.
Water: Drought tolerant to occasional.
Natural Habitat and Range: Dry coastal slopes in chaparral; Santa Barbara County south to northwestern Baja California.

Summer holly blossoms resemble those of manzanita, Rancho Santa Ana Botanic Garden, Claremont. BART O'BRIEN

If you adore manzanita flowers and fancy the orange-red berries of toyon, you'll want to save a spot to plant summer holly. This uncommon native combines some of the best attributes of these two plants and can easily hold its own as a focal point. Summer holly in full bloom is a glorious sight, and the late-summer spectacle of birds dining on the vivid red fruits is further incentive to include it in your garden.

Summer holly's colorful fall berries, Regional Parks Botanic Garden, Berkeley. SAXON HOLT

At first glance summer holly's foliage resembles toyon's, with its serrated, leathery leaves, but summer holly's leaves are paler below. Both shrubs attain a similar size and reach 8 to 20 feet in height and width. Summer holly's arching inflorescences of nodding, urn-shaped white flowers reveal its taxonomic kinship with manzanitas. Blossoms appear in late winter or spring and are followed by bumpy red fruits that hang gracefully at the branch tips. The fibrous, gray-brown trunk shreds as the plant matures and exposes the cinnamon-colored layer beneath.

The multi-trunked summer holly can be trained into a tree. It may also serve as an informal hedge or screen, and its dark, shiny leaves provide an effective backdrop for plants with pale flowers or silver gray foliage. For a satisfying design, try combining summer holly with irises, low-growing manzanitas, and gray-leaved sages and buckwheats; for extra effect, place a sweep of silvery dudleyas in the foreground.

Summer holly has not reached the same heights in popularity as other native shrubs due to its slow growth rate and limited availability. For those willing to wait, its numerous attributes are worthy rewards, especially since this undemanding shrub needs no special care. An older plant that becomes sparse with age rejuvenates when pruned back to the basal burl, a result of its adaptation to fire. Aphid galls can disfigure the foliage, and it is susceptible to *Botryosphaeria* fungus (see page 52).

Coreopsis gigantea
GIANT COREOPSIS
Sunflower Family (Asteraceae)

Plant Type: Semi-evergreen to deciduous shrub.
Geographic Zones: Immediate coast to warm interior valleys of central and southern California.
Light: Sun to partial shade.
Soil: Adaptable; well-drained preferred.
Water: Drought tolerant.
Natural Habitat and Range: Coastal dunes and sea bluffs in coastal scrub below 200 feet; San Luis Obispo County to Los Angeles County, most of the Channel Islands, and Guadalupe Island.

It would be difficult to come up with another California native to top giant coreopsis in the weird-looking plant category. The peculiar appearance of this shrubby daisy endears it to many gardeners, some of whom liken giant coreopsis to a character from a Dr. Seuss book. Its ungainly, branched, 3- to 6-foot-tall form looks dead during the long dry summer months, but the onset of the rainy season triggers a flush of succulent,

Giant coreopsis becomes a garden focal point in spring, Santa Barbara Botanic Garden. STEPHEN INGRAM

lacy leaves at the tips of its chunky, naked branches. By late winter, a spray of 3-inch-wide yellow flowers emerges above the green foliage. The flowers bloom for about a month, then fade to chocolate brown.

A blooming giant coreopsis makes a striking focal point in any garden. Use it in perennial borders, on slopes, or in a garden full of succulents. Out-of-season water easily rots the fleshy roots, so plant it away from areas receiving summer irrigation. Some complementary partners are blue-eyed grass, annual lupines (especially those with deep blue flowers), any number of bunch-grasses, or low-growing ceanothus, sages, and buck-wheats. The summer-blooming buckwheats, in particular, are perfect for drawing attention away from giant coreopsis during its awkward summer doldrums. If the plant gets too tall for your taste, start over with newly purchased plants, or try growing some from seed. Protect young plants from predation by snails, slugs, rabbits, and ground squirrels.

Other Species: Sea dahlia *(Coreopsis maritima)* is easier to use in the garden than giant coreopsis but is much more restricted in the wild, growing only in San Diego County and south into northwestern Baja California. This cheery perennial requires the same growing conditions as giant coreopsis but has coarser foliage and a fleshy taproot from which the leafy stems emerge. Its flower stalks arc 8 to 24 inches tall and hold solitary, 3- to 5-inch-wide bright yellow blossoms in late winter and early spring. With judicious supplemental irrigation and regular deadheading, sea dahlia may continue to flower throughout the summer in cool areas, but be careful—too much water will be fatal. Plant several in drifts in perennial borders or meadows, and use them as cut flowers. Sea dahlia is often grown as an annual, but avoid sowing seeds in fall in frost-prone areas. It is susceptible to the same predators as giant coreopsis.

Cornus sericea
CREEK DOGWOOD
Dogwood Family (Cornaceae)

Plant Type: Deciduous shrub.
Geographic Zones: All except deserts.
Light: Sun to shade.
Soil: Adaptable.
Water: Occasional to regular.
Natural Habitat and Range: Streambanks and moist places in many plant communities below 9000 feet; across most of North America.

The numerous common names of *Cornus sericea*, such as creek dogwood, American dogwood, red-osier dogwood, Colorado dogwood, and redtwig dogwood,

Creek dogwood's attractive flowers, leaves, and stems, private garden, Oakland. STEPHEN INGRAM

testify to its variable nature and widespread distribution. Although it lacks the broad, showy bracts (often mistaken for flower petals) of some dogwood species, creek dogwood offers four-season interest and serves many functions in the landscape.

In California, creek dogwood is an aggressive, spreading shrub to 15 feet tall with a broad, rounded habit. The smooth stems and long branches are whip-like and often bright red. Unrestrained, it will spread via rhizomes or layering of lower branches to form large expanding thickets. The flat green leaves are 2 to 3 inches long and broadly lance-shaped or elliptic, with prominent parallel veins. Small cream or white flowers appear in tight, flat-topped, 2- to 3-inch-wide clusters in spring and then sporadically into the fall. Birds are attracted to the fleshy white- or blue-tinged, ¼-inch-wide berry-like fruits.

A versatile shrub, creek dogwood is particularly useful bordering lawns or planted along streams and creeks to stabilize banks. Away from the immediate coast, its autumn leaves offer a splash of red, yellow, orange, plum, and pink. Combine creek dogwood with big-leaf maple, Fremont cottonwood, and California wild grape for a bounty of fall color. In winter its wine red stems stand out against light-colored walls and fences or snowy mountain landscapes. Include the stems in winter floral bouquets for extra color.

Creek dogwood thicket in winter, Regional Parks Botanic Garden, Berkeley. SAXON HOLT

Creek dogwood is generally free of diseases and pests. It requires little maintenance beyond removal of undesirable rooting stems or occasional pruning late in the dormant season to control size. Pruning also improves the stem color, as the younger wood exhibits a richer color. Some Native Americans use the stems of creek dogwood in basketry.

Cultivars: Numerous selections have been made of creek dogwood, but few of these are California natives. 'Stinson Beach' is a large California cultivar with rich purple-red stems.

Cupressus forbesii
TECATE CYPRESS
Cypress Family (Cupressaceae)

Plant Type: Evergreen tree.
Geographic Zones: All except cool, foggy coasts and high mountains.
Light: Sun.
Soil: Adaptable.
Water: Drought tolerant to occasional.
Natural Habitat and Range: Forms isolated forests on dry slopes in chaparral from 1500 to 5000 feet; Peninsular Ranges from Orange County to northwestern Baja California.

Tecate cypress fits the California cypress profile well. This fire-adapted, California Floristic Province endemic is fast growing, has closed cones and scale-like leaves, and is confined to localized populations. What sets it apart from other California cypress species is its extraordinary bark. On mature trunks distinct colors of

Above: Tecate cypress (about 10 years old) planted as a screen, private garden, Ballard. JOHN EVARTS
Left: Beautiful bark on older, pruned Tecate cypress, Santa Barbara Botanic Garden. STEPHEN INGRAM

maroon, amber, pink, silver, gray, and metallic lime green appear together in a mosaic. As the bark peels, one color slips into another and, like the bark of California sycamore, its multicolored pattern continues to change as the tree grows.

Tecate cypress is a small tree to 30 feet tall and is often multi-trunked. Young trees grow rapidly and put out open sprays of light green, scale-like leaves. Lacking a resin gland on the leaf surface, the foliage doesn't emit the sharp fragrance found in other California species. Initially the branches are upright and produce a narrow, conical form. With age it develops horizontal branches and a picturesque open habit. The marble-sized cones age dull gray and persist on the tree for years.

Unlike the widely planted Monterey cypress (*Cupressus macrocarpa*), Tecate cypress can be used reliably in hotter interior sites, with only an occasional deep summer watering. It is particularly suitable as a specimen in small gardens and seldom outgrows its welcome. The rapid, dense growth of Tecate cypress recommends it for informal screens and windbreaks, and it readily accepts shearing to create more formal hedges. When developing Tecate cypress into a more arboreal form, selective pruning and thinning will improve its shape and structure and expose its appealing bark.

Cypress canker (*Coryneum cardinale*) can pose a serious problem for Tecate cypress, although it is not as susceptible as coastal species in the genus. Weakened or stressed trees are most vulnerable, and infections can be avoided if water applications and pest populations are carefully monitored. Copious water produces rank growth and top-heavy specimens that are easily toppled in strong winds.

Datura wrightii
SACRED DATURA
Nightshade Family (Solanaceae)

Plant Type: Semi-evergreen herbaceous perennial or annual.
Geographic Zones: As annuals, all. As perennials, all except cool northern coastal and high mountains.
Light: Sun.
Soil: Adaptable.
Water: Drought tolerant.
Natural Habitat and Range: Widespread in many plant communities below 4000 feet; central and southern California, to Utah, Texas, and South America.

Georgia O'Keefe, Edwin Weston, and many other artists of the Southwest have been transfixed by the considerable beauty and symmetry of the flowers of sacred datura. All parts of this plant are deadly poisonous, but a number of Native American peoples use it for ceremonial purposes.

Sacred datura grows so well in most sunny gardens that it is sometimes labeled a weed. Plants are either annuals or short-lived perennials. Mature plants reach 2 to 3 feet in height and 6 feet across. They grow vigorously in the heat of the summer and flower from this time until early fall. The variously lobed, coarse-textured, dark gray-green leaves have pointed tips and are up to 6 inches long. Crushed or bruised stems and foliage have

Above: Sacred datura thrives in hot, sunny sites, Furnace Creek, Death Valley National Park. DAVID FROSS
Left: Sacred datura flowers open in early evening, private garden, Borrego Springs. JOHN EVARTS

an unpleasant smell. The foliage provides an excellent foil for the luminescent flowers, whose color may vary considerably from pure white to creamy white to pale lavender. The upturned trumpet-shaped flowers may reach 4 to 5 inches across and 6 to 10 inches in length. Flowers open early in the evening and are sweetly scented to attract pollinating hawkmoths. By midmorning of the following day, the flowers usually collapse, and removing them will encourage further blooms. Pollinated flowers develop into a nodding, round, spine-covered fruit, which drops numerous tan or black seeds. Be sure to place these plants where their exquisite blooms may be enjoyed on moonlit nights. For a dramatic evening garden, combine it with Our Lord's candle, white sage, and California evening primrose.

Sacred datura is not susceptible to disease and has few insect pests. The most frequently encountered pest is the cucumber beetle; it resembles a green ladybug and eats holes in both foliage and flowers. Plantings may rot in gardens with heavy, rich soil if given excessive amounts of summer water. Cut sacred datura back hard in early winter, as it looks bedraggled by that time of year. New shoots will appear in spring.

Dendromecon harfordii
ISLAND BUSH POPPY
Poppy Family (Papaveraceae)

Plant Type: Evergreen shrub.
Geographic Zones: All except high mountains and deserts.
Light: Sun to partial shade.
Soil: Well-drained.
Water: Drought tolerant to occasional.
Natural Habitat and Range: Dry slopes in chaparral below 2000 feet; endemic to the Channel Islands.

Above: Island bush poppy in full bloom, Regional Parks Botanic Garden, Berkeley.
STEPHEN INGRAM
Left: Island bush poppy flower detail, Santa Barbara Botanic Garden.
STEPHEN INGRAM

Poppies are garden favorites, and island bush poppy is simply one of the best. Its flowers are a brilliant uniform yellow and appear year-round. You might think such floral profusion would preclude a season of super-abundance, yet in high spring these plants bloom with an exuberance that defies logic. The clean, waxy blue-green foliage provides a stunning backdrop for the yellow flowers. Individual leaves are quite variable in size and range from 2 to 6 inches long and 1 to 3 inches wide. Garden plants typically mature as open, hemispheric shrubs that vary in size from 5 to 10 feet high and equally wide, though larger specimens are sometimes seen.

Island bush poppy enhances gardens of all sizes. In larger landscapes, plant it in front of a tall blue-flowering ceanothus to display the drama of California's official blue and gold colors. This shrubby poppy may also be used as an informal hedge or screen, or in a large mixed border with other shrubs and perennials. Island bush poppy is such an all-season performer that it can hold the center of attention in smaller gardens. In such plantings, island bush poppy may be pleasingly combined with island snapdragon, blue witches, or low-growing species of ceanothus, such as Hearst ceanothus or maritime ceanothus. It also goes well with blue-, silver-, or gray-foliaged plants, such as David's Choice sandhill sagebrush, Montara California sagebrush, Canyon Silver island snowflake, and royal penstemon.

Bush poppy can be difficult to establish in a garden. Its root system, like most poppies, is especially brittle and will not tolerate rough handling. Most plants that die within the first year are lost due to damaged roots or excessive watering. Mature plants may be pruned hard, but senescent specimens may not always recover. Dry old leaves have a tendency to remain on the stems and should be removed by hand. Once established, island bush poppy has few pests or diseases.

Other Species: Island bush poppy's mainland relative, bush poppy *(Dendromecon rigida)*, has pale, stiff, upright to arching branches that are sparsely clothed with willow-like, leathery blue-green leaves. This shrub blooms once a year in spring.

Dryopteris arguta
COASTAL WOOD FERN
Wood Fern Family (Dryopteridaceae)

Plant Type: Evergreen fern.
Geographic Zones: All except high mountains and deserts.
Light: Partial shade to shade.
Soil: Adaptable; humus-rich and well-drained preferred.
Water: Drought tolerant to occasional.
Natural Habitat and Range: Shaded slopes and open woods in many plant communities below 5000 feet; California Floristic Province from San Diego County north to British Columbia.

Coastal wood fern is one of the few native ferns that is both evergreen and drought tolerant. Despite these desirable attributes, this lush-looking, adaptable fern is difficult to obtain.

Coastal wood fern with new growth, Santa Barbara Botanic Garden. STEPHEN INGRAM

The erect fronds of coastal wood ferns are arranged in appealing vase-like clusters. Each dark green frond is 1 to 2 feet long and 4 to 6 inches wide. In northern California, one finds substantial clonal colonies, whereas farther south, the stout rhizomes barely spread and plants appear to be randomly scattered individuals. This recalcitrant rhizome may explain the scarcity of coastal wood fern in commerce; there's precious little material for vegetative propagation.

Since coastal wood fern can withstand competition from the roots of mature trees, use it to soften the understory of coast live oak, California bay, pines, and other trees. The leafy green fronds serve as a soothing backdrop for California fescue, foothill sedge, coral bells, irises, and shade-tolerant annuals. Older fronds should be removed as they become tattered or brown.

Thrips are the one pernicious insect pest of coastal wood fern. Infestations of these minute insects are easy to detect because their feeding turns the fronds silvery. Once the fronds change color it is too late to save them, but a stream of water directed to their undersides can help dislodge the insects and keep them from spreading. One method of biological control involves releasing lacewings, a natural predator of thrips, but this must be timed carefully to coincide with the correct developmental stage of the pest. Another form of natural control uses coppicing to disrupt the thrips' life cycle.

Dudleya species
DUDLEYAS
Stone-crop Family (Crassulaceae)

Plant Type: Succulents.
Geographic Zones: Varies with species.
Light: Sun to partial shade.
Soil: Varies with species.
Water: Drought tolerant to infrequent; usually essential to avoid summer watering.
Natural Habitat and Range: Rocky, clayey, or sandy sites in coastal scrub, chaparral, mixed-evergreen forests, and deserts to 9000 feet; California Floristic Province, with a few species in Arizona, Oregon, and the cape region of Baja California.

One of the common names for *Dudleya* is "liveforever," which speaks volumes about this western North American genus that thrives on neglect. Some species reputedly live as long as 50 to 100 years, others a "mere" 20. This genus contains a number of California's most rewarding succulents for use in horticulture. Its numerous species offer a dizzying array of leaf shapes, sizes, habits, and flower colors for the garden.

Garden forms of dudleyas come in two distinct types: branching and unbranching. Both types are ideal for succulent and rock gardens. Branching species develop multiple rosettes that form low, tufted colonies, while unbranched species produce a solitary rosette. The colony formers are valuable groundcovers in the front of a border, whereas the single rosettes make excellent container specimens and focal points in beds.

Most of the myriad habitats dudleyas occupy become dry in summer. Therefore, it is important to cut off water to dudleyas in your garden during summer. Plants grown in sandy soils or containers are exceptions; they will accept infrequent summer watering

Chalk dudleya tucked between rocks bordering steps, private garden, Montecito. STEPHEN INGRAM

as long as the soil drains well. The onset of fall or winter rains reawakens dudleyas from drought-induced dormancy. Their shriveled leaves plump up quickly, growth resumes, and flowering occurs during the next spring or summer. Dudleyas are amazingly resilient; if a portion of a colony sloughs off a cliff face or is uprooted by a burrowing animal, it can persist for months until soil contact is reestablished. Species that naturally grow on ocean bluffs are also salt-spray tolerant.

Dudleyas have their share of disease and pest problems. If you can prevent Argentine ants from introducing mealybugs or aphids to your dudleyas, they will be healthier. Mealybugs nestle in the deep recesses of the leaves, and their feeding weakens the plants. They may also be vectors, along with aphids, for a virus that disfigures the foliage. Aphids commonly attack emerging flower stalks, and should be washed off carefully with soapy water or a strong jet of water.

Snails and slugs relish the juicy foliage of dudleyas and leave telltale holes. Avoid overwatering, which attracts these creatures and also favors root-rotting, soil-borne pathogens that may kill the plants. Provide ample air circulation to minimize fungal disease organisms, such as powdery mildew and *Alternaria*. Powdery mildew invades leaf tissues and causes browning and scarring of the upper surface; *Alternaria* produces ugly brownish black spots. Dudleyas are particularly susceptible to rot above ground if moisture accumulates in the rosette; plant them on a slight angle to drain water away more quickly. Browsing by rabbits and deer can reduce dudleya rosettes to nubs; to ensure your dudleyas have a chance to grow, you will need to exclude these animals from your garden.

Only a handful of the roughly 40 species of dudleya are reliably available. Several species are quite rare in the wild and are now protected by law. Thankfully, a number of nurseries and botanic gardens continue to responsibly propagate many choice species. For greatest success in cultivation, choose species from your local area.

Britton dudleya in a decorative pot, private garden, Sebastopol.
PHILIP VAN SOELEN

Britton dudleya (*Dudleya brittonii*) is prized for its strikingly beautiful 6- to 12-inch-wide solitary rosette. The whitish coating (rarely green) on the flattened 1- to 2-inch-wide leaves accounts for its luminous appearance. In spring, the flower

Catalina Island dudleya in a rock garden, Leaning Pine Arboretum, Cal Poly, San Luis Obispo. DAVID FROSS

stalk, which measures 1½ to 2½ feet, elongates and turns dark red as the pale yellow flowers open. This native of northwestern Baja California occurs primarily on steep bluffs in maritime coastal scrub. Possibly the most popular dudleya in cultivation, Britton dudleya makes a perfect accent in beds or containers. Plant it in well-drained soil, provide full sun near the coast or some shade inland, and protect it from freezing temperatures.

Candleholder dudleya (*Dudleya candelabrum*), one of many island-endemic dudleyas, is restricted to Santa Cruz, Santa Rosa, and San Miguel islands. Found on rocky ridges and slopes, its solitary rosettes average 6 to 10 inches across. The flattened 3- to 6-inch-long and 1- to 2½- inch-wide green leaves have a chunky look. The species gets its common name from its candelabra-like inflorescences, which bear numerous pale yellow flowers in tight clusters. It is somewhat frost tolerant.

Canyon dudleya (*Dudleya cymosa*) is a highly variable, diminutive dudleya esteemed for its colorful floral display. The flowers range from pale to bright yellow to orange or red. The wide, flattened leaves are also variable in color and the caudex may be branched or simple. Canyon dudleya occurs in rocky outcrops on slopes throughout the California Floristic Province, except the Central Valley. Try growing this challenging species in containers, and keep it dry during its summer dormancy.

Chalk dudleya (*Dudleya pulverulenta*) is spectacular in bloom. It has foliage similar to Britton dudleya, and its red flowers contrast handsomely with the white stalks. This widespread species occurs in coastal scrub and chaparral plant communities from San Luis Obispo County south to northwestern Baja California. It typically grows on slopes and appears to defy gravity by adorning steep cliff faces. Try several nestled in the crevices of a rock wall for a dramatic look. Chalk dudleya is more

Frank Reinelt dudleya with flowering stalks, Native Sons Nursery, Arroyo Grande. BART O'BRIEN

frost tolerant than Britton dudleya. Plant it in part shade, and leave it completely dry in summer.

Catalina Island dudleya *(Dudleya virens* ssp. *hassei)* is endemic to Santa Catalina Island. The densely clustered rosettes of grayish white leaves are 3 to 6 inches across. This profusely branching species is the best groundcover dudleya and is also valued for its tolerance of heavy soils.

Cultivars: 'Frank Reinelt' (also known as 'Anacapa') forms tight, low mounds about 6 to 8 inches tall and 12 or more inches wide. It has very silvery leaves, which flush to rose-purple in winter.

Encelia californica
CALIFORNIA SUNFLOWER
Sunflower Family (Asteraceae)

Plant Type: Evergreen subshrub.
Geographic Zones: Central coastal; southern coastal to interior valleys, but not areas with a hard frost.
Light: Sun.
Soil: Adaptable.
Water: Drought tolerant to moderate.
Natural Habitat and Range: Coastal scrub below 1600 feet; Santa Barbara County south to northwestern Baja California.

California sunflower is a garden stalwart that blooms profusely for months on end. It is best adapted to southern California gardens, where it typically produces flowers prolifically in spring and again in autumn. Few flowers are produced during hot, dry summer months or the coldest winter periods.

Inflorescences have golden yellow rays and chocolate brown centers, though plants with either pale yellow rays or green-colored centers are sometimes seen. For best performance and appearance, California sunflower should be deadheaded regularly—about every 2 weeks will suffice. Garden-grown plants that receive some additional water are typically much more lush, vigorous, and longer blooming than plants in the wild. The coarse green leaves clothe young stems and provide an excellent foil for gray and silver foliage.

Cut California sunflower back hard annually in winter after it flowers, otherwise this vigorous shrub can become ungainly and floppy. Pruned garden specimens may reach 2 to 4 feet tall and 3 to 5 feet wide. Like most of the plants in the sunflower family, California sunflower attracts numerous bees, butterflies, and other insects. Aphids are sometimes noteworthy pests, but generally this plant is pest free.

California sunflower is an excellent choice for use on hillsides and for erosion control. Plant it at the base of any of the medium to large shrub forms of ceanothus or with Cleveland sage and its hybrids to create a brilliant blue and yellow floral palette.

Cultivars: 'El Dorado' has especially large flower heads with overlapping ray flowers.

Other Species: Incienso *(Encelia farinosa)* has broad silvery leaves and blooms profusely during spring. This plant is especially characteristic of California's Colorado Desert, though it extends into the eastern Mojave Desert and to southwestern Utah, Arizona, and northwestern Mexico. In drought conditions, plants lose nearly all of their foliage. If it is planted near the coast or receives too much water, incienso has a rank and less satisfactory appearance. Grow it in full sun, well-drained soil, and with limited water, and you will be rewarded with a beautiful spring flower show. In California this plant is typically grown only in dry southern portions of the state.

California sunflower growing beside a path, Santa Barbara Botanic Garden. JOHN EVARTS

Epipactis gigantea
STREAM ORCHID
Orchid Family (Orchidaceae)

Plant Type: Deciduous herbaceous perennial.
Geographic Zones: All.
Light: Sun to partial shade.
Soil: Adaptable; moisture-retentive preferred.
Water: Moderate to regular.
Natural Habitat and Range: Streambanks, wet meadows, and seeps in most plant communities throughout California and north to British Columbia, and to South Dakota, Texas, and Mexico.

Orchids are the most diverse group of flowering plants on earth and have legions of devotees. Serious enthusiasts spend considerable time and money building their collections. Although most people associate orchids with the tropics, the California flora includes about 30 orchid species. Of these, only stream orchid has successfully made its way into nurseries and gardens.

Stream orchid occasionally appears in nursery catalogs and at botanic garden plant sales. Surprisingly easy

Stream orchid flowers, private garden, Swall Meadows.
STEPHEN INGRAM

to grow, especially for an orchid, this rhizomatous perennial has much to offer. In late winter, the plant awakens from dormancy and sends up light green shoots along the buried rhizome. Stream orchid reaches 1 to 2 and occasionally 3 feet tall when in bloom. Each flower stalks bears 3 to 15 blossoms that are 1 inch wide and have muted green, purple, maroon, and yellow colors. Even the fresh seedpods are an attractive shade of green.

Once stream orchid becomes established, it begins to spread slowly in all directions. Drier soil helps keep this traveler in check, or plant it in a generous-sized container and place it in the garden during its active growth period. If you plant stream orchid directly in the ground, be prepared for that spot to be empty during its fall and winter dormancy, unless you interplant it with another herb or low-growing shrub that can compete with its rhizomes, such as giant chain fern,

scarlet monkeyflower, or wild ginger. Stream orchid's attractive foliage and unusual flowers are worth the effort, especially as part of a moist woodland or water garden design.

Cultivars: 'Serpentine Night' has darker flowers and deep purple-black leaves that are particularly attractive when paired with silver-leaved plants. It isn't quite as strong as the species, however, and seems to lose its intense color as the weather warms.

Erigeron glaucus
SEASIDE DAISY
Sunflower Family (Asteraceae)

Plant Type: Evergreen herbaceous perennial.
Geographic Zones: All except high mountains and deserts.
Light: Sun.
Soil: Adaptable, except poorly drained.
Water: Drought tolerant to moderate.
Natural Habitat and Range: Coastal bluffs, dunes, and beaches in coastal scrub below 500 feet; northern Channel Islands and Santa Barbara County north to Oregon.

Seaside daisy is an easily grown, reliable perennial that produces cheerful daisy-like flowers at the tips of leafy stalks from spring to summer. The outer ring of ray flowers may be white, pink, rose, lavender, or violet and surrounds a central yellow-green disk. The dusty green leaves of seaside daisy are typically oval-shaped and have several coarse teeth along their margins.

Seaside daisy performs best in coastal gardens and works well in mixed borders, meadows, or containers. In richer, heavier soils it looks better and blooms more profusely than it will in sandy or rocky soils. In inland gardens plants grown in full sun flower spectacularly

W. R. seaside daisy brightens up a white wall, Rancho Santa Ana Botanic Garden, Claremont. BART O'BRIEN

*Cape Sebastian seaside daisy in a mixed border, Leaning
Pine Arboretum, Cal Poly, San Luis Obispo.* DAVID FROSS

throughout the spring but often burn to a crisp during
summer. For best appearance and to promote additional flowers, remove dead flower heads as they become
unsightly. Long bare stems with rosettes of foliage at
the tip can be cut back to 1 or 2 inches in late fall.
Individual seaside daisy plants have a useful garden life
span of two to seven years. Plants are typically pest free,
but when stressed by drought or heat, they are susceptible to spider mite and mealybug infestations.

Cultivars: Plants sold as 'Arthur Menzies' vary considerably from one source to the next. Nearly all are good
garden subjects, but they range from giants (2½ feet
tall and 4 feet wide) to near dwarf proportions (8 inches
tall and 12 inches wide). 'Cape Sebastian' is a dense,
low-spreading selection ideal for use as a small-scale
groundcover or in rock gardens. W. R. seaside daisy
(*Erigeron* 'W. R.'), also know as Wayne Roderick daisy
(*Erigeron* 'Wayne Roderick'), produces a thick mat of
lanceolate leaves to a height of 6 inches and spreads
from 2 to 3 feet wide. Flowers are produced on 6- to
10-inch-long stems in abundance throughout the year,
though fewer are produced during the hottest summer
and coldest winter months. This hybrid is longer-lived
and much more durable than seaside daisy. It has
thrived in California gardens with winter temperatures
of -6°F and summer temperatures of 115°F.

Eriogonum species
BUCKWHEATS
Buckwheat Family (Polygonaceae)

When it comes to buckwheats, few places can rival
the botanic richness of California. More than 125 species
make their home in the Golden State, and they range

in size from tiny annuals to 8-foot-tall shrubs. With the
possible exception of sedges, buckwheats make up the
largest genus in the California flora. Such diversity
challenges many botanists; gardeners, however, will find
that the buckwheats commonly used in horticulture are
fairly easy to distinguish from each other. They also
happen to be some of our most ornamental natives.

As garden subjects buckwheats are in an elite class.
Few ornamentals have such showy flowers, handsome
seed heads, attractive foliage, and pleasing forms, all in
one package. In the native garden, buckwheats seamlessly link one season to the next. By choosing as few as
three species, you can have buckwheat blossoms from
midspring to autumn, plus several months more of
attractive drying inflorescences.

Buckwheats are found from the seashore to alpine
peaks and occur in just about every plant community.
They are essentially sun-loving, drought-enduring
species that occupy drier, well-drained sites and favor
steep rocky slopes, coastal bluffs, and sandy, desert
soils. Many have gray or silvery foliage. The masses of
tiny flowers can be spectacular, ranging in color from
creamy white to pale or bright yellow and including
varying shades of pink and red. What really distinguishes buckwheats, however, are the arrangements of
the inflorescences, which can be densely packed rounded heads, airy wand-like spikes, or intricately branched
flattened sprays. As the flowers fade, they turn dark
yellow, deep red, or earthy hues of tan, russet, or
chocolate.

Buckwheats are a versatile element in the dry garden. They can be used as a sculptural focal point in a
container or rock garden, as an informal hedge or
groundcover, to edge a pathway or garden bed, or to
control ero-
sion. Their
utility extends
indoors as well
for fresh or
dried floral
arrangements.
Buckwheats
attract benefi-
cial insects and
are of substan-
tial value to
wildlife: they
provide food
for butterflies,
pollen and nec-
tar for bees,
seeds for birds
and mammals,
and cover for
many creatures.

*California buckwheat with creamy
white flowers, Regional Parks Botanic
Garden, Berkeley.* SAXON HOLT

When siting buckwheats in the garden, avoid areas where activities can break their brittle branches. Some species recover poorly, if at all, once broken, and are best replaced. Pest problems are relatively minor. An occasional infestation of aphids on the new growth is easy to control. Of more concern are mildew fungi, which can affect all or part of a plant. Refrain from overhead watering to reduce this problem. The following species descriptions include specific recommendations for plant care.

Eriogonum arborescens
SANTA CRUZ ISLAND BUCKWHEAT

Plant Type: Evergreen shrub.
Geographic Zones: All except Central Valley, high mountains, and deserts.
Light: Sun to partial shade.
Soil: Well-drained.
Water: Drought tolerant to moderate.
Natural Habitat and Range: Coastal bluffs, rocky slopes, grassy hillsides, and floodplains in coastal scrub, chaparral, and grasslands below 500 feet; Santa Cruz, Anacapa, and Santa Rosa islands.

Santa Cruz Island buckwheat, landscape planting, Santa Ynez Elementary School, Santa Ynez. STEPHEN INGRAM

Of all the native shrubby buckwheats, Santa Cruz Island buckwheat is the most elegant and refined. As a juvenile, this densely mounded shrub is all leaves and flowers, but with age it reveals its sinuous, shredding bark. Less bold than Saint Catherine's lace, but more stately than California or ashleaf buckwheat, this species is a long-lived beauty.

Like so many other members of the genus, Santa Cruz Island buckwheat has bifacial leaves. The linear 1- to 2-inch-long leaves are pale gray-green on top and whitish underneath. Clustered at the tips of the branches, they are held erect, giving the plant a grayish cast. Depending upon the habitat, plants vary in size from prostrate mounds less than 1 foot tall to arborescent individuals 6 feet or greater. Their widths range from 3 to 5 feet across. In summer the asymmetrical 3- to 6-inch-wide inflorescences begin their mutable display. The pinkish buds unfold, revealing creamy white or pink flowers. On close inspection, much of the pink comes from the tiny anthers. While some flowers fade to russet, others continue to open. This bisque-colored phase lasts for several weeks until finally the entire flat-topped cluster turns cinnamon brown.

When planted in windy, exposed sites, Santa Cruz Island buckwheat tends to stay compact and low, making it ideal for rock gardens where these conditions prevail. In more protected locations, plants become open and gnarled with age, and the roughened bark adds a textural element. You can plan ahead to highlight this living sculpture by siting the shrub as a focal point; this works especially well when Santa Cruz Island buckwheat is placed in an attractive pot that has a cascading companion plant spilling over the edge. Other options are to use it in a row as a medium-sized unclipped hedge or mass it on banks to aid in erosion control.

Santa Cruz Island buckwheat is a low-maintenance plant. To keep it looking good, all you need to do is remove the disintegrating flower stalks. Be grateful if a few seedlings pop up to replace specimens past their prime. Occasional aphid infestations on the new growth are more annoying than troublesome, but downy mildew can be problematic during cool springs and summers.

Eriogonum cinereum
ASHYLEAF BUCKWHEAT

Plant Type: Evergreen shrub.
Geographic Zones: All except Central Valley, high mountains, and deserts.
Light: Sun.
Soil: Well-drained.
Water: Drought tolerant to occasional.
Natural Habitat and Range: Steep slopes, canyons, and coastal bluffs in coastal scrub; Los Angeles County to Santa Barbara County and Santa Rosa Island.

One doesn't have to garden near the coast to appreciate the attributes of ashleaf buckwheat. Despite its natural affinity for seaside areas, this buckwheat also grows well in many interior locales. Use it along with other buckwheats to achieve a blooming season that spans nine months.

Ashyleaf buckwheat produces a long-lasting floral display, Santa Barbara Botanic Garden. STEPHEN INGRAM

Eriogonum crocatum
SAFFRON BUCKWHEAT

Plant Type: Evergreen subshrub.
Geographic Zones: Coastal, and intermediate and interior valleys.
Light: Sun.
Soil: Well-drained.
Water: Drought tolerant to occasional.
Natural Habitat and Range: Rocky slopes in coastal scrub below 500 feet; restricted to one region of the Santa Monica Mountains in Ventura County.

Saffron buckwheat with buds and flowers, Santa Barbara Botanic Garden. STEPHEN INGRAM

Ashyleaf buckwheat is a billowing shrub that puts forth numerous slender stems from its base. It creates a shapely mound and ranges in size from 3 to 6 feet tall and 3 to 10 feet across. The soft, ovate leaves are angled upward, exposing the lower ashen surfaces and causing plants to appear gray from a distance. As summer draws to an end, countless flower stalks begin to elongate. Each fork of the irregularly branched inflorescence holds small, fuzzy, pink to cream ball-like flower heads. The floral display lasts for months, and the color often intensifies to a deeper pink before fading to rosy tan.

A utilitarian shrub, ashyleaf buckwheat looks better in mass plantings than alone. For gardeners with challenging slopes to cover, it should rank high on the list of candidates. Use it with impunity at the beach; the salt and wind won't bother it. Take advantage of its late blooming period by mixing it in a perennial border with other water-thrifty species, such as red-flowered buckwheat, golden yarrow, any of the coastal manzanitas or ceanothus, and some colorful monkeyflowers. Removing the spent flower stalks can be a bit daunting due to their copious numbers, but if you want to tackle this non-essential task, try using shears.

As its common name suggests, saffron buckwheat has yellow flowers—not just any yellow, but an eye-catching chartreuse yellow. At first glance, the color looks a bit jarring against the plant's fuzzy white stems and leaves, but eventually it segues into a deep chocolate brown that makes for an appealing contrast with the foliage.

Saffron buckwheat is a rare plant in the wild, and its bright foliage and cushiony shape make a lasting impression when first seen in its natural habitat. This wavy-leaved buckwheat forms mounds 1 to 2 feet tall and 2 to 3 feet wide. The downy white flower stalks elongate in spring into flattened inflorescences. Watching the flowers' progression from rusty buds to chartreuse blossoms to brown seed heads is part of the visual pleasure in growing this perennial.

Saffron buckwheat is quite versatile. Plant several as a small-scale groundcover or to edge the front of a perennial border; use a few to soften a rock garden; or feature one alone in a favorite container. Saffron buckwheat can even serve as an informal, low hedge surrounding an herb or knot garden. Remove the flower stalks after they have shed their seeds, and prune back leggy branches every few years to retain this buckwheat's compact habit. If you are lucky, seedlings will sprout at random, insuring saffron buckwheat's continual presence in your garden.

Eriogonum fasciculatum
CALIFORNIA BUCKWHEAT

Plant Type: Evergreen shrub.
Geographic Zones: All except high mountains.
Light: Sun to partial shade.
Soil: Adaptable; well-drained preferred.
Water: Drought tolerant to occasional.
Natural Habitat and Range: Dry slopes and canyons in coastal scrub, chaparral, desert woodland, and desert scrub below 8000 feet; Alameda County south to northwestern Baja California and east to southwestern Utah and Arizona.

California buckwheat (gray-leaved variety) in a drought-tolerant garden, Santa Ynez Valley Union High School. JOHN EVARTS

As the state's most widespread shrubby buckwheat species, California buckwheat is aptly named. This evergreen shrub probably doesn't make it onto many "favorite plants" lists, but don't let that be a deterrent. This tough plant offers an abundance of flowers,

benefits for wildlife, and serves many functions in a garden or landscape.

The needle-like, ½- to ¾-inch-long leaves of California buckwheat are clustered in bundles similar to pine needles. All are felty white below, but the color of the upper surface varies from medium green to silvery gray, depending upon the amount of pubescence. The leaf hairs play a role in cooling plants exposed to harsh sunlight and dry conditions and are just one of many drought adaptations the plant possesses.

California buckwheat rarely exceeds 4 feet in height and has many growth habits. Some forms have arching branches that root where they touch the ground, creating low, spreading mounds. This rooting tendency makes California buckwheat ideal for erosion control. Other forms are prostrate and are useful in rock gardens or as a groundcover. With some effort, you can even clip California buckwheat into a low hedge, but this much pruning would sacrifice most of the flowers.

California buckwheat bears a superficial resemblance to rosemary and chamise due to similarities in their foliage, but once it flowers, California buckwheat looks vastly different from these plants. Its wiry flower stalks are branched near the top and bear one to several capitate clusters. The flower clusters are usually so numerous that they literally cover the entire plant and mask the foliage below with their fuzzy blossoms. Blooming begins in spring and continues through summer, often extending into fall. The cream to white flowers are occasionally tinged with pink, and as they mature, the plant's appearance changes from cream to rust or brown. Viewing wild hillsides covered with the coppery seedheads of California buckwheat is a uniquely Western experience and lends a touch of fall color to our state.

Cultivars: Most selected forms of California buckwheat are from the immediate coast and were chosen for their low-growing habit. 'Bruce Dickenson', 'Dana Point', 'Theodore Payne', and 'Warriner Lytle' are cultivars that are occasionally available; 'Warriner Lytle' is likely the most adaptable.

Eriogonum giganteum
SAINT CATHERINE'S LACE

Plant Type: Evergreen shrub.
Geographic Zones: All except high mountains and deserts.
Light: Sun.
Soil: Adaptable; well-drained preferred.
Water: Drought tolerant to occasional.
Natural Habitat and Range: Dry slopes and ridges in coastal scrub and chaparral below 1500 feet; Santa Catalina, San Clemente, and Santa Barbara islands.

Top: Saint Catherine's lace covered with blooms, Rancho Santa Ana Botanic Garden, Claremont. BART O'BRIEN
Bottom: Saint Catherine's lace with dried inflorescences, private garden, Ballard. JOHN EVARTS

Undisputedly the giant of its genus, Saint Catherine's lace is prized for the size and delicate beauty of its lacy inflorescences and for its bold stature. The common and scientific monikers of this species allude to these notable characteristics, and this much-admired, easy-to-grow shrub has graced gardens in California for decades.

A young Saint Catherine's lace is rounded in outline, eventually becoming 4 to 8 feet tall and 6 to 10 feet wide. As the plant matures, it becomes more irregular, and the gnarled, dark gray limbs take on a sculptural quality. Its 2- to 3-inch-long egg-shaped leaves are silvery green on top and felty white underneath. The enormous, intricately branched inflorescences hover over the foliage and are awesome to behold. Upwards of 2 feet in diameter and bearing masses of tiny off-white flowers in summer, the sprays age to a warm reddish brown.

Its size alone recommends Saint Catherine's lace as a focal point in a mixed border or in a large container.

It makes an effective informal screen or backdrop for a border and, as its native habitat suggests, works well on slopes and within range of salt spray. Lightly prune the branch tips to keep it somewhat contained, but do not cut into old wood, which doesn't reliably resprout. Don't be afraid, however, to selectively remove a branch here and there to accentuate its strong character. At any stage, snip off the inflorescences and bring them indoors; when dry, they will remain whatever color they were when cut and will last for many years. Be sure to allow a few flowers to mature if new seedlings are desired.

Eriogonum grande var. *rubescens*
RED-FLOWERED BUCKWHEAT

Plant Type: Evergreen subshrub.
Geographic Zones: Coastal region and intermediate and interior valleys.
Light: Sun to partial shade.
Soil: Well-drained.
Water: Drought tolerant to occasional.
Natural Habitat and Range: Coastal bluffs and rocky slopes in coastal scrub and grasslands below 700 feet; northern Channel Islands.

Red-flowered buckwheat in a mixed border, Santa Barbara Botanic Garden. STEPHEN INGRAM

Characterizing the flower color of red-flowered buckwheat as red is a bit hyperbolic, but that doesn't detract from its beauty. With its frothy pink to cherry red inflorescences, this island species is another terrific plant for the garden.

Red-flowered buckwheat has a lot in common with saffron buckwheat. Both share an affinity for well-drained, sunny sites, flower from spring to summer, and form low mounds. Red-flowered buckwheat grows 1 to 3 feet tall and about as wide. The ovate leaves are green to gray-green on top and white underneath. Flower color, size, and shape are unpredictable due to natural variation and hybridization with other closely related species, but in general, blossom color will vary from pale pink to deep rose.

Think of red-flowered buckwheat as filler, and plant it liberally around the garden. Its modest size and relatively short life—typically 3 to 5 years—suggest this strategy. Drifts of it weaving through a perennial border or tucked between rocks are pretty in late spring and summer. The pink flowers are never garish and blend gracefully with other colors, save perhaps true reds and intense oranges. Of the many suitable companions, try saffron buckwheat, purple sage, golden yarrow, seaside daisy, clarkias, and dudleyas. The blossoms of red-flowered buckwheat don't age well; remove them as they fade unless seedlings are desired. If plants become leggy, prune them back to lateral buds, replace them, or let volunteer seedlings take over.

Eriogonum latifolium
COAST BUCKWHEAT

Plant Type: Evergreen subshrub.
Geographic Zones: Coastal regions and intermediate valleys.
Light: Sun to partial shade.
Soil: Well-drained.
Water: Drought tolerant to occasional.
Natural Habitat and Range: Coastal bluffs and dunes in coastal scrub below 500 feet; from San Luis Obispo County north to Washington.

If coast buckwheat had less hairy leaves and pinker flowers, it could pass for red-flowered buckwheat. Indeed, botanists previously treated these two plants as the same species. Still, coast buckwheat is a desirable plant in its own right. Its form, foliage, and flowers are attractive additions to rock gardens and mixed borders.

The oval leaves of coast buckwheat are invitingly soft. A touch of green may show through the mat of white hairs on the upper surface, but the lower surface is always densely felted. It forms low mounds 1 to 2 feet tall and often wider, and the pubescent flower

Coast buckwheat (foreground) and Emerald Carpet manzanita flanking a stairway, private garden, La Honda.
BART O'BRIEN

stalks that begin to elongate in late spring enhance the pleasing shape. Whether simple or branched, the stalks are topped with tight, 1-inch-wide pompoms of creamy white to light pink (occasionally deep rosy red) flowers. Some gardeners actually prefer the cream-colored blossoms, as they mirror the foliage below so seamlessly. Coast buckwheat partners well with seaside daisy, David's Choice sandhill sagebrush, quail bush, and Cape Mendocino reedgrass.

Eriogonum umbellatum var. polyanthum
SULFUR BUCKWHEAT

Plant Type: Semi-evergreen subshrub.
Geographic Zones: All.
Light: Sun to partial shade.
Soil: Adaptable; well-drained preferred.
Water: Infrequent to occasional.
Natural Habitat and Range: On dry slopes and openings in forests from 700 to 10,000 feet; northern Sierra Nevada, Klamath and Cascade ranges, Modoc Plateau, and into Oregon.

If you come upon a yellow-flowered buckwheat while hiking in the mountains of California, chances are it will be one of the more than twenty varieties of sulfur buckwheat. Horticulturists have selected a few

Sulfur buckwheat with Dr. Hurd manzanita and woolly blue curls, private garden, Lafayette. STEPHEN INGRAM

choice forms of this widespread and highly variable species to use in the garden. Most of these come from the variety *polyanthum,* which grows in the northern mountains of the state. Despite its origins in montane habitats, sulfur buckwheat is surprisingly adaptable to garden culture at lower elevations. It also tolerates shade better than most buckwheat species.

Sulfur buckwheat is a long-lived, mat-forming or mounding subshrub that grows ½ to 1½ feet tall and 1 to 3 feet wide. Its sage green to gray-green leaves are whitish underneath. Some forms of the species are semi-deciduous and lose most of their leaves in late summer or fall. The bright yellow flowers, arranged in dense pom-pon heads, start blossoming in spring. The leaves and blossoms are subtler than those of saffron buckwheat and therefore a bit easier to blend into a perennial border or rock garden. Its faded flowers, however, don't hold up well, nor do they provide as strong a contrast to the foliage.

Cultivars: 'Shasta Sulphur' performs well throughout California and offers a profusion of bright yellow flowers in very dense heads. It forms tight mounds that reach 1½ feet in height when in bloom and measure 2 to 3 or more feet across. The gray-green leaves may turn an appealing plum brown in winter.

Eriophyllum nevinii 'Canyon Silver'
CANYON SILVER ISLAND SNOWFLAKE
Sunflower Family (Asteraceae)

Plant Type: Evergreen subshrub.
Geographic Zones: Immediate coast and warm interior valleys of central and southern California.
Light: Sun to partial shade.
Soil: Adaptable; well-drained preferred.
Water: Drought tolerant to occasional.
Natural Habitat and Range: A selection from the Santa Barbara Botanic Garden. The species is a rare plant that occurs on rocky bluffs in coastal scrub below 100 feet; Santa Catalina, Santa Barbara, and San Clemente islands.

Canyon Silver island snowflake is an eye-catching cultivar with beautiful foliage, interesting texture, colorful summer flowers, and attractive seed heads. More reliable in cultivation than the species, 'Canyon Silver' grows 3 to 5 feet tall and equally wide.

Silvery white, deeply lobed lacy leaves are Canyon Silver island snowflake's best feature. In summer the foliage is augmented by dense clusters of deep golden yellow flowers in heads 4 to 8 inches across. These butterfly- and bee-attracting blossoms dry a wonderful

Canyon Silver island snowflake, flowers and foliage, private garden, Montecito. STEPHEN INGRAM

chocolate brown, contrasting with the silver leaves below. Remove the spent flowers as they disintegrate and prune older stems in fall or late winter, using the newly emerging shoots to guide you. If its stems are not cut back, the plant becomes leggy and unable to support next year's heavy flowers, resulting in a floppy habit.

Use this remarkably versatile shrub as a focal point in a mixed border, or go all out and plant several to form a medium-sized, informal hedge. It merits a prime spot in a silver or white garden. For maximum effect, contrast Canyon Silver island snowflake with a glossy dark green partner like Oregon grape or blue blossom ceanothus to accentuate its arresting foliage.

Like many plants with gray or silver foliage, Canyon Silver island snowflake grows best in full sun. If you use its bright foliage to lighten up a shady spot, expect reduced flowering. Aphids may infest the new foliage, but are easily controlled by hand or with a strong jet of water. Gardeners in areas with frost will need to replant Canyon Silver island snowflake annually.

Other Species: Golden yarrow *(Eriophyllum confertiflorum)* is a semi-evergreen subshrub common to dry sites in many plant communities of the California Floristic Province. This diminutive gray- to green-leaved species averages 1 to 2 feet tall and forms loosely upright to mounded cushions. In spring and summer, many 1- to 2-inch-wide domed flower clusters crown the plant with golden yellow. This charming, cold-hardy, incredibly drought-tolerant native is an ideal filler in dry borders, where its fine texture complements grasses, wildflowers, and bold-leaved shrubs. It also makes an attractive cut flower. Retain its compact habit by deadheading or pruning plants down to 3 or 4 inches.

Festuca californica
CALIFORNIA FESCUE
Grass Family (Poaceae)

Plant Type: Semi-evergreen, cool-season perennial grass.
Geographic Zones: All except high mountains and deserts.
Light: Sun to partial shade.
Soil: Adaptable.
Water: Drought tolerant to moderate.
Natural Habitat and Range: Open and shaded woodlands and forests below 5000 feet; northwestern and central western California, San Bernardino Mountains, Sierra Nevada, Coast and Cascade ranges to Oregon.

California fescue aligns its growth to match the rhythm of California's Mediterranean climate. After the first autumn rains it sends forth silver blue or verdant green new blades from its clump of dry-season leaves. This cool-season grass grows quickly through winter and early spring before its inflorescences stretch above the leaves to present first florets and then seeds.

The mature, stiffly arching blades of California fescue can be dull green or silver blue, and they form a large, graceful clump to 2 feet or more in height. The elegant flowering stems rise 1 to 3 feet above the foliage in spring and early summer. They produce delicate sprays, which at first have a gray-blue blush and then bleach to a wheat color with age.

Plant California fescue as a groundcover in woodland gardens among oaks, California bays, or pines, or site it as a specimen to help mark the turn of the seasons. Selections with blue-gray leaves make an effective foil for the bright flowers of seaside daisy, checkerbloom, or Douglas iris. Groom plants with a stiff rake to remove old foliage and freshen summer and fall appearance. In the warmer, dryer portions of southern California it has a more cultivated appearance when moderate or occasional summer water is supplied. California fescue is seldom troubled with diseases or pests, although a number of insects may eat the foliage in heavily irrigated gardens.

Cultivars: All of the selections of California fescue have been made for foliage color. There are a number of cultivars with silver or blue-gray foliage. 'Horse Mountain

Above, left: California fescue with flowering stalks, private garden, Arroyo Grande. DAVID FROSS
Above, right: Red fescue covering a gentle slope, private garden, Solvang. JOHN EVARTS

Green' is one of the most vigorous and has a tall vertical habit and unusual bicolored foliage; the blade's top surface is green and its underside is chalky blue. Its wheat-colored seed heads can reach as much as 6 feet tall. Even with summer irrigation it is difficult to prevent full dormancy with 'Horse Mountain Green' or any of the California fescue cultivars.

Other Species: Idaho fescue *(Festuca idahoensis)* is one of the most common and widely distributed grasses of the western states. It occurs in northwestern California, in the central and northern Coast Ranges, and in the Sierra Nevada and Cascade Range north to Canada and east across northern Nevada, Utah, and Colorado. As with most widespread species, it is found in many plant communities, but usually in open, dry habitats below 5000 feet.

Idaho fescue has a tight, clump-forming habit and reaches 12 to 18 inches tall. The basal leaves are narrow and often colored an appealing blue, green, gray or silver. Flowers are borne in spring on 1- to 2-foot-tall stems that occasionally are blushed pink or rose. The dense gray-green heads become straw-colored with age.

Idaho fescue grows best in well-drained soils in full sun or partial shade and requires occasional dividing to maintain vigorous clumps. When massed, Idaho fescue makes a bold statement, or when repeated in borders it can unify a garden with both color and texture. The intense blue-colored selections combine well with purple-leaved shrubs. A daring gardener might try planting drifts of Idaho fescue with Diamond Heights ceanothus to complement its variegated foliage.

The turf industry makes extensive use of the 100-plus cultivars of red fescue *(Festuca rubra)*. This species grows naturally in a broad range of habitats across the cooler portions of North America and Eurasia. In California, it is found in moist habitats below 9000 feet in the Sierra Nevada and Cascade and Transverse ranges and extends south in the Coast Ranges to Monterey County.

Red fescue forms tufted drifts 3 to 12 inches high and spreads by creeping rhizomes. The leaf blades have a lax character and a reddish or purplish basal sheath and range in color from yellow-green to blue-green or deep green. The flowering stems rise 4 to 12 inches above the foliage in loose panicles that open with a purple tint before maturing to blonde. On some selections flowering is infrequent.

Use red fescue in full sun or light shade. Effective in meadow gardens or as a small-scale lawn, red fescue requires no maintenance but can be clipped with a mower or string trimmer when it reaches a height of 2 to 3 inches. Like most other fescues, it is disease and pest free.

Cultivars: 'Jughandle' has chalk gray foliage to 6 inches high and forms a tight clump. 'Patrick's Point' is blue-gray and grows to 1 foot tall with an equal spread. Both are suitable for rock gardens, containers, or the spaces between stepping-stones and require less water than typical red fescues.

Fragaria chiloensis
BEACH STRAWBERRY
Rose Family (Rosaceae)

Plant Type: Evergreen herbaceous perennial.
Geographic Zones: All except high mountains and deserts.
Light: Sun to partial shade.
Soil: Adaptable; well-drained preferred.
Water: Infrequent to occasional.
Natural Habitat and Range: Sand dunes and bluffs in coastal scrub below 1000 feet; Santa Barbara County north to Alaska and in coastal South America.

Beach strawberry is a vigorous and fast-growing perennial that will quickly cover the ground with a mat of glossy dark green foliage and bright white flowers. Although it is the parent of commercial strawberries, beach strawberry's genetic contribution to agricultural varieties is vigor, not fruiting character; its small, edible, seed-flecked crimson berries are only about ½ inch long.

Beach strawberry's thick, leathery, compound leaves have three coarsely toothed leaflets. The flowers vary in size up to 1¼ inches in diameter. They are held on leafless stalks and have white petals surrounding numerous yellow stamens and carpels. Plants can be male or female and some are bisexual.

Primarily used as a groundcover, beach strawberry has long, robust, rose-colored stolons that terminate with a rooted plantlet. The easily established plantlets spread rapidly in favorable sites, but patches of them can be contained with a mower or string trimmer. Left unmowed, the plant can grow to 10 inches tall. An annual spring pruning will freshen plantings and prevent thick-layered colonies.

Effective on any scale, beach strawberry works with equal success on broad hillsides or in smaller gardens as a lightly trafficked turf. Combine it with other dune and sea bluff perennials like seaside daisy, David's Choice

Woodland strawberry grown as a groundcover, private garden, Montecito. STEPHEN INGRAM

sandhill sagebrush, and dune sedge to create a colorful coastal garden. It requires shade in interior gardens.

Replace older plants that show declining vigor, as they may be infected with strawberry virus. Stunted plants with dying leaves are often the sign of strawberry root weevil. These small, fat grubs with light brown heads eat the plant's roots and can kill entire plantings over time. There are no environmentally safe treatments available to control root weevils.

Cultivars: 'Aulon' is a male selection that has long, vigorous stolons and larger leaves and flowers than typical beach strawberry.

Other Species: Woodland strawberry (*Fragaria vesca* ssp. *californica),* is found primarily in shaded places in chaparral, woodlands, and forests below 7000 feet in much of the California Floristic Province. Woodland strawberry has lighter green leaves than beach strawberry and produces smaller but more flavorful fruit. It serves as an excellent groundcover in partial shade. Plant it under the canopy of mature trees with foothill sedge, giant chain fern, and Douglas iris. Divide older drifts on occasion to maintain vigor and increase strawberry production. A cultivar of woodland strawberry, 'Montana de Oro', is a vigorous female selection with flavorful fruit.

Aulon beach strawberry beginning to flower, Rancho Santa Ana Botanic Garden, Claremont. BART O'BRIEN

Fraxinus dipetala
FLOWERING ASH
Olive Family (Oleaceae)

Plant Type: Deciduous tree or shrub.
Geographic Zones: All except high mountains and deserts.
Light: Sun to partial shade.
Soil: Adaptable.
Water: Drought tolerant to occasional.
Natural Habitat and Range: Dry slopes, canyons, and streambanks in chaparral and woodland below 4000 feet; foothills of the Sierra Nevada, and Coast, Transverse, and Peninsular ranges, to Utah and Arizona.

Most species in the ash genus produce an abundance of small, unremarkable blossoms. Flowering ash is a delightful exception that bears fragrant blooms for a brief few weeks in spring. The creamy white blossoms, which resemble lilac flowers, cascade below the four-angled twigs in 2- to 6-inch-long airy panicles.

Flowering ash grows as a broadly upright, multi-trunked tree or shrub to 7 to 25 feet tall. Its bark becomes dark gray and furrowed with age. The pinnately compound leaves emerge shortly after flowering begins. In some years, the leaves exhibit a pleasing array of coppery orange and plum hues before they drop in midsummer.

Flowering ash is easy to grow and requires no maintenance, although some pruning of young plants will encourage better form. It has no significant insect problems, but it is susceptible to anthracnose and verticillium diseases. In some areas mistletoe *(Phoradendron macrophyllum)* is a nuisance. Flowering ash's only drawbacks are a rather slow rate of growth, a long dormant period, and limited availability.

Flowering ash, close-up of flower clusters, Santa Barbara Botanic Garden. J. R. HALLER

To play up its billowing blossoms, site flowering ash as a focal point in a mixed border. Frame it with evergreen companions, such as coffeeberry, manzanitas, and low-growing barberries, to draw attention away from its dormant phase. It combines well with hummingbird sage, monkeyflowers, irises, and bunchgrasses or clumping sedges. Try flowering ash as a patio tree in situations where a deciduous tree is desirable. The birds that visit to harvest the seeds from its one-winged samaras add yet another reason to seek out this little-used native.

Flowering ash, showing multiple-trunk growth habit, Rancho Santa Ana Botanic Garden, Claremont. STEPHEN INGRAM

Fremontodendron californicum
CALIFORNIA FREMONTIA
Mallow Family (Malvaceae)

Plant Type: Evergreen shrub.
Geographic Zones: All except low deserts.
Light: Sun to partial shade.
Soil: Well-drained.
Water: Drought tolerant.
Natural Habitat and Range: Rocky soils and slopes in sunny open chaparral or woodland between 1200 and 6500 feet; inner North Coast Ranges of Tehama County and the foothills of the Sierra Nevada and Cascade Range from Shasta County south to northwestern Baja California and central Arizona.

A California fremontia in full bloom is an unforgettable sight. The waxy, 3-inch-wide bright yellow flowers are produced with such abandon that they may

California Glory fremontia in full bloom, U.C. Davis Arboretum. BART O'BRIEN

Above: Pine Hill fremontia on a hillside beneath Dr. Hurd manzanita, private garden, Berkeley. STEPHEN INGRAM
Left: Pacific Sunset fremontia flowers, Santa Barbara Botanic Garden. KAREN MUSCHENETZ

obscure the foliage. Almost always, the flowers develop orange or rusty tints as they age. Hybrid fremontias are generally considered superior to the species for use in horticulture. All fremontias demand dry conditions, and violating this requirement results in the premature death of plants from a host of fungal root or crown rots.

Though nearly all fremontias have the potential to reach enormous size, they rarely live long enough to do so. Their short-lived proclivity is offset by the fact that even year-old plants are free flowering and spectacular. If a plant grows too large for the available space, it can be removed, replaced, or pruned.

Gardeners should be aware of fremontia's shallow, wide-spreading roots. Young plants are particularly fast growing and are especially vulnerable to blowing over in windy areas; toppled plants usually don't recover. Also, a fremontia's roots may spread into a more water-ed portion of the garden or landscape, providing an avenue for root rots that kill the plant. Fremontias are frequently recommended as candidates for espaliers, but due to their extremely fast rate of growth this is impractical in much of California.

Careful placement of fremontias in gardens is additionally important due to their dense coating of skin-irritating brownish stellate hairs. If you need to perform a gardening chore near or under a fremontia, it should be the last task of the day, as you will likely feel the need to shower and launder your clothing afterwards.

Other Species: Mexican fremontia (*Fremontodendron mexicanum*) is federally listed as an endangered species and is only known from two locations—one in Baja California and the other in San Diego County. Mexican fremontia is typically easier to grow in most gardens than the other *Fremontodendron* species,

although it is still a challenging plant. Its blossoms are similar to those of California fremontia but are larger and become more prominently marked with orange as they age. Mexican fremontia blooms over a long period of time, but the flowers are often obscured by its green-er and much larger foliage.

Cultivars: The named selections of fremontia are the most commonly grown. These cultivars are widely regarded as some of the most spectacular California native plants. 'California Glory' is likely the best of them all and has bright yellow flowers and three-lobed dark green leaves. It is grown in temperate and Mediter-ranean climates around the world. Plants initially have an upright growth habit but develop a mounding to arching form with age and may reach 20 feet with a spread twice as wide.

'Pacific Sunset' and 'San Gabriel' are similar large fremontias that may reach 20 feet tall and 40 feet wide. The former has a bit more orange in the flowers, and the latter typically branches in a distinctive, nearly two-dimensional herringbone pattern. Both plants rarely attain full size and may be appreciated in smaller gardens until they either get too big or die prematurely.

Pine Hill fremontia *(Fremontodendron decumbens)* is a rare and difficult-to-grow plant from the Sierra Nevada foothills that has contributed its smaller size and rusty orange flowers to a number of strikingly beautiful cultivars. 'El Dorado Gold' and 'Ken Taylor' are two hybrids with downward-facing flowers that are the result of crosses between 'California Glory' and Pine Hill fremontia. 'El Dorado Gold' is the most garden-tolerant of the fremontias. Its mounding to spreading growth may reach 4 to 6 feet in height, and it typically spreads twice as wide. The flowers are yellow-orange, the small leaves are dark green, and the leaves and stems are densely coated with golden brown hairs.

'Ken Taylor' has showy, large orange-yellow blossoms. The blue-green to gray leaves are slightly three-lobed, and the stems and leaves are lightly coated with brown hairs. Its cascading to arching form is attractive and distinctive. Ken Taylor fremontia is particularly effective when grown on a slope or atop a retaining wall where the flowers and foliage may be seen and appreciated.

Galvezia speciosa
ISLAND SNAPDRAGON
Figwort Family (Scrophulariaceae)

Plant Type: Evergreen shrub.
Geographic Zones: All except high mountains and deserts.
Light: Sun to partial shade.
Soil: Adaptable.
Water: Drought tolerant to occasional.
Natural Habitat and Range: Rocky canyons and bluffs in coastal scrub below 3000 feet; San Clemente and Santa Catalina islands and Guadalupe Island, Mexico.

Red-flowered shrubs in the California flora are precious commodities, and island snapdragon is one of the most ornamental members of this elite group. Its lipstick-red blossoms weigh down the tips of the lanky branches, act as beacons for hummingbirds, and add refreshing color to the garden.

Island snapdragon forms a spreading, open mound 3 to 4 feet tall and 5 to 7 feet wide. If its long, brittle stems receive support, island snapdragon may grow up to 15 feet through the branches of nearby shrubs or

Top: Bocarosa island snapdragon bordering a pathway, Rancho Santa Ana Botanic Garden, Claremont. STEPHEN INGRAM
Bottom: Firecracker island snapdragon in bloom, Rancho Santa Ana Botanic Garden, Claremont. KAREN MUSCHENETZ

trees, creating a vine-like effect. The somewhat succulent, medium to yellow-green leaves are either glabrous or hairy. Clusters of 1-inch-long flowers terminate the arching branches. They are most abundant in late winter and spring but appear almost any time of year. The saturated red blossoms strongly resemble those of its annual, non-native cousin, the common snapdragon.

Despite its narrow distribution in the wild, island snapdragon is an adaptable, easy-to-grow shrub. It benefits from regular pinching to encourage a bushy habit, and some gardeners like to prune it annually, in late winter, all the way back to the crown to prevent build-up of woody tissue. Avid pruners can use island snapdragon as a native alternative to boxwood hedges. Other than an infrequent aphid infestation, island snapdragon is a pest-free plant. Although cold sensitive, it tolerates occasional frosts.

To make the most of the rich red flowers, plant island snapdragon where it can spill down a bank or drape over a low wall. It is useful in containers, as a large-scale groundcover, or trained against a trellis, but keep in mind its pruning requirements. Although flowering will be reduced, it grows well beneath the high canopy of coast live oak.

Cultivars: 'Firecracker' reaches 2 to 3 feet tall and about 3 feet wide, has softly pubescent leaves, and is more erect and compact than island snapdragon. 'Bocarosa' is a floriferous selection.

Other Species: Baja bush snapdragon *(Galvezia juncea),* as its Latin name implies, has rush-like (as in the genus *Juncus*) stems with ephemeral to much-reduced leaves. Plants vary in color from medium green to blue-green. The abundant, bright red flowers are smaller and narrower than island snapdragon's. The vase-shaped plants are 3 to 6 feet tall; from the base, they develop masses of stems that may layer naturally to form thickets. Culture for this Baja native is comparable to island snapdragon, but it does not tolerate frost.

Garrya elliptica
COAST SILK-TASSEL
Silk-tassel Family (Garryaceae)

Plant Type: Evergreen shrub or small tree.
Geographic Zones: All except interior valleys, high mountains, and deserts.
Light: Sun to partial shade.
Soil: Adaptable; well-drained preferred.
Water: Infrequent to occasional.
Natural Habitat and Range: Dry slopes and ridges in chaparral and mixed-evergreen forests below 2000 feet; Coast Ranges from Ventura County to southwestern Oregon.

James Roof silk-tassel in the background of a mixed border, private garden, Dorset, England. DAVID FROSS

James Roof silk-tassel covered with male catkins, highway landscaping, Colma. BART O'BRIEN

Few native shrubs can match the visual drama provided by a male coast silk-tassel in full winter bloom, when its pendulous, silver green catkins hang from the stems like delicately arranged tinsel on a Christmas tree. Along with the flowers of manzanitas and currants and the emerging spikes of hummingbird sage, coast silk-tassel's catkins decorate the early days of winter.

In the wild, coast silk-tassel can grow to 24 feet high with an equal spread, but in gardens, 8 to 12 feet is more common. Its oval or elliptic 1½- to 3-inch-long leaves have a thick, leathery texture, wavy margins, and a smooth, dark green surface. The undersides are felted with woolly hairs. Male and female flowers appear on separate plants. On male plants, catkins form near the ends of stems in loose, dangling 3- to 12-inch-long clusters. Their pollen induces an allergic reaction in some people. Female catkins measure 2 to 4 inches and when fertilized, elongate into 6-inch-long clusters of fleshy, grape-like fruits, which have a vivid purple pulp.

The winter catkins and evergreen foliage of coast silk-tassel combine well in the garden with deciduous shrubs like spicebush and western azalea to add seasonal interest and contrast. Complementary herbaceous partners include western meadow rue, western columbine, and Douglas iris. Coast silk-tassel serves equally well as a foundation shrub, informal hedge or screen, or trained as an espalier. Mature specimens can be pruned into handsome small trees.

Water molds can be a problem for coast silk-tassels grown in poorly drained soils, and branch dieback will affect drought-stressed shrubs, particulary in warmer climates away from the coast. (See *Botryosphaeria* on page 52.) In these areas coast silk-tassel requires additional irrigation and partial shade to avoid damage from the sun. Annual pruning is recommended to shape the plant and to remove old dried leaves and dead branches. Shear plants to the basal burl to rejuvenate older, leggy specimens. Flowering is variable and can be light one year and heavy the next.

Cultivars: Most of the plants available in California are from two male clones selected for their long, elegant catkins. 'James Roof' is a prolific bloomer with 1-foot-long tassels. 'Evie' is a dense, robust selection. Its catkins are a bit shorter than those of 'James Roof', and the smaller leaves are held closer along the stems.

Grindelia stricta var. *platyphylla*
SPREADING GUM PLANT
Sunflower Family (Asteraceae)

Plant Type: Evergreen herbaceous perennial.
Geographic Zones: All except intermediate and interior valleys, high mountains, and deserts.
Light: Sun to partial shade.
Soil: Adaptable.
Water: Drought tolerant to moderate.
Natural Habitat and Range: Dunes, marshes, and bluffs in coastal scrub below 700 feet; throughout coastal California.

Spreading gum plant brings color to the garden after many species in the California native flora have already finished flowering. Along with buckwheats and California fuchsias, it brightens the landscape during the warm, dry summer months.

A prostrate groundcover that remains under a foot tall, spreading gum plant easily reaches 6 to 10 feet across as its decumbent stems take root. The thickened, shallowly toothed leaves are incredibly variable in size, but are generally widest at the tip. In summer, the inflorescences extend slightly beyond the foliage. The center of each fat green bud holds a pool of gummy white resin, which glistens in the sun and protects the blossoms from predators. The daisy-like flowers practically cover the plant with a mantle of bright yellow; they eventually fade to dark brown but persist for several months.

Spreading gum plant is well suited to gardens exposed to salt spray. It is free of pests, with the exception of unsightly but harmless spittlebugs, and requires minimal maintenance. Shear the spent blossoms in autumn for a cleaner appearance, and prune wayward stems to keep plants in bounds. Older plants that become woody at the crown or leggy can sometimes be rejuvenated with a hard pruning in fall or winter. If this fails, simply start over with healthy young specimens, which will quickly fill the space.

Use spreading gum plant in a meadow garden with other perennials. It makes a complementary green foil for Douglas iris, blue-eyed grass, checkerbloom, David's Choice sandhill sagebrush, and seaside daisy. For a mosaic of green groundcovers in a larger garden, try spreading gum plant with low-growing forms of manzanita, ceanothus, and buckwheat, and add an occasional silvery counterpoint, such as Canyon Gray California sagebrush, Canyon Silver island snowflake, or Silver Carpet California aster.

Other Species: Great Valley gum plant *(Grindelia camporum)* and hairy gum plant *(Grindelia hirsutula)* are erect 1- to 3-foot-tall herbaceous perennials with 2-inch-wide bright yellow heads that bloom from spring well into summer. Utilize these two upright gum plants in meadow gardens, mixed borders, and as cut flowers. Great Valley gum plant can grow in warm interior valleys.

Spreading gum plant, South Coast Watershed Resource Center, Santa Barbara. STEPHEN INGRAM

Hesperoyucca whipplei
OUR LORD'S CANDLE
Agave Family (Agavaceae)

Plant Type: Evergreen subshrub.
Geographic Zones: All except high mountains.
Light: Sun to partial shade.
Soil: Adaptable; well-drained preferred.
Water: Drought tolerant.
Natural Habitat and Range: Slopes in chaparral and coastal scrub below 8000 feet; southern Sierra Nevada, South Coast Ranges from Monterey and San Benito counties south to northwestern Baja California.

Our Lord's candle in bloom, Leaning Pine Arboretum, Cal Poly, San Luis Obispo. DAVID FROSS

Our Lord's candle adds its distinctive form to a sunny slope, Santa Barbara Botanic Garden. JOHN EVARTS

Never a shy or retiring plant in the garden, Our Lord's candle is best suited for making a bold statement. This plant is also at home in a diversity of garden styles, from the abstract and avant-garde to minimalist desert plantings. One might expect the flowers of Our Lord's candle always to be creamy white, but plants growing in the wild from Riverside and Orange counties southward may have stunning dark purple flowers or even pale pink blossoms, although these variants are rarely seen in gardens. Emerging flower stalks are often strikingly colored red and resemble giant asparagus spears.

Our Lord's candle is quite variable in the wild. Some populations produce enormous foliage rosettes from 3 to 8 feet across, but the plants die after they flower. Others produce up to 3-foot-wide rosettes, and although the flowering rosette dies after blooming, several basal shoots emerge to form new rosettes. These perennial types may, over the course of time, form large, impenetrable colonies, making them an excellent choice for long-term barrier or security plantings.

Enjoy the beautiful silver to blue-gray or green foliage while you wait for flowers. Our Lord's candle can take anywhere from 3 to 15 years or more to bloom—typically, the older the plant, the more impressive the bloom. Young plants produce flowering stalks that are 6 feet tall, while the spires of older specimens may attain heights of 15 to 20 feet.

The stiff, extremely sharp-tipped leaves and the ultimate size of the plant must be taken into account when placing Our Lord's candle in your garden. Plants pose an extreme hazard to unwary children, garden visitors, and pets. Eliminate problem weeds well in advance of planting, and add a deep gravel or rock mulch around these potentially dangerous plants to assist with weed suppression.

Our Lord's candle is the perfect garden companion for boulders. Placed on a gentle south-facing slope among large dark-colored volcanic rocks, the starbursts of foliage are spectacular. Accentuate Our Lord's candle's striking form by planting it along a wall or where you can see its silhouette against the sky. These plants are especially effective in moonlit gardens, where their rosettes appear to glow.

Heteromeles arbutifolia
TOYON
Rose Family (Rosaceae)

Plant Type: Evergreen shrub or small tree.
Geographic Zones: All except high mountains and deserts.
Light: Sun to partial shade.
Soil: Adaptable.
Water: Drought tolerant to occasional.
Natural Habitat and Range: Chaparral and woodlands below 4000 feet; Sierra Nevada foothills from Shasta County to Tulare County; Humboldt County south to the Sierra San Pedro Martir of northwestern Baja California, then on widely scattered mountain ranges to the Sierra de la Laguna of the cape region of Baja California Sur.

Toyon makes an effective screen, Santa Barbara Botanic Garden. JOHN EVARTS

Toyon in front of a garden wall, Los Angeles County Arboretum, Arcadia. SAXON HOLT

Toyon is the only California native plant that continues to be commonly known by a Native American name. It retains the name given to it by the Ohlone, who along with other California tribes use parts of this plant for food, medicines, and implements. Toyon's resemblance to the European holly and its abundance in the hills of southern California were the genesis of the name "Hollywood" for the now world-famous film capital.

This widely adaptable, easy-to-grow shrub is treasured for its evergreen foliage and bounty of winter berries. These fruits are preceded in early summer by showy terminal bunches of small white flowers. In the wild, toyon displays an astonishing variability in leaf size and shape, berry size and color, and growth habit. Plants are most often seen as large shrubs, which reach from 8 to 15 feet in height and width, but older specimens may develop into multi-trunked trees that display smooth to fissured gray bark and branches. The leathery leaves have serrated margins and may be narrow or wide as well as long or short.

Like many plants in the rose family, toyon's showy fruits are initially unpalatable due to the presence of

cyanide compounds. After about two months of ripening, the toxic chemicals in the berries begin to ferment. The fruits then attract both resident and migratory birds. Sometimes birds appear drunk or otherwise impaired after gorging themselves on large numbers of berries, but they usually recover their bearings quickly.

In cultivation, young toyons are frequently weak, spindly plants and usually take a year or two to settle into the garden. Young plants are also susceptible to numerous fungal pathogens that may disfigure the foliage and occasionally kill them. After establishment, toyons become long-lived backbone elements of a garden. Toyons can be used as informal large hedges or screens, as specimen shrubs, or as multi-trunked small trees. They are not recommended as single-trunked specimens, as they typically produce numerous water sprouts from the base. Established plants may be coppiced or pruned to rejuvenate or enhance their appearance.

Toyon plantings normally harbor insignificant infestations of a wide array of pests and diseases, including aphids, scales, mealybugs, white flies, thrips, and leaf spot. Gardeners should monitor pest levels and take appropriate action as each situation warrants. Fireblight may appear occasionally and must be dealt with promptly or the plants may be lost or permanently disfigured. Affected branches retain their dead leaves and appear burnt. Such growth should quickly be removed and burned or otherwise disposed of (do not add it to your compost or mulch). Sterilize your pruning shears or saw between each cut to prevent spreading this pathogen.

Cultivars: 'Davis Gold' is an outstanding cultivar of yellow-berried toyon (*Heteromeles arbutifolia* var. *cerina*), a form that is rarely seen in the wild. It has remarkably clean foliage and profuse yellow fruits that are burnished with a touch of orange.

Davis Gold toyon has distinctive yellow fruits, private garden, Solvang. JOHN EVARTS

Heterotheca sessiliflora ssp. *bolanderi*
'San Bruno Mountain'
SAN BRUNO MOUNTAIN GOLDEN ASTER
Sunflower Family (Asteraceae)

Plant Type: Evergreen herbaceous perennial.
Geographic Zones: All except high mountains and deserts.
Light: Sun to partial shade.
Soil: Adaptable.
Water: Drought tolerant to moderate.
Natural Habitat and Range: Golden aster is found on coastal dunes and headlands in coastal scrub below 1500 feet; Mendocino to San Mateo counties. The selection is from San Bruno Mountain, which straddles the boundary between San Francisco and San Mateo counties.

San Bruno Mountain golden aster, private garden, Montecito.
STEPHEN INGRAM

San Bruno Mountain golden aster is the best of the golden asters for California gardens. It produces abundant ½-inch-wide golden yellow flowers from spring through fall. Their massed effect gives this plant its charm.

This easy-to-grow and long-lived perennial forms a tight bun of oval-shaped, light green leaves that are covered with long white hairs. A mature plant reaches about 6 inches high and 12 inches wide. Use San Bruno Mountain golden aster at the front of mixed or perennial borders, in rock gardens, or in sand. It combines well with other small, sun-loving plants, such as David's Choice sandhill sagebrush, seaside daisy, foothill penstemon, blue-eyed grass, blue witches, and native irises.

For best garden appearance, this cultivar requires regular deadheading since its spent flowers quickly turn an unappealing brown color. Some gardeners leave the mature seedheads to attract birds. You can cleanup and rejuvenate the plant in late fall by cutting it back to 2-inch-long stubs with a string trimmer. However, when grown in frosty areas such care is often unnecessary. San Bruno Mountain golden aster has no pests or diseases.

Heuchera species
CORAL BELLS
Saxifrage Family (Saxifragaceae)

Coral bells are always near the top of any list of favorite California native plants for gardens and landscapes. They range in size from tiny, compact alpine species to lush, airy woodland species. Coral bells are excellent choices for use as groundcovers or massed plantings, though the size of individual plants will dictate the scale of the planting. They are wonderful subjects for containers, where they may be grown singly, grouped, or in combination with other partial-shade-loving plants. Suitable garden companions for the larger-sized coral bells include Douglas iris, Canyon Prince wild rye, snowberry, hummingbird sage, gooseberry, currants, and ferns. Smaller coral bells combine beautifully with Patrick's Point fescue, coyote mint, cliff-maids, smaller manzanitas, and less vigorous iris species and hybrids.

Coral bells have several important insect pests. Mealybugs are the most frequently encountered, and heavy infestations will cause serious damage. Thrips can disfigure the foliage, especially if the plants are growing near the coast or in humid gardens. Strawberry root weevils may attack the root system of coral bells; they are particularly damaging to the smaller species and hybrids. Affected plants appear to shrink in size as the older leaves wilt and die, leaving only small young leaves.

In early spring, mildew may make an unwelcome appearance on the foliage of the larger-sized coral

Lillian's Pink coral bells (center) and other natives, private garden, Lafayette. STEPHEN INGRAM

Hybrid coral bells from the Canyon Quartet series, Santa Barbara Botanic Garden. CAROL BORNSTEIN

bells—island alum root and its hybrids—but most plants recover completely without intervention by early summer. Rust has become a problem with some of the larger hybrids. Leaves of affected plants develop powdery rust-colored spots on their undersides, while their tops are spotted with dead tissue.

Heuchera elegans
ELEGANT CORAL BELLS

Plant Type: Evergreen perennial.
Geographic Zones: All except deserts.
Light: Sun to partial shade.
Soil: Adaptable; well-drained preferred.
Water: Occasional to moderate.
Natural Habitat and Range: Partially shaded steep, rocky slopes in pine forests above 4000 feet; San Gabriel Mountains.

Aptly named, elegant coral bells is an excellent choice for small perennial beds, containers, rock gardens, and edging paths. In gardens it forms dense foliage mats composed of tightly packed rosettes of bright green leaves and may reach 10 to 24 inches across and 1 to 3 inches high. Soft-haired, rose-tinted flower stalks are 6 to 12 inches high and carry loosely arranged clusters of ⅛- to ¼-inch-wide flowers. The flowers have a bicolor appearance due to their pinkish calyces and white petals. Flowers of elegant coral bells bloom for a three to four week period from spring to early summer. Due to its showy flowers and easy culture, elegant coral bells has often been used in breeding programs.

Rosada coral bells in a mass planting, Rancho Santa Ana Botanic Garden, Claremont. BART O'BRIEN

Canyon Melody coral bells, Santa Barbara Botanic Garden. STEPHEN INGRAM

Other Species: Santa Rosa Mountains coral bells (*Heuchera hirsutissima*) grows in coniferous woodlands in the Santa Rosa Mountains; mountain coral bells (*Heuchera rubescens*) is found above 5000 feet in elevation in California and is widespread in the west. Both species are closely related to elegant coral bells, and all three may be substituted in gardens for one another. Other than overall height and size, which are variable within each species, the most obvious differences between these plants is the degree of hairiness on the stems, leaves, and calyces.

Crevice alum root (*Heuchera micrantha*) is found on shaded rock outcrops and hillsides from the Coast Ranges of southern Oregon south to San Luis Obispo County and in the Cascade Range and Sierra Nevada from Siskiyou County south to Tulare County. This species grows best in central and northern California as it prefers cooler conditions. Plants typically have 8- to 24-inch-long airy inflorescences that carry numerous tiny white to pale pink flowers. Foliage is typically green, though some forms have foliage that is attractively marbled with silver, purple, or reddish brown. The cultivar 'Martha Roderick' is especially notable for its pink blossoms.

Cultivars: 'Bella Blanca' is the only named selection of elegant coral bells and unlike typical specimens, has pure white flowers and bright green stems. It is an excellent counterpoint to the pink- and rose-colored flowers of the numerous other small coral bells species and hybrids.

Since the late 1970s, breeding programs have yielded excellent garden-worthy cultivars of coral bells using elegant coral bells, or California's other smaller species of coral bells, and frequently involving scarlet coral bells (*Heuchera sanguinea*)—a familiar garden perennial from the state of Arizona. These outstanding plants may be used as small-scale groundcovers, in mixed borders and containers, or to edge pathways.

In 1985, Dara Emery of the Santa Barbara Botanic Garden introduced the first of his California hybrids, 'Canyon Delight' and 'Canyon Pink'. Both are showy, mat-forming perennials with 8- to 16-inch-long flower stalks. The flowers of 'Canyon Delight' have white petals and deep pink calyces, whereas those of 'Canyon Pink' are uniformly deep pink. When conditions are favorable, these two selections are long-lived, durable garden performers. In cooler areas, the more sun they receive, the better they bloom. Plants growing in full sun in hot or inland gardens, however, tend to burn up and die during the long summer months.

The most recent California hybrids are known collectively as the Canyon Quartet series: 'Canyon Belle', 'Canyon Chimes', 'Canyon Duet', and 'Canyon Melody'. They range in height from 12 to 18 inches. 'Canyon Belle' is the most distinctive, with its rich red flowers; 'Canyon Chimes' produces dark pink flowers; 'Canyon Duet' has strongly bicolored flowers of pink and white; and 'Canyon Melody' sends forth medium pink flowers with a touch of white.

A little-known charmer, 'Pink Wave', has tight, shiny rosettes of wavy-margined leaves that form 1- to 2-inch-high vigorous spreading mats up to 18 inches across. In the spring, 6- to 8-inch-tall flower stalks appear in abundance. Because of its small size, 'Pink Wave' is best grown in containers or rock gardens.

'Chiqui' has the largest individual flowers of any of the hybrid coral bells; each blossom may reach ½-inch long. The flower's color varies with sun exposure and soil type and is either salmon-pink or apricot-pink. These uniquely colored flowers are held in 8- to 18-inch-long narrow spike-like inflorescences. Clumps of loose, hairy, pale green foliage reach about 3 to 6 inches tall and 6 to 18 inches wide. In most gardens, 'Chiqui' requires sun for at least half of the day. Be sure it has good air circulation, as it is particularly susceptible to mildew.

The smallest of all is Chiquita coral bells (*Heuchera parishii* 'Chiquita'). Young plants display delicate, 3-inch-long pink-blushed flower clusters and are perfectly at home in a 2-inch pot.

Heuchera maxima
ISLAND ALUM ROOT

Plant Type: Evergreen perennial.
Geographic Zones: All except frost-prone valleys, high mountains, and deserts.
Light: Sun to partial shade.
Soil: Adaptable; well-drained preferred.
Water: Occasional to moderate.
Natural Habitat and Range: Rocky outcrops and woodlands below 1500 feet; Anacapa, Santa Cruz, and Santa Rosa islands.

Island alum root and its hybrids are formidable treasures of the richly endowed *Heuchera* genus. For maximum garden effect, plant them in masses under trees; their 2-foot-wide rosettes of soft, pale green hairy foliage are lush and soothing. During the spring months numerous 2- to 3-foot-long upright to spreading, branched flower stems emerge and create an airy cloud of tiny greenish white to pale pink flowers. These plants bloom particularly well when they are located under deciduous trees, where they receive full sun in winter and partial shade during hot summer months. Another successful strategy is to place plants along the south or west side of a large evergreen tree, so they receive shade in summer but plenty of sunshine in winter due to the lower sun angle. Island alum root will grow and flower in dense shade, but its hybrids require more light.

Island alum root does not produce nearly as many side branches as its more diminutive cousins. Leafy stems typically continue to elongate, and plants gradually decrease in vigor, size, and flower production. To counteract this tendency, cut longer stems back to inch-long stubs during fall every two to five years. For large plantings, accomplish this task with a string trimmer.

Cultivars: Hybrids between island alum root and Arizona scarlet coral bells *(Heuchera sanguinea)* are glorious

additions to the garden. In 1953, Lee Lenz of Rancho Santa Ana Botanic Garden initiated the breeding program that gave rise to many of these plants. These vigorous hybrids inherited the large size of the flower stems and rosettes from island alum root and the larger individual flowers and various tones of red from scarlet coral bells. The following discussion of some of the best cultivars arranges them in order from largest to smallest.

'Old La Rochette' has broadly lobed and wavy-margined pale green leaves and pale pink flowers. 'Opal' features soft, hairy, pale green leaves and white flowers that turn pink as they age. 'Wendy' displays open rosettes of pale green leaves and exceptionally profuse rosy pink blooms. 'Santa Ana Cardinal' and the indistinguishable 'Susanna' have lush, shiny dark green foliage and deep red flowers. 'Rosada' features dense rosettes of pale green foliage and rosy pink blooms. 'Genevieve' bears rich magenta flowers and dark green leaves often highlighted with silvery markings; it has a tendency to rebloom periodically through late fall. Of different hybrid origin, but definitely in the class of large hybrids, is 'Lillian's Pink', which has dense rosettes of green foliage and a profusion of pink flowers on 12- to 18-inch-long stems. All of these hybrids look good when they are

Island alum root in a shady woodland, Santa Barbara Botanic Garden. STEPHEN INGRAM

planted in large drifts. They are also effective in mixed borders, as path edgings, and in container plantings. Hybrids with shiny green foliage (as opposed to pale green) tolerate more sunlight in the summer months, but even these burn if they receive too much sun.

Hyptis emoryi
DESERT LAVENDER
Mint Family (Lamiaceae)

Plant Type: Evergreen to semi-evergreen shrub.
Geographic Zones: Warm southern coastal, intermediate and interior valleys, and low desert.
Light: Sun.
Soil: Well-drained.
Water: Drought tolerant to infrequent.
Natural Habitat and Range: Gravelly washes and slopes in desert scrub below 3000 feet; Sonoran and lower Mojave deserts to Arizona and northwestern Mexico.

The intensely perfumed French, Spanish, and English lavenders are ubiquitous in California gardens. These shrubs are prized for their essential oils and profuse floral display. Yet few gardeners realize that California has a native plant that bears a remarkably similar fragrance. The leaves of our native species, desert lavender, often have a zesty hint of grapefruit aroma as well.

California's sole representative of this mostly Central and South American genus is a common and variable desert shrub. Either upright or spreading, desert lavender attains 3 to 10 feet in height and a comparable width. The irregular growth habit and widely spaced leaves create an open, airy impression. The finely toothed leaves are densely hairy and range from ashy gray to silvery white in color. Desert lavender will shed most of its leaves during prolonged dry spells in the desert and will releaf when the rains resume. Its 1- to 3-inch-long clusters of tiny, pale to deep violet woolly blossoms attract bees, butterflies, and hummingbirds.

Although a desert native, this lavender is remarkably easy to grow in coastal southern California when given a warm site, good drainage, and dry conditions. An occasional deep watering in summer will keep plants in desert gardens more presentable. Established plants typically resprout from the crown following an occasional hard frost. Prune as desired to control size and shape, as well as to harvest the aromatic flowers and foliage for floral arrangements and potpourri. No other maintenance is required.

Place desert lavender along a dry streambed or near a path or bench to allow contact with the fragrant foliage. Its height makes it a useful backdrop in an herb

Desert lavender with an upright habit, Santa Barbara Botanic Garden. STEPHEN INGRAM

garden or dry border. Turn desert lavender into a pleasing focal point by pruning to accentuate its vase-shaped form, or shear it into a hedge. The soft leaves and fuzzy flower clusters complement spiky agaves, yuccas, and succulents. Combine it with purple three-awn or alkali sacaton and a carpet of desert annuals to create a simple but effective composition.

Iris species
IRISES
Iris Family (Iridaceae)

Plant Type: Evergreen herbaceous perennial.
Geographic Zones: All except high mountains and deserts.
Light: Sun to partial shade.
Soil: Douglas iris and cultivars are adaptable; Oregon iris needs well-drained soil.
Water: Drought tolerant to occasional; moderate in intermediate and interior valleys.
Natural Habitat and Range: Depending upon species, in open places or shady wooded slopes in grasslands, forests, and woodlands; west of the Sierra Nevada/ Cascade crest from the San Bernardino Mountains north to Washington. The species used to breed Pacifica hybrids occur from the Transverse Ranges north to Washington.

Our native irises are practically *de rigueur* for California gardens. Iris means rainbow in Greek and is a fitting name for plants that display such a wide spectrum

Douglas iris is an attractive, durable native, Santa Barbara Botanic Garden. STEVE JUNAK

of springtime colors. Their lovely flowers, graceful bearing, and rich green to blue-gray foliage are outstanding additions to both formal and informal settings.

California irises are potentially long-lived, mostly evergreen perennials with thin rhizomes. In autumn, new clusters of sword-shaped to linear leaves in a fanlike arrangement begin to grow, and by late winter or early spring, the first blossoms appear. Each inflorescence bears one to three flowers that open one at a time. The outer whorl of three sepals, known as falls, are either reflexed or spreading; the middle three petals, called standards, are erect, and the inner whorl of petal-like stigmas hide the stamens underneath. In some species, the flower stalks are short and tucked within the foliage, which partially obscures the floral display. In others, the stalks rise above the foliage and offer a better view of each blossom.

The two most widely grown species are Douglas iris *(Iris douglasiana)* and Oregon iris *(Iris innominata)*. Douglas iris is larger and is the more common, vigorous, and durable of the two. It occurs primarily in open grassy habitats along the coast from southwestern Oregon to Santa Barbara County at elevations typically below 350 feet but as high as 3000 feet. Its dark, glossy, sword-like evergreen leaves are ½ to ¾ inches wide and 1 to 3 feet long. Flower color ranges from creamy white to blue, lavender, reddish purple, and deep purple. Douglas iris is not fussy; it accepts sun or shade, occasional or no summer water, and all but soggy soils. Oregon iris is dainty in comparison. It has narrower, more grass-like, glossy arching leaves that reach a maximum of 16 inches in length. Flowers are typically deep yellow, with occasional purples or lavenders. Oregon iris is uncommon in the wild and is found only in extreme northwestern California and adjacent parts of Oregon at elevations between 1000 and 6000 feet. This iris needs well-drained, preferably humus-rich soil and summer water to thrive in most garden situations, and it requires some shade in inland areas.

Use irises in a mixed border, woodland garden, meadow, or as edging near a pool or stream. They make an excellent groundcover, especially in the shade of oak trees. Flowering will decrease, however, as shade deepens. The more diminutive species and cultivars are also effective in rock gardens. Plant them in masses and use one color or an assortment. The warmer toned russet- and maroon-colored cultivars work well with barberries, manzanitas that produce bronzy new growth, and other plants with burgundy foliage. Irises with pastel-colored flowers are wonderful with just about everything, but are especially effective with ceanothus, native sages, and coral bells. Take some flower stalks indoors for floral arrangements; each blossom lasts 2 to 3 days, and the buds will continue to open after the stalks are cut.

Native irises are easy to grow as long as their cultural requirements are met. For gardeners in intermediate and interior valleys, the most important factors are protection from the hot afternoon sun and modest watering in summer. Douglas iris tolerates an array of soil conditions, but a combination of heavy soil and over-watering can still kill it. Some species and cultivars are prone to fungal rust diseases, particularly in coastal

Douglas iris hybrids along the edge of a driveway, private garden, Walnut Creek. STEPHEN INGRAM

Canyon Snow Douglas iris, Golden West College Native Garden, Huntington Beach. DAN SONGSTER

and unless the wholesale nursery sorts them by color or they're in bloom, it is difficult to know what you're getting at the time of purchase.

Many PCH irises are fussy garden subjects, having often been bred for gorgeous flowers at the expense of disease resistance. If you buy them in spring, consider holding them in the container until fall or winter, which are safer times to plant them in open ground. If they are root-bound, however, transplant them to a larger pot for the summer.

'Canyon Snow', a selection of Douglas iris, is a dazzling pure white iris with golden yellow spots on the falls. This is one of the most dependable and floriferous selections and is therefore grown by many wholesale nurseries.

areas; these are more unsightly than debilitating. A borer that tunnels into the flower stalks and rhizomes is cyclically troublesome in the San Francisco Bay Area, but vigorous plants usually rebound. The only other pests of concern are snails and slugs, which can damage the flowers and foliage.

Maintenance depends upon personal preference. Snap off the spent flowers one at a time if their wilted visages offend, or wait for the entire inflorescence to finish blooming. If you want to encourage new seedlings, let the fruits ripen and spill their seeds. You may be rewarded with a delightful new color form, but volunteer plants usually have lavender-purple flowers. Depending upon the exposure and watering regime, the tips of the leaves may turn brown in summer and can be snipped off. Some gardeners annually cut the foliage back in autumn to 1 or 2 inches before new growth emerges; this can help break the life cycle of rust fungi. Do not pull out dead leaves if there is any resistance, as this can wound the plant. To increase or rejuvenate a favored specimen, carefully divide the clump in fall shortly after the first soaking rains, when the new white roots begin to grow. Attempting to divide irises at other times will usually kill them. Be sure to replant or pot them promptly after they are divided.

Cultivars: Enticed by their beauty, plant breeders have dabbled with the native irises for years, attempting to improve upon nature. Most gardeners choose the Pacifica, or Pacific Coast Hybrid (PCH) irises over the wild species because they have vivid, splashy flowers in a wider range of colors, more frilly petals and sepals, and typically larger blossoms. Although hundreds of cultivars have been developed over the years, few are sold by name except through specialty mail order nurseries. Instead, they are lumped under the PCH label,

Isomeris arborea
BLADDERPOD
Caper Family (Capparaceae)

Plant Type: Semi-evergreen shrub.
Geographic Zones: All except northern coastal and high mountains.
Light: Sun to partial shade.
Soil: Adaptable; well-drained preferred.
Water: Drought tolerant to occasional.
Natural Habitat and Range: Dry ridges, slopes, and sandy washes in many plant communities below 4000 feet; San Luis Obispo, Fresno, and Inyo counties southward to northwestern Baja California.

Bladderpod is an easily grown shrub familiar to botanists due to its widespread distribution, peculiar smell, and unusual fruit. Along the coast of San Diego County it is found in a range of plant communities from oak woodland to coastal scrub, while in the Mojave Desert it grows in desert scrub and woodlands.

Bladderpod has some flowers almost year-round, Santa Barbara Botanic Garden. JOHN EVARTS

The foliage has an odd, pungent scent, and for gardeners seeking the uncommon, its inflated fruit makes this plant distinctive.

In the wild, bladderpod can grow to 6 feet tall, but in most garden settings, this open shrub is generally smaller. The leaves are palmately compound and have three blue-green leaflets that are up to 1½ inches long and fold along a central axis during periods of drought. Its yellow-gold flowers attract hummingbirds and are held in terminal racemes. Bladderpod blooms heaviest in spring, with occasional flowers year-round. The lantern-like fruits are blue-green like the leaves at first, but as they mature they become translucent and appear to be lit from within. These 1- to 2-inch-long pods contain pea-sized brown seeds.

As bladderpod's broad range suggests, it is an adaptable shrub. It is also relatively fast growing and can be used with other shrubs, such as California barberry and quail bush, as an informal hedge or screen. The blue-green foliage combines well with both gray-foliaged species like purple sage and Indian mallow and the dark greens of Leatherleaf coffeeberry and ceanothus. Use it for erosion control on dry slopes and banks, as it requires little maintenance or water. Bruised foliage gives off a strong scent, which some people find disagreeable or even repulsive. Take this into consideration when selecting a planting site.

In the garden, bladderpod has few disease and pest problems, although snails and slugs will occasionally attack young plants and tender new growth. Pruning requirements are minimal, but older plants can be coppiced to encourage fresh new growth. Seedlings are common in many gardens, and although it is not invasive, bladderpod does have the potential to naturalize freely in open ground.

Iva hayesiana
POVERTY WEED
Sunflower Family (Asteraceae)

Plant type: Evergreen subshrub.
Geographic Zones: All except high mountains and deserts.
Light: Sun to partial shade.
Soil: Adaptable.
Water: Drought tolerant to infrequent.
Natural Habitat and Range: Alkaline flats and seasonally moist riparian corridors in coastal scrub below 1000 feet; southern San Diego County to northwestern Baja California.

With nondescript green foliage, unassuming flowers, and a less-than-enticing common name, poverty weed would seem to be difficult to sell in nurseries.

Poverty weed used on a steep slope, Santa Barbara Botanic Garden. JOHN EVARTS

Yet this low, spreading plant is noted for its capacity to grow in either heavy or sandy soils and for its exceptional drought tolerance. Poverty weed's ability to perform in many difficult situations may explain its continued, albeit limited, appeal. Unfortunately, the native habitat of this tough plant is threatened by development.

Poverty weed typically grows 1 to 3 feet tall and may spread 8 to 12 feet wide as the trailing stems take root. Its loosely arching branches are clothed with oblong, fleshy green leaves that are 1 to 2½ inches long. Lightly press the leaf's sticky surface and you will release a pungent aroma that is reminiscent of sagebrush.

Use poverty weed for erosion control on slopes where a durable and low-maintenance groundcover will be highly appreciated. Try interplanting it with bush poppy or Matilija poppy, medium-sized ceanothus, or Our Lord's candle. This fast-growing native has virtually no pest problems and requires only occasional pruning to shape or rejuvenate it. Shear or mow it back to the crown about every five years when the stems begin to show more woody tissue than foliage.

Juncus patens
WIRE GRASS
Rush Family (Juncaceae)

Plant Type: Evergreen perennial.
Geographic Zones: All except high mountains.
Light: Sun to partial shade.
Soil: Adaptable.
Water: Drought tolerant to regular.
Natural Habitat and Range: Moist places in most plant communities below 5000 feet; California Floristic Province.

Wire grasses are ideal for gardeners who love to water, as it is impossible to over-water them. Even though they prefer wet or moist sites and full sun, established plants are remarkably tolerant of drought and shade. Like other rushes, wire grasses evoke the presence of water, especially when planted along dry stream courses.

Wire grass typically forms dense clumps of rigid, upright to slightly arching stems from 1 to 2 feet tall. It gradually spreads to form large colonies over time, but its growth rate is primarily dependent upon the

Occidental Blue wire grass with seed heads at the tips of its stems, private garden, Petaluma. SAXON HOLT

amount of water it receives. Stem color varies from medium green to dark blue-, or gray-green. Loose clusters of small star-like brown bracts and flowers emerge from the top of the stem.

Wire grass's strong vertical growth habit effectively contrasts with the rounded forms of western columbine, island alum root, and any of the low-growing species of ceanothus. It also complements the paler green upright to spreading form of western giant chain fern, as well as scarlet and seep monkeyflowers. Wire grass is an excellent container plant, and its flowering stems work well as accents in floral arrangements.

Cultivars: All of the cultivars of wire grass are easily grown, and like these three examples—'Carman's Gray', 'Elk Blue', and 'Occidental Blue'—they have been selected for the color of their stems.

Other Species: Spiny rush (*Juncus acutus* ssp. *leopoldii*) and soft rush (*Juncus effusus*) are easily grown species that tolerate heavy soils but require ample water and sunshine for best performance. Spiny rush typically averages 3 to 6 feet in height and usually forms large colonies. Be careful how you site it in the garden to avoid inadvertent contact with its spear-tipped, arching stems. Soft rush is typically brighter green and has a finer, softer texture than wire grass.

Justicia californica
CHUPAROSA
Acanthus Family (Acanthaceae)

Plant Type: Deciduous shrub.
Geographic Zones: Southern and central coastal, southern intermediate and interior valleys, and low desert.
Light: Sun.
Soil: Adaptable; well-drained preferred.
Water: Drought tolerant to occasional.
Natural Habitat and Range: Washes and alluvial fans in desert scrub below 2500 feet; Colorado Desert south to Baja California.

Chuparosa's narrow, tubular, nectar-rich flowers are some of the best for attracting hummingbirds to your garden. *Chuparosa* is the Spanish word for hummingbird, and these birds are sure to visit when this desert shrub begins to bloom. While most chuparosa flowers are in the orange to red spectrum, striking yellow or yellow-orange flowered specimens are occasionally seen.

In its native environment chuparosa resembles a disheveled pile of greenish to blue-gray twigs for most of the year. But in a garden setting occasional water can transform it into an upswept, rounded shrub covered with dense flower clusters for months on end. Even

Top: Tecate Gold chuparosa, a golden-flowered cultivar, Rancho Santa Ana Botanic Garden, Claremont. BART O'BRIEN
Bottom: Chuparosa blossoms, Anza-Borrego Desert State Park. MICHAEL WALL

when it is grown in gardens with adequate water, the few leaves chuparosa produces fall quickly. The key to maintaining a healthy and decorative chuparosa is pruning. Flowers are produced only on relatively young branches, so older (less green) stems and branches should be thinned out during late summer or early fall months. Old flower clusters frequently hang on after they've bloomed. To remove them, give mature plants a careful shaking with a rake, or wash them off with a jet of water.

Chuparosa is pest and disease free but requires protection from heavy frost. It is not particular about soil conditions as long as the soil is warm and relatively well drained. Be careful when planting because young chuparosas are brittle. Try combining chuparosa with other heat-loving natives that thrive in full sun, such as desert lavender, Indian mallow, jojoba, and native sages.

Cultivars: All of the named selections of chuparosa are yellow-flowered forms. Two widespread cultivars are 'Dick Tilforth', which has pure lemon-rind yellow blossoms, and 'Tecate Gold', which produces yellow flowers burnished with orange.

Keckiella cordifolia
HEARTLEAF KECKIELLA
Figwort Family (Scrophulariaceae)

Plant Type: Deciduous to semi-evergreen shrub.
Geographic Zones: All except high mountains and deserts.
Light: Sun to partial shade.
Soil: Adaptable.
Water: Drought tolerant to occasional.
Natural Habitat and Range: Dry slopes and canyons in chaparral below 4000 feet; San Luis Obispo County to northwestern Baja California.

Although heartleaf keckiella appears conflicted as to whether it wants to be a vine, a perennial, or a shrub, it always knows the season. Even before the first rains arrive, cooler fall nights and shorter days often encourage it to produce thin, ovate, light to medium green leaves. Winter rains stimulate an abundance of new foliage and stems, which grow throughout the spring. As temperatures reach toward the century mark, the stems explode with branched terminal clusters of brilliant red-orange blossoms. California summers are usually much too hot for the delicate leaves of heartleaf keckiella to endure, so the plant quickly sets seeds, sheds some or all its leaves, and shows off its

Heartleaf keckiella's twining stems weave through other plants, Santa Barbara Botanic Garden. STEVE JUNAK

brassy arching stems. It will go completely dormant for the summer months in the hotter, drier parts of California, but it may remain semi-evergreen in coastal areas of central and northern California.

Plant heartleaf keckiella with medium to large, robust spring-blooming shrubs and let it weave its way through and around its neighbors. This will allow you to get two seasons of bloom in the same space. Glossy-leaved species of ceanothus, redberry, Saint Catherine's lace, coast silk-tassel, coyote brush, and spicebush are excellent companions. Bare stems may be cut back to 6-inch-long stubs at any time during the summer months. Do not be discouraged if heartleaf keckiella looks poorly in nursery containers. It will rebound when planted and is pest and disease free.

Other Species: Yellow keckiella *(Keckiella antirrhinoides)* has terminal clusters of stout, bright yellow blossoms, which are pollinated by bumblebees. It reaches 3 to 5 feet tall and has a nearly equal spread. This shrub's 1-inch-long narrow green leaves give the plant a pleasing, fine-textured appearance. Plants will grow in full sun or partial shade, and they perform best in hotter geographic zones. Like heartleaf keckiella, yellow keckiella loses its leaves during summer dormancy. Combine yellow keckiella with blue-flowered plants that bloom in late spring, such as foothill penstemon and Skylark ceanothus.

Lavatera assurgentiflora
MALVA ROSA
Mallow Family (Malvaceae)

Plant Type: Evergreen shrub.
Geographic Zones: Coastal and intermediate valleys of California and interior valleys of southern California.
Light: Sun to partial shade.
Soil: Adaptable; well-drained preferred.
Water: Drought tolerant to occasional.
Natural Habitat and Range: Sandy or rocky sites on coastal bluffs in coastal scrub below 1000 feet; Channel Islands.

Malva rosa is a rare shrub with showy blossoms and bold texture. This fast-growing island endemic quickly reaches 5 to 10 feet tall and brings a lush, tropical look to the garden. Reminiscent of hibiscus, but more drought tolerant, malva rosa works well in informal settings.

Everything about malva rosa is big. Its maple-like, 2- to 6-inch-wide leaves are medium green on top and paler below. The leaves partially obscure the 2- to 3-inch-wide flowers that sway underneath them. The prominently veined, rose to lavender flowers are present

during all but the coldest months of the year and have a glazed sheen.

Malva rosa's rank growth and coarse appearance make it a poor choice for formal garden settings, but try it where a quick hedge or informal screen is needed. The large flowers and leaves create an arresting focal point in mixed borders. Gardeners along the

Purisima mallow with showy, hibiscus-like flower, Santa Barbara Botanic Garden. STEPHEN INGRAM

immediate coast value malva rosa for its tolerance of salt spray and wind. The plant is so well adapted to this environment that it has naturalized along the central and southern coasts. Some compatible partners are purple sage, red-flowered buckwheat, Canyon Prince wild rye, low or medium-sized ceanothus, and shrubby monkeyflowers. For a special visual display, pick some flowers and let them float in a decorative bowl filled with water.

Although malva rosa is easy to grow, it requires pruning to retain a pleasing habit. It is relatively short-lived and also susceptible to a virus specific to the mallow family. A number of insect pests feed upon the leaves, including spider mites, thrips, lace bugs, psyllids, and giant whiteflies. To reduce the potential for insect problems, do not plant it in nutrient-rich soils and avoid excess irrigation. When necessary, use soap sprays to reduce pest infestations. Malva rosa will need protection from gophers, which are particularly fond of it, and from deer, mice, rats, and rabbits, which favor its tender green stems and new foliage.

Cultivars: Purisima mallow *(Lavatera* 'Purisima') is the most reliably available of several cultivars and much less prone to the above insect pests. It is broader than tall and bears richly colored red-violet flowers. Purisma mallow is a durable hybrid of malva rosa and San Benito Island mallow *(Lavatera venosa),* a rare species from the San Benito Islands off the west coast of Baja California.

Lepechinia species
PITCHER SAGES
Mint Family (Lamiaceae)

Plant Type: Semi-evergreen shrubs.
Geographic Zones: All except deserts and high mountains.
Light: Sun to partial shade.
Soil: Adaptable, except poorly drained.
Water: Drought tolerant to occasional.
Natural Habitat and Range: In chaparral and woodlands below 4000 feet; range varies by species.

Pitcher sages are best known for their softly hairy, strongly fragrant leaves and long racemes of large, showy white to lavender-pink flowers. Like their relatives the sages, these plants occupy the boundary between woody shrub and herbaceous perennial. Similar to a number of California's plants, pitcher sages exhibit two distinctive types of foliage over the course of a year. Lush foliage is exuberantly produced from winter to early summer. Shortly after the plant blooms, in late spring or early summer, most of the larger leaves are shed. They are replaced by much smaller, grayer leaves, which last through autumn or until conditions are favorable for new growth. These plants frequently are short-lived in gardens, but are valuable for their scent, foliage, and flowers. Bumblebees pollinate the wide-mouthed flowers. Plants are generally pest and disease free.

Of the few species and selections of pitcher sages, the most valuable for the home gardener is Rocky Point pitcher sage (*Lepechinia calycina* 'Rocky Point'). A selection from Rocky Point in Monterey County, this plant has a graceful arching to mounding habit. It is densely branched, compact, and quickly reaches 3 feet tall and 4 to 5 feet wide. The luxuriant leaves of 'Rocky Point' are particularly attractive and carry an intriguing medicinal aroma. This selection is favorably disposed to hard pruning. Established plants that are cut back to 4- to 6-inch-long stubs in late fall rapidly respond with an incredible display of new foliage and flowers. The large white flowers are blushed with lavender and are produced in pairs along the 6-inch-long terminal inflorescences. Typically, only two flowers in the same inflorescence are open at the same time, so the color effect is muted.

Rocky Point pitcher sage may be used in many ways in gardens. It performs admirably when it is massed along a garden path with California poppy, blue-eyed grass, El Dorado California sunflower, and mules ears. If left unpruned it provides durable structure in mixed borders or plantings on coastal bluffs. During spring, this plant is an excellent choice for display in a large container.

Fragrant pitcher sage (*Lepechinia fragrans*) has the most attractive flowers and most pleasing scent of all our native species. Showy, foxglove-like lavender flowers

Top: El Tigre pitcher sage, like other pitcher sages, has fragrant, soft hairy leaves, private garden, Sebastopol. PHILIP VAN SOELEN
Bottom: El Tigre pitcher sage with an open habit, Rancho Santa Ana Botanic Garden, Claremont. BART O'BRIEN

are produced along lax 1- to 2-foot-long inflorescences in spring and early summer. The fruity scent of the foliage is hard to place, yet delightful. Plants left on their own often develop a rather open, gangly habit, reaching a height of 6 feet. To produce plants with a full, dense appearance, frequently pinch back the foliage of young plants. The only fragrant pitcher sage cultivar, 'El Tigre', originates from Santa Cruz Island and has even more richly colored flowers with a flush of deep purple on the stems, calyces, and bracts.

Lessingia filaginifolia 'Silver Carpet'
SILVER CARPET CALIFORNIA ASTER
Sunflower Family (Asteraceae)

Plant Type: Evergreen herbaceous perennial.
Geographic Zones: All except high mountains and deserts.
Light: Sun to partial shade.
Soil: Adaptable; well-drained preferred.
Water: Infrequent to occasional.
Natural Habitat and Range: This cultivar was selected from coastal scrub along the Big Sur coast. The species occurs in coastal scrub, oak woodlands, and grasslands up to 7800 feet throughout much of California, southwestern Oregon, and northwestern Baja California.

Silver Carpet California aster produces flowers through summer, private garden, Arroyo Grande. DAVID FROSS

During the long days of summer, plants that offer an abundance of flowers and attractive foliage are particularly desirable. Silver Carpet California aster is one such candidate. From summer into fall its copious floral display may temporarily obscure the plant's silvery foliage. Gardeners eager to attract butterflies will want to try this perennial, which provides food for both larval and adult stages.

Once in the ground, Silver Carpet California aster makes up for its lackluster appearance in a gallon can, becoming an attractive ground-hugging mat 4 to 8 feet wide. The 1-inch-wide daisy-like flowers have a central yellow disk surrounded by "petals" of lavender-pink. The pastel blossoms and softly pubescent leaves are a welcome addition to the perennial border or meadow garden. They can be used to tone down the warm colors of summer-flowering California fuchsias and goldenrods or to complement other silver-, blue-, or gray-leaved plants in a cool-color scheme. Silver Carpet California aster makes an effective groundcover in the front of a border or spilling over a wall. Lilac verbena or bright yellow shrubby monkeyflower are pleasing partners.

Silver Carpet California aster is easy to grow. If the spent flowers are objectionable, remove them in fall. A light pruning around the plant's perimeter will help maintain its dense habit. Insect and disease problems are seldom encountered.

The parent species, California aster *(Lessingia filaginifolia)* is a terrifically variable and widespread plant. Its flower color ranges from light purple to pink or occasionally white. Plants typically grow 1 to 3 feet tall and equally wide and exhibit either an upright or trailing growth habit. The taller forms become leggy and less attractive unless you prune them back to a height of 3 or 4 inches when the season's new growth appears. Try weaving several of the upright forms through other plants, or mass them for a bolder impact.

Lewisia cotyledon
CLIFF-MAIDS
Purslane Family (Portulacaceae)

Plant Type: Succulent perennial.
Geographic Zones: All except low deserts.
Light: Sun to partial shade.
Soil: Well-drained.
Water: Infrequent to occasional.
Natural Habitat and Range: Rock outcrops, open sandy slopes, and canyon walls in forests above 1500 feet; Klamath and Siskiyou mountains of northwestern California and southwestern Oregon.

The delicate, festive flowers and attractive rosettes of species in the genus *Lewisia* have long made these plants a favorite choice for rock and alpine gardens.

Cliff-maids featured in a rock garden, Garden in the Woods, Framingham, Massachusetts. SAXON HOLT

Their popularity has led to myriad hybrid strains—primarily from *Lewisia cotyledon*—and a carnival of flower colors. Floriferous seedlings of cherry red, hot pink, salmon, apricot, purple, orange, and white are available to western gardeners; veins or striations of darker hues mark some of the pastel-colored blossoms. The genus is named in honor of Meriwether Lewis of the Lewis and Clark expedition, who returned from his western explorations with many new botanical specimens, including bitterroot (*Lewisia rediviva*).

Cliff-maids' fleshy, strap-shaped leaves are 2 to 6 inches in length and rise from a succulent caudex or crown to form a flattened rosette. Typical cliff-maids have smooth-edged leaves and striated flowers on 6- to 10-inch-long stems. The hybrid Sunset Strain cliff-maids (*Lewisia* 'Sunset Strain') shares a genetic heritage with cliff-maids. It has variable leaves that can be wide or narrow with wavy or smooth margins and features a spectrum of flower colors.

Colorful and drought tolerant, cliff-maids are particularly useful in containers as solitary specimens or mixed in bold multicolored displays. They can be nestled into rock retaining walls or massed in raised beds with other rockery plants, such as canyon dudleya, scarlet monardella, and native bulbs. Cliff-maids will usually survive on rainfall alone, although an occasional summer watering will improve vigor and appearance. Container-grown plants require additional water, but plant them on an angle to shed excess water and exercise care to keep the crown area dry. Repotting and an application of a low-nitrogen fertilizer with occasional irrigation may stimulate repeated bloom. Provide some shade for plantings in areas away from the coast, as they often burn in full sun. Infestations of mealybugs are easily treated with soap products. Red, orange, or mottled leaves indicate a fungal disease that spreads rapidly to other cliff-maids. Destroy infected plants to prevent further infection.

Leymus condensatus 'Canyon Prince'
CANYON PRINCE WILD RYE
Grass family (Poaceae)

Plant Type: Evergreen, cool-season perennial grass.
Geographic Zones: All except high mountains and deserts.
Light: Sun to partial shade.
Soil: Adaptable.
Water: Drought tolerant to occasional.
Natural Habitat and Range: A selection found in coastal scrub on Prince Island, an islet located off San Miguel Island. The species is widespread below 5000 feet in dry habitats in western central and southern California, the Mojave Desert, and Mexico.

Top: Canyon Prince wild rye planted in a front yard, private garden, near San Luis Obispo. DAVID FROSS
Bottom: Flowering stalks of Canyon Prince wild rye, Leaning Pine Arboretum, Cal Poly, San Luis Obispo. DAVID FROSS

The bold, icy blue foliage of Canyon Prince wild rye commands attention. Whether this stunning grass is used alone for accent or planted in large colonies in a meadow garden, it blends well with any color scheme.

A popular and adaptable selection, Canyon Prince wild rye has a compact habit that rarely exceeds 5 feet in height even when in bloom. It spreads slowly by rhizomes to produce ever-wider colonies, but can be contained by periodic removal of runners or by installing a root barrier. In summer, a few powdery blue flower stalks emerge on younger plants and add a dramatic exclamation point to the mounded foliage below. The stalks are an attractive wheat color when dry, and they hold up well in floral arrangements.

'Canyon Prince' is exceptionally easy to grow and tolerates all but soggy soils and extreme drought. The intensity of blue in the foliage deepens with increasing light, so place it in full sun to enhance this key attribute. Cut the foliage back to the ground between late summer and early winter when clumps become lax or build up dead leaves. The surprisingly green new growth eventually turns blue as temperatures rise.

Giant wild rye *(Leymus condensatus)* is typically a coarse-textured, medium-green bunchgrass that soars to 9 feet tall when in bloom. It is principally used in revegetation projects or to stabilize slopes. Unlike 'Canyon Prince', the species is considered too rangy for most gardens, but may be used effectively in some cases. Both the cultivar and the species are pest and disease free.

Other Species and Cultivars: Great Basin wild rye *(Leymus cinereus)* attains 6 to 8 feet in height when flowering. This upright, warm-season grass usually lacks rhizomes and looks best planted in naturalistic drifts. For gardeners in colder regions, Great Basin wild rye is a reliable replacement for Canyon Prince wild rye, as its foliage remains blue-gray regardless of temperature. *Leymus triticoides* 'Grey Dawn' is a rhizomatous selection of wild rye that has attractive glaucous blue foliage. When in bloom, it reaches 2 to 4 feet tall. 'Grey Dawn' needs supplemental water to thrive in southern parts of the state and has potential as a native turf, but beware of its aggressive, spreading habit.

Lupinus albifrons
SILVER BUSH LUPINE
Pea Family (Fabaceae)

Plant Type: Evergreen shrub.
Geographic Zones: All except high mountains and deserts.
Light: Sun.
Soil: Well-drained.
Water: Drought tolerant to occasional.
Natural Habitat and Range: Dry slopes and flats in many plant communities below 5000 feet; Southern Oregon, California's Coast Ranges from Humboldt to Santa Barbara counties, north slope of the Western Transverse Ranges of Ventura and Los Angeles counties, and Sierra Nevada foothills from Shasta to Tulare counties.

Lupines are among the most ubiquitous and well-loved California wildflowers. There are literally dozens of species ranging from bright annuals to beautiful perennials and gorgeous shrubs. Silver bush lupine exemplifies the qualities of this genus and has stunning silver gray stems and foliage year-round. This shrub usually grows 5 to 6 feet tall and equally wide to somewhat wider. Silver bush lupine is truly spectacular in the spring when it produces numerous erect spires of blue to violet (rarely pink or white) flowers.

Due to a few horticultural quirks, most perennial and shrub species of the genus *Lupinus* are rarely available in nurseries. Nearly all lupines resent root disturbance,

Silver bush lupine, Goodwin Education Center garden, Carrizo Plain National Monument. JOHN EVARTS

so take special care when planting them. Most lupines perform best when grown in nutrient-poor, well-drained soils. Plants are often short-lived, but those in gardens with favorable conditions may provide seedlings; those in rich, fertile soils are often rank, especially short-lived, and generally unsatisfactory. Protect young specimens and seedlings from birds, ground squirrels, rabbits, and deer. In cool coastal gardens, snails, slugs, and caterpillars can be devastating. Birds and small mammals are particularly fond of large nutritious lupine seeds, but a few species have seeds that are toxic to livestock. Many insects, especially bumblebees, are attracted to the pea-like blossoms. A change in the color of the center of the flower from white or pale yellow to violet or dark purple signals that the blossom has already been pollinated.

Nurseries sometimes carry a beautiful prostrate form of silver bush lupine, *Lupinus albifrons* var. *collinus.* This small plant has large blossoms and is an excellent choice for a rock garden or dry border.

Other Species: (For annual lupines, see page 205 within the Annuals.) Yellow bush lupine *(Lupinus arboreus)* is native to plant communities of the immediate coast from Sonoma to Ventura counties. Plants have green foliage and canary yellow blossoms, although lilac- and purple-flowered specimens sometimes occur. Yellow bush lupine is an excellent choice for coastal gardens, but it performs poorly or may die in summer when grown in hot inland situations. This lupine was once planted to help stabilize coastal dunes to the north of its natural range. It has since naturalized in these fragile communities, where its rapid spread disrupts the local ecology and threatens the survival of several rare plant species.

Due to its propensity to become an invasive weed, this lupine is not a good choice for gardens in coastal Mendocino County and northward.

Grape soda lupine *(Lupinus excubitus)* is treated by many gardeners as a southern California equivalent of silver bush lupine. This smaller silver-foliaged shrub may reach 2 to 3 feet tall. Its richly scented flowers smell like grape soda, hence its common name.

Lyonothamnus floribundus ssp. *aspleniifolius*
SANTA CRUZ ISLAND IRONWOOD
Rose Family (Rosaceae)

Plant Type: Evergreen tree.
Geographic Zones: All except high mountains and deserts.
Light: Sun to partial shade.
Soil: Adaptable; well-drained preferred.
Water: Drought tolerant to occasional.
Natural Habitat and Range: Rocky, mostly north-facing slopes and canyons in woodlands and chaparral below 2000 feet; Santa Cruz, Santa Rosa, and San Clemente islands.

Widespread on the mainland of California until about 6 million years ago, Santa Cruz Island ironwood now grows wild only on three of the Channel Islands. This odd and rare member of the rose family is a collage of unusual parts that make it one of our most alluring and picturesque trees. It has fern-like leaves, sinuous peeling bark, and pancake-flat inflorescences reminiscent of shrubby buckwheats.

Santa Cruz Island ironwood is a slender, single- to multi-trunked tree that grows 20 to 50 feet tall and about 15 to 20 feet wide. At first glance, its compound leaves look remarkably like marijuana. Reddish twigs enhance the dark green glossy leaf surfaces. In spring or summer, 4- to 8-inch-wide flattened flower clusters cap the higher branches. Initially creamy white, the clusters ripen to chocolate brown and then turn gray. They persist for several years, which some gardeners find objectionable. The twigs and red-brown to grayish bark begin to exfoliate when the trees are young, revealing deeper red tones underneath; the shredded strips eventually weather to an ashy gray. As old leaves drop and carpet the ground, their warm earthtones create a beautiful mulch.

This fast-growing island endemic is fairly easy to cultivate, although it is prone to chlorosis when planted in heavy soils. Prolonged freezing temperatures may damage a recently planted ironwood, but an established tree will tolerate light frosts. When grown in hot inland sites, protect it from drying winds and irrigate it deeply but infrequently in summer. Pests and diseases are uncommon, and maintenance consists of removing dead branches and, if deemed offensive, the dried flowers. If the canopy of an older tree becomes too thin, cut it

Above: Santa Cruz Island ironwood grown in a front yard, private garden, Santa Ynez. JOHN EVARTS *Left: Santa Cruz Island ironwood, multi-trunked specimen and leaf litter, Santa Barbara Botanic Garden.* STEPHEN INGRAM

back to the basal burl to encourage a flush of new growth. The hard wood removed during pruning is useful for rustic railings, garden ornaments, or firewood.

Santa Cruz Island ironwood is a desirable specimen tree, though it is particularly stunning when planted in groves. Suitable companions include island ceanothus, island alum root, manzanitas, and any of the island buckwheats. You can espalier ironwood against a wall or fence, but this requires annual or semiannual pruning and support.

Malacothamnus species
BUSH MALLOWS
Mallow Family (Malvaceae)

Plant Type: Evergreen shrubs.
Geographic Zones: All except deserts and high mountains.
Light: Sun.
Soil: Adaptable; well-drained preferred.
Water: Drought tolerant to occasional.
Natural Habitat and Range: Recently burned sites mostly in chaparral below 8500 feet; Mendocino, Tehama, and Amador counties south to northwestern Baja California.

Bush mallows are fast-growing fire-followers with some remarkable characteristics. They make ideal candidates for erosion control on dry, sunny slopes due to

Above: Edgewood bush mallow covered with blossoms, Yerba Buena Nursery, Woodside.
BART O'BRIEN
Left: Palmer bush mallow, close-up of rosebud-like flower, Rancho Santa Ana Botanic Garden, Claremont.
BART O'BRIEN

their widely spreading root systems and ever-expanding thickets of new stems. While these qualities often make them too exuberant for either formal settings or small sites, several bush mallows perform admirably in the garden. Most species produce showy spring- to summer-blooming inflorescences and all have attractive maple-like foliage in shades of white, gray, or green.

Bush mallows with white to gray leaves are spectacular when grown among dark-foliaged plants.

One might expect that such vigorous spreading plants would be long-lived, but this is rarely the case. Parent plants frequently take a year or more before rapidly establishing a broad colony. Just when there seems to be an endless supply of bush mallow plants, some of the older stems begin to die. Often, this is the beginning of a rapid decline of the whole colony, and the entire planting may disappear over the course of one or two years. The cause of this demise is unknown, but some plantings are more durable. Coppicing seems to extend the life of these colonies indefinitely. Even short-lived colonies are useful for filling in space and controlling erosion while other slower-growing plants are getting established.

All parts of these evergreen shrubs, except the flowers, are variously covered with star-like white- or rust-colored hairs that require close inspection to be seen. Some people may develop a skin rash from contact with them. Older woody stems may be cut to the ground after flowering or during fall or early winter to help rejuvenate the colony, although this is not a good idea if there are only one or two stems.

Bush mallows attract a wide variety of garden pests. Deer, ground squirrels, rabbits, grasshoppers, and caterpillars eat their leaves, stems, and flowers. Installing cages around the plants deters the vertebrate pests; manual removal of insects helps keep them in check. Weevils almost inevitably attack developing and mature seeds. Rust may disfigure the foliage.

Other Species and Cultivars: No single bush mallow species or cultivar predominates in the nursery industry. The following are occasionally sold and are excellent choices for large gardens and landscapes that can accommodate their tendency to spread. Most have showy wand-like flower stalks.

Edgewood bush mallow (*Malacothamnus arcuatus* 'Edgewood', also known as *Malacothamnus fasciculatus* 'Edgewood') sometimes produces underground stems. The deeply veined leaves appear gray due to the heavy frosting of white hairs. Inflorescences are 2 to 3 feet long, densely packed with pink flowers, and cover the 4- to 6-foot-tall plant in late spring and early summer. 'Edgewood' is spectacular where summer temperatures rarely top 100°F, but is often short-lived and disappointing in hot inland gardens.

San Clemente Island bush mallow (*Malacothamnus clementinus*) has long inflorescences that carry discrete clusters of fragrant, white to pink, 1-inch-wide hollyhock-like flowers. Plants in cultivation reach from 3 to 5 feet tall. Although this plant is grown in southern California gardens, it is a federally listed endangered species in its native habitat on San Clemente Island.

When in bloom, Santa Cruz Island bush mallow (*Malacothamnus fasciculatus* var. *nesioticus*) is a particularly beautiful member of the genus. It produces lavender-rose flowers in 6-inch-long branched terminal clusters. This rare plant is a federally listed endangered species.

Jones bush mallow (*Malacothamnus jonesii*) is grown for its distinctive buff to white foliage and pale pink flowers that appear in mid- to late summer.

Palmer bush mallow (*Malacothamnus palmeri*) produces dense, head-like clusters of pink blossoms. Before they fully open, these flower heads resemble miniature bouquets of rose buds.

Melica imperfecta
COAST MELIC GRASS
Grass Family (Poaceae)

Plant Type: Semi-evergreen to deciduous, cool-season perennial grass.
Geographic Zones: All except high mountains.
Light: Sun to partial shade.
Soil: Adaptable.
Water: Drought tolerant to occasional.
Natural Habitat and Range: Dry, open woods and rocky slopes in many plant communities below 5000 feet; California Floristic Province from San Francisco Bay south to northwestern Baja California and east to the Mojave Desert.

Coast melic grass is a cool-season grass that comes to life immediately after the fall rains begin. In the coastal foothills of southern California, its bright green, lax foliage softens slopes and lines trails through chaparral and oak woodland. In designed landscapes, this graceful, understated bunchgrass adds quiet beauty to woodland or meadow gardens.

The clumps of coast melic grass can be either loosely or densely tufted, with culms typically 1 to 2 feet tall. Its medium green or yellow-green leaves are occasionally softly pubescent but are more often glabrous. The delicate, 4- to 16-inch-long flower stalks are either erect or nodding and vary from slender to open and spreading. The small seeds are quite beautiful; rub off the bracts to reveal the shiny, dark amber grains. Coast melic grass readily self-sows but is not hard to contain.

Cultivating coast melic grass is easy. It is not fussy about light exposure or soil type, and judicious watering keeps plants nearly evergreen year-round. One of our earliest grasses to green up in the fall, it is also one of the first to go dormant as the soil naturally dries out in summer. The entire plant dries to an appealing straw color and holds its shape all summer long. Cut it back at the first sign of new green shoots or earlier if desired.

Coast melic grass with flowering stalks, Cleveland National Forest, near Mission Viejo. DAN SONGSTER

To make the most of its subtle features, plant several coast melic grasses along the edge of a shady path or where their leaves can cascade over the top of a low retaining wall. It partners easily with California buttercup, hummingbird sage, western meadow rue, golden yarrow, coffeeberry, toyon, and oaks. This grass mixes well with wildflowers and needle grasses in a meadow planting, where it provides an early green backdrop for the colorful annuals. In a spare, Zen-inspired garden, a gently swaying solitary coast melic grass will bestow a calming effect.

Although coast melic grass has no pest problems, gardeners should be aware of a pernicious weed, panic veldt grass (*Ehrharta erecta*), which resembles it. This grass from South Africa has broader leaf blades and seeds that are cream or green rather than brown, but the easiest way to distinguish it from melic grass is by its behavior. *Ehrharta* typically grows up through other plants, making it time-consuming to eradicate without disturbing the desired plant. Unfortunately, it has spread rapidly throughout much of California, often to the detriment of native vegetation in coastal and riparian habitats. At present there are no successful control methods other than hand weeding.

Mimulus species
SHRUBBY MONKEYFLOWERS
Figwort Family (Scrophulariaceae)

Plant Type: Evergreen to nearly deciduous subshrubs.
Geographic Zones: All except high mountains and deserts.
Light: Sun to partial shade.
Soil: Adaptable; well-drained preferred.
Water: Drought tolerant to moderate.
Natural Habitat and Range: Coastal scrub, chaparral, and woodland and forest edges below 5000 feet; California Floristic Province, including Cedros and Guadalupe islands of Baja California.

With their large showy flowers and preference for partial shade, shrubby monkeyflowers are often mistaken for azaleas. They exhibit an astonishing range of flower colors, including pure reds, yellows, oranges, apricots, whites, creams, and even pinks and purples. Flowers vary in size from 1 to 3 inches across and from 1 to 2 inches long.

Shrubby monkeyflowers (sometimes called *Diplacus*) are quite variable in nature and are the cause of much taxonomic controversy. If you are looking for a reason for the common name, monkeyflower, look no further—there isn't any. Some botanists say there is a single variable species while others choose to recognize as many as 13 different kinds. This diversity is particularly evident in southern California and bodes well for gardeners, as there is a great degree of natural variation to choose from. In contrast, shrubby monkeyflowers found in the Coast Ranges from Santa Clara County and northward are remarkably uniform.

All shrubby monkeyflowers and their hybrids produce a pair of opposite, often sticky leaves and flowers at each node along unbranched flowering stems. The lowest pair of flowers opens first and is followed by subsequent pairs of blossoms up the stems. The length of the flowering stems is indeterminate, and the plants continue blooming from spring into summer as long as conditions are favorable. In suitable mild climates, blooming plants that are cut back in May or early June produce another wave of flowers in July and August. These profusely blooming plants require attention to perform their best. All are brittle and need light pinching and pruning to produce well-balanced plants that effectively display and support their beautiful flowers. Plants rarely recover from pruning back into old wood. Well-grown garden specimens may vary from 2 to 3 feet tall and 2 to 4 feet wide.

Shrubby monkeyflowers have many garden uses. They are excellent choices for small drifts in partial shade, in mixed borders, or in containers. Plant them with California fuchsias, blue witches, sages, buckwheats, coyote mints, and smaller manzanitas for best

Above: Shrubby monkeyflower hybrids, such as the three shown here, come in a wide array of colors, private garden, Oakland.
STEPHEN INGRAM
Left: Shrubby monkeyflower hybrid, Chelsea Garden show, London, England. DAVID FROSS

effect. Most plants are not long-lived. Expect them to last an average of 2 to 5 years before you will need to replace them with fresh new specimens.

Monkeyflowers are among the most deer-proof of California native plants, and rabbits and ground squirrels rarely bother them. They are occasionally subject to aphid infestation, but the only other problem insects of note are the painted lady butterfly caterpillars, which can defoliate a young plant. Unfortunately, the hybrids often fall victim to numerous fungal and viral attacks. Place them in areas with good air circulation, and avoid purchasing plants with puckered or distorted leaves.

The round, two-lipped white stigma of these plants may be used to demonstrate rapid movement in plants.

Sticky monkeyflower with orange-colored blossoms typical to the species, private garden, Arroyo Grande. DAVID FROSS

When the lips are gently touched, the plant assumes that it has been pollinated and the stigma closes. After a short while, when the plant "realizes" that pollination has not taken place, the stigma opens again—waiting for bees or hummingbirds to deliver pollen.

Other Species: Though all of the following have been lumped into a single widely variable species *(Mimulus aurantiacus)*, the forms listed here are expected to persist in horticulture due to their distinctive flowers and growth habits. Sticky monkeyflower *(Mimulus aurantiacus)*, when more narrowly defined, has soft orange flowers about ¾ inch across. Azalea-flowered monkeyflower *(Mimulus bifidus)* has the largest flowers of the species. The buff- to apricot-colored blossoms are deeply lobed and may reach over 2 inches across. Plants are often lax. Island monkeyflower *(Mimulus flemingii, also known as Diplacus parviflorus)* has rather small red to red-orange flowers and is only found on California's Channel Islands. Southern monkeyflower *(Mimulus longiflorus)* has hairy leaves, and the flowers may be either soft yellow, pale orange, or brick red. Red monkeyflower *(Mimulus puniceus)* has dark red flowers and typically dark stems and long internodes.

Cultivars: The wondrous variety of hybrid shrubby monkeyflowers has beguiled horticulturists and gardeners since the 1940s. Of the dozens of named selections, the following are recommended: 'Burgundy' is long-lived and has deep red flowers; 'Eleanor' is durable, lives for a long time, and has pale yellow flowers with central orange lines and shiny, deep green leaves; 'Elliot's Verity Red' features small, vividly red flowers, dark green leaves, and short internodes; 'Pumpkin' produces rich orange flowers that are darker on the outside; 'Sam' has large, buttery yellow flowers; and 'Verity White' features huge flowers that emerge pale cream and quickly become pure white.

Mimulus cardinalis
SCARLET MONKEYFLOWER
Figwort Family (Scrophulariaceae)

Plant Type: Evergreen herbaceous perennial.
Geographic Zones: All except high mountains.
Light: Sun to partial shade.
Soil: Adaptable.
Water: Moderate to regular.
Natural Habitat and Range: Moist places and streambanks in many plant communities below 6500 feet; throughout California to Oregon, Utah, Nevada, New Mexico, and northwestern Baja California.

Scarlet monkeyflower is an ideal candidate for edging a small perennial stream or pond, as it prefers to have wet, or at least moist, roots. This robust, easily grown perennial has large, pale green, softly hairy leaves. The showy flowers are typically orange-red, but occasional bright yellow-flowered individuals are seen. These plants are variable in size, but generally range from 2 to 3 feet tall and wide.

The unusual shape of scarlet monkeyflower blossoms evolved to accommodate their hummingbird pollinators. The lower three petals are folded back while

Scarlet monkeyflower planted along a garden pathway, private garden, Montecito. STEPHEN INGRAM

the upper two arch forward to protect the plant's anthers and stigma, as the anthers deposit and the stigma collects pollen from the back of the hummingbird's head.

Grow scarlet monkeyflower with other moisture-loving plants, such as meadowfoam, western columbine, stream orchid, and wire grass, or place it in front of giant chain fern or larger shrubs like creek dogwood and Pacific wax myrtle.

Plants often look bedraggled after the long hot summer and are best cut back hard during fall or early winter. Individual plants are short-lived, but healthy plants tend to produce new seedlings. Any unwanted seedlings are easily removed.

Other Species: Seep monkeyflower *(Mimulus guttatus)* is widely distributed in moist habitats throughout most of western North America and may be either annual or perennial. It readily adapts to and reseeds in well-watered gardens and landscapes. Volunteer seedlings are nearly always welcomed, but are easily removed if necessary. This species is quite variable in the wild, and mature plants may reach from 1 inch to 4 feet tall. Most plants are strictly erect and typically produce side branches from their base only after the main stem has begun to bloom. The cheerful, brilliant yellow flowers are variously spotted with red dots or markings.

Monardella macrantha 'Marian Sampson'
MARIAN SAMPSON SCARLET COYOTE MINT
Mint Family (Lamiaceae)

Plant Type: Evergreen perennial.
Geographic Zones: All except deserts.
Light: Sun to partial shade.
Soil: Well-drained; lightly acidic preferred.
Water: Occasional to moderate.
Natural Habitat and Range: The species grows in chaparral, woodlands, and forests from 2000 to 7000 feet; Santa Lucia Mountains of Monterey County south to the Sierra San Pedro Martir of Baja California. The cultivar originated as a chance seedling at Mourning Cloak Ranch and Botanic Garden in Tehachapi.

Any time from late spring through fall, the meek, creeping stems of scarlet coyote mint can explode with 2- to 4-inch-wide starbursts of tubular yellow, orange, or red flowers. The beautiful inflorescences attract the attention of hummingbirds seeking summer sustenance. This rhizomatous plant creates loose trailing mats of foliage up to 4 inches high. Its leaves are quite variable in size and shape, and frequently have purplish highlights on their undersides.

Until recently this desirable California plant was almost never seen in low-elevation gardens because it usually succumbed to a rust organism. Fortunately, a vigorous, rust-resistant clone has been discovered and is now available. This free-flowering selection has red-orange blossoms and is named 'Marian Sampson' in honor of one of the co-founders of Mourning Cloak Ranch and Botanic Garden in Tehachapi. The shape of the inflorescences of Marian Sampson scarlet coyote mint resemble an old-fashioned shaving brush and are not as widely spreading as those seen on most plants in the wild.

Marian Sampson scarlet coyote mint, close-up of flower, Rancho Santa Ana Botanic Garden, Claremont.
BART O'BRIEN

Grow Marian Sampson scarlet coyote mint in a hanging basket or a container, place it in a choice foreground position in a raised bed, or plant it in a rock garden where viewers can appreciate its spectacular flowers. In gardens with hot, dry climates, this plant requires moderate supplemental irrigation for best results. Marian Sampson scarlet coyote mint needs little maintenance except to lightly pinch young stems in early spring and selectively remove long sprawling stems in early winter. Plants resent alkaline soils and water. Even when well situated, Marian Sampson scarlet coyote mint typically has a garden life span of only two to four years. It is easily grown from cuttings or division.

Monardella villosa
COYOTE MINT
Mint Family (Lamiaceae)

Plant Type: Evergreen subshrub.
Geographic Zones: All except high mountains and deserts.
Light: Sun to partial shade.
Soil: Well-drained.
Water: Drought tolerant to moderate.
Natural Habitat and Range: Rocky slopes in many plant communities below 4000 feet; Humboldt County south to Santa Barbara County, and Sierra Nevada foothills.

Coyote mint edging a pathway, private garden, Los Altos.
SAXON HOLT

With its showy dense heads of lavender-pink to purple blossoms and its pungent minty fragrance, coyote mint is a refreshing presence in the garden. In the wild, flowers typically appear from late spring to early summer, but this 1-foot-tall and -wide subshrub may blossom at any time from spring to fall in garden settings. Butterflies and other insects are particularly attracted to these blooms.

Coyote mint's compact size makes it an excellent choice to place at the front of a dry border, along the edge of a path, or where it can tumble over a low wall. Coyote mint also works well in containers and rock gardens. The green, oval-shaped leaves are arranged opposite one another along the stem and may be hairy or smooth. Coyote mint can be grown in full sun. It looks good throughout the year in gardens along the immediate coast, but elsewhere it often appears worn out and ragged from midsummer through fall. Drought-stressed plants that shed most of their foliage during the hottest months of the year will quickly leaf out with fall rains and cooler temperatures. Nurseries occasionally offer plants that slowly spread by underground runners; these unusual specimens are never invasive.

Cut plants back lightly during the fall to winter months to encourage full, dense growth, otherwise they may become sprawling and leggy after a couple of years. Dead-headed plants present a much tidier look. If aphids, mealybugs, and spider mites cause problems, control them with soap sprays.

A favorite form, San Luis Obispo coyote mint (*Monardella villosa* var. *obispoensis*) has nearly round, gray leaves that are enveloped in soft white fuzz.

Other Species: There are many coyote mints to experiment with in gardens. Most have not been widely grown, and due to their complex taxonomy their names are often confused. Nearly all bring pleasing scents and flowers to the garden. Flax-leaved monardella (*Monardella linoides*) is found growing on slopes on the western edge of California's deserts from Mono to San Diego counties. The plants have gray-green foliage and rosy lavender summer blossoms. They may reach 2 feet tall and present an open, willowy appearance.

Muhlenbergia rigens
DEER GRASS
Grass Family (Poaceae)

Plant Type: Evergreen, warm-season perennial grass.
Geographic Zones: All except high mountains.
Light: Sun to partial shade.
Soil: Adaptable.
Water: Drought tolerant to moderate.
Natural Habitat and Range: Dry or moist places in many plant communities below 7000 feet; widespread in California—except northwestern California and the northern and central Coast Ranges—and into Texas and Mexico.

Deer grass is the most cherished species in California's vast treasure trove of grasses. Established plants resemble gigantic pincushions and may reach 5 feet tall and 3 to 6 feet wide. The tightly packed shoots produce gray-green leaves that bend and spill outwards,

Deer grass planted in a drift, Leaning Pine Arboretum, Cal Poly, San Luis Obispo. DAVID FROSS

Deer grass makes a bold statement in this poolside planting, private garden, Sonoma. BART O'BRIEN

creating the impression of a fountain of leaves. Dozens of spike-like flowering stems are held stiffly vertical and persist for several years.

Single specimens of deer grass are dramatic, but large drifts are stunning. Crowded plants look pinched, so be sure to allow enough space for them to develop properly. Use deer grass with large boulders and coarse-textured foliage for maximum contrast; showy milk-weed, Saint Catherine's lace, and Pigeon Point coyote brush are excellent companions. The reliable growth form and durable character of deer grass lends itself to pattern plantings and commercial landscapes. It is one of the best choices for difficult transition areas between regularly watered lawns and drier sites. Deer grass performs well even on seasonally dry soils and is useful for erosion control on banks and slopes.

Gardeners can rely on deer grass to maintain its striking appearance throughout the year. It is truly our most carefree and easy-to-grow native grass and can be left on its own with no grooming for years at a time; all it needs is sunshine. Deer grass performs unreliably in the shade, so use caution when planting it under estab-lished trees with aggressive surface roots. From late summer to fall, some gardeners use a heavy stiff-tined rake to pull out long-dead shoots, leaves, and flower stalks. Others employ a string trimmer to cut the entire clump down to 3 to 4 inches. You can even burn it back. Native Americans use this method to reduce the plant to a dense, crown-like stubble in order to improve production of the flowering stems highly prized for bas-ketry. As new growth begins to appear, plants that are cut or raked, rather than burned, may be given a light dose of nitrogen fertilizer to compensate for the removed nutrients.

Despite its common name, deer generally avoid eating this grass. Young plants do require protection from rabbits and ground squirrels until they are well established, which might take up to a year or more.

Myrica californica
PACIFIC WAX MYRTLE
Wax Myrtle Family (Myricaceae)

Plant Type: Evergreen shrub to small tree.
Geographic Zones: All except high mountains and deserts.
Light: Sun to partial shade.
Soil: Adaptable.
Water: Occasional to regular.
Natural Habitat and Range: Moist slopes, streamsides, and canyons in many plant communities near the coast below 500 feet; Santa Monica Mountains to Washington.

Pacific wax myrtle is a handsome large shrub capa-ble of performing in demanding situations. Resilient enough to use in freeway landscaping, this plant is also called upon to soften the visual impact of cinder block walls and foundations or to screen utility installations. Its bright green foliage and erect, rounded form grace many formal or natural hedges in urban California.

Densely branched to 30 feet tall, Pacific wax myr-tle has smooth gray bark and leathery ¾-inch-wide and 4-inch-long leaves. Spring leaves flush apple green then darken as they mature to a rich forest green. The glossy leaves have a subtle spicy fragrance and can be used like bay leaves to flavor sauces and other foods. Inconspicu-ous yellow-green flowers are borne in axillary male and female catkins. The fragrant, waxy, purple-brown fruits attract birds.

Pacific wax myrtle responds favorably to light or heavy pruning. Coppice older, excessively woody

Pacific wax myrtle (background) blocks street noise and visibility, private garden, Lafayette. STEPHEN INGRAM

Pacific wax myrtles pruned as small trees, private garden, Solvang. JOHN EVARTS

specimens to encourage a vigorous new appearance. You can feature its attractive gray bark by shaping the plant into a small tree; this treatment is particularly effective when a specimen is sited in front of a light-colored building. Pacific wax myrtle has a fresher appearance when it receives regular water. Plants grown in coastal areas with strong prevailing winds and salt spray are smaller but still maintain their bright green color.

Thrips and spider mites can quickly disfigure plants and require monitoring during the warm season. Thrips are problematic in coastal climates, while spider mites tend to be found in sunny, interior sites and drought-stressed plantings. Reduce drought stress and apply horticultural oils or soaps to prevent serious problems.

Nassella species
NEEDLEGRASSES
Grass Family (Poaceae)

Plant Type: Deciduous to semi-evergreen, cool-season perennial grasses.
Geographic Zones: All except high mountains and deserts.
Light: Sun.
Soil: Adaptable.
Water: Drought tolerant to occasional.
Natural Habitat and Range: Dry slopes in open grasslands, coastal scrub, chaparral, and oak woodlands below 4500 feet; Channel Islands, Coast Ranges, Sacramento Valley, and Sierra Nevada foothills south to northwestern Baja California.

Our needlegrasses reinforce the basic tenets of California's Mediterranean climate and live by its fundamental code: rest during the warm, dry summer and grow during the cool, moist winter. These grasses have an elegant spring character, which is more fully appreciated after viewing the flaxen husks of dormant plants in August and September. California's three species—*Nassella cernua, N. lepida,* and *N. pulchra*—all become dormant as temperatures rise and soils dry out. During this period, water, fertilizer, and special attention may not counter their obligate summer dormancy and are more likely to kill needlegrasses than prevent their natural summer rest.

Needlegrasses form dense, tufted clumps 2 to 3 feet high with narrow green leaves. The delicate inflorescences are produced in late winter through early spring on tall, airy spikes that measure up to 3 feet in length. Individual flowers are held in a loose, nodding fashion, creating a relaxed character. Each floret emerges with a distinctive rose-purple thread-like awn 2 to 4 inches in length. These awns twist and take on a silver cast as they dry. The small, narrow seeds ripen in early summer and usually produce a few new seedlings each year.

Above: Purple needlegrass with dried flowering stalks, U.C. Santa Barbara Sedgwick Reserve, Santa Ynez. JOHN EVARTS
Left: Purple needlegrass setting seed in late winter, Santa Barbara Botanic Garden. JOHN EVARTS

Nodding needlegrass (*Nassella cernua*) is effective used with other native perennials like checkerbloom, blue-eyed grass, and California poppy in dry meadows or informal borders. It naturalizes easily, which makes it a good choice for use on slopes and hillsides, for erosion control, or in large drifts along highways and median strips.

Foothill needlegrass (*Nassella lepida*) is similar to nodding needlegrass but has thinner blades and a more refined character. It also lacks the consistent nodding habit of *Nassella cernua* and is more tolerant of partial shade.

Purple needlegrass (*Nassella pulchra*) is the state grass of California, and its widespread distribution reminds us that California's grasslands were dominated by perennial grasses before the introduction of exotic annual grasses. Like foothill and nodding needlegrass, it has a delicate, airy appearance combined with a durable, drought-tolerant character. It is still found in much of its original range and competes successfully with introduced weeds.

All three needlegrass species are disease and pest free. They combine well with native bulbs and annuals on dry slopes. If you consider the dormant phase objectionable, prune these grasses back after flowering. In fire-prone areas they should be cut back in early summer due to the flammable nature of the dried stalks.

Parry beargrass blooms after many years of growth, Rancho Santa Ana Botanic Garden, Claremont. KAREN MUSCHENETZ

Nolina species
BEARGRASSES
Nolina Family (Nolinaceae)

Plant Type: Evergreen shrubs.
Geographic Zones: All except immediate coast, northern coastal, and high mountains.
Light: Sun.
Soil: Well-drained.
Water: Drought tolerant.
Natural Habitat and Range: In desert scrub and desert woodland below 6000 feet; range varies with species.

If you yearn for yuccas but are afraid to invite them into your garden due to their fierce terminal spines, your craving will be sated by planting California beargrasses. Their glorious inflorescences are similar in appearance to Our Lord's candle, though the individual cream-colored to greenish flowers are smaller and much more numerous. Beargrasses form attractive bold clumps of stiff to lax, narrow leathery leaves. They are extremely long-lived plants and are pest and disease free. Maintenance requirements for them are minimal—the only necessary task is the removal of spent inflorescences.

Parry beargrass (*Nolina parryi*) is the largest Californian species. It is an outstanding accent plant and is especially recommended for large, long-term landscapes and gardens. For several decades the plants form stiff fountain-like rosettes of olive green foliage that may grow to 15 feet across. Singleleaf pinyon, incienso, beavertail cactus, banana yucca, jojoba, and agaves are a few of the many excellent garden companions for this giant beargrass. Magnificent single-trunked specimens found in the Kingston Mountains in the eastern Mojave Desert resemble palm trees and were formerly known as giant nolina (*Nolina parryi* ssp. *wolfii*), a name that persists in horticulture. These plants take their time to flower and develop noticeable trunks. Records show that it takes 35 years for the first blooms to appear on seed-grown plants. Parry beargrass grows in chaparral, desert scrub, and desert woodlands on the Kern Plateau and in the Santa Rosa, San Jacinto, Kingston, Eagle, and Little San Bernardino mountains.

Desert beargrass (*Nolina bigelovii*) is found in widely scattered populations in desert mountain ranges and the Mojave Desert from southern Nevada and San Bernardino County, California south to northwestern Mexico. Older leaves of this species have notably shredded or fibrous margins. Single plants not in bloom are 1 to 3 feet tall and equally wide; an inflorescence can extend the plant's height to over 8 feet. Simple massed plantings of desert beargrass set among large decomposed granite boulders create a majestic impression.

Oenothera californica
CALIFORNIA EVENING PRIMROSE
Evening Primrose Family (Onagraceae)

Plant Type: Deciduous herbaceous perennial.
Geographic Zones: All except northern coastal and high mountains.
Light: Sun.
Soil: Well-drained.
Water: Drought tolerant to occasional.
Natural Habitat and Range: Sandy soils in many plant communities below 8000 feet; Coast, Transverse, and Peninsular ranges from Ventura County south to northwestern Baja California, and desert areas from Mono to Los Angeles counties and east into Nevada.

California evening primrose is noted for its prostrate, spreading mats of gray foliage and its 2- to 3-inch-wide crystalline white blossoms. Its narrow leaves are coarsely and irregularly serrated. All parts of the plant are densely hairy, except for those glorious, sweetly scented flowers (*oenothera* is Greek for "wine scented"). Each moth-pollinated ephemeral bloom bursts forth in a matter of minutes during early evening and lasts a single night before collapsing into a formless pinkish mass the next morning. Numerous flower buds are produced, so the show often continues for a month or more in spring or early summer. A mature plant may reach 4 inches tall and 2 to 3 feet across.

California evening primrose is long-lived and is an excellent choice for a hot, dry garden with well-drained soil. Plants completely disappear and are dormant from midsummer until they emerge in late winter. Several species of evening primrose become invasive in the garden, but this species does not share that tendency. The few seedlings of California evening primrose that may appear will always be welcome.

Plant California evening primrose together with sacred datura; its welcome spring blossoms are precursors to sacred datura's summer flowers. Placed at the base of a woolly blue curls, California evening primrose's spent flowers are curiously complementary, while the foliage of the two

California evening primrose in a private garden, Swall Meadows.
STEPHEN INGRAM

plants provides contrast. California evening primrose is typically pest and disease free.

Other Species: Hooker evening primrose *(Oenothera elata)* is an aggressive biennial found in moist places throughout most of California. Showy 1- to 6-foot-high flower stalks display many 2- to 4-inch-wide bright yellow flowers, which open late in the afternoon and wither the following morning. Plants spread quickly by seed. It is easy to grow in full sun to partial shade and tolerates a range of watering regimes.

Top: California evening primrose with masses of sweet-scented flowers, roadside in Antelope Valley. STEPHEN INGRAM
Bottom: Hooker evening primrose in a meadow planting, Santa Barbara Botanic Garden. STEVE JUNAK

Opuntia basilaris
BEAVERTAIL CACTUS
Cactus Family (Cactaceae)

Plant Type: Evergreen succulent shrub.
Geographic Zones: All except for immediate coast and high mountains.
Light: Sun to partial shade.
Soil: Well-drained.
Water: Drought tolerant to infrequent.
Natural Habitat and Range: Widespread on well-drained soil in desert scrub and desert woodland below 9000 feet; southeastern San Joaquin Valley, southern Sierra Nevada, Tehachapi, San Gabriel, and San Bernardino mountains, eastern Peninsular Ranges, and the Mojave and Colorado deserts to Utah, Arizona, and Sonora, Mexico.

Beavertail cactus with a showy display of flowers and buds, private garden, Borrego Springs. BILL EVARTS

Cacti are often noted for their beautiful and evanescent blossoms, and those of California's beavertail are highly prized. In a good year, a mature plant may produce dozens of 3- to 4-inch-wide flowers. Brilliant magenta is the most prevalent flower color, but plants with white, pink, rose, yellow, or red blossoms are sometimes found. The floral excesses of cacti are amply illustrated by beavertail's rich blooms. Silky 1½-inch-long petals surround dozens of golden yellow anthers and a single, creamy white, star-like stigma.

Beavertail is one of California's most variable cacti. Its thick, succulent, typically flattened stems (pads) vary in color and may be green, blue-green, gray, or purple. Beavertail typically lacks the rigid spines that are found on nearly all of California's cacti. At each small dot on the pad, known as an areole, there is a dense tuft of ⅛-inch-long brown hair-like spines called glochids. The spacing of these glochid-rich areoles creates the characteristic pattern seen on the pads.

Placing, planting, and moving beavertail requires just as much thought and caution as planning for its ongoing maintenance requirements. Bumping into this cactus or accidentally brushing against a typical glochid-rich pad while weeding or watering is memorable. Glochids often remain in gloves or clothing even after repeated cleaning and washing. Use beavertail in containers, dry rock gardens, and desert plantings where the need for weeding is minimal. For a desert-themed garden, plant beavertail with desert willow, palo verde, desert lavender, and Louis Hamilton apricot mallow. In desert or other hot interior valley gardens, plants perform best when grown in light shade. Mature beavertail cactus plants may reach up to 18 inches tall. Due to their ability to root wherever their pads touch the soil, they will spread, albeit slowly.

Cochineal scales *(Dactylopius coccus)* appear as small, cottony clumps on the surface of the pads or at joints between pads and are a significant pest. When dried and crushed, these pests become the source material for a highly prized bright red dye. Using horticultural oils may control this insect, as well as infestations of other types of scale and mealybugs.

Crown rot and root rots may be problematic if this cactus is planted too deeply or in heavy soils. When you set it in the ground, take special care to keep it slightly higher than the surrounding soil to avoid these fungal diseases.

Ornithostaphylos oppositifolia
PALO BLANCO
Heath Family (Ericaceae)

Plant Type: Evergreen shrub or small tree.
Geographic Zones: All except the immediate coast and high mountains.
Light: Sun.
Soil: Adaptable, except poorly drained.
Water: Drought tolerant when established.
Natural Habitat and Range: Slopes in chaparral below 2500 feet; Tijuana Hills of San Diego County south to northwestern Baja California.

Palo blanco is unfamiliar to most Californians, but it has too many enticements to ignore. This durable plant may reach 15 feet high and wide. It shares the smooth sinuous bark and growth habit of the largest manzanitas, but with a magnificent difference. As the cinnamon-colored bark peels in early summer, the newly revealed bark is chalky white. This is the origin

Top: *Palo blanco, used as a specimen plant, Rancho Santa Ana Botanic Garden, Claremont.* BART O'BRIEN
Bottom: *Palo blanco, pruned to reveal its handsome bark, Rancho Santa Ana Botanic Garden, Claremont.* DAVID FROSS

of its common name *palo blanco,* Spanish for "white stick." When palo blanco's new bark is exposed, the trunks and main branches have a granular or sandy texture. By the time the fall rains arrive, they have aged to a warm cinnamon brown and are smooth to the touch.

Palo blanco foliage is fine textured, and its nearly see-through appearance makes it an ideal choice for use as a small multi-trunked tree in a patio or atrium garden. Its narrow, dark green leaves are paler beneath and are generally produced in threes. Tiny, urn-shaped cream-colored flowers are produced in short terminal clusters during the winter months and are followed by small manzanita-like fruits that are eaten by birds.

Palo blanco is best used as a specimen plant and is particularly striking when placed in front of dark foliage or walls. It is also effective when used in mass plantings with other evergreen chaparral shrubs as an informal screen. Pleasing companions include

California evening primrose, sacred datura, incienso, deer grass, and dudleyas.

Plants grow at a moderate to fast rate, but specimens located in cool coastal climates are often slow growing. The most significant pest is scale, which can be controlled with horticultural oils. Manzanita branch dieback *(Botryosphaeria dothidea)* also affects palo blanco, and there is no known cure for this pathogen.

Several of our chaparral plants, palo blanco among them, develop a woody basal burl at ground level that enables these plants to survive periodic wildfires that would otherwise kill them. Gardeners may take advantage of this attribute to rejuvenate an older or unsatisfactory specimen by drastically pruning the plant to the ground in late summer or fall. Typically, plants respond quickly by producing a flush of new growth.

Oxalis oregana
REDWOOD SORREL
Wood Sorrel Family (Oxalidaceae)

Plant Type: Evergreen herbaceous perennial.
Geographic Zones: All except interior valleys, high mountains, and deserts.
Light: Shade.
Soil: Adaptable; rich soil preferred.
Water: Occasional to regular.
Natural Habitat and Range: Cool shade of coniferous and mixed-evergreen forests below 3000 feet; Monterey County to British Columbia.

The delicate, clover-like appearance of redwood sorrel belies the tenacious character and specialized adaptations it requires to compete for light, nutrients, and water on the shaded floor of redwood and Douglas-fir forests. Gardeners can take advantage of redwood sorrel's attributes by choosing it when they need a plant that will thrive in mature gardens with deep shade and plenty of root competition from established trees.

Redwood sorrel is a fleshy perennial that grows 4 to 8 inches high and has spreading rhizomes. Its compound leaves are divided into heart-shaped leaflets that rise on thin stems from basal clumps. The stems and undersides of the leaves are burgundy-colored. Redwood sorrel's flowers, which are often hidden in the foliage, reach up to 1 inch in diameter and are held on solitary stalks. They range in color from white to pink, often with reddish or lavender venation. The main bloom is in the spring, but redwood sorrel frequently produces flowers again in fall.

Primarily used as a groundcover, redwood sorrel can be slow to establish when planted in areas with heavy root competition or clay soils. Once firmly rooted,

Redwood sorrel (with clover-like leaves) and wild ginger, private garden, Berkeley. STEPHEN INGRAM

it can spread rapidly and may overwhelm other ground-covers. Perennials from the understory of redwood forests, such as giant chain fern, western sword fern, wild ginger, and western meadow rue, are fitting companions. It can also be used in entryways and alcoves with low-light levels.

When stressed by drought or heat, redwood sorrel's leaflets fold along a central axis, which helps it conserve moisture. They also fold in heavy rain, perhaps to reduce the impact of the droplets. To freshen older plantings, cut them back with a string trimmer in the fall. Severely drought-stressed plants drop peripheral leaves and are reduced to the basal clumps. Under these conditions they will need supplemental irrigation, or they will not produce more leaves until the winter rains arrive. Diseases and pests are few, but monitor snails and slugs to prevent heavy infestations.

Redwood sorrel and other species in the genus *Oxalis* contain oxalic acid. The acid gives the leaves and stems of redwood sorrel a sour, tangy flavor. Some people like to add them to a salad, but consumption of large quantities is potentially harmful.

Penstemon species
PENSTEMONS
Figwort Family (Scrophulariaceae)

Plants that inspire their own plant society have a lot going for them. Roses, orchids, ferns, conifers, irises, and succulents each have one, and so do penstemons. The American Penstemon Society was established to celebrate these colorful perennials that form the largest genus of flowering plants endemic to North America. Penstemons are highly prized ornamentals, particularly

for western gardeners, due to their incredible diversity, gorgeous blossoms, and wealth of species to choose from.

California alone has over 50 species and a great many varieties of penstemons. Relatively few of these have become commonplace at specialty nurseries and botanic garden plant sales, perhaps because most penstemons are rather exacting in their growing requirements. Still, they are worth the challenge. Their tubular, two-lipped, open-throated blossoms come in endless hues. Arranged either on long, wand-like branches or on congested spikes, they are delightful to behold. Hummingbirds and bumblebees seek them out, as do gardeners.

Give penstemons plenty of sun, good air circulation, and gravelly soil, and be careful not to overwater them. To promote a second bloom, prune off the fading stalks and water judiciously. After flowering is finished, cut the stalks back almost to the ground, but first allow the seeds to ripen to encourage volunteer seedlings. Once established, penstemons are gems that truly thrive on neglect. Some gardeners grow them as annuals or biennials due to their typically short-lived nature.

Penstemon centranthifolius
SCARLET BUGLER

Plant Type: Evergreen herbaceous perennial.
Geographic Zones: All except high mountains.
Light: Sun.
Soil: Well-drained.
Water: Drought tolerant to occasional.
Natural Habitat and Range: Dry, often disturbed sites in chaparral and oak woodlands below 6000 feet; North Coast Ranges south to Mexico and inland to the Sierra Nevada.

Consider scarlet bugler when creating a warm color scheme in your garden. From spring to summer, the inflorescences of this showy perennial are laden with narrowly tubular, 1-inch-long bright orange-red blossoms. The glaucous, blue-gray to gray-green leaves measure 2 to 4 inches long, have smooth margins, and are attractive in their own right. Plants can reach 2 to 5 feet tall when in bloom. Although

Scarlet bugler in bloom, San Felipe Valley, eastern San Diego County. RICHARD FISHER

specimens in cultivated situations rarely replicate the masses of flower stalks produced by plants in the wild, a garden display is still impressive. Grow scarlet bugler in a border with other blue-leaved partners, such as Canyon Prince wild rye, Our Lord's candle, and Matilija poppy. Or plant it in a decorative terra cotta pot; some container specimens thrive for years.

Penstemon heterophyllus
FOOTHILL PENSTEMON

Plant Type: Evergreen herbaceous perennial.
Geographic Zones: All except high mountains and deserts.
Light: Sun.
Soil: Well-drained.
Water: Drought tolerant to occasional.
Natural Habitat and Range: Dry places in grasslands, chaparral, and woodland and forest clearings below 5000 feet; Coast Ranges inland to the Sierra Nevada.

Of all the native penstemons, foothill penstemon is probably the most widely known and grown, due no doubt to its greater tolerance of heavy soils and summer watering. The unexpectedly yellow buds suggest nary a hint of the colors to follow. Each blossom of this floriferous perennial offers a shimmering blend of blues, purples, and pinks. To picture the overall impression these blooms create, imagine a piece of crystal that changes color based on the angle of refracted light.

Foothill penstemon forms a loose mound of thin, leafy branches. It reaches 1 to 3 feet high in bloom and is topped in spring and summer by the multi-hued 1½-inch-long flowers. The linear leaves are 1 to 3 inches long and may turn maroon in late summer and fall.

Foothill penstemon's tufted shape works well in rock gardens and in the foreground of mixed borders. As a bonus, the cut flowers hold up well in arrangements. Plant it with saffron or red-flowered buckwheat, California poppies, and a wide array of sun-loving bunchgrasses. Be sure to grow it in full sun and with good air circulation to reduce the likelihood of powdery mildew.

Other Species: In areas of northern California where the climate makes foothill penstemon marginally successful, consider trying the equally beautiful mountain blue penstemon *(Penstemon laetus)*. Growing naturally in desert scrub or coniferous forest, it accepts both sun and light shade in gardens.

Cultivars: Several selections have been introduced through the years, but by far the most reliable and garden tolerant is 'Margarita BOP'. What sets this clone apart from the others is its disease resistance and staying power; it blooms profusely for several months.

Margarita BOP penstemon provides a splash of color in a border planting, private garden, Ballard. JOHN EVARTS

Penstemon spectabilis
ROYAL PENSTEMON

Plant Type: Evergreen herbaceous perennial.
Geographic Zones: All except high mountains and high deserts.
Light: Sun.
Soil: Well-drained.
Water: Drought tolerant to occasional.
Natural Habitat and Range: Dry, gravelly slopes and washes in chaparral, coastal scrub, and oak woodlands below 6500 feet; Transverse and Peninsular ranges south to Mexico.

This southern California penstemon lives up to its common name. When in bloom it can reach 3 to 6 feet tall, and each flower stalk bears upwards of 100, 1-inch-long blossoms, creating a regal display of blue, pink, lilac, lavender-purple, violet, or white. This floral performance can last from spring to fall.

Royal penstemon is a rather coarse-textured perennial due to its large, irregularly toothed leaves. Just one specimen can serve as a focal point in a mixed border, but for maximum effect plant several as a ribbon running through a bed, complemented by Canyon Silver island snowflake, sages, and ceanothus.

When you plant both scarlet bugler and royal penstemon together, don't be surprised to find future generations of volunteer seedlings that appear to be hybrids of these two. Known as Parish penstemon *(Penstemon × parishii)*, this form occurs in the wild where the two species overlap. It more closely resembles scarlet bugler, but its tubular flowers are shocking pink. It is a welcome addition to any garden.

Other Species: The list of native penstemons for California gardens continues to expand, thanks to specialty nurseries and botanic gardens. Look for the following species in mail-order nurseries, at plant sales, and offered as seed by the American Penstemon Society. All require excellent drainage and/or some winter chill to thrive.

The name of azure penstemon *(Penstemon azureus)* says it all. The brilliant flowers of this woodland species line the leafy stalks, and the whole plant reaches 1 to 2 feet high. Unlike the species described above, this one appreciates a bit of summer water.

Alpine gardeners will want to try timberline penstemon *(Penstemon davidsonii)*. This mat-forming beauty rarely exceeds 4 inches tall and has outsize, richly purple flowers atop 3- to 4-inch-long stems. Low-elevation gardeners must settle for appreciating it in the wild.

Mountain pride penstemon *(Penstemon newberryi)* grows naturally on rocky outcrops. In alpine regions, it sports electrifying cherry-red flowers. Flatlanders should opt for Sonoma penstemon *(Penstemon newberryi var. sonomensis)*. Its flowers tend toward rosy purple, and it is easier to grow than the species, although it blooms sparingly at low elevations.

Palmer penstemon *(Penstemon palmeri)* is a must for desert gardeners. It has handsome glaucous foliage and reaches a height of 4 feet when in bloom. The inflated, intensely fragrant flowers have a scent reminiscent of grape soda and are pale pink with darker nectar guides. Palmer penstemon may succeed in coastal gardens if placed in a hot, dry, well-drained spot.

Two forms of Grinnell penstemon *(Penstemon grinnellii)* occur in chaparral, forest edges, and dry woodlands. They resemble Palmer penstemon, but have a lighter scent, greener leaves, and a shorter stature (½ to 2½ feet tall). Flower color varies and includes white, pink, and purple.

Perityle incana
GUADALUPE ISLAND ROCK DAISY
Sunflower Family (Asteraceae)

Plant Type: Evergreen subshrub.
Geographic Zones: Immediate coast and warm intermediate valleys of central and southern California.
Light: Sun to partial shade.
Soil: Well-drained.
Water: Infrequent to occasional.
Natural Habitat and Range: Coastal bluffs and canyons in chaparral below 4000 feet; Guadalupe Island, Baja California.

Gardeners who are partial to cooler colors will find a treasure trove of species in the California flora with leaves that are silver, white, blue, or gray. A little known yet highly desirable plant in this category is Guadalupe Island rock daisy, which originates from the southernmost corner of the California Floristic Province. As with other silver-foliaged species, this plant blends well with just about everything. Its sunny yellow blossoms look equally attractive when combined with both warm and cool colors.

Royal penstemon in a mass planting, Rancho Santa Ana Botanic Garden, Claremont. BART O'BRIEN

Guadalupe Island rock daisy with flower heads, Leaning Pine Arboretum, Cal Poly, San Luis Obispo. DAVID FROSS

In the wild, Guadalupe Island rock daisy hugs steep cliffs and nestles its trunk into rock crevices. Looking like a smaller version of island snowflake, this frost-tender island endemic reaches 3 to 4 feet in height and width. The deeply lobed leaves are about 2 inches long and bluish or silvery gray. Masses of yellow, dome-shaped, 1- to 2-inch-wide flower clusters hover above the foliage from spring into summer.

The common name for this uncommon plant suggests an effective way to site it in a garden. Guadalupe Island rock daisy's fine-textured foliage is ideal for softening the strong character of boulders. Use it in larger rock gardens, perennial borders, or gardens with a gray color scheme. Plant it behind a carpet of saffron buckwheat and dudleyas and in front of Winifred Gilman sage or Sierra Blue ceanothus. For a livelier, warmer grouping, try combining Guadalupe Island rock daisy with royal penstemon, island snapdragon, California fuchsias, and gum plants.

Maintenance of this practically carefree plant consists of deadheading the dark brown dry flowers and cutting it back by one-third each year to retain youthful vigor and a compact shape. Insect and disease problems are seldom encountered.

Philadelphus lewisii
WESTERN MOCK ORANGE
Mock Orange Family (Philadelphaceae)

Plant Type: Deciduous shrub.
Geographic Zones: All except deserts.
Light: Sun to partial shade.
Soil: Adaptable; heavy and rich preferred.
Water: Infrequent to moderate.
Natural Habitat and Range: Slopes and canyons in forests and chaparral below 4500 feet; Lake, Mendocino, and Tulare counties north and east to British Columbia and the Rocky Mountains.

What is the state flower of Idaho doing in California? Northern California is the southern limit for the widely distributed western mock orange, and we are indeed fortunate to have it grace our gardens and wild landscapes.

Western mock orange is a large deciduous shrub reaching up to 12 feet tall, with a pleasing fountain-like growth habit. Leaves are light green and may have entire or coarsely serrated margins. Flowers are produced in clusters toward the end of the arching branches from late spring to early summer. Individual blossoms up to 1½ inches wide have four to five white petals and a central brush of cream-colored stamens. The blooms' sweet fragrance is reminiscent of citrus flowers, hence the common name, mock orange.

Western mock orange's blossoms have a scent like citrus flowers, private garden, Novato. SAXON HOLT

Popular during Victorian times, mock orange has lost favor in today's smaller gardens. It is most often seen as a specimen plant, although it is useful in an informal hedge, especially when mixed with broadleaf evergreen shrubs and trees such as coffeeberry, Golden Abundance barberry, mountain mahogany, toyon, and California bay. Massed plantings of western mock orange are especially effective on lightly shaded slopes.

Western mock orange is easy to grow. It requires at least half a day of sunlight to bloom well and performs poorly when sited on nutrient-deficient, coarse soils. Western mock orange is attractive when left unpruned, though it may be cut back hard, or even coppiced, at roughly five-year intervals.

Cultivars: 'Goose Creek' is the most distinctive cultivar of western mock orange. It is a vigorous plant with long-lasting, fully double flowers.

Other Species: The main attraction of littleleaf mock orange *(Philadelphus microphyllus)* is its powerful fragrance, generally acclaimed as the strongest and best in this aromatic genus. It is no surprise to learn that it has been widely used in breeding programs for its scent. As the specific epithet suggests, this rounded deciduous shrub has small leaves. Plants may reach 3 to 5 feet tall and wide. Flowers are borne singly or in small clusters, and each blossom is about ½ inch across. It inhabits several mountain ranges in and adjacent to California's deserts and extends south into the mountains of northern Mexico and as far east as Texas.

Pinus species
PINES
Pine Family (Pinaceae)

Pines represent the largest genus of tree species found in California. Of the 19 species that occur here, 11 are endemic to the California Floristic Province. Within this distinctive collection of pines are many worthy of superlatives: Torrey pine, the rarest pine in the United States; bristlecone pine, the oldest living tree on earth; sugar pine, the tallest pine; and Coulter pine, the pine with the heaviest cones. Species in this diverse genus grow in many habitats, from granitic headlands just above the Pacific Ocean to alpine deserts at 11,500 feet in the White Mountains.

Pines are distinguished from other conifers by their evergreen needles that are held in sheath-wrapped bundles. The needles vary in length from 1 to 14 inches. Pines emit a pleasing aroma due primarily to the oils that evaporate through their needles. This scent is especially prevalent in warm weather or with species that have resinous cones. Cone size ranges from 2 to 18 inches, with some exceptional sugar pine cones measuring 24 inches long. The seeds of many pines have a wedge of membranous tissue attached to the seed coat. This paper-thin tissue acts like a

Foothill pine, needles and male pollen cones, Henry W. Coe State Park, Santa Clara County.
J. R. HALLER

wing, spinning and slowing the seeds in their descent, allowing a form of flight. Pine species lacking this wing-like tissue usually have evolved a mutually beneficial relationship with Clark's nutcracker or various species of jays; the trees' seeds provide food to the birds and the birds disperse the trees' seeds. Pine seeds have traditionally been an important food source for many Native Americans. Although all pines produce edible seeds, indigenous people tend to favor the larger-seeded species with the easiest-to-open cones. Pines in wildland habitats and in the garden also offer food and shelter to many animal species.

Most of the California pines are drought tolerant and require little water once established. Applying fertilizer is not recommended, because heavy inputs of nutrients produce rank, fragile growth. The characteristic pine duff found under mature trees will slowly acidify the soil and is a fine complement to acid-loving species growing in the understory.

Pruning can improve the shape of pines and is best accomplished in spring as spires of new growth, called candles, elongate. A partial cut of the candles will create a denser, stouter tree, and if they are removed entirely, the tree's size can be limited without distorting its natural form. An annual pruning allows pines to be used in containers or as hedges and screens.

Diseases and pests can pose considerable challenges for pines, although healthy, vigorous trees seldom have serious problems. Bark and engraver beetles can harm or kill stressed trees. Sawdust-like frass found near small holes or at the base of a tree indicates their presence. Maintaining trees free of drought stress is the best strategy to prevent beetle damage. Pruning pines during the cool season when beetle activity is at a minimum will also lessen the chance of infestation. Pitch canker is a debilitating fungal disease affecting many species of pines. Monterey pine is one of the most susceptible species, and this once-popular landscape tree is no longer recommended for use in most coastal counties of California.

Pinus coulteri
COULTER PINE

Plant Type: Evergreen tree.
Geographic Zones: All except deserts.
Light: Sun.
Soil: Adaptable, well-drained preferred.
Water: Drought tolerant to infrequent.
Natural Habitat and Range: Dry slopes and ridges in woodlands and forests from 2500 to 7000 feet; Northern Contra Costa County south through the South Coast and Peninsular ranges to northwestern Baja California. Also the Transverse Ranges except in Ventura and western Los Angeles counties.

Coulter pine is an excellent choice for dry, sunny gardens of interior California. This conifer has a symmetrical habit and will develop a broad crown when not crowded by other trees. It can reach up to 75 feet, but rarely achieves that size when used in cultivation. Trees

Coulter pine can form a broad base in open habitat, Figueroa Mountain, Los Padres National Forest. JOHN EVARTS

in inland sites grow faster than those along the coast.

Coulter pine's thick, attractive dark blue-green needles are arranged three to a bundle, and measure 6 to 12 inches long. Its oval 12- to 14-inch-long cones are the heaviest in the world. They persist on the tree and have sharply hooked cone scales that are often encrusted with pitch. Winged seeds are held tightly within the cones for years by some stands of Coulter pine. In the wild, the timing of the release of these seeds varies: some populations have cones that open on warm days in late summer and fall, while in other populations the cones open only when exposed to the heat of a wildfire.

Plant Coulter pine in groves or as a specimen tree. Its cones are ornamental but dangerous, and trees should be sited away from areas where the falling cones could cause injuries. This durable pine withstands heat, drought, wind, and air pollution.

Pinus monophylla
SINGLELEAF PINYON

Plant Type: Evergreen tree.
Geographic Zones: All except northern coastal and immediate coasts.
Light: Sun.
Soil: Adaptable, well-drained preferred.
Water: Drought tolerant to infrequent.
Natural Habitat and Range: Dry, rocky slopes and ridges in woodlands below 9500 feet; the Great Basin from western Utah to the eastern Sierra Nevada; Tehachapi Mountains and inner South Coast Ranges, and Transverse and Peninsular ranges to Baja California.

Singleleaf pinyon is unique among the pines of the world because it produces only a single needle in each

Singleleaf pinyon in circular driveway, private residence, Swall Meadows. STEPHEN INGRAM

fascicle. One of the most widespread trees in the Great Basin, it often grows with Utah, Sierra, or California juniper in a plant community known as pinyon-juniper woodland. These woodlands cover 40 million acres of the Great Basin at elevations between 3000 and 9000 feet, including large areas of eastern California.

A handsome, broad-crowned tree with upturned branches, singleleaf pinyon grows to 30 feet tall with a 15- to 25-foot spread. The ash gray, 1- to 2-inch-long needles are stiff, slightly curved, and held in a dense, brush-like arrangement along the stems. Mature trees may produce bountiful crops of knobby, 3- to 5-inch-long cones bearing large nutritious seeds. The tasty seeds remain an important food for Native Americans of the Great Basin and are a significant dietary element for pinyon, scrub, and Steller's jays and for Clark's nutcracker—the only nutcracker native to North America.

Singleleaf pinyon does best in warmer interior climates that provide adequate heat. It can serve as a specimen tree, informal hedge, or screen, but trees are slow growing at first and may take 10 to 15 years to achieve a height of over 10 feet. Young trees usually have a slender, symmetrical habit and striking blue needles that complement gray-foliaged plants, such as Great Basin sagebrush or purple sage. You can plant singleleaf pinyon in containers, and it makes a fine bonsai subject.

Pinus sabiniana
FOOTHILL PINE

Plant Type: Evergreen tree.
Geographic Zones: All except northern coastal, high mountains, and deserts.
Light: Sun.
Soil: Adaptable, well-drained preferred.
Water: Drought tolerant to infrequent.
Natural Habitat and Range: Dry slopes in woodlands and forests mostly between 1000 and 3000 feet and below 7000 feet; Coast Ranges and Sierra Nevada foothills around the Central Valley.

Foothill pine naturally occurs in open stands where it often grows with blue oak, interior live oak, or California buckeye. In these woodlands, the oddly tilted trunks and wispy gray crowns of the pines appear ghost-like above the other trees, imparting an illusory look to the landscape.

A medium-sized pine with an irregular to round silhouette, foothill pine can reach over 100 feet high,

Foothill pine showing characteristic forked trunk, private garden, Ballard. JOHN EVARTS

although 40 to 80 feet is more typical in gardens. The silver or olive gray needles are 6 to 12 inches long and held loosely, three to a bundle. Chocolate brown cones vary in size but can easily attain the size of a pineapple. Each cone scale has a sharply pointed tip, and some are armed with a claw-like spur. The seed has a short, thick wing and a dense shell that encloses an edible nut. Rich in protein and fat, the seeds are still harvested annually by members of California's indigenous tribes.

Also known as gray pine, this California endemic offers the gardener a number of unusual qualities. The trunks are often forked and support airy, almost transparent foliage that casts a modest, but feathered, shade. When planted against the south or west side of a tall building, the tree's thin shade creates an ornamental pattern as it falls across walls of concrete. Foothill pine makes an excellent specimen tree; it is also a good choice for roadside plantings and lightly used areas of parks, where its cones are unlikely to fall on people. It combines well with most native oaks, and it adds an appealing contrast to the lacy foliage of Santa Cruz Island ironwood. Fast growing and broadly tolerant of heat, drought, air pollution, and varied soils, it is recommended for both coastal and interior gardens.

Pinus torreyana
TORREY PINE

Plant Type: Evergreen tree.
Geographic Zones: All except high mountains and deserts.
Light: Sun.
Soil: Adaptable, well-drained preferred.
Water: Drought tolerant to infrequent.
Natural Habitat and Range: Dry slopes and bluff tops in coastal scrub and woodland along the immediate coast below 500 feet; San Diego County near Del Mar and Santa Rosa Island.

Torrey pine is the rarest pine found in the United States. It occurs naturally in two populations that are separated by 175 miles of ocean. One contains about 2000 trees and is located on the northeast side of Santa Rosa Island. The other, comprising roughly 7000 trees, stretches along seven miles of coastline just north of the city of San Diego. Each stand has its own unique group of associate species.

Exposure to salt-laden winds in its natural habitat gives Torrey pine a gnarled appearance with twisted, sprawling branches. If it is grown away from the immediate coast, Torrey pine has a straight trunk and can attain over 70 feet in height. Its 6- to 13-inch-long needles are dark green to gray-green and come five to a bundle. The cones are large, armed with sharply pointed cone scales, and contain thick-coated edible seeds.

Torrey pine, a mature specimen in a backyard, private garden, Santa Ynez. JOHN EVARTS

Torrey pine exhibiting the more rounded form typical of trees from Santa Rosa Island, Santa Barbara Cemetery. JOHN EVARTS

Torrey pine is useful in open areas, parks, and along roadsides where its large size can be accommodated. A fast-growing tree, it quickly develops a broad crown that can reach up to 50 feet across at maturity. Even though it is a coastal species, Torrey pine will tolerate the heat, wind, and air pollution of interior southern California, and with adequate drainage, it is recommended for use in the Central Valley.

Other Species: Monterey pine *(Pinus radiata)* is easily the most recognized California pine and remains a common tree of the urban landscape. It is found naturally only near the town of Cambria in San Luis Obispo County, around Monterey peninsula in Monterey County, and in the vicinity of Año Nuevo State Reserve in San Mateo and Santa Cruz counties. Mature wildland specimens can reach 100 feet tall or more. Fast growing, it has been bred for its lumber potential and is an important timber tree in New Zealand and Australia. In California, pitch canker *(Fusarium circinatum)* has spread through 22 California coastal counties; Monterey pine is highly susceptible to this pathogen and is no longer a recommended tree in these areas. Infections are extremely difficult to prevent because disease spores are vectored by insects and spread via air, soil, and wood wastes. Pitch canker can only be reliably diagnosed in the laboratory, but to reduce the risks of disseminating it, learn to recognize symptoms of the disease. First, pine needles change in color from dark green to a paler lime green, next they turn yellow, and finally they become reddish brown. The result is "tip die back" or death. Restricting pruning to the cool months, disinfecting pruning tools, and keeping trees in a healthy condition may help prevent contamination.

Shore pine *(Pinus contorta* ssp. *contorta)* is relatively small in size and has a handsome dark green color and a rounded crown. It grows to 35 feet tall and is found along the coastal bluffs, dunes, and headlands of Del Norte, Humboldt, and Mendocino counties. Shore pine's tolerance of salt spray makes it a good choice for windswept coastal landscapes and gardens. It requires afternoon shade when it is planted in hotter sites away from the coast.

Parry pinyon *(Pinus quadrifolia)* is a small pine to 35 feet tall with dark blue-green foliage, a rounded or pyramidal crown, and reddish brown bark. It is found on the dry, desert-facing slopes of the Peninsular Ranges into northwestern Baja California. One of our most drought-tolerant pines, Parry pinyon is an excellent choice for smaller gardens in hot interior valleys.

Platanus racemosa
CALIFORNIA SYCAMORE
Sycamore Family (Platanaceae)

Plant Type: Deciduous tree.
Geographic Zones: All except high mountains.
Light: Sun.
Soil: Adaptable.
Water: Occasional to moderate.
Natural Habitat and Range: Creeks, springs, and other riparian areas below 4000 feet; Central Valley from Shasta County south to Kern County; South Coast, Transverse, and Peninsular ranges to northwestern Baja California.

The much loved and easily grown California sycamore has many distinctive features. This long-lived, fast-growing tree makes a unique impression with its mottled flaking bark, chains of three to five ball-like flower and seed heads, and large pale green, maple-like leaves. While many other trees develop predictable outlines, California sycamore often grows as a single- or multi-trunked specimen with wildly tilted or twisted trunks and broken branches.

California sycamore is best planted in large park-like settings, since mature plants reach a height of 40 to 80 feet and quickly outgrow small spaces. It must always have access to water, but never plant it near water pipes, sewer lines, or septic systems—its voracious roots unfailingly find and ruin them.

If attempting to garden beneath an existing grove of sycamores, your choices should include vigorous plants that can compete with California sycamore's formidable root system and its ongoing deposition of leaves. Although deciduous riparian shrubs, such as spicebush, creek dogwood, and golden currant, are ecologically compatible with California sycamore, gardeners should also consider Pacific wax myrtle, coffeeberry, malva rosa, and other broad-leaved evergreens.

Throughout California, this tree is extremely susceptible to sycamore blight, also called anthracnose, which is caused by the fungus *Gloeosporium platani.* In cool, moist spring conditions, this affliction infects young twigs and leaves and causes them to fall. In bad years, infected trees drop several sets of leaves before this fungus is checked by warm, dry conditions. The ongoing waves of fallen leaves are a maintenance headache, as they do not decompose quickly. Some people are allergic to California sycamore's pollen or the dense hairs that coat the leaves, or to both.

California sycamore frequently hosts infestations of mistletoe, which should be dealt with promptly by a professional arborist before they compromise the structural integrity and health of the tree. The sycamore bark beetle may damage the aesthetic appeal of the bark,

Above: California sycamore grows well at the edge of an irrigated lawn, private garden, Ballard. JOHN EVARTS
Left: Cluster of young California sycamore trunks, Dripping Springs campground, Cleveland National Forest. JOHN EVARTS

although this pest is rarely fatal. California sycamore is a survivor, and even though many pests and diseases attack it, they rarely kill the tree.

Recently, there has been much discussion about the genetic integrity of California sycamore. Botanists are concerned that the survival of this species is threatened by hybridization with the ubiquitously planted, non-native London plane tree *(Platanus × acerifolia).*

Polypodium californicum
CALIFORNIA POLYPODY
Polypody Family (Polypodiaceae)

Plant Type: Deciduous fern.
Geographic Zones: All except high mountains and deserts.
Light: Partial shade to shade.
Soil: Well-drained.
Water: Drought tolerant to occasional.
Natural Habitat and Range: Scrublands, woodlands, and forests below 4000 feet; Humboldt and Butte counties south to northwestern Baja California.

California polypody grows on a cool shaded slope, Santa Barbara Botanic Garden. JOHN EVARTS

California polypody emerges from summer dormancy and unfurls its 4- to 12-inch-long bright green fronds at the first sign of cool nights and fall rains. This characteristic fern of coastal and southwestern California enlivens any winter garden. Grow it on slopes in rock gardens, in the cracks of stone walls or steps, in rock outcrops, or in any shady, seasonally moist but not wet portion of the garden. This fern makes a spectacular cool-season groundcover when planted under trees.

The rhizomes of California polypody creep along at, or just below, the surface of the soil. In nature these stems are often hidden by mosses, lichens, and decaying organic material. In your garden, be sure to remove heavy layers of leaves or excessive debris that cover the rhizomes. The fronds of California polypody wither and dry in late spring or early summer even if there is adequate moisture, although plants grown near the coast may be nearly evergreen. When planting California polypody on flat sites, make sure it has good drainage, or it may succumb to root rot. Good garden companions for California polypody include yerba buena, Oregon iris, Humboldt lily, western meadow rue, coral bells, and dudleyas.

Ferns are an excellent choice for gardens besieged by vertebrate pests such as deer, wood rats, squirrels, scrub jays, raccoons, or gophers, because these pests rarely bother ferns. Watch for infestations of thrips, especially in coastal gardens.

Cultivars: Sarah Lyman California polypody (*Polypodium californicum* 'Sarah Lyman') has spectacular, finely divided leaves. It was discovered in Napa County in the 1800s and has been vegetatively propagated ever since by its admirers. Well worth the search, this long-lived plant is a beautiful addition to the shady garden. Unlike the typical forms of California polypody, 'Sarah Lyman' has a more clumping growth habit. This vigorous selection is sterile and is only propagated by division.

Other Species: In the wild, leather leaf polypody (*Polypodium scouleri*) grows in cool, foggy coastal environments. Its stiff, upright evergreen fronds are dark green. This choice fern is slow growing in gardens, though it is an excellent container specimen. Infestations of scale insects are sometimes difficult to control.

Polystichum munitum
WESTERN SWORD FERN
Wood Fern Family (Dryopteridaceae)

Plant Type: Evergreen fern.
Geographic Zones: All except interior valleys, high mountains, and deserts.
Light: Partial shade to shade.
Soil: Adaptable; acidic preferred.
Water: Occasional to regular.
Natural Habitat and Range: Moist, shaded forests and wooded slopes below 5000 feet; throughout much of the non-desert regions of California, north to Alaska and Montana, and south to northwestern Baja California.

Western sword fern is a robust fern capable of reaching 5 feet tall in favorable conditions. Its lance-shaped, forest green fronds rise from a stout crown that has papery, russet brown scales. Large, mature specimens can produce as many as 75 to 100 fronds that are initially erect and then develop an arching form. The thick fronds are laddered with leaflets shaped like swords and arranged in parallel rows on each side of the stalk.

This tough, adaptable species is capable of enduring cool, dry conditions, but maximum growth comes with regular, or at least occasional, water. Full sun is tolerated along the immediate coast of northern and central California; shade is required in southern California and interior sites. In the wild, western sword fern grows in cool, shaded canyons and in the forest understory. This makes it a good choice to use in the deep shade on the north side of a building or under the

Western sword fern surrounding a bird bath, private garden, Oakland. STEPHEN INGRAM

canopy of an urban forest. Western sword fern is tolerant of tree root competition and works well when massed in drifts under coast redwood, California bay, or alders. In shady borders, it complements giant chain fern, coral bells, and sedges. Single specimens are effective container subjects in shady alcoves. The cut fronds are long lasting and make an excellent contribution to flower arrangements. Frayed and senescent fronds should be removed from plants.

Native Americans have utilized western sword fern in a number of innovative ways. The fronds can serve as protective layering in pit ovens and between foods in storage boxes and baskets; they also make excellent non-stick mats on berry-drying racks. Children play a game counting the leaflets on a frond in a single breath, and some tribes eat peeled and baked rhizomes. Historically, the fronds were tied with maple bark to serve as bedding and mattress.

Thrips often attack western sword fern when it is grown in coastal environments; a silvery tan cast on the leaves easily identifies the damage they cause. Early detection and application of insecticidal soaps and horticultural oils will help prevent disfiguring infestations; coppicing is an effective alternative to sprays.

Populus fremontii
FREMONT COTTONWOOD
Willow Family (Salicaceae)

Plant Type: Deciduous tree.
Geographic Zones: All.
Light: Sun.
Soil: Adaptable; moisture-retentive preferred.
Water: Occasional to regular.
Natural Habitat and Range: Along alluvial flats, rivers, and streams in riparian woodlands and forests below 6000 feet; throughout California, with the exception of the Modoc Plateau, to southern Colorado, western Texas, and northern Mexico.

Fremont cottonwood with autumn foliage, private garden, Ballard. JOHN EVARTS

The poet Merrill Gilfillan said of cottonwoods, "Where there is any hope at all there are cottonwoods on the horizon." Anyone who has sought the shelter of a Fremont cottonwood on a hot summer afternoon can understand the wisdom of these words. In western North America, these graceful trees mark the course of water; their presence reminds us of water's meaning in an arid land.

Fremont cottonwood has a spreading, open crown and grows from 50 to 75 feet tall. Occasionally trees will reach 90 feet, but this is rare in gardens. The young bark is silver gray, with plated furrows and small amber fissures. Mature trunks develop a thick, rough bark that is deeply furrowed and colored an appealing russet-gray. The leaves are copper green at first but quickly become a bright yellow-green; they have a glossy surface and leather-like texture when mature. The 2- to 4-inch-long triangular leaves have coarsely serrated margins and are held on flattened petioles. When the wind blows, the leaves sound like a cascading stream. Autumn turns them a brilliant lemon yellow.

Fremont cottonwood, cottony seeds on a female tree, Santa Ynez River, Los Padres National Forest. STEVE JUNAK

Fremont cottonwood is fast growing and easy to cultivate in the garden. Some trees will require pruning to improve their form and to counteract a weak branching structure. In summer a mature tree casts a mantle of shade that creates a perfect site to place a garden bench. This tree is also a good choice for the edges of streams or watercourses, such as drainage basins or irrigation canals. Fremont cottonwood requires thoughtful placement, as it produces many suckers and its wide-spreading surface roots will aggressively seek a water source. Female trees produce masses of cottony seed; although beautiful, the quantity of seed can be a nuisance. Trees planted near the coast are prone to rust and do not produce significant fall color. Tent caterpillars sometimes attack the foliage, and mistletoe may colonize the branches.

Cultivars: 'Nevada' is the best known of the male clones and was selected for its non-suckering habit, broad columnar form, and bright autumn color. It seldom needs pruning.

Other Species: Black cottonwood *(Populus balsamifera* ssp. *trichocarpa)* is similar to Fremont cottonwood, but the leaves are rounded and have finely serrated margins. It is widespread across western North America from Alaska to Baja California where it occurs in mixed riparian woodlands or in open stands along streams below 10,000 feet. Quaking aspen *(Populus tremuloides)* is a small tree from 25 to 50 feet tall and up to 30 feet wide. Many trees are multi-trunked with light gray or white bark. Found in the mountains of western North America below 9000 feet, it has round leaves and vertically flattened stalks that in windy conditions create the rustling sound, or "quake", for which the tree is named. Quaking aspen is also recognized for its autumn displays of brilliant golden yellow to reddish foliage. It is best used in mountain environments.

Prunus ilicifolia ssp. *ilicifolia*
HOLLYLEAF CHERRY
Rose Family (Roseaceae)

Plant Type: Evergreen shrub or small tree.
Geographic Zones: All except high mountains and deserts.
Light: Sun to partial shade.
Soil: Adaptable.
Water: Drought tolerant to occasional.
Natural Habitat and Range: Chaparral and woodlands below 5000 feet; Napa County through the Coast Ranges to northwestern Baja California.

Hollyleaf cherry's form and size varies depending on its surrounding environment. In the shallow rocky soils found in much of California's chaparral, hollyleaf cherry typically grows 3 to 8 feet high and has a tight, rounded habit. In heavier valley soils or along riparian corridors it can be tree-like, reaching 30 feet tall with a broad crown and thick trunk. This adaptability recommends hollyleaf cherry for a broad range of garden and landscape uses.

Above: Hollyleaf cherry forming a screen at the edge of a lawn, private garden, Montecito. STEPHEN INGRAM
Left: Hollyleaf cherry fruits, private garden, Ballard. JOHN EVARTS

This tightly branched evergreen shrub has glossy green foliage. As the common name suggests, its ¾- to 2-inch-long leaves resemble those of the non-native holly. They have a serrated, wavy edge, leathery texture, and an almond-like scent when crushed. In spring, fragrant cream-colored flowers are held in clusters that measure 1 to 2 inches long; the flowers yield ½-inch-wide dark red to blackish fruits in summer and fall. Especially attractive to scrub jays, mockingbirds, and robins, these cherries provide an ample food source, as well as a generous crop of seedlings.

A remarkably easy plant to grow, hollyleaf cherry is drought tolerant, durable, and seldom troubled by disease or pests. It has a high tolerance for soils infected with oak root fungus and can be grown in these areas with confidence. Manage occasional problems with fireblight by pruning out infected branches, removing and disposing of all diseased tissue, and sterilizing pruning tools to avoid spreading the bacteria. Similar control measures are required for Western X disease, which causes constricted internodes and tiny leaves.

With regular pruning, you can sculpt hollyleaf cherry into a variety of shapes or shear it into an attractive formal hedge. An individual specimen is easily trained into a small tree. It also combines well with toyon, Pajaro manzanita, and sugar bush as an informal screen. Be careful to place plants far enough away from paved surfaces to avoid staining them with fallen cherries.

California's indigenous people have traditionally found many uses for hollyleaf cherry. The fruit has a thin pulp with a sweet flavor and a bitter aftertaste; it is highly prized and even considered a delicacy by some. The cherry is eaten raw or dried, and the large seed within can also be consumed after it is treated to remove the toxic cyanide it contains. The leaves, bark, and roots have medicinal value, and the wood is utilized in bow construction.

Other Species: Catalina cherry *(Prunus ilicifolia* ssp. *lyonii)* is found in chaparral and oak woodlands in Baja California and on four of California's Channel Islands: Santa Catalina, San Clemente, Santa Rosa, and Santa Cruz. It is considerably larger than hollyleaf cherry and often grows as a tree reaching 45 feet. The flat, shiny, 2- to 5-inch-long leaves often lack the serrated margins characteristic of hollyleaf cherry. The cream-colored flowers open in 2- to 5-inch-long spikes and are followed by blue-black cherries.

Catalina cherry and hollyleaf cherry hybridize freely in gardens and nurseries; consequently, many of the plants sold in the nursery trade are hybrids. The cultural needs of Catalina cherry are similar to those of hollyleaf cherry, and it tolerates a wide range of landscape conditions. It has a fresh appearance through the

Catalina cherry, pruned as a small tree for a street planting, Buellton. JOHN EVARTS

seasons, and the glossy green leaves are useful as contrast to the dull green of chaparral currant or lemonade berry. With supplemental water, Catalina cherry grows rapidly. It makes an effective screen and is easily trained into a formal hedge or foundation shrub.

Quercus species
OAKS
Oak Family (Fagaceae)

Oaks characterize much of California. Landscapes filled with the muscled trunks and broad crowns of these majestic trees inspired Spanish-speaking settlers to adopt community names such as Encino, Encinitas, and Paso Robles. Later, English-speaking residents adopted names like Oakland and Thousand Oaks. Today, expansive oak savannas and woodlands, although diminished and exploited, continue to encompass the state's communities, valleys, and fields, bearing silent witness to our history.

The rich oak woodlands of California once provided a primary food source for most of the state's indigenous people. Acorn harvesting, storing, and cooking methods varied, but nearly every tribe in California collected acorns each fall and held harvest ceremonies. Communities and territories were based, in many cases, upon the distribution of acorn-producing oak groves, and acorns remain a central symbol to many California tribes.

Twenty species of oak are found across a wide expanse of California, ranging from arid woodlands of the Mojave Desert to moist coniferous forests in the

Klamath Mountains. They grow at elevations from sea level to 9000 feet and occupy wildly diverse habitats; the result is oak forests, woodlands, and scrublands of varying structure, appearance, and species composition. Even within a species, considerable variation occurs as a result of extensive ecological tolerances. In addition, the tendency of oaks to hybridize adds to the challenge of identifying individual oaks.

California oaks range in size from 3-foot-high shrubs to stately 100-foot-tall trees. The foliage is equally varied from thick, rolled 1-inch-long leaves to lobed leaves 6 inches long. Leaf margins can be entire, serrated, or deeply lobed, and colors vary from deep green and olive to matte blue. Acorns come in an assortment of sizes and shapes as well, from fat and egg-shaped to thin and conical. Plated or deeply fissured, the bark can be light gray, whitish, brown, or almost black, with a smooth or corrugated texture. All oaks are wind pollinated, and some people are allergic to the spring pollen.

The oak-studded landscapes of California provide a rich and bountiful environment for wildlife. Bears and bushtits, scrub jays and salamanders, ants and alligator lizards are just a few of the many species that come to oaks for food and shelter. Some live their entire lives in a few trees, while others are transient or seasonal visitors, such as Townsend warblers. Some are obvious, like the ubiquitous scrub jay, while others, like the secretive arboreal salamander, are rarely encountered. The acorns and leaves of oaks are the nutritional foundation of oak-based ecological communities, but it is the physical structure and size of the shrubs and trees that create complexity and myriad opportunities for shelter.

All of the California species have landscape and garden applications, but few are commonly available in retail nurseries. The uses of oaks are limited only by our imagination, as there are species suitable to most garden needs, from bonsai subjects to spreading shade trees. Oaks also offer gardeners an opportunity to reconnect their landscape to regional oak woodlands and help to join fragmented ecosystems and wildlife corridors. Planted widely through suburban developments or urban neighborhoods, they can even define communities and bestow a coherent sense of place.

Thousands of insects are associated with oaks and form an essential part of complex oak ecosystems. Only a few are problematic; these pests usually attack a weakened or stressed tree, but left untreated, they can lead to the death of the tree. Large infestations of oak pit scale (*Asterolecanium* sp.), a small green scale, can overwhelm a mature tree, causing twiggy growth and a thinning canopy. Oil and soap sprays are effective if treatment is initiated at the outset of an infestation. Western oak bark beetle (*Pseudopithiphorus agrifoliae*)

Above: Engelmann oak, shown here growing as a specimen tree, has wildland populations that have been greatly reduced by development, Santa Barbara Botanic Garden. JOHN EVARTS *Left: Coast live oak acorn, private land, Ballard.* JOHN EVARTS

lays its eggs in the bark and twigs in spring and early summer. After hatching, the larvae tunnel just below the surface of the bark into the phloem, producing reddish frass and an oozing wound. They can quickly kill a tree if not controlled. Another pest, sycamore bark moth *(Ramosia resplendens),* has a black body and clear wings with yellow bands on the tips. It lays eggs on the lower trunks of usually older or drought-stressed trees, and its larvae tunnel below the bark, producing a reddish frass.

Above: Valley oak, mature specimen with lichen-draped branches, private ranchland, Santa Ynez Valley.
JOHN EVARTS
Left: Valley oak serves as a granary for acorn woodpeckers, private land, Ballard.
JOHN EVARTS

oozing lesions at the bottom of their trunks. Informed management of oaks in gardens and landscapes is usually sufficient to prevent the onset of these pathogens, but once a tree shows signs of infection, it is difficult to counter the progression of these diseases.

The fungus-like organism *Phytophthora ramorum* causes a disease that poses a severe threat to oaks in counties on or near the coast of northern and central California. Named "sudden oak death" (SOD) for its ability to bring about seemingly rapid mortality, this disease is responsible for the death of tens of thousands of trees. Coast live oak, black oak, Shreve oak, and tanbark oak all show susceptibility to SOD and exhibit similar symptoms when infected: a thick, reddish brown or black sap oozes from cracks in the trunk; leaves yellow, then turn brown; wood-boring beetles may attack the weakened tree; and small, dome-shaped fruiting bodies of the associated wood-decaying fungus *Hypoxylon thouarsianum* may emerge on the outside of the bark.

At this point there is no known preventative or cure for SOD, and its spread is likely facilitated by the fact that several native and exotic plant species are susceptible to, and act as hosts for, *Phytophthora ramorum*. Humans may also inadvertently serve as important vectors of the disease by transporting the pathogen in soil adhering to the soles of shoes or vehicle tires, or in firewood cut from dead or dying trees. The discovery of exotic plants infected with SOD in southern California nurseries has raised fears that the pathogen could spread to native plants in the southern part of the state. The pathogen's apparent preference for cooler temperatures and higher humidity, like those found in central and northern Californina, will hopefully keep it from spreading to southern California, where hotter and drier conditions prevail.

To keep oaks from becoming stressed and more susceptible to diseases, it is important to adhere to some precautionary horticultural practices and pay attention to how the trees grow. Although oak trees depend on a central taproot when young, they develop wide spreading roots that often extend beyond the area beneath a tree's canopy. When gardening in the vicinity of oaks, use plants that have cultural requirements similar to oaks and set them at least 6 to 10 feet away from the trunks. (See "Under Oaks Trees" on page 237 for recommendations.) Ample leaf litter should remain under the trees but not in the immediate trunk area. Also avoid changing the grade; burying the surface roots, mounding soil at the crown, and removing roots will often lead to the death of the tree. Trenching through the soil under the canopy area is equally damaging and, if necessary, should be done as far from the trunk as possible. Keep summer water to a minimum to prevent root rots.

Pruning of oaks is best accomplished in the dormant season—late summer and early fall for the evergreen species and winter for the deciduous types. Pruning should be minimal. Whether removing dead material or damaged limbs, controlling form, or opening the canopy, be sure only 15% of the tree's mass is removed at one time. Heavy pruning can create numerous problems and often results in deformed specimens with excessive growth in the remaining branches. Improperly pruned trees are susceptible to witches' brooms caused by powdery mildew.

Oak root fungus *(Armillaria mellea)* and crown rots *(Phytophthora* spp.) are serious pathogens affecting oaks. These organisms thrive in warm, moist conditions and are especially common in poorly drained soils. The symptoms of these pathogens are similar and include loss of vigor, leaf drop, chlorosis, twig dieback, and eventual death of the tree. There are some differences, however: trees with oak root fungus have amber-colored mushrooms at their base in winter; trees infected with crown rot produce dense clusters of sweetly scented,

Quercus agrifolia
COAST LIVE OAK

Plant Type: Evergreen tree.
Geographic Zones: All except high mountains and deserts.
Light: Sun to shade.
Soil: Adaptable.
Water: Drought tolerant to occasional.
Natural Habitat and Range: From coastal bluffs to mountain ridges in many plant communities below 5000 feet; Mendocino County south to northwestern Baja California, also Santa Cruz and Santa Rosa islands.

Coast live oak is the most popular and commonly grown of the California oaks. Primarily a coastal species, it seldom occurs farther than 50 miles from the ocean. A mature coast live oak may have a single or multi-branched trunk and massive, sprawling limbs that arch towards the ground. It forms a broad, billowing crown of dense foliage and attains 20 to 60 feet in height and width. The cupped, oval leaves are 1½ to 2 inches long with numerous small spiny teeth and a distinctly leathery texture. Fresh spring leaves, often flushed with a rosy tint, appear just as the oldest leaves are shed. The spring flowers are held in short chartreuse catkins that add a brief but graceful contrast to the dark green leaves. Its narrow acorns measure 1 to 2 inches long and ripen in less than one year. Mature trees can produce up to 500 pounds of nuts in a plentiful year.

A remarkably versatile landscape tree, coast live oak serves equally well as a shade or street tree, specimen, or pruned screen. This handsome and stately oak can be grown in most California gardens large enough to accommodate its broad spread. Coast live oak is one of the fastest growing of California's native oaks; under favorable conditions it can reach 40 feet high with an equal spread in just 20 years.

Top, right: Coast live oak, a younger tree with typical dense canopy, church landscape, Los Olivos. JOHN EVARTS
Bottom: Mature coast live oak shading a path and groundcover of Hearst ceanothus, private garden, Montecito. STEPHEN INGRAM

Gardening beneath the canopy of a mature coast live oak is challenging because an older tree has an aggressive root system and sheds copious quantities of leaves. Leaf drop under a large tree adds considerable debris to a garden and is especially heavy in spring. The leaf mulch that builds up beneath a coast live oak is a valuable resource that can be used in other parts of the garden; however, never remove the entire insulating layer of leaves from under a tree's canopy.

New growth that is distorted and covered with a downy white coating indicates the presence of powdery mildew. This fungal disease poses a problem in coastal gardens, especially when trees are forced into out-of-season growth by summer watering or heavy pruning. Infestations of California oak moth occur cyclically in coast live oaks of the central and southern portions of the state. These insects cause conspicuous defoliation of trees. Although a nuisance, their feeding rarely causes significant long-term damage to the trees.

Quercus douglasii
BLUE OAK

Plant Type: Deciduous tree.
Geographic Zones: All except high mountains and deserts.
Light: Sun.
Soil: Adaptable.
Water: Drought tolerant to occasional.
Natural Habitat and Range: Dry, interior foothills in woodlands and savannas below 3500 feet; Coast Ranges and Sierra Nevada.

Blue oak is a California endemic that grows primarily in the foothills and is the dominant tree in

Blue oak showing distinctive linear bark, U.C. Santa Barbara Sedgwick Reserve, Santa Ynez. JOHN EVARTS

a band of nearly continuous woodlands and savannas around the Central Valley. It tolerates thin, poorly developed soils, extended periods of hot summer temperatures, and annual precipitation as low as 12 to 15 inches. Blue oak's common companions in this demanding environment are foothill pine and California buckeye.

In favorable sites blue oak can reach up to 60 feet tall, but it typically grows as a 15- to 30-foot-high tree. The crooked branches and stems of mature trees have a gnarled, twisted grace that adds a picturesque quality to their rounded form. As its common name implies, blue oak's lobed 1- to 3-inch-long leaves are usually blue-green; they have a pale green underside and a wavy margin. In colder regions the leaves turn an attractive yellow-orange color in the fall. The oval-shaped acorns are up to 1½ inches long and mature in one year.

Considering blue oak's remarkable drought tolerance and its ability to grow in the poorest soils, it is surprising that this admirable tree has not found a home in more California gardens. Blue oak's exceptionally slow growth rate probably helps to explain its lack of popularity. But for gardeners with patience, this tenacious tree is a good choice to plant on dry, rocky slopes or in hot interior gardens.

Quercus durata
LEATHER OAK

Plant Type: Evergreen shrub.
Geographic Zones: All except high mountains and deserts.
Light: Sun.
Soil: Adaptable.
Water: Drought tolerant to occasional.
Natural Habitat and Range: Dry slopes and ridges primarily on serpentine soils in chaparral and woodlands below 6000 feet; northern Sierra Nevada foothills, Klamath and Coast ranges to Santa Barbara County with an outlying population in the San Gabriel Mountains.

In its native habitat leather oak is mostly restricted to serpentine soils. This California endemic forms intermittent colonies on nutrient-poor, almost toxic serpentine soils, where it often grows in the company of rare and unusual plants. Like many species that occur naturally on these soils, leather oak will perform well in most soils found in California gardens.

A rigid, intricately branched shrub, leather oak will attain a height of up to 10 feet. In many wild populations, it forms dense mounds and appears as if it has been pruned with regularity. Its leaves are curled or rolled and ¾ to 1 inch long, with toothed or smooth

Leather oak (lower right), Cuesta Ridge Botanical Area, Los Padres National Forest. JOHN EVARTS

margins. The olive or gray-green foliage has a dusty appearance that stems from the delicate white hairs that cover both leaf surfaces. Acorns are cylindrical, measure ½ to 1 inch long, and ripen in one year.

Leather oak is rarely bothered by diseases or pests and can be grown in more challenging garden sites with confidence. Slow growing and long-lived, it is effective as the foundation of a dry garden or pruned as a formal hedge. Leather oak is also useful in containers or rock gardens, particularly when pruned to accentuate its inherently sculptural form.

Quercus engelmannii
ENGELMANN OAK

Plant Type: Semi-evergreen tree.
Geographic Zones: All except high mountains and deserts.
Light: Sun.
Soil: Adaptable.
Water: Drought tolerant to occasional.
Natural Habitat and Range: Dry slopes, mesas, and valleys in woodlands and savannas mostly below 4000 feet; southeastern Los Angeles County to northwestern Baja California.

Engelmann oak is perhaps the most threatened of California's oaks because its restricted distribution corresponds with the most developed portions of southern California. Scattered populations are found along the base of the San Gabriel Mountains, with massive relict specimens located in suburban landscapes from

Engelmann oak's attractive foliage makes it a good landscape tree, private garden, Solvang. JOHN EVARTS

Pasadena to San Dimas. Most remaining stands occur in San Diego County.

Engelmann oak is an irregular tree to 40 feet tall with an open, spreading crown. The thick, leathery blue-green leaves are 1 to 3 inches long and can be flat or wavy with a smooth, toothless margin. In dry years the leaves begin to drop early, leaving trees with a modest canopy of foliage. In years with adequate winter rains or occasional summer water Engelmann oak will hold its foliage until the spring flush of new growth. The cylindrical, 1-inch-long acorns mature in one year, and the thick, deeply furrowed bark is separated into pale gray-brown plates.

Foliage color alone recommends Engelmann oak; the blue-green leaves work well in gray-themed gardens and complement Mediterranean shrubs like rosemary, rockrose, and lavender. The blue-green color is also suitable combined with Ray Hartman ceanothus, Leatherleaf coffeeberry, and the broad leaves of coast silk-tassel. The magnificent specimens found in Pasadena and San Marino clearly demonstrate Engelmann oak's tolerance of metropolitan conditions as well as its remarkable longevity. Diseases or pests seldom trouble Engelmann oak.

Quercus kelloggii
BLACK OAK

Plant Type: Deciduous tree.
Geographic Zones: All except deserts.
Light: Sun to partial shade.
Soil: Adaptable.
Water: Drought tolerant to occasional.
Natural Habitat and Range: Primarily foothills and mountains in woodlands and forests between 3000 and 8000 feet; from central Oregon to the Laguna Mountains in southern San Diego County, with some outlying populations.

Above: Black oak with Great Basin sagebrush (foreground), Inyo National Forest near Independence.
JOHN EVARTS
Left: Black oak foliage with fall color, Yosemite National Park.
J. R. HALLER

Black oak makes a good specimen tree in every season: spring heralds its colorful leafing-out; summer brings a mantle of glossy dark green leaves; autumn turns the foliage golden; and winter reveals its gnarled, dark silhouette. Black oak's common name is derived from the blackish, deeply plated bark, but it could just as easily be called "rose" or "crimson" oak after the color of its emerging spring leaves. Although this hue only lasts about two weeks, it adds to black oak's list of desirable attributes.

This graceful deciduous tree grows 35 to 80 feet tall and has an ascending habit and rounded crown. The leaves measure 2 to 6 inches long and are deeply lobed, with a soft bristle at the pointed tips. They turn orange-yellow or gold in the fall, and their colors are especially vivid in cold regions. The oblong acorns are 1 to 1½ inches long and mature 18 to 20 months after flowering.

Black oak is effective in many landscape applications; use it as a shade or street tree, position it as a specimen, or plant it in groves. Paired with the rich green of conifers, such as incense cedar or western red cedar, black oak's pink-rose spring leaves and yellow-orange fall foliage add subtle seasonal character to gardens large enough to accommodate multiple trees. Black oak's growth rate is slow until it becomes well established. It requires moisture-retentive soils and occasional summer water when grown in southern California. Diseases and pests rarely cause problems for black oak.

Quercus lobata
VALLEY OAK

Plant Type: Deciduous tree.
Geographic Zones: All except immediate coast, high mountains, and deserts.
Light: Sun.
Soil: Adaptable.
Water: Infrequent to occasional.
Natural Habitat and Range: Valleys, mesas, foothills, and riparian corridors in woodlands often below 2000 feet but up to 5500 feet; Coast Ranges, Central Valley, Sierra Nevada foothills to northern Los Angeles County, and Santa Cruz and Santa Catalina islands.

Valley oak, the elder statesman of California's oaks, possesses a quiet dignity derived from its size, longevity, and grace. Mature trees can reach a height of 100 feet, with massive trunks 6 to 7 feet in diameter. These impressive, elegant trees are survivors. They have faced droughts, fires, diseases, and pests, yet they persist, some reaching 400 to 600 years of age. Giants of the earth, they seem to govern the landscape.

While young trees have a straight, rigid form, older valley oaks develop a rounded, spreading crown with thick, twisted limbs that occasionally sweep to the ground. The deeply lobed 2- to 4-inch-long leaves are covered in downy hairs. Their upper surface is a dull green, and their underside is pale green. Acorns are conical, 1 to 2 inches long, and mature in one year.

Valley oak losing its leaves in late fall, private garden, Solvang. JOHN EVARTS

Established trees tend to produce a significant crop every other year. Older trees develop thick, deeply fissured, ash gray or dark brown bark with a checkered pattern.

Valley oak is at home in the heat of interior valleys, but it is an adaptable tree and will grow in a broad range of conditions. It prefers rich alluvial soils and a constant supply of ground water. Renowned botanist Willis Linn Jepson commented that valley oaks are a "sign of the richest soils." Under favorable conditions it grows rapidly and can achieve a height and spread of 40 feet in 25 years. Remarkably handsome, this deciduous tree is particularly effective as a shade tree; it casts an appealing high shade in summer and allows welcome light to penetrate throughout the winter months. It is generally pest and disease free, although oak pit scale (*Asterolecanium minus*) can reduce its growth and thin the canopy.

Quercus tomentella
ISLAND OAK

Plant Type: Evergreen tree.
Geographic Zones: All except high mountains and deserts.
Light: Sun.
Soil: Adaptable.
Water: Drought tolerant to occasional.
Natural Habitat and Range: Canyons and north-facing slopes in chaparral and woodlands below 2000 feet; on five of the Channel Islands and Guadalupe Island, Baja California.

Island oak is a classic relictual species. Fossil records provide evidence of past mainland populations, but now island oak is confined to the mesic, maritime conditions found in its island environment. This handsome

Island oak in a street planting, private garden, Solvang. JOHN EVARTS

evergreen tree and other island relicts, such as Santa Cruz Island ironwood, give us an intriguing glimpse at components of the state's prehistoric flora.

In sheltered sites in the wild, island oak has a broad, rounded crown and can reach 60 feet high. Along the coast, where it is exposed to salt-laden winds, it develops a smaller, twisted form. The thick, 2- to 6-inch-long leaves are elliptic and have prominent parallel veins and toothed margins. New leaves are covered with fine hairs; their silvered or lime green color presents a brief but interesting contrast to the dark glossy green older leaves. Oval acorns are 1 to 1½ inches long and mature about 18 months after pollination.

Island oak is a moderate-growing tree, suited to areas of coastal California where the environment is similar to its island habitat. Well-sited landscape trees can attain 40 feet in height and width within 20 years. Island oak's attractive form recommends it as a street, shade, or specimen tree. It is also effective used as a natural screen. Although it tolerates many soil conditions, island oak will grow more rapidly and attain a fuller size in deep, well-drained soils. It has few disease and pest problems.

Ranunculus californicus
CALIFORNIA BUTTERCUP
Buttercup Family (Ranunculaceae)

Plant Type: Deciduous herbaceous perennial.
Geographic Zones: All except deserts.
Light: Sun to partial shade.
Soil: Adaptable.
Water: Drought tolerant to occasional.
Natural Habitat and Range: Vernally moist sites in grasslands, coastal scrub, woodlands, and forests below 7000 feet; throughout California excluding deserts, and in southern Oregon and northwestern Baja California.

California buttercup blooming in early spring, Santa Rosa Plateau Ecological Reserve, Murrieta. BART O'BRIEN

One of our most widespread perennials, California buttercup is a welcome harbinger of spring. As early as February, these delicate beauties are lighting up the natural landscape in some parts of the state. California buttercup is easy to cultivate, but not easy to find in nurseries or at plant sales.

The bright green shoots of California buttercup appear shortly after the fall rains begin. This deciduous perennial starts to bloom in winter and keeps going well into spring. The rather wispy plant has a few, mainly basal, delphinium-like leaves, but most of its substance is carried on the slender and fragile 1- to 2-foot-tall flower stalks. These divide into wiry stems that bear several 1-inch-wide shiny yellow blossoms. Some flowers appear double due to a profusion of petals. California buttercup starts to shut down as the soil begins to dry out, but it leaves behind a few withered leaves and stems and lots of viable seed.

California buttercup makes a perfect filler, whether it is brightening up the shady understory of a coast live oak or dotting a grassy slope. In well-drained soil it may be able to withstand summer watering, but it is better to site it away from summer irrigation to avoid root rot. Wait to remove the flower stalks until after the seeds have dropped to ensure a new wave of seedlings the following autumn.

Use California buttercup liberally in meadows, woodland gardens, and perennial borders. Due to its sensitivity to summer watering, place California buttercup with other natives that demand similar dry conditions, such as woolly blue curls and most of our native bulbs. Or, if you use a drip irrigation system that allows you to control where moisture is emitted, you can mix in other plants, such as strawberries, alum roots, and irises, that will appreciate some extra summer water. This will create a composition that continues to please all summer long.

Rhamnus californica
COFFEEBERRY
Buckthorn Family (Rhamnaceae)

Plant Type: Evergreen shrub.
Geographic Zones: All except high mountains and deserts.
Light: Sun to shade.
Soil: Adaptable; well-drained preferred.
Water: Drought tolerant to occasional.
Natural Habitat and Range: Widespread in many plant communities below 7000 feet; from southwestern Oregon to southern California through the Klamath, Coast, western Transverse, and Peninsular ranges.

Coffeeberry is one of the most common evergreen shrubs encountered in coastal California. Its wide distribution in many plant communities helps explain why coffeeberry is so variable and can adapt to many garden conditions. In cooler, moister sites, coffeeberry's leaves tend to be larger and greener, while in warmer, drier areas, they are smaller with gray-green or olive-green

Coffeeberry with ripening fruits, private garden, Arroyo Grande. DAVID FROSS

coloration. This evergreen shrub's size and form are also habitat dependent; a coffeeberry growing as an understory plant is commonly open and sprawling or arborescent, while a plant found on an exposed coastal bluff or dry ridge usually has a dense, mounded structure.

Seasonal color changes augment coffeeberry's rich green foliage. The young stems are ruby-colored and the small spring flowers, which attract an array of pollinating insects, are yellow-green. The berries develop through a series of interesting colors—lime green, rose, and red—before turning burgundy-black in autumn. The ripe berries are attractive to small mammals and birds, especially mockingbirds. This often results in a generous distribution of garden seedlings.

Coffeeberry does not have showy flowers like its close relative ceanothus, but instead contributes to the garden with its reliable, functional character. It is particularly useful in transitional areas where the exposure can change from deep shade to full sun with the day or season. Pliant, it serves equally well as an informal hedge or screen, or it can be trained as a formal foundation shrub with occasional pruning or shearing. Coffeeberry combines effectively with toyon and native oaks to create a woodland theme; its foliage provides contrast to the sage-colored leaves of sandmat manzanita or the burgundy heads of purple three-awn.

Few diseases or pests trouble coffeeberry, although water molds can be a problem in heavy soils and branch dieback infects some populations. Beetles and weevils will occasionally scallop the leaves but seldom do serious damage. Healthy, established plants that become woody or too large for their location can be cut to the ground and allowed to crown sprout. Coffeeberry's fruit can litter and stain patios and concrete paths, so consider this shrub's occasionally heavy fruit production before siting it in the landscape.

Cultivars: 'Eve Case' is the best known and most commonly grown of the coffeeberry cultivars. It features broad leaves that are 3 inches long and 1 inch wide and round berries with a ½-inch diameter. A mature specimen can form a large, 8- to 10-foot-high dusky green mound, but you can control the size with selective pruning. Vigorous and fast growing in well-drained soils, it can be a challenging selection in heavy clay soils and outside of the marine influence. 'Leatherleaf' is a mounding shrub to 5 feet high and 6 feet across with black-green foliage. In full sun its leaves are 2 inches long; in shade they occasionally reach as much 6 inches long and 3 inches wide. The dark, almost brooding foliage of 'Leatherleaf' is a strong presence in the garden and is particularly useful as a contrast to gray-leaved plants like California sagebrush, purple sage, and Canyon Silver island snowflake. 'Mound San Bruno' features narrow light green leaves and a tightly

Top: *Eve Case coffeeberry hedge growing beneath coast live oaks, private garden, Montecito.* STEPHEN INGRAM
Bottom: *Leatherleaf coffeeberry has vivid, dark green foliage, private garden, Arroyo Grande.* DAVID FROSS

branched, mounding habit to 5 feet tall with an equal spread. Plants may grow larger in shade or against a wall, but still retain a dense character. 'Mound San Bruno' is a remarkably versatile and garden-tolerant coffeeberry selection.

Other Species: Redberry *(Rhamnus crocea)* is a more diminutive relative of coffeeberry that grows in dense thickets or scattered in coastal scrub, chaparral, and oak woodlands below 3000 feet from the North Coast Ranges to northwestern Baja California. The dark glossy green leaves are small, rounded, and held on stiff, almost spine-like stems. Inconspicuous yellow-green flowers appear in small clusters each spring, followed in summer by luminous red berries. The fruit is favored by birds, especially western blue birds, and seldom persists once it has ripened.

Redberry is a durable and adaptable shrub with an attractive, although irregular, habit. It grows slowly to 3 to 8 feet tall with a wider spread. Plants sited in full sun have a dense form, whereas plants in shade tend to be open and lax but retain a handsome character. Redberry is useful as a low screen or informal hedge and provides contrast when used with gray-leaved shrubs, such as purple sage or California sagebrush. It is a good choice for the habitat garden because the seasonal fruits provide food and the intricately branched form offers cover.

Rhododendron occidentale
WESTERN AZALEA
Heath Family (Ericaceae)

Plant Type: Deciduous shrub.
Geographic Zones: All except deserts.
Light: Sun to partial shade.
Soil: Adaptable; prefers acidic to neutral soils.
Water: Occasional to regular.
Natural Habitat and Range: Moist places and streambanks in many plant communities below 7500 feet; Cascade Range and the Sierra Nevada from Siskiyou to Kern counties; Klamath and Coast ranges from southwestern Oregon to San Benito and Monterey counties; Peninsular Ranges of California.

Western azalea growing in a decorative pot, private garden, Cupertino. STEPHEN INGRAM

Many gardeners associate rhododendrons with moist environments and are surprised to learn that the California flora contains not one, but two native *Rhododendron* species: western azalea and California rose-bay. Western azalea is the more garden tolerant of the two native species. It is also one of the most desirable plants in this incredibly diverse genus due to two special attributes: it blooms later than most rhododendrons, and unlike the majority of *Rhododendron* species and hybrids that have no fragrance, it is deliciously scented. For these reasons, western azalea continues to be a mainstay of a number of breeding programs.

The thin, lightly hairy leaves of western azalea are wider at the tip than at the base. They are deciduous in the winter months and may turn yellow before falling. The funnel-shaped flowers have long protruding stamens and are held in dense terminal clusters in spring. Typically, the flowers are pure white with a showy yellow-orange splotch on the uppermost petal, but pink-flowered forms also exist. This variable shrub may reach from 3 to 10 feet tall and will spread equally wide.

Western azalea can be fussy about its garden requirements, but it is well worth extra attention. This shrub prefers partial shade, but if it receives too much shade it will die quickly or produce few if any blooms. In excessive sunlight western azalea may flower heroically through spring but promptly burn and collapse during the summer months. It requires acid to neutral soils and will not tolerate alkaline or salty soils or water. To increase soil acidity, add acid organic matter such as peat moss or compost. Mildew often attacks the foliage in spring and early summer. Root weevils sometimes damage the plant; adult insects make scalloped cuts along the edges of the leaves, while juvenile grubs may girdle the roots.

Grow western azalea against a backdrop of conifers or other dark-foliaged evergreen plants, as these accentuate the azalea's flowers and foliage. It also makes a beautiful specimen in a glazed pot.

Cultivars: 'Irene Koster' is probably the most adaptable and satisfying selection. Plants freely produce compact terminal clusters of pale pink flowers that have yellow-orange flashes on their upper two petals. Especially fragrant blossoms emit a delightful spicy scent that is often detected some distance away from the plant.

Rhus integrifolia
LEMONADE BERRY

Rhus ovata
SUGAR BUSH
Sumac Family (Anacardiaceae)

Plant Type: Evergreen shrub or small tree.
Geographic Zones: All except high mountains and deserts.
Light: Sun to partial shade.
Soil: Adaptable.
Water: Drought tolerant to occasional.
Natural Habitat and Range: Lemonade berry: coastal bluffs, slopes, and canyons in coastal scrub and chaparral below 2500 feet; Santa Barbara County south to northwestern Baja California. Sugar bush: dry slopes, canyons, and foothills in chaparral below 4000 feet; Santa Barbara County to northwestern Baja California and inland to the western edge of the Colorado Desert, and Arizona.

Lemonade berry in a parking lot landscape, El Capitan State Beach, Goleta. JOHN EVARTS

Top: Sugar bush in full flower, private garden, Ballard.
JOHN EVARTS
Bottom: In winter, sugar bush displays its red bracts, private garden, Ballard. JOHN EVARTS

Lemonade berry and sugar bush are widely grown for good reason: these handsome shrubs are workhorses in the garden, fulfilling utilitarian functions and providing many years of reliable service. Gardeners in coastal areas can choose from either species, whereas those in hotter inland areas tend to favor sugar bush.

Lemonade berry and sugar bush are so closely related that they hybridize in the wild and in gardens. They both range in size from 4 to 20 feet tall and often wider. Their petioles and at times their young twigs are maroon, adding a subtle but welcome bit of color. These resinous, aromatic shrubs have thick leathery leaves that are dark green above and paler below. Those of lemonade berry are more or less flat and have entire or sharply toothed margins. The darker, egg-shaped leaves of sugar bush have entire margins, are often folded along the midrib, and are considered more attractive by many gardeners. The stout inflorescences are similar, but sugar bush has more reddish bracts that are quite prominent in winter against its deep green foliage. The white to pink flowers of both species bloom in late winter to spring. Of the two, lemonade berry has larger and stickier reddish fruits. Many animals consume the fruit, and some people harvest them and soak them in water to make a refreshing drink, from which the shrub takes its common name.

These versatile shrubs are incredibly adaptable in gardens. Although they thrive in full sun, they grow surprisingly well in dense shade. They respond well to pruning, with the frequency dictated by how you want them to function in your garden. Specimens that become sparse with age or too much shade will benefit from a late winter or spring pruning back to the crown; the coppiced plants will typically resprout with vigor. Gardeners are advised to wear long sleeves and gloves when pruning these shrubs, as their oils can cause a rash in some individuals.

Lemonade berry and sugar bush are ideal for screens and hedges. Taller, informal screens need little to no pruning. Both shrubs are utilized in slope plantings for erosion control, and both are effective as windbreaks or espaliered on fences or walls. You can shape them into single- or multiple-trunk specimens and allow them to serve as handsome patio trees or, in modest-sized gardens, as a substitute for coast live oak. Lemonade berry also tolerates salt-laden ocean winds and makes a fine, naturally sheared groundcover on coastal bluffs.

Branch dieback may occur in lemonade berry during excessively wet winters due to verticillium wilt; the effects of this fungal disease appear after the first hot days of spring. Otherwise, both species have few disease or pest problems and are long-lived. (A regularly sheared 4-foot-high by 3-foot-wide hedge of lemonade berry that was planted at the Santa Barbara Botanic Garden in the 1940s continues to thrive today.)

Other Species: Pink-flowering sumac *(Rhus lentii)* is an especially attractive shrub from the maritime deserts of central Baja California. It differs from its cousins in having bluish gray foliage and rich pink to cherry red flowers. The sticky, flattened fruits are larger than those of lemonade berry. Culture and use are the same as above. Basket bush *(Rhus trilobata)* is a deciduous, rhizomatous, many-branched shrub that closely resembles poison oak. Both share three-parted leaves, but basket bush has yellowish terminal flowers and red fruits, whereas poison oak has greenish white axillary flowers and white fruits. Basket bush is widespread in California and extends into Canada, the central United States, and northern Mexico. Varying from upright to sprawling in habit, it provides several months of color, from the sticky red fruits in summer to its multihued fall foliage of yellow, orange, and red. Use basket bush as a groundcover on slopes or along seasonally moist streambeds. Several Native American tribes coppice basket bush to promote growth of the long, unbranched shoots that they favor for basketry.

Ribes species
CURRANTS and GOOSEBERRIES
Gooseberry Family (Grossulariaceae)

Ribes is a variable genus of evergreen and deciduous shrubs. Species with spines are called gooseberries, while the unarmed types are known as currants. The California species range in size and form from the 12-foot-high erect, vase-shaped, pink-flowering currant to the 3- to 5-foot-tall arching, sprawling Catalina perfume. Many species have resinous leaves with a pleasant, although pungent, scent. Fruits can be glaucous or covered with dense, glandular bristles; their color varies from translucent yellow and orange-red to purple and black. The berries of a number of species are edible, fresh or dried.

Most of the California species of *Ribes* are adaptable, and the ones included here have proven garden tolerance across a broad range of conditions. Some will accept full sun, but most perform best in filtered or partial shade. Well-drained soils are recommended, but many will succeed in heavier soils that have at least moderate drainage.

Currants and gooseberries are an excellent choice for gardeners who want to attract birds. Their shrubby form provides avian shelter, and their small berries appeal to mockingbirds, cedar waxwings, and a variety of other fruit-eating species. *Ribes* are also important to resident hummingbirds because many have flowers that bloom in early winter and supply a critical nectar source that lasts well into spring.

Several California currant species have demonstrated a resistance to mildew and have been used in breeding programs designed to improve the mildew resistance of currants grown for commercial harvest. Some types of water molds can still pose a problem for native currants, especially when northern California species, such as red-flowering currant *(Ribes sanguineum* var. *sanguineum),* are used in interior portions of southern California. Well-drained soils and informed irrigation practices can prevent or moderate water mold damage. Spider mites and thrips occasionally trouble a number of species. Treat the thrips with horticultural soaps and oils, and remove the spider mites with a strong spray of water. Rust may infect some species. *Ribes* provide an alternate host to white pine blister rust *(Cronartium ribicola).* This introduced disease completes its life cycle on currants and gooseberries but spreads to pines, so be careful not to plant *Ribes* near susceptible pine species, such as singleleaf pinyon, western white pine, sugar pine, and other pines in the white pine subgenus.

Claremont currant flower clusters, private garden, Los Osos. KAREN MUSCHENETZ

Ribes aureum var. *gracillimum*
GOLDEN CURRANT

Plant Type: Deciduous shrub.
Geographic Zones: All except high mountains and deserts.
Light: Sun to partial shade.
Soil: Adaptable.
Water: Drought tolerant to occasional.
Natural Habitat and Range: Slopes and alluvial places in many plant communities below 2500 feet; South Coast Ranges south to western Riverside County.

Golden currant is a broad, sprawling shrub reaching as much as 10 feet tall. Clusters of yellow flowers form in midwinter and develop a reddish cast as they fade. Combined with the glossy green, 1- to 2-inch-wide leaves, they offer bright, early season color. The foliage of golden currant complements the dark greens of coast live oak, coffeeberry, and toyon; it also contrasts handsomely with the blue flowers of ceanothus. The translucent yellow-orange or black berries attract birds, and seedlings are common as a result.

Golden currant also spreads via layering stems and rhizomes, and unless pruned it tends to form rangy thickets. Fungal rust will develop on the leaves by early summer in most parts of California. Infected plants quickly lose their foliage, leaving behind a tangle of woody stems. Still, golden currant's vivid yellow flowers and fresh spring foliage compensate for the summer and fall dormancy. You can encourage flowering by siting golden currant in full sun.

Top: Golden currant espaliered against a building, California Flora Nursery, Fulton. PHILIP VAN SOELEN
Bottom: Golden currant berries in various stages of ripeness, Santa Barbara Botanic Garden. CAROL BORNSTEIN

Ribes malvaceum
CHAPARRAL CURRANT

Plant Type: Deciduous shrub.
Geographic Zones: All except high mountains and deserts.
Light: Sun to partial shade.
Soil: Adaptable.
Water: Drought tolerant to occasional.
Natural Habitat and Range: Dry slopes, canyons, and arroyos in coastal scrub, chaparral, and woodlands below 5000 feet; Channel Islands, Sierra Nevada foothills, San Francisco Bay Area, and Coast, Tranverse, and Peninsular ranges to northwestern Baja California.

Chaparral currant is a tough, reliable shrub from 4 to 10 feet high with an upright, slightly rounded to vase-shaped form. Multiple stems rise from the crown and hold 1- to 3-inch-wide leaves that have a viscid, rough surface and a pungent, resinous scent. Chaparral currant blooms early and often flowers from December through March. The pendulous flower clusters are 2 to 6 inches long and range in color from dusty pink to rose red. The berries have a waxy, powder-like coating on their blue-black surface.

Dancing Tassels currant, Rancho Santa Ana Botanic Garden, Claremont. BART O'BRIEN

The species is divided into two varieties, southern chaparral currant (*viridifolium*) and chaparral currant (*malvaceum*). Southern chaparral currant occurs naturally in the Santa Monica, San Jacinto, and Santa Ana mountains and southward, while chaparral currant grows in the wild from Tehama to Los Angeles counties and on the Channel Islands. Of the two, *viridifolium* is perhaps more attractive for garden use. It features larger, brighter-colored leaves and longer flower clusters.

Both varieties are drought tolerant. With age they may become woody, but their exfoliating bark adds compelling detail to their gnarled stems. Combine them with redberry, Pacific wax myrtle, and toyon to create an informal screen, or plant them as a backdrop to a perennial bed of hummingbird sage, alum roots, and irises.

Cultivars: 'Montara Rose' is the most commonly grown chaparral currant selection. It features an open habit and has upright stems growing to 6 feet high and short clusters of dark rose flowers. 'Dancing Tassels' can reach 8 feet in height and has 8- to 12-inch-long clusters of pale pink flowers. There are two cultivars of southern chaparral currant: 'Ortega Beauty' and 'Ortega Ruby'. Both grow 5 to 8 feet tall with an equal spread and produce 4- to 6-inch-long clusters of deep pink flowers.

Ribes sanguineum var. glutinosum
PINK-FLOWERING CURRANT

Plant Type: Deciduous shrub.
Geographic Zones: All except high mountains and deserts.
Light: Sun to shade.
Soil: Adaptable.
Water: Infrequent to moderate.
Natural Habitat and Range: Open slopes, chaparral, and moist woodlands below 2000 feet; Del Norte County through the Coast Ranges to Santa Barbara County and in Oregon.

The many selections of pink-flowering currant available attest to the popularity of this versatile shrub. Plants range in size from 5 to 12 feet high and are vase-shaped or rounded. The flowers are held in pendulous clusters 2 to 8 inches long and vary in color from silver pink to carmine red. The medium to dark green, maple-like leaves are 1½ to 3 inches wide and have lobed, irregularly toothed margins. The powdered, blue-black berries are edible, although the seeds are bitter, and to get a taste of this fruit you will have to compete with the birds.

Pink-flowering currant grows best in partial shade in all but coastal conditions, where it benefits from full sun. Supplemental irrigation is recommended to give this adaptable shrub a fuller, fresher appearance.

Spring Showers currant in full sun, Leaning Pine Arboretum, Cal Poly, San Luis Obispo. THOMAS ELTZROTH

Combine it with toyon, coffeeberry, and oaks in a woodland garden; plant it in the understory of California sycamore or alders; or mix it with hummingbird sage, western columbine, and western meadow rue. Its upright form makes pink-flowering currant a good choice to use in breezeways or along narrow corridors.

Cultivars: Among the many cultivars, two have proven particularly tolerant of the warmer and drier conditions of southern California: 'Claremont' grows to 8 feet and features pale pink flowers that darken as they age; 'Tranquillon Ridge' can reach 10 feet in height and has shorter flower clusters of rose pink. Others include 'Inverness White', which has large white flower clusters and an open form to 8 feet tall, and 'Spring Showers', which is a floriferous selection to 6 feet tall that produces light pink flowers in pendent, 8-inch-long clusters.

Ribes speciosum
FUCHSIA-FLOWERED GOOSEBERRY

Plant Type: Deciduous shrub.
Geographic Zones: All except high mountains and deserts.
Light: Sun to shade.
Soil: Adaptable.
Water: Drought tolerant to occasional.
Natural Habitat and Range: Coastal scrub, chaparral, and woodlands below 2500 feet; Santa Clara County to northwestern Baja California.

Fuchsia-flowered gooseberry at its best, California Flora Nursery, Fulton. PHILIP VAN SOELEN

Fuchsia-flowered gooseberry was one of the first California native plants to receive horticultural attention and yet, viewing a wild specimen in late summer or early fall, it would be fair to wonder why. During this dormant period, fuchsia-flowered gooseberry, which has three sharp spines at each node, appears to be little more than a gathering of thorns. It takes the onset of winter rains to initiate an abundance of new, apple green foliage. The leaves quickly cover the arching branches and develop a thick, leathery texture and a glossy upper surface. Lobed slightly and pale on the underside, they measure ¾ to 1½ inches long. The crimson flowers resemble fuchsia blossoms and give this plant its common name. They are held on drooping stalks that are partially hidden by the flush of leaves and often bloom before Christmas. Stamens are exerted far beyond the throat of the flowers, as if extending an invitation to the hummingbirds that are sure to seek out their nectar. Spiny fruits hang from the stems in early summer.

Due to its sharp spines and its period of summer dormancy, fuchsia-flowered gooseberry requires careful placement in the garden. You may want to keep it away from pathways, or you can turn its spines into an advantage by situating it as a barrier to discourage foot traffic. Combine it with evergreen species to minimize the effect of its summer dormancy. Fuchsia-flowered gooseberry makes an elegant companion to woodland species like California barberry, western meadow rue, and coast melic grass. It can also be used as a foil in a gray-themed garden with California sagebrush and Canyon Silver island snowflake. Train its arching stems to create a formal espalier against walls and fences, or consider planting fuchsia-flowered gooseberry on a hillside or slope where its graceful flowers can be viewed from below.

Diseases and pests seldom trouble fuchsia-flowered gooseberry, although rust can be a problem in humid gardens receiving regular summer water. Rust rarely persists in dry gardens, as the leaves are shed just as the rust begins to develop. It is best to allow the plant to go dormant in the summer; a plant receiving summer water tends to produce water-sprout-type growth.

Ribes viburnifolium
CATALINA PERFUME

Plant Type: Evergreen shrub.
Geographic Zones: All except high mountains and deserts.
Light: Partial sun to shade.
Soil: Adaptable.
Water: Drought tolerant to moderate.
Natural Habitat and Range: Shaded canyons and arroyos in coastal scrub, chaparral, and woodlands below 1000 feet; Santa Catalina Island and northwestern Baja California.

Catalina perfume is often the first plant mentioned in answer to the question, "What can I plant under my oaks?" A sprawling, evergreen groundcover, it can reach up to 5 feet high with support, but more typically the branches arch to 3 feet in height before bending back towards the ground. The leathery, ¾- to 1½-inch-wide glossy green leaves have an ovate to round shape and a spicy fragrance. Stems are equally fragrant and display a reddish color that provides a pleasing contrast to the dark coloring of the leaves. Individual maroon flowers are star-like and held in small clusters. The fruit is a ⅛-inch-wide red-orange to yellow berry but is seldom seen in gardens.

Catalina perfume has a long history of use in California gardens as a groundcover on sites with

Catalina perfume planted above a retaining wall, Santa Barbara Botanic Garden. JOHN EVARTS

filtered light or full shade. It is suitable for erosion control on dry slopes and as a manicured groundcover in the company of California sycamore and cottonwoods. Plants require some tip pruning to produce a dense cover, and older plants can be cut with a string trimmer to encourage fresh growth. Catalina perfume may take some time to get established, especially when it is planted in the understory of mature trees that present heavy root competition. Spider mites can cause problems for Catalina perfume in coastal gardens, but it is otherwise disease and pest free.

Romneya coulteri
MATILIJA POPPY
Poppy Family (Papaveraceae)

Plant Type: Semi-evergreen herbaceous perennial.
Geographic Zones: All except high mountains and deserts.
Light: Sun to partial shade.
Soil: Adaptable, except poorly drained.
Water: Drought tolerant to occasional.
Natural Habitat and Range: Chaparral below 4000 feet; Ventura County south to northwestern Baja California.

Though justly and thoroughly praised through the years as the queen of California's wildflowers, Matilija poppy is both finicky and aggressive in the garden. Getting it established is difficult; too much water causes root rot, whereas minimal water often results in terminal wilt. Once it gains a foothold, however, Matilija poppy's underground stems spread quickly in sandy, gravelly, or rocky soil and more slowly in heavy loam or clay soil. Do not even bother trying to contain this plant, as it always escapes. You may be forgiven when you curse the day that you invited Matilija poppy into your garden; but the plant's flowers and foliage are so beautiful that nearly everyone eventually succumbs to its charms.

In spring and summer, tall stems reaching 6 to 10 feet high carry expansive blooms that are the largest displayed by any California native plant. These 6- to 12-inch-wide flowers feature pure white, crepe-paper-like petals surrounding a crown of golden stamens. A heady fragrance of fresh apricots wafts from the blooms, but look before you sniff, as bees are frequent visitors. The clean, steely blue-gray leaves are deeply cut.

Matilija poppy's exuberant, unpredictable growth may make it unsuitable for small, tailored gardens, but it is very effective for erosion control. In a large garden, plant Matilija poppy along barely cultivated margins, on slopes, in dry areas, or beside parkways. Surround it with large shrubs that can withstand its ability to spread, such as sugar bush, Nevin barberry, ceanothus,

Above: White Cloud Matilija poppy with Margarita BOP penstemon at its base, Rancho Santa Ana Botanic Garden, Claremont.
BART O'BRIEN
Left: Matilija poppy flowers and buds, Leaning Pine Arboretum, Cal Poly, San Luis Obispo.
THOMAS ELTZROTH

fremontias, and manzanitas. From late fall to early winter, prior to the emergence of new lush foliage, cut the plant back to 3- to 4-inch-long stubs so it will look and bloom better. Gardeners are advised to wear gloves during this process as the stems and leaves have a few prickles.

Rosa californica
CALIFORNIA WILD ROSE
Rose Family (Rosaceae)

Plant Type: Deciduous shrub.
Geographic Zones: All except deserts.
Light: Sun to partial shade.
Soil: Adaptable.
Water: Drought tolerant to moderate.
Natural Habitat and Range: Along streambanks and in seasonally moist areas in many plant communities below 6000 feet; California Floristic Province.

Many gardeners are not aware that California has several native rose species. As a result, most California rose gardens fail to include specimens of our native

Above: California wild rose grown along a fence, Rancho Santa Ana Botanic Garden, Claremont.
CAROL BORNSTEIN
Left: Schoener's Nutkana rose, a Nootka rose hybrid, Rancho Santa Ana Botanic Garden, Claremont.
BART O'BRIEN

although rarely fatal. Aphids often attack tender new growth and flower buds, but are easily removed by insecticidal soaps or a strong jet of water. To rejuvenate them, prune native roses to the ground in late summer or fall.

Cultivars: The selection 'Plena' is delightful, although some botanists are skeptical of its relationship to California wild rose. In springtime the pink, completely double blossoms appear atop arching, cane-like stems. Plants may exceed 5 feet in height and form slowly spreading clumps.

Other Species: Wood rose (*Rosa gymnocarpa*) is most notable for its ability to thrive in the shade of California's coniferous and mixed-evergreen forests. Plants are typically 3 to 5 feet tall and have solitary, pale pink flowers in spring. Nootka rose (*Rosa nutkana*) has the largest showy pink flowers of any of our native roses. On warm days nearly year-round, glands on its leaves, sepals, and flower stalks release volatile oils that perfume the air for considerable distance with a pungent, spicy fragrance. Nootka rose requires some summer water for best performance. Baja littleleaf rose (*Rosa minutifolia*) commonly occurs in northwestern Baja California; it also existed in California until recently, when the last population in the state was extirpated. Baja littleleaf rose typically forms broad colonies of low, arching stems up to 2 to 4 feet in height. It is the earliest of the native roses to bloom; the deep to pale pink (rarely white) flowers appear in late winter. As its name suggests, this rose has the tiniest leaves in the entire genus.

roses, even though they require far less pampering than their Asian and European cousins. Among the native species, California wild rose is especially easy to grow.

California wild rose forms thickets that increase in size with age, to the point where it may require a root barrier. Stems range from very thorny to nearly smooth, and weeding among a jumble of spiny stems is quite difficult. Fragrant pink blossoms with five petals appear from spring to early summer. By fall, the flowers develop into small, decorative, ¼- to ½-inch-wide orange-red fruits known as rose hips.

California wild rose is an excellent choice for wildlife gardens where its thickets of 3- to 6-foot-tall stems provide cover for a variety of birds. This rose is also effective in barrier plantings and in hedgerows. Combine it with deciduous or evergreen plants, such as pink-flowering currant, western azalea, western mock orange, coffeeberry, giant chain fern, and Oregon grape.

California's native roses are subject to the same or similar disease and pest problems as their widely grown non-native cousins, yet they always thrive. From late winter through spring, they may have problems with rust and mildew that can be seriously disfiguring,

Salvia species
SAGES
Mint Family (Lamiaceae)

Sages belong to a large genus of roughly 900 species that encompasses plants with a wide diversity of sizes, shapes, and colors. California sages make up a mere 2%

Pozo Blue sage puts on a floriferous display, Rancho Santa Ana Botanic Garden, Claremont. BART O'BRIEN

Purple sage, close-up of whorls of bracts and flowers, Los Padres National Forest near Santa Barbara.
STEVE JUNAK

of this worldwide bounty; most of these natives are true shrubs, but two species are annuals and a few are sub-shrubs. The woody species are so different from other sages that, for years, botanists put them in their own genus, *Audibertia*. Several *Salvia* species cross-pollinate freely in the wild and in cultivation, yielding a number of enticing cultivars.

Our native sages, without exception, are plants of dry places. Some clothe entire hillsides, permeating the air with their aromatic oils. A few of the desert species are uncommon to rare and have exacting horticultural requirements; these are best appreciated in their natural setting or left to botanic gardens or serious collectors to cultivate. Most sages, however, are easy to grow, readily available in nurseries, and serve a multitude of functions in the garden.

The genus name *Salvia* is Latin for "to save," and sages are prized by many cultures for their culinary and medicinal value. The commercial variety sold for use in cooking is from a Mediterranean species, *Salvia officinalis*. Native American tribes make teas from sage leaves to help cure illness, and they traditionally toasted and ground the seeds to make a thin gruel.

The primary visual attraction of sages is their spectacular floral displays. The blossoms of native species range in color from white to pinkish purple, magenta, and numerous shades of blue. All are magnets for hummingbirds and bees. Beekeepers seek out apiary sites located near slopes covered with white, black, or purple sage in hopes of collecting a crop of the clear, mild-flavored honey produced from their nectar. The drying flowers bear copious seeds that are relished by goldfinches and quails, and the stiffly erect seed stalks of some species are lovely in dried flower arrangements.

Many sages are potentially long-lived plants that thrive on neglect. The recipe for cultivating them is straightforward: give them plenty of sun (exceptions noted below), reasonably well-drained soils, little to no supplemental water, and skip the fertilizer. Too rich a "diet" will result in excessive growth that causes woody species to fall apart; it also encourages aphid infestations and root rot. Most sages perform best with annual pruning, especially the larger shrubs. For these, remove up to one third of the plant in late summer or fall to retain youthful vigor and prevent splitting at the crown. (Note that older, never-pruned shrubs typically do not respond to a hard pruning.) The thinner branches on woody species are rather brittle; site plants carefully to avoid potential damage.

California's sages come in many shapes and sizes, from prostrate creepers to 6-foot-tall mounding shrubs. Every California garden should have at least one. Use them as groundcovers, for bank plantings, as accents or container specimens, massed in borders or raised beds, or for wildlife habitat.

Salvia apiana
WHITE SAGE

Plant Type: Evergreen shrub.
Geographic Zones: All except northern coastal and high mountains.
Light: Sun.
Soil: Adaptable; well-drained preferred.
Water: Drought tolerant to occasional.
Natural Habitat and Range: Dry slopes and flats in coastal scrub, chaparral, and some woodlands and forests below 4500 feet; western edges of the Colorado and Mojave deserts, Transverse and Peninsular ranges, and from Santa Barbara County to northwestern Baja California.

White sage has something for everyone. Gardeners treasure this strikingly handsome shrub for its bold foliage, dramatic floral display, and powerful scent.

White sage showing striking, silvery white foliage, private garden, Ballard. JOHN EVARTS

White sage flowers appear in loosely spaced spikes rather than in whorls, private garden, Ballard. JOHN EVARTS

Some California Indian tribes hold white sage sacred, burning the leaves as incense in purification ceremonies. Bees produce a delicate and flavorful honey from its flowers (*apios* means bee in Latin).

On average, white sage grows 2 to 3 feet tall and 3 to 6 feet across. In spring it sends up flower stalks that easily add another 2 to 6 feet in height. The occasionally lavender-tinged white flowers are clustered in interrupted spikes, rather than in the distinct whorls characteristic of our other sages. In some plants the stalks are pinkish to maroon, adding still more color. The broad, silvery white leaves are 3 to 4 inches long, and their scent is incredibly pungent, even overpowering to some.

An exceptionally drought-tolerant plant, white sage does not need summer water to improve its clean good looks. It makes an arresting focal point in a border and can be massed on slopes to help curb erosion. The white foliage is luminous in the early evening, especially on moonlit nights. Prune the flower stalks back to the most robust new buds to keep plants from becoming leggy and to avoid wind damage. Combine it with other sages, any number of buckwheats and penstemons, deep blue-flowered ceanothus, and California fuchsias. It is virtually pest free.

Salvia clevelandii
CLEVELAND SAGE

Plant Type: Semi-evergreen shrub.
Geographic Zones: All except northern coastal, high mountains, and high deserts.
Light: Sun.
Soil: Well-drained.
Water: Drought tolerant to occasional.
Natural Habitat and Range: Dry slopes in coastal scrub and chaparral below 3000 feet; Riverside County south to northwestern Baja California.

Sages are known for their fragrance, which varies from inconsequential in some species to overwhelmingly potent in others. Cleveland sage tops the list of many sage enthusiasts for having the sweetest "nose." Some gardeners use the foliage as a substitute for culinary sage. The rich violet-blue flowers, however, account for its enduring popularity.

In comparison to white, black, and purple sage, Cleveland sage is more refined in appearance. This 3- to 5-foot-tall, rounded shrub has ½ to 1½-inch-long sage green leaves. In late spring, the delicate-looking flower stalks begin to bloom, producing clusters of pale to vivid blue blossoms that dry to an attractive cocoa brown.

Gardeners in cooler areas of coastal northern California may have trouble growing Cleveland sage. To increase success, place it in the hottest, driest, fastest-draining site available. Even southern California gardeners should heed this advice. Use Cleveland sage as a focal point in a decorative pot or dry border, as an informal low hedge, or in an herb garden. The blue flowers combine favorably with both warm and cool colors. For a lovely composition, try planting Cleveland sage in front of island bush poppy and behind red-flowered buckwheat, foothill or royal penstemon, and groundcover manzanitas.

Cleveland sage grown in a private garden, Cupertino.
STEPHEN INGRAM

Cultivars: 'Winifred Gilman' is an outstanding selection; its deep violet-colored flowers emerge from ruby bracts spaced along dark maroon stems. 'Betsy Clebsch' has an unpredictable array of blue, white, and bicolored flowers held separately or in the same whorl. This temperamental cultivar does well in containers, where its whimsical flowers can be viewed up close.

Salvia leucophylla
PURPLE SAGE

Plant Type: Semi-evergreen shrub.
Geographic Zones: All except high mountains and deserts.
Light: Sun.
Soil: Adaptable.
Water: Drought tolerant to occasional.
Natural Habitat and Range: Common on dry, open hills and slopes in coastal scrub and chaparral below 2000 feet; Monterey County south to northwestern Baja California.

Purple sage is one of the easiest native sages to grow. Despite its misleading common name, this whitish gray shrub produces copious 6- to 10-inch-long spikes of light to rosy pink flowers in spring. After petal drop, whorls of bracts persist, adding a stiff, decorative element that small birds love to perch on. The juxtaposition of these charcoal gray bracts with the foliage below is reason enough to plant purple sage.

This semi-evergreen shrub is quite variable in shape, size, and flower color. Upright forms typically grow 4 to 7 feet tall and are equally wide; shrubs in some coastal populations top out at 3 feet and may spread 10 to 15 feet across, their stems occasionally rooting where they touch the ground. Purple sage produces two sets of leaves. The lush, new, apple green spring leaves are 1 to 3 inches long and somewhat bumpy. They are eventually replaced by smaller, silvery white foliage as the weather heats up.

Purple sage borders a path in a native plant landscape, private garden, Berkeley. SAXON HOLT

Purple sage covers sunny, steep slopes in the wild, and it makes an excellent plant for erosion control. It is equally useful on level ground; the low-growing cultivars are particularly effective when planted in masses. Taller forms can serve as a backdrop in mixed borders or as solo specimens in large pots. The foliage and flowers of purple sage blend well with almost any other color. Try it with western redbud, blue-eyed grass, golden yarrow, California aster, ceanothus, and the darker green manzanitas. Lightly prune this long-lived species after it flowers to maintain vigor and a pleasing form.

Cultivars: Purple sage hybridizes freely with black, white, and Cleveland sage. Hybrids with Cleveland sage are described on page 177. Listed here are selections of purple sage, all from the wild in Santa Barbara County. 'Point Sal' (note that plants sold under this name are variable) and 'Point Sal Spreader' are two selections from coastal bluffs in the northern part of the county. Both grow as low mounds and produce pale pink flowers. 'Amethyst Bluff', another selection from this same locale, reaches 3 to 5 feet tall and can spread well over 10 feet wide. Its dark rosy pink flowers are held on mauve-tinged stems.

Salvia spathacea
HUMMINGBIRD SAGE

Plant Type: Semi-evergreen herbaceous perennial.
Geographic Zones: All except high mountains and deserts.
Light: Sun to partial shade.
Soil: Adaptable.
Water: Drought tolerant to occasional.
Natural Habitat and Range: Shady or open grassy slopes in coastal scrub, chaparral, and woodlands below 2500 feet; Solano County south through the Coast Ranges to Orange County.

Hummingbird sage is one of the few herbaceous groundcovers that grows well in dry shade. It is easy to cultivate and has fabulous flowers and an intensely fruity fragrance. This first-rate sage satisfies on all counts and truly lives up to its common name by attracting hummingbirds to your garden.

The only red-flowered native sage, hummingbird sage begins to bloom in late winter and continues into summer. Its pagoda-like stalks, typically 1 to 3 feet tall, are punctuated with several dense whorls bearing showy dark maroon or ruby red bracts. The bracts offset the 1- to 1½-inch-long magenta to salmon (rarely pale yellow) flowers. The drying, dark brown stalks provide conspicuous vertical accents.

Hummingbird sage is a reliable groundcover. It spreads slowly by rhizomes, carpeting the soil with its

Hummingbird sage with tiered whorls of showy bracts and flowers, Santa Barbara Botanic Garden. JOHN EVARTS

3- to 8-inch-long, slightly wavy leaves. It does particularly well in the shady understory of oak trees. Rarely does it get out of bounds, and if it does, its rhizomes are easy to dig up and harvest for starting a new colony. The best time for this task is late fall or winter. Soft, sticky hairs that cover the entire plant are bothersome when performing maintenance chores, but deadheading is still advisable. Cut the spent flower stalks to the ground when they are no longer attractive to avoid leggy stalks that might flop over in the following year. Hummingbird sage looks good in a decorative pot and mixes well with plants that won't be smothered by its large leaves, such as coarse or dense bunchgrasses, vigorous irises, manzanitas, and coffeeberries.

Insects and diseases are a minor concern. Plants occasionally get a mild case of powdery mildew that usually clears up quickly, especially if plants are cut back to the ground and diseased foliage is removed. You may be disappointed if you wish to collect seed, as an insect often gets there first, eating right through each seed.

Cultivars: A few selections have been made, but 'Powerline Pink' is the most distinctive. This robust clone grows

well in full, hot sun, even inland. Its flowers, which are actually crimson red, are borne on 4- to 5-foot-long stalks.

Other sage species: Three closely related species of sage are worth noting. Black sage *(Salvia mellifera)* is California's most common sage, occurring in coastal scrub and chaparral plant communities from the San Francisco Bay Area south into northwestern Baja California. Although it is an important bee plant in the wild, it is not as popular with gardeners as other sages, perhaps because its unremarkable green foliage and pale blue to white flowers are eclipsed by other species. A few low-growing selections are useful groundcovers, even in part shade. 'Terra Seca' is roughly 2 feet tall by 8 or more feet wide. Brandegee sage *(Salvia brandegeei)*, in contrast to the wide-ranging black sage, is restricted to Santa Rosa Island and a few coastal locations in northwestern Baja California. Its shiny upper leaf surface has an appealing, pebbled texture and the underside is a felted white; otherwise Brandegee sage is superficially similar to black sage. Munz sage *(Salvia munzii)* resembles a diminutive version of black sage, rarely exceeding 4 feet in height and width. Its smaller leaves are ashy green and its petite flowers are pale to deep blue. Munz sage occurs from San Diego County to northwestern Baja California. A selection of Munz sage called 'Emerald Cascade' forms mounds 2 to 3 feet tall and 3 to 5 feet wide; its arching branches make this selection ideal for spilling over boulders in a rock garden. Some gardeners, however, consider 'Emerald Cascade' temperamental, possibly due to its sensitivity to cold temperatures.

Other Cultivars: Of the many hybrids between Cleveland and purple sage introduced over the years, 'Allen Chickering' is still the most popular. Others include 'Whirly Blue', 'Aromas', and 'Pozo Blue'. All have the robust character of purple sage and the

Mrs. Beard sage is a reliable, low-growing sage, Rancho Santa Ana Botanic Garden, Claremont. BART O'BRIEN

A hybrid sage in full flower, private garden, Ballard.
JOHN EVARTS

Above: *Western elderberry in an entry garden of California natives, private garden, Oakland.*
SAXON HOLT
Left: *Western elderberry covered with flower umbels, private garden, Ballard.*
JOHN EVARTS

bright blue-purple flowers of Cleveland sage. Prune these rapid-growing, brittle shrubs fairly hard in early fall to create a more compact habit and to promote increased flowering. 'Bee's Bliss' is an outstanding light gray groundcover with lovely periwinkle blue flowers on 1-foot-long stalks. This hybrid reaches 1 to 2 feet tall and spreads quickly to 8 feet wide. It is subject to powdery mildew during cool weather, but the mildew disappears as temperatures heat up. 'Dara's Choice' and 'Mrs. Beard' are hybrids of creeping sage *(Salvia sonomensis)* and black sage that are available in nurseries. 'Dara's Choice' grows quite well in partial shade. It has glaucous green leaves, a loosely mounded form, and is topped with dark blue flowers held on congested spikes. This 2-foot-tall by 3- to 6-foot-wide cultivar is susceptible to verticillium wilt. Plant it on a slope in well-drained soil to ward off this potentially lethal disease. 'Mrs. Beard' has masses of pale blue flowers and a similar form, and it is more reliable than 'Dara's Choice'.

Sambucus mexicana
WESTERN ELDERBERRY
Honeysuckle Family (Caprifoliaceae)

Plant Type: Deciduous shrub or small tree.
Geographic Zones: All except deserts.
Light: Sun to partial shade.
Soil: Adaptable.
Water: Drought tolerant to moderate.
Natural Habitat and Range: Widespread in many plant communities below 10,000 feet; California to British Columbia, Utah, New Mexico, and northwestern Baja California.

Western elderberry is often planted for its wildlife value, but it also offers considerable ornamental appeal.

The expanding, bright green leaves are a promising sight in late winter, and the clouds of flowers at the branch tips are quite showy in spring. In summer, the glossy fruits attract an incredible number of birds, including flickers, flycatchers, grosbeaks, nuthatches, orioles, tanagers, and warblers.

Western elderberry is typically multi-trunked and grows 8 to 25 feet tall with an equally broad spread. The handsome ochre-brown bark of older specimens is lined with silvery gray streaks, and the coarse, pinnately compound leaves consist of three to nine leaflets. The flat-topped, 2- to 8-inch-wide inflorescences contain hundreds of creamy white flowers, which are rarely without a swirl of bees and other pollinators. Its purple-black berries have a whitish coating that imparts a bluish cast. These fruits are used in jams, pies, and wine-making, but most other parts of the plant are poisonous.

Some western elderberries develop into single-trunked trees on their own. To retain this form, simply remove the occasional wayward stems that sprout. Arborescent specimens show off western elderberry's handsome bark and allow room for planting beneath their boughs with colorful perennials, such as western columbine, hummingbird sage, irises, coral bells, and fine-textured bunchgrasses or sedges.

Western elderberry is easy to grow and accepts a wide range of cultural situations. Although plants look more luxuriant and hold their leaves longer with periodic summer water, they do not need it except in hot inland locations. Flowering and berry production is more abundant when plants are grown in full sun. Aphids occasionally target the new leaves, but they can be rinsed off with a strong stream of water.

Other Species: Red elderberry (*Sambucus racemosa*) is primarily a coastal species from northern California that needs regular moisture. Birds relish its showy scarlet berries.

Satureja douglasii
YERBA BUENA
Mint Family (Lamiaceae)

Plant Type: Evergreen herbaceous perennial.
Geographic Zones: All except high mountains and deserts.
Light: Partial shade to shade.
Soil: Adaptable; well-drained preferred.
Water: Infrequent to moderate.
Natural Habitat and Range: Slopes and flats in many plant communities to 3000 feet; British Columbia south to Los Angeles County.

The fresh minty fragrance of yerba buena stands out, even in a native flora filled with scented foliage. Native Americans in California have long used a tea made from its leaves to reduce fever, cure colds and insomnia, and to settle the stomach. Yerba buena is still found today in teas and potpourris. The abundance of the plant in San Francisco gave the city its original name, Yerba Buena, which means "good herb" or "good mint" in Spanish.

This prostrate, trailing herb has heart-shaped, pale to medium green leaves that are ½ to 1 inch long. Its tiny white flowers appear in late spring and early summer. Well-established plants root at the nodes and form dense mats of foliage; less vigorous plantings spread erratically. Yerba buena benefits from pinching to encourage branching.

Use this versatile plant as a component of a small-

Yerba buena extends its prostrate, trailing stems across a boulder, Santa Barbara Botanic Garden. STEPHEN INGRAM

scale mixed groundcover or border combined with elegant coral bells. Plant it in shaded crevices in rock walls and steps, between widely spaced stepping stones, at the foot of chaparral plantings, or in an entry garden where its scent may be carried into the home on shoes and clothing.

Unfortunately, yerba buena is often unpredictable in gardens. Plants yellow and die when grown in heavy, poorly drained soils or when planted in excessive shade. If faced with these conditions, try growing yerba buena in a large container with a taller companion and allow it to spill over the edge, or place it alone in a hanging basket.

Other Species: Monkeyflower savory (*Satureja mimuloides*) is strikingly different from yerba buena. It is an erect herbaceous perennial to 3 feet tall with a wider spread. This hummingbird-pollinated plant carries clusters of tubular, inch-long burnt-orange flowers from late spring to early summer. It favors streamside or springy sites in the wild and needs summer irrigation in gardens. Plants should be cut back hard in the late fall or early winter; they quickly resprout from slowly spreading rhizomes.

Sequoia sempervirens
COAST REDWOOD
Bald Cypress Family (Taxodiaceae)

Plant Type: Evergreen tree.
Geographic Zones: All except high mountains and deserts.
Light: Sun to partial shade.
Soil: Adaptable; moisture-retentive preferred.
Water: Occasional to regular.
Natural Habitat and Range: Fog-dominated canyons, slopes, and alluvial flats in mixed-evergreen and coniferous forests to 3200 feet; coastal southwestern Oregon to San Luis Obispo County.

Coast redwood with new growth on branch tips, Myers Flat, Humboldt Redwoods State Park. JOHN EVARTS

Above: Coast redwood in a planting with dogwood (left) and Pacific wax myrtle (foreground), private garden, Hillsborough. STEPHEN INGRAM

Left: A mature coast redwood towers over this private garden, Woodside. BART O'BRIEN

Coast redwood is the world's tallest tree and the state tree of California. Planted in gardens from Redding to San Diego, coast redwood elicits alluring images of silent, towering forests and fog-shrouded glades. Products from the redwood timber industry permeate our lives: redwood timber is found in houses, fences, and decks across the state; many nurseries use redwood shavings as the foundation of their growing media; and new landscapes are commonly finished with a blanket of fresh redwood mulch.

Coast redwood is capable of living hundreds of years—the oldest recorded specimens were over 2200 years old—and reaching heights in excess of 300 feet. In landscape plantings coast redwood commonly grows 70 to 100 feet high; outside of its native range it is usually considerably shorter. Coast redwood's massive columnar trunk is clothed with thick, furrowed, gray to reddish brown bark. Its narrow crown supports horizontal or weeping branches with flat sprays of foliage. The broad lower branches typically spread 20 to 30 feet wide. The sharp-pointed, ½- to 1-inch-long leaves are linear (although some are awl-like) with a shiny green, blue-green, or gray surface and a blue-green underside. In winter, egg-shaped cones form singly or in small clusters at the ends of stems; they turn a decorative chocolate brown color and measure up to 1 inch long by the time they mature in autumn.

In cultivation, coast redwood is surprisingly flexible and can lend a rich, sylvan character to the garden. Use it in groves, as a specimen or large screen, or, with regular shearing, prune it into a hedge. Redwood sorrel, woodland strawberry, giant chain fern, and wild ginger grow well in the deep shade that coast redwood provides. For an especially verdant combination, add shrubs such as coffeeberry, bush anemone, Pacific wax myrtle, and pink-flowering currant.

Coast redwood responds favorably to the frequent watering regime common to many urban landscapes and performs well in or near a lawn. It will require regular water to sustain a healthy appearance when planted in warmer, drier interior sites. Stressed trees will yellow and burn in areas with dry winds, poor water quality, alkaline soils, or low humidity. Scale insects are occasionally found on trees and can give specimens a brownish, unhealthy appearance. Treatment with horticultural oils or soaps will usually remedy the problem.

Cultivars: Natural variability has produced several distinct and handsome coast redwoods that have been reproduced clonally. These two clonal selections were made primarily for foliage color and growth habit: 'Aptos Blue' has blue-green foliage and horizontal branches with weeping branchlets; 'Soquel' is a fine-textured tree with dark, royal green leaves that have a blue-gray underside. It has a compact, symmetrical habit with horizontal to upswept branches and upturned tips.

Sidalcea malviflora
CHECKERBLOOM
Mallow Family (Malvaceae)

Plant Type: Deciduous to evergreen herbaceous perennial.
Geographic Zones: All except deserts.
Light: Sun to partial shade.
Soil: Adaptable.
Water: Drought tolerant to moderate.
Natural Habitat and Range: Dry slopes in coastal scrub, grasslands, and woodlands below 7000 feet; California Floristic Province.

Checkerbloom with hollyhock-like flowers, Leaning Pine Arboretum, Cal Poly, San Luis Obispo. THOMAS ELTZROTH

Checkerbloom is a remarkably variable species found throughout most of California. Horticulturists have taken advantage of this bountiful variation by making a number of outstanding—although unnamed—selections for gardens.

Plants can be prostrate and spreading or stiffly upright to 6 to 24 inches high with a thickened base. Checkerbloom's dark olive to blue-green leaves are often hairy, yet can be glossy or dull. The generally lobed or divided leaves differ in size along the stems, with the basal leaves usually growing larger. The spring-blooming, ½- to 1½-inch-wide flowers resemble small hollyhocks and range in color from silver pink to dark rose, commonly with white veins.

The prostrate forms of checkerbloom are particularly useful at the front of a mixed perennial border or lining the edge of a walkway. Combine them with dune sedge, seaside daisy, and blue-eyed grass as part of a meadow you can mow, or weave them into a bed of beach or woodland strawberry to create a small-scale turf substitute. Checkerbloom is reliable and generally free of diseases and pests. Trim it after flowering or as needed for a fresh appearance. Away from the coast, most forms are deciduous through late summer and early fall.

Other Species: Point Reyes checkerbloom (*Sidalcea calycosa* ssp. *rhizomata*) is a groundcover from moist marshy areas near the coast. Useful for its low form and vigorous nature, it is recommended for moist sites or poorly drained soils. Try planting it with dune sedge and wire grass. Oregon checkerbloom (*Sidalcea oregana*) is an upright to prostrate species that typically has small pink to rose flowers. It fares best in northern California gardens and is effective when mixed with grasses, such as Cape Mendocino reedgrass, or as part of a meadow planting.

Simmondsia chinensis
JOJOBA
Jojoba Family (Simmondsiaceae)

Plant Type: Evergreen shrub.
Geographic Zones: All except northern coastal, high mountains, and high deserts.
Light: Sun.
Soil: Well-drained.
Water: Drought tolerant to occasional.
Natural Habitat and Range: Arid slopes in coastal scrub, chaparral, and deserts below 5000 feet; Riverside and San Diego counties through the Sonoran Desert to Arizona and northern Mexico, and on San Clemente Island.

Jojoba (center) planted with other desert species, Tohono Chul Park, Tucson, Arizona. STEPHEN INGRAM

For the conservation-minded gardener, planting jojoba has a special significance. The rich oil derived from the jojoba fruit makes its way into an amazing variety of products—from shampoos to auto lubricants—and substitutes for the high quality oil that was once harvested from sperm whales. This cultivated crop of arid regions of the Southwest also has lesser-known ornamental value for the designed landscape.

Jojoba is the only species in the entire jojoba plant family. This rounded, stiffly branching shrub grows slowly to 3 to 10 feet tall and usually broader. Its thickened, dull green leaves are often bluish or gray-green. Lester Rowntree, an early proponent of California native plants, described the leaves whimsically: "Besides listening goats' ears—or listening fawns' or rabbits' ears—the leaves have always reminded me of some mistletoe leaves."

Male and female flowers develop on separate plants. To produce the 1-inch-long nutlike fruits, you need to grow both male and female plants. The bright green fruit follows insignificant flowers and ages to brown. These edible "nuts" can be roasted and ground into a coffee substitute and are important forage for wildlife.

Jojoba grows naturally in sandy or gravelly soils in warm, dry, sunny situations. Replicate these conditions for best results in the garden. This undemanding shrub needs minimal maintenance and has no pest problems of consequence. Plants grow faster and look better with modest supplemental irrigation. Jojoba makes an unassuming windbreak or hedge, with or without shearing, and is tough enough to use along freeways. Older plants can be coppiced. It is a pleasing foil for spiky or spiny succulents and desert annuals.

Sisyrinchium bellum
BLUE-EYED GRASS
Iris Family (Iridaceae)

Plant Type: Semi-evergreen to deciduous herbaceous perennial.
Geographic Zones: All except high mountains and deserts.
Light: Sun to partial shade.
Soil: Adaptable.
Water: Infrequent to moderate.
Natural Habitat and Range: Widespread in many plant communities below 6000 feet; throughout California to Oregon and northwestern Baja California.

Whether bordering a small perennial bed or massed on a grassy slope, blue-eyed grass will brighten any garden with its festive flowers and fresh green to blue-green leaves. The common name comes from its thick, flattened, grass-like foliage, and many people mistake this iris relative for a grass, especially when it is not in bloom.

Above: Golden-eyed grass borders a curving path, private garden, Santa Barbara.
CAROL BORNSTEIN
Left: Blue-eyed grass, Rancho Santa Ana Botanic Garden, Claremont.
STEPHEN INGRAM

The leaf blades rise from a basal fan and grow 4 to 12 inches high. The ephemeral, six-petaled flowers form on branched stems in spring and range in color from pure white to violet blue. The petals are tinged with yellow at their base and surround a central cluster of yellow stamens. The bead-like, dark brown fruits form in late spring or summer and later release copious amounts of seed, which enables blue-eyed grass to naturalize freely in many gardens.

Blue-eyed grass is a good choice for sites with heavier soils. It is useful in meadow and grassland gardens as well as mixed borders. For an attractive meadow planting, try combining it with seaside daisy, coast melic grass, and Cape Mendocino reedgrass, or for simplicity, use it with nothing more than dune sedge. You can also place it in containers mixed with annual wildflowers or mass it with purple needlegrass and checker-bloom in a broad, informal border. Blue-eyed grass colonizes easily and will fill in spaces between shrubs and other perennials.

Blue-eyed grass is completely summer dormant in dry gardens, although dormancy can be delayed with summer irrigation and is not as pronounced in coastal gardens. For a tidier appearance cut plants to the ground to remove dried summer foliage. Blue-eyed grass is disease and pest free.

Cultivars: A number of interesting selections have been made from blue-eyed grass but most are short-lived in gardens. 'Californian Skies' is a robust selection to 12 inches tall with large, sky blue flowers. 'Rocky Point' is a diminutive selection to 8 inches high with broad-bladed leaves and large purple-blue flowers. 'San Simeon' (often incorrectly sold as *S. macounii* 'Album') is a Lester Rowntree selection with bright white flowers and a yellow center. Free flowering, it grows to 4 inches high and produces young plantlets at the ends of the stems.

Other Species: *Sisyrinchium californicum,* golden-eyed grass, is found in moist coastal areas below 2000 feet from Monterey County to British Columbia. Growing 6 inches to 2 feet tall, it has chalky green leaves and bright yellow spring flowers. It is an excellent choice for sun or partial shade in wet, poorly drained areas or regularly watered gardens. In moist environments it will reseed freely.

Solanum parishii, Solanum umbelliferum,
Solanum xanti
BLUE WITCHES
Nightshade Family (Solanaceae)

Plant Type: Deciduous subshrub.
Geographic Zones: All except high mountains and deserts.
Light: Sun to partial shade.
Soil: Adaptable.
Water: Drought tolerant to moderate.
Natural Habitat and Range: These species occur in many plant communities to 5000 feet; primarily in the California Floristic Province and Arizona.

Three species in the nightshade family share the same common name—blue witch. Some people consider them to be perennials, others think of them as shrubs. Not only are they hard to categorize, they are difficult to tell apart. From a gardener's perspective,

they are interchangeable; all are good choices for use in containers, rock gardens, and dry sunny borders or for filling in nooks and crannies among sun-loving shrubs.

Members of this trio of blue witches have green stems and leaves that may appear gray due to a covering of soft, short hairs. They bloom over long time periods—sometimes throughout the year—and display showy blue, purple, or lavender (rarely white) flowers. The

Blue witch flower close-up, Cuesta Ridge Botanical Area, Los Padres National Forest.
STEPHEN INGRAM

blossoms are round in outline, about an inch across, and composed of five fused petals. Small tomato-like fruits are produced abundantly and mature to a greenish white or dark green. Be careful, especially if children have access to your garden; all parts of this plant, notably the fruits, are poisonous.

Blue witches thrive in containers, but for inexplicable reasons they are often difficult to establish in gardens. Sadly, even if you plant several, few are likely to thrive. In favorable conditions where the plants take hold, they spread by underground runners but are never invasive. Plants are often summer dormant and show twiggy, leafless stems from summer to fall. Shrubby monkeyflowers, buckwheats, sages, and California fuchsias are excellent garden companions for blue witches. Flea beetles are known to skeletonize the leaves, but otherwise blue witches have no significant pests or diseases.

Cultivars: A number of floriferous, compact-growing selections are available. Indians Grey blue witch (*Solanum umbelliferum* var. *incanum* 'Indians Grey') has gray stems and foliage and pale lavender flowers. Navajo Creek blue witch (*Solanum xanti* 'Navajo Creek') has dark purple flowers and crinkly, dark green leaves. Purple Haze blue witch (*Solanum parishii* 'Purple Haze') has narrow, wavy-edged foliage and purple flowers. Salmon Creek blue witch (*Solanum xanti* 'Salmon Creek') is notable for its dark violet-blue flowers and dark green leaves and stems. Spring Frost blue witch (*Solanum umbelliferum* var. *incanum* 'Spring Frost') has white flowers and gray stems and leaves.

Solidago californica
CALIFORNIA GOLDENROD
Sunflower Family (Asteraceae)

Plant Type: Semi-evergreen herbaceous perennial.
Geographic Zones: All.
Light: Sun to partial shade.
Soil: Adaptable.
Water: Drought tolerant to moderate.
Natural Habitat and Range: Dry or moist sites in clearings or woodland margins in many plant communities below 7000 feet; California Floristic Province and Modoc Plateau.

California goldenrod adds summer and fall color to the landscape, Santa Barbara Botanic Garden. JOHN EVARTS

Gardeners in the eastern United States associate goldenrod with summer, butterflies, and meadows. In California, unfortunately, our namesake goldenrod barely registers on gardeners' radar screens and is hard to find in nurseries. We consequently miss out on a carefree and valuable native for summer and fall color.

Although fairly nondescript until it blooms, California goldenrod is transformed in summer when it sends up 1- to 4-foot-long stalks whose masses of golden yellow flowers come alive with bees, butterflies, and other insects. The stalks may be slender and wand-like or resemble inverted pyramids. The softly pubescent leaves are 2 to 4 inches long and ½ to 1½ inches wide.

To achieve the best floral display, give California goldenrod plenty of sun and occasional water during the summertime. This perennial is a particularly good candidate for planting in a large-scale meadow. If part shade is all that is available, it will still serve as a useful green groundcover, especially beneath the canopy of both evergreen and deciduous oak trees. California goldenrod's creeping rhizomes can help curb erosion, but it spreads aggressively if it receives additional irrigation.

To use it in a perennial border, consider installing a root barrier to keep it within bounds. In desert gardens it requires moderate supplemental watering to survive.

Care of this undemanding perennial is easy: prune it annually after flowering to remove the spent stalks and drying foliage. For a colorful bouquet, mix a few stalks with royal penstemon and blue-flowered sages. Contrary to common belief, goldenrod does not induce hay fever symptoms; this false notion stems from the fact that goldenrod is in bloom at the same time as the real culprit: ragweed.

Other Species: Canada goldenrod *(Solidago canadensis* ssp. *elongata)* and southern goldenrod *(S. confinis)* are two variations on this summer-blooming theme. Their care is similar to California goldenrod. Canada goldenrod looks best with occasional summer water, but is not suited for hot inland valleys. Southern goldenrod has a shorter rhizome, or none at all, and is more manageable than either California or Canada goldenrod.

Sphaeralcea ambigua
APRICOT MALLOW
Mallow Family (Malvaceae)

Plant Type: Evergreen subshrub.
Geographic Zones: All except immediate coast and high mountains.
Light: Sun.
Soil: Adaptable; well-drained preferred.
Water: Drought tolerant to occasional.
Natural Habitat and Range: Dry rocky places in desert scrub and desert woodland below 7500 feet; throughout the California deserts to Utah, Arizona, and Baja California and Sonora, Mexico.

Apricot mallow in a desert wash, public land (BLM), northern Imperial County. STEPHEN INGRAM

Apricot mallow is a garden favorite for all the right reasons: it is easy to grow, has showy distinctive flowers, and blooms for months at a time. If it is grown in warm areas and receives additional water during the summer months, apricot mallow often blooms nearly year-round. This plant tolerates cold, dry conditions, but it can never get too much heat or sunshine.

Louis Hamilton apricot mallow flowers, Rancho Santa Ana Botanic Garden, Claremont. CAROL BORNSTEIN

Apricot mallow's gray to olive-colored leaves are deeply veined and variously coated with stellate hairs. The textured foliage is typically sparse and forms a loose shrublet from 6 to 18 inches tall and about half again as wide. Add to that height the numerous, wand-like, 1- to 4-foot-long inflorescences, and you have a good idea of the presence that apricot mallow can bring to the garden. Though one might expect solely apricot-colored flowers, the hibiscus-like blossoms range from pale orange through salmon to red-orange. Flower size varies tremendously, from ½ inch to over 2 inches wide.

Apricot mallow may be used as a specimen in a dry border or massed in a desert-themed garden. It is an excellent choice to combine with desert lavender, incienso, beavertail cactus, and Shaw agave. Prune apricot mallow back to 3- to 6-inch-long stubs after it blooms. Occasionally it will produce welcome volunteer seedlings. Rabbits, ground squirrels, and deer relish apricot mallow plants and eat them to the ground; you may need to protect your plants with a wire cage. Although apricot mallow adapts to many garden environments, cold moist conditions, especially in combination with heavy soils, are invariably fatal.

Pink mallow (*Sphaeralcea ambigua* ssp. *rosacea*) has large showy flowers in many shades of pink, rose, and lavender. In the wild, this species is found along the western edge of California's Colorado Desert and in Arizona and Baja California. Sometimes these pink-flowered forms will turn up within groups of apricot mallows sold in nurseries.

Cultivars: 'Louis Hamilton' has distinctive grenadine-colored flowers and is a noteworthy selection reaching 3 to 4 feet tall. The blooms have an especially luminescent quality.

Sporobolus airoides
ALKALI SACATON
Grass Family (Poaceae)

Plant Type: Deciduous, warm-season perennial grass.
Geographic Zones: All except northern coastal.
Light: Sun.
Soil: Adaptable.
Water: Drought tolerant to moderate.
Natural Habitat and Range: Seasonally moist alkaline flats in alkali sink and coastal scrub below 7000 feet; Sierra Nevada foothills, Central Valley, South Coast Ranges, and southwestern California through the deserts to eastern Washington, central and southern United States, and Mexico.

Alkali sacaton with airy panicles backlit by the sun, Santa Barbara Botanic Garden. CAROL BORNSTEIN

This warm-season bunchgrass is saddled with a bland common name, yet it rivals most of California's grasses in beauty. As spring passes, the panicles of alkali sacaton begin their graceful display. Masses of shimmering pink stalks appear above the mounded foliage, adding texture, movement, and color to the garden during the long days of summer.

This densely tufted, 1- to 3-foot-tall and slightly wider grass forms arching mounds of narrow gray-green leaves that turn light tan in winter. The 4- to 16-inch-long airy panicles emerge with a rose pink to purple hue, fade to gold, and finally become a pale straw color before shattering. Thousands of tiny seeds fall to the ground or are carried by the wind, yet few germinate in cultivated situations.

Alkali sacaton is a versatile grass in the landscape. A sinuous drift in a meadow or dry border is an arresting sight, especially when juxtaposed with the contrasting foliage of bush poppy, Canyon Prince wild rye, wire grass, or a dark green manzanita. The pinkish flowers are exquisite against the purple-mahogany bark of Louis Edmunds manzanita. Consider planting several in a narrow sunny strip, flanked on one or both sides by red-flowered or saffron buckwheat. The delicate panicles are impressive in both fresh and dried flower arrangements.

Alkali sacaton was a common component of the grasslands in California's Central Valley before intensive agriculture altered the natural landscape. "Sacaton" is derived from the Spanish word for "grass" or "hay," and as the modifier "alkali" suggests, this bunchgrass tolerates soils with a high pH. Alkali sacaton will thrive in almost any soil, however, and accepts a wide range of watering regimes. Plants in coastal gardens do not need summer water, whereas those in arid interior locations will be more attractive with irrigation. To rejuvenate them, mow or shear the clumps to 3 or 4 inches in height every few years in fall.

Symphoricarpos mollis
CREEPING SNOWBERRY
Honeysuckle Family (Caprifoliaceae)

Plant Type: Deciduous shrub.
Geographic Zones: All except deserts.
Light: Sun to shade.
Soil: Adaptable.
Water: Drought tolerant to occasional.
Natural Habitat and Range: Shaded slopes in chaparral and woodlands below 9000 feet; Cascade Range and the Modoc Plateau to British Columbia; Coast Ranges and the Sierra Nevada to northwestern Baja California, and many mountain ranges in the western United States.

Creeping snowberry growing beneath a dense canopy of coast live oak, Santa Barbara Botanic Garden. JOHN EVARTS

Few shrubs work as well as creeping snowberry when situated under the dense canopy of a coast live oak. This low, trailing shrub spreads by rhizomes and layering

Above: Creeping snowberry foliage moistened by rain, Santa Barbara Botanic Garden. JOHN EVARTS
Left: Snowberry fruits, Montaña de Oro State Park, Los Osos. PHILIP VAN SOELEN

stems and can withstand heavy root competition. It will eventually form an attractive, open thicket 6 to 24 inches high. In sites with dry shade, plant creeping snowberry with woodland strawberry, foothill sedge, and coastal wood fern to create a pleasing woodland.

Creeping snowberry is multi-branched with arching to upright stems. The leaves are round-ovate with occasional lobes and measure ½ to 1 inch in length. The pink, ⅛-inch-long bell-shaped flowers hang in pairs or small groups from the leaf axils and provide a delicate detail against the muted blue-green of the leaves. The matte white, ¼-inch berry-like fruit hangs in clusters along the leafless stems from late fall into winter. Berry production differs from year to year, and when available, the fruit is a valuable food source for varied thrushes, robins, and quails.

Creeping snowberry is easy to grow and seldom troubled by disease or pests. Try combining it with other woodland species, such as hummingbird sage, coffeeberry, and fuchsia-flowered gooseberry. It makes an ideal choice for the habitat garden, as the thicket-forming growth provides nesting cover for birds as well as protective shelter for other wildlife. Creeping snowberry requires only an occasional coppicing to freshen growth.

Other Species and Cultivars: Snowberry (*Symphoricarpos albus* var. *laevigatus*) is similar to creeping snowberry, with pink flowers and showy white fruit, but has a more erect habit. Snowberry also spreads by suckering stems and forms open colonies on north slopes, along streams, and in shaded woodlands of the Coast Ranges and Sierra Nevada to Alaska. Snowberry is an excellent choice to use in the dry shade of oak trees. 'Tilden Park' is a reliable selection with large fruit.

Tanacetum camphoratum
DUNE TANSY
Sunflower Family (Asteraceae)

Plant Type: Semi-evergreen herbaceous perennial.
Geographic Zones: All except high mountains and deserts.
Light: Sun.
Soil: Adaptable; moisture-retentive preferred.
Water: Occasional to moderate.
Natural Habitat and Range: Coastal dunes below 100 feet; San Francisco Bay Area north to British Columbia.

Dune tansy has fern-like, aromatic foliage, Santa Barbara Botanic Garden. CAROL BORNSTEIN

Any good book on herbs will have a page devoted to tansy enumerating its many uses, from medicinal to cosmetic to culinary. Although these herbals describe the European tansy, our California native reputedly shares some of these qualities. For gardeners, however, dune tansy is most appreciated as an easy-to-grow, durable groundcover that doesn't need much attention.

Dune tansy spreads by thickened, almost woody rhizomes. Its fern-like, twice- or thrice-divided foliage is 3 to 10 inches long and comes in two distinct colors. The vibrant yellow-green form, which some authors classify as *T. douglasii,* is decidedly more vigorous than the light gray form. Like the common European tansy, our native species has aromatic foliage that imparts a medicinal scent. The flattened, button-like, yellow flower heads appear in 1- to 2-inch-wide clusters. They bloom in late spring to summer and quickly fade to a chocolate brown that provides contrast to the foliage. They are also effective in small flower arrangements.

Despite the fact that it occurs naturally only in coastal dunes, dune tansy grows surprisingly well in heavy clay soil. Indeed, it may spread further afield than intended, but can be controlled without difficulty. In sandy, well-drained soil, it needs water regularly beyond the rainy season to retain a lush appearance; in clay soil, summer watering should be reduced considerably. To curb dune tansy's tendency to spread beyond its allocated space, irrigate less often. If it still gets out of bounds, install a root barrier or simply pull out unwanted runners—the roots are not tenacious. At summer's end, prune off the spent flower stalks and any leggy branches to improve appearance and rejuvenate the colony. Dune tansy has no disease problems, and the foliage is said to repel insects, which no doubt accounts for its lack of insect pests.

Thalictrum fendleri var. *polycarpum*
WESTERN MEADOW RUE
Buttercup Family (Ranunculaceae)

Plant Type: Semi-evergreen to deciduous herbaceous perennial.
Geographic Zones: All except high mountains and deserts.
Light: Sun to shade.
Soil: Adaptable.
Water: Drought tolerant to occasional.
Natural Habitat and Range: Common in forests and woodlands below 3000 feet; from Washington to the Klamath and North Coast ranges and south to the Peninsular Ranges, and occasional in the Sierra Nevada.

The fine-textured foliage of western meadow rue is always a delight to the eye. This graceful plant could be easily mistaken for western columbine until you bruise the leaves and smell its malodorous foliage. The scent may account for the reason this perennial is not more widely known and grown. If you are lucky enough to find it in a nursery, keep your car windows open during the drive home.

Western meadow rue awakens from its summer rest at the onset of autumn rains, blooms the following spring, and shuts down by summer's end. The green or blue-green leaves are divided into many segments, giving the foliage a delicate, fern-like appearance. Adding to this effect are the tiny unisexual flowers, which are showy by virtue of their sheer numbers. Great masses dance at the tops of 2- to 5-foot-high stalks, responding to the slightest breeze. Male and female flowers occur on separate plants, and the male flowers—with their pendulous stamens and intriguing color combination of green, light purple, and cream—are more noteworthy and colorful than the erect, club-like female flowers. The plant's overall impression is one of delicate beauty.

Western meadow rue thrives in the dry understory of trees, especially coast live oaks. It also accepts a fair amount of watering in summer. Plants are programmed to go dormant in late summer, regardless of one's watering practices, and the foliage may turn a pleasing mosaic of soft yellow, tan, and brown. Group several plants together for best effect, and keep them slightly back from the bed's edge to avoid brushing against the pungent leaves. Western meadow rue partners well with western columbine, coffeeberry, coral bells, ferns, grasses,

Western meadow rue in a dry site beneath oaks, Santa Barbara Botanic Garden. STEPHEN INGRAM

and trees. Undemanding in every way, western meadow rue needs only an annual pruning to remove the dried flower stalks and leaves. Do this after the seeds ripen if new plants are desired, as it readily self-sows. The occasional damage from mealybugs or leaf miners is inconsequential.

Thuja plicata
WESTERN RED CEDAR
Cypress Family (Cupressaceae)

Plant Type: Evergreen tree.
Geographic Zones: All except deserts.
Light: Sun or partial shade.
Soil: Adaptable.
Water: Occasional to regular.
Natural Habitat and Range: Moist forests from sea level to 7000 feet; northwestern California to Alaska and in the Rocky Mountains of Idaho, Montana, and British Columbia.

Western red cedar slips into the moist temperate fringe of northwestern California as if testing the region for adequate rainfall and cool summers. Although unable to naturally penetrate the Mediterranean portions of the state, western red cedar is grown in warmer, drier regions as a lawn tree and in other regularly watered landscapes.

Western red cedar is a graceful, pyramidal tree that, in the wild, can reach 200 feet high with a 60 foot spread. A height of 50 to 100 feet and spread of 25 to 50 feet are more typical in garden settings. Flattened sprays of rich green, scale-like leaves have a glossy sheen and are suspended on drooping branchlets. The trunk is thick and buttressed with deep vertical seams, and the gray or reddish brown bark peels in long fibrous strips. Masses of brown ½-inch-long egg-shaped cones hang from the trees in autumn.

With adequate water, western red cedar will grow in most areas of the state. Its elegant, formal appearance works well in parks, spacious lawns, or even in large decorative containers. Tolerant of shearing, it can also be used as a hedge or dense screen with a couple of prunings per year. The wide-spreading lower branches require adequate space to develop their characteristic grace; removing them results in an awkward form. Western red cedar is disease and pest free when grown in moist, well-drained soils. Like other scale-leaved conifers, the branchlets will die at points of continuous contact with other leaves.

Cultivars: A remarkable range of horticultural selections is available from specialty growers and includes cultivars with dwarf, conical, or globose habits and dense or

Above: Woolly blue curls adds its alluring blossoms to a water-wise landscape, private garden, Arroyo Grande. DAVID FROSS
Left: Woolly blue curls' flowers are pollinated by hummingbirds, Rancho Santa Ana Botanic Garden, Claremont. RICHARD FISHER

Western red cedar's characteristic drooping branchlets, Rancho Santa Ana Botanic Garden, Claremont. KAREN MUSCHENETZ

pendulous branches. Others have golden, white, or bronze foliage. 'Emerald Cone' is currently the most commonly grown California form; it features brilliant green foliage, has a pyramidal habit, and grows to 80 feet tall.

Trichostema lanatum
WOOLLY BLUE CURLS
Mint Family (Lamiaceae)

Plant Type: Evergreen shrub.
Geographic Zones: All except high mountains and deserts.
Light: Sun.
Soil: Adaptable, except poorly drained.
Water: Drought tolerant to occasional.
Natural Habitat and Range: Coastal scrub and chaparral below 3500 feet; Coast Ranges from Monterey and San Benito counties south to southwestern California and into northwestern Baja California.

Woolly blue curls' stunning floral display makes it one of the most gorgeous California native plants. Its inflorescence is a study in excess. A dense coat of soft magenta to blue or white hairs thickly covers the stems and calyces, while numerous short-stemmed clusters of flowers are spaced along the length of the flower spike.

Each vivid blue to pink or off-white flower has distinctive white nectar guides that lead into the center of the bloom. A set of four long, curving, showy anthers and a single stigma, held slightly higher, top off each flower. The blooms are pollinated by hummingbirds and visited by bumblebees.

Woolly blue curls is a perfect size for most home gardens. As a mature flowering shrub it reaches 3 to 4 feet tall and 3 to 4 feet wide. All vegetative parts of this beautiful plant carry a pungent resinous aroma. The shiny, narrow, bright green leaves are incongruous when compared to the typical olive to gray-green foliage of its chaparral compatriots. Foliage amply covers stems of young, actively growing plants, but is scant on older specimens.

In most gardens, young plants and plants that are transplanted from containers may require surprising amounts of water to become well established. When you set woolly blue curls in the ground, make sure its crown remains slightly higher than the surrounding soil to avoid crown rot. Keep organic mulches far away from the plant, though inorganic mulches, such as rocks and gravel, are welcome. Pinch vigorous young plants to develop bushier specimens and more flowering stems. Typical rejuvenation techniques, such as cutting back to old wood, do not work with woolly blue curls. Once the plant starts to decline, it continues in a downward spiral until death. In some gardens, woolly blue curls naturalize; in others, plants are often short-lived and need to be replaced every two to five years. They bloom nearly year-round, and in worst-case scenarios woolly blue curls can still be successfully grown as a highly satisfactory annual.

Cultivars: Five selections of woolly blue curls have been named; none are easy to find, but all are exceptional plants. 'Cuesta Ridge' is especially vigorous and is the easiest cultivar to grow in most gardens. Its large inflorescences are coated with dark purple fuzz. 'Fremont Peak' has more and broader foliage than the species and other selections. Its large inflorescences are densely covered with magenta fuzz and carry many dark blue flowers. 'Lion Den' has narrow inflorescences with dark blue flowers. The flower clusters on the long, candle-like inflorescences of 'Salmon Creek' are more closely spaced, giving them a denser appearance. 'Ted's Select' has sizeable inflorescences covered with dark blue hairs.

Umbellularia californica
CALIFORNIA BAY
Laurel Family (Lauraceae)

Plant Type: Evergreen tree or shrub.
Geographic Zones: All except high mountains and deserts.
Light: Sun to shade.
Soil: Adaptable; moisture-retentive preferred.
Water: Drought tolerant to moderate.
Natural Habitat and Range: Common in canyons and valleys in many plant communities below 5000 feet; southwestern Oregon and throughout California, except the Central Valley and deserts, to northwestern Baja California.

California bay is an intensely aromatic tree familiar to hikers of chaparral, woodland, and forest. On a warm day, its distinctive odor may announce its presence before it comes into view. The scent is pleasant but strong—a few people even get headaches just walking through a grove of California bays. In the kitchen, a mere pinch of California bay is a pungent substitute for the leaves of its Mediterranean relative, sweet bay laurel.

Also known as Oregon myrtle, myrtlewood, or California bay laurel, the wood of California bay is used to make furniture, cabinets, bowls, plates, and other items. As a tree, it can attain a height of 100 feet or more in the wild and has either a globular or conical silhouette. In drier parts of its range or on ocean bluffs buffeted by salt-laden winds, California bay takes on a

Above: California bay pruned into an open, multi-trunked specimen, private garden, Santa Barbara.
ROBERT MULLER
Left: Small, fragrant flowers on California bay in late winter, private garden, Solvang. JOHN EVARTS

shrubby form. The medium to yellowish green, oblong, leathery leaves are 1 to 5 inches in length and have a glossy upper surface. In late winter, the small rounded clusters of fragrant yellow-green flowers may stand out from the foliage, but often go unnoticed. The inch-long fruits, reminiscent of plump green olives or tiny avocados, weigh down the branches. Some people find the roasted nuts to be a taste treat. Others are sensitive to the foliar oils of bay and should avoid exposure to the cut leaf surface.

In gardens California bay grows slowly or moderately to 30 to 50 feet high. With age, the tree develops a massive basal burl, whose dormant buds resprout following a wildfire, drought, or severe pruning. The smooth, light to dark gray bark eventually furrows at the burl. California bay makes an excellent tall screen or clipped hedge. Use it in place of non-native shrubs, such as eugenia or pittosporum, especially where pittosporum might become invasive and escape into adjacent wildlands. It makes a handsome specimen tree, especially if allowed to grow unfettered and the lower limbs are left intact. The foliage casts a dense shade that limits understory plantings.

California bay is an incredibly adaptable plant with relatively few pest and disease problems. Laurel aphids often attack the leaves; they secrete sugary honeydew that supports the unsightly growth of sooty mold fungus, which blackens the leaf surface. Use soap spray to keep the aphids in check. In addition, bays are also susceptible to the *Botryosphaeria* fungus, which kills affected branches.

Canyon sunflower in bloom between a pair of coast live oak trunks, private garden, Santa Barbara. CAROL BORNSTEIN

Venegasia carpesioides
CANYON SUNFLOWER
Sunflower Family (Asteraceae)

Plant Type: Semi-evergreen subshrub.
Geographic Zones: Immediate coast to warm interior valleys of central and southern California.
Light: Sun to shade.
Soil: Adaptable; moisture-retentive preferred.
Water: Drought tolerant to moderate.
Natural Habitat and Range: Shaded slopes in canyons and along streambanks near the coast in coastal scrub, chaparral, and oak woodlands below 3000 feet; Monterey County south to Baja California and the Channel Islands.

Native plants that flower in dry shade are prized commodities, and canyon sunflower offers up its golden blooms virtually cost-free. This under-used perennial lights up the shade when it flowers, displays bold leaves well into summer, and demands little in return.

Canyon sunflower is the only species in its genus. It grows 3 to 6 feet tall and equally wide. The thin, green, deltoid leaves vary from 1½ to 5 inches long, depending upon the amount of light and water provided. From late winter well into summer, charming lime green buds that resemble cabbage roses give way to 1½- to 2-inch-wide sunflower-like, crayon yellow blossoms.

Although canyon sunflower tolerates and even thrives in deep shade, it grows equally well in full sun. This is one drought-tolerant native that doesn't mind surplus irrigation, so to keep up its appearance in exposed locations, supply it with fairly regular amounts of water. If the soil begins to dry out, canyon sunflower's leaves will shrivel but hang on—giving the plant a bedraggled appearance. Prune it hard after it blooms, leaving just a few inches of stem tissue. New shoots will emerge from ground level the next growing season, yielding a bushy specimen. Skip this late-summer grooming and the plant will be much less attractive in the following season, with almost naked stems and a puff of foliage and flowers at the tips. If you want volunteer seedlings, allow the seeds to ripen and disperse before you deadhead or prune.

Canyon sunflower is a coarse-textured plant that works well in the middle or back of a perennial border, as its cheerful blossoms combine easily with many other colors. It is also valuable in the shade of oak trees, where the size and vivid colors of the flowers and leaves command attention. In inland sites, treat canyon sunflower as a short-lived perennial. In coastal gardens, leaf miners occasionally tunnel through the leaves, creating intricate whitish patterns. The damage they do is primarily cosmetic, so think of the tunnels as nature's doodles and don't worry about the plant's health.

Verbena lilacina
LILAC VERBENA
Verbena Family (Verbenaceae)

Plant Type: Evergreen subshrub.
Geographic Zones: All except high mountains and deserts.
Light: Sun to partial shade.
Soil: Adaptable.
Water: Occasional to moderate.
Natural Habitat and Range: Canyons and bluffs in maritime desert scrub below 3500 feet; Cedros Island, Baja California.

Lilac verbena is endemic to Cedros Island, where parts of the natural landscape look like a veritable flower garden in springtime. This loosely mounded plant dots the island's canyons and bluffs and produces fragrant, pastel-colored blooms from spring through

De La Mina verbena, covered with fragrant blossoms, Leaning Pine Arboretum, Cal Poly, San Luis Obispo. THOMAS ELTZROTH

fall. Its flowers attract myriad butterflies, making it an exceptional plant for butterfly gardens.

Lilac verbena reaches 2 to 3 feet high and 3 to 6 feet wide. The deeply divided, medium green leaves give the plant its lacy texture. Simple or branched inflorescences terminate the squarish stems, bearing dense heads of light purple blossoms. As the flowers open, the head elongates, eventually becoming a 2-inch-long spike. Each individual flower is almost a half-inch wide.

Lilac verbena adapts to many garden conditions. In hot, dry climates, additional watering will help rejuvenate plants with leaves that have begun to brown. In other areas, lilac verbena accepts fairly regular watering as long as the soil is well-drained. If your soil is heavy, however, be sparing with the supplemental irrigation. Too much water may lead to somewhat lanky, less tidy plants. An overall light shearing during the summer months will make plants denser; otherwise the only maintenance chore is an annual pruning to remove spent blossoms and to retain the compact habit. Pest problems are nil.

An outstanding container plant, lilac verbena offers copious flowers for months on end. It is an excellent choice for mixed borders and blends easily into either a cool or warm color scheme. Plant several in the midborder, leaving one or two up front so you can capture a whiff of the mildly spicy, clove-like scent of the flowers. It is a must for butterfly gardens. Due to its fast growth rate and early flowering, gardeners in cold-winter areas can use it as an annual. The soft purple flowers look vibrant paired with seaside daisy, white- and pink-colored native yarrows, yellow monkeyflowers, and gum plants.

Cultivars: The selection 'De La Mina' is distinguished by the darker purple color of its blossoms.

Vitis californica
CALIFORNIA WILD GRAPE
Grape Family (Vitaceae)

Plant Type: Deciduous vine.
Geographic Zones: All except high mountains.
Light: Sun to partial shade.
Soil: Adaptable.
Water: Infrequent to moderate.
Natural Habitat and Range: Canyons and streambanks in riparian woodlands below 4000 feet; western foothills and east side of the Sierra Nevada, Central Valley, and Coast Ranges to southern Oregon.

Finding plants that display bold, colorful fall foliage is a challenge for native plant gardeners. Although there are some excellent choices, including Fremont cottonwood, big-leaf maple, spicebush, and creek dogwood, options are limited, especially where autumn nights are seldom cold. California wild grape is particularly useful in these situations, as it will provide autumn color even in gardens with the mildest winter temperatures. A vigorous, willful vine, California wild grape can quickly cover a fence or climb over trees and shrubs but is easily controlled with pruning. Adaptable, it can be trained up a formal trellis or used as a large, rambling groundcover.

California wild grape, like commercial wine and table grapes, is a deciduous vine with clasping tendrils. Swollen spring buds open on woody stems, giving rise to broad, fan-shaped leaves up to 6 inches wide and 3 to 4 inches long. The new leaves are silver green and quickly mature to a fresh apple green color; they have shallowly lobed margins and small blunt teeth. Spring flowers are yellow-green and held in short clusters. Although they are not showy and are often hidden in the foliage, they have a pleasing fragrance. Tight, purple bundles of spherical ¼-inch grapes are produced in late summer. The edible grapes are much smaller than

Roger's Red wild grape, close-up of foliage beginning to show fall color, private garden, Arroyo Grande. DAVID FROSS

Roger's Red wild grape trained against a wall in a landscape of California natives, private garden, Montecito. STEPHEN INGRAM

domesticated varieties, but they are quite attractive to birds. Autumn foliage is usually gold or yellow, and the older wood has shredding, cinnamon brown bark.

Diseases and pests seldom trouble California wild grape, although the spread of the glassy-winged sharpshooter may change that. Sharp shooters serve as vectors for Pierce's disease, which is fatal to grapes. The only effective control is preventing infection, and this disease has already caused serious damage to the wine industry in southern California.

Cultivars: A number of selections have been made of California wild grape for fall color. 'Roger's Red' is a particularly robust selection with vines that grow to 40 feet in length. The verdant green summer leaves of this selection turn bright crimson in autumn. 'Russian River' has plum red fall foliage that persists well into winter. 'Walker Ridge' is smaller—climbing to 15 feet—and has gray-green leaves and yellow to orange-red fall color.

Other Species: Desert wild grape *(Vitis girdiana)* is a closely related species from streamside and canyon bottoms of the desert Southwest. It is a better choice for hotter, drier gardens and features a silvered appearance on the new growth caused by the short hairs covering the foliage.

Washingtonia filifera
CALIFORNIA FAN PALM
Palm Family (Arecaceae)

Plant Type: Evergreen tree.
Geographic Zones: All except immediate coast, high mountains, and high deserts.
Light: Sun.
Soil: Adaptable.
Water: Drought tolerant to occasional.
Natural Habitat and Range: Desert oases below 4000 feet; Colorado Desert from San Bernardino County east to Arizona's Sonoran Desert and south to central Baja California.

California fan palm is a state icon. In southern California, palms seem to go with everything. Found from desert oases to roadside colonnades, palms also serve as exclamation points in avant-garde landscapes or as exotic ornaments in the gardens of Victorian mansions. In some areas they are a nearly ubiquitous feature of the suburban skyline. Early settlers throughout much of the state planted California fan palms as beacons of civilization to guide early travelers to their homes and ranches. Desert-dwelling Native Americans make use of California fan palm's fruits, seeds, fronds, and petioles for numerous purposes ranging from food to shelter and clothing.

California fan palms line a driveway, private garden, Borrego Springs. STEPHEN INGRAM

California fan palm is one of the hardiest and most massive palm trees in the world. Mature specimens can attain heights of nearly 80 feet with trunks that are 3 to 4 feet across. It has a fibrous root system and does not produce a taproot. During the summer months, numerous 10- to 15-foot-long inflorescences cascade from near the summit of the plant and carry hundreds of tiny, creamy white blossoms that are followed by small, hard, blackish fruits. These are attractive to birds and other wildlife that consequently spread the seeds considerable distances from the parent trees.

The fan-like leaf blade is nearly round in outline and is deeply cut and pleated. A number of birds, especially orioles, collect the abundant fibrous strands produced by the leaves to create their nests. The petioles of young plants have conspicuous spiny margins. As the plants attain greater age and height, the spines are no longer produced. One theory to explain this suggests that a now-extinct prehistoric animal ate the palm fronds and that the spines on the lower fronds were a deterrent to such browsing.

Dead fronds are held indefinitely and create the palm's characteristic gray-brown skirt. In urban areas palm skirts have a reputation for harboring roof rats and other unwanted creatures. While this is true, palm skirts also provide housing for desirable wildlife, including owls. The skirt of dead fronds may be removed if care is taken not to damage the trunk. Unlike most trees, palm trunks will not expand in thickness with age, so any wounds to the trunk will remain exposed. Under no circumstances should live palm fronds be pruned, as such removals frequently compromise the tree by providing an easy avenue for infection by fungal and bacterial pathogens.

This long-lived palm is easy to grow. It thrives in the intense heat and sunlight characteristic of its native habitat in the low desert, but it must have ready access to water. California fan palm even tolerates alkaline conditions and windy areas. It is easy to procure from nurseries, and large specimens are commercially available. When grown in coastal climates, California fan palm is almost always afflicted by diamond scale (*Sphaerodothus neowashingtoniae*), which is actually a fungal pathogen. Infested palm fronds are dotted with diamond-shaped areas of dead tissue. There is no known cure for this disfiguring but non-lethal disease. In such climates, try the smaller Guadalupe Island fan palm.

Woodwardia fimbriata
GIANT CHAIN FERN
Deer Fern Family (Blechnaceae)

Plant Type: Evergreen fern.
Geographic Zones: All except high mountains.
Light: Sun to shade.
Soil: Adaptable; moisture-retentive preferred.
Water: Occasional to regular.
Natural Habitat and Range: Moist places in many plant communities below 7000 feet; California, except Great Basin and Central Valley, to British Columbia, Arizona, and northwestern Mexico.

Giant chain fern, California's largest native fern, is an excellent choice for planting in the understory of the state's diverse urban forests. The generous shade cast by large established trees in older metropolitan communities like Pasadena, Palo Alto, and Santa Barbara mimic giant chain fern's natural habitat. Not surprisingly, this graceful fern has become one of the most frequently encountered ferns in California gardens.

Giant chain fern became popular with southern California gardeners early in the 20th century, as it was considered an excellent match for the Victorian homes of this period. Collectors sought out wild plants to supply the demand, and giant chain fern has still not recovered from this harvest. Its current wildland population and distribution is reduced to a fraction of its previous numbers and range.

In spring, apple green fronds rise from the fern's

Giant chain fern thrives beneath the canopy of a coast live oak, private garden, Montecito. STEPHEN INGRAM

dense cinnamon brown crowns of short, stout rhizomes. The plant develops an arching, upright form to 8 feet high in favorable sites, but heights of 4 to 6 feet are more typical in gardens. Individual fronds are divided into coarse segments and lined on the underside with chain-like spore cases that are the source of the common name.

Use giant chain fern to face the north side of buildings, or combine it with pink-flowering currant, coffeeberry, Humboldt lily, and sedges in a woodland setting. In coastal gardens it is surprisingly drought tolerant, but if conditions are drier it will not grow as tall. In fog-belt gardens it can be sited in full sun, but additional degrees of shading and regular summer water are required to maintain a fresh appearance in warmer interior sites. Once it is established, this long-lived fern requires little maintenance, although toward the end of late summer or fall fronds frequently become frayed with unsightly brown edges. This effect is more pronounced where conditions are drier, as sunnier sites tend to bleach the fronds. These older, tattered fronds can be selectively pruned, or the entire plant can be

sheared to the crown before the flush of new spring growth emerges.

Thrips and mites occasionally present problems with giant chain fern and are more pronounced in drought-stressed plants growing in hot, dry climates. Cleaning the plants with water and keeping them dust free will help to control these pests.

Wyethia species
MULES EARS
Sunflower Family (Asteraceae)

Plant Type: Deciduous herbaceous perennial.
Geographic Zones: All except deserts.
Light: Sun to partial shade.
Soil: Adaptable; heavy preferred.
Water: Drought tolerant to occasional.
Natural Habitat and Range: Dry open places in grasslands, chaparral, and woodlands below 11,500 feet. Varies by species, but collectively this genus is found throughout the state except in the Central Valley and desert regions.

All of mules ears' features are bold: large leaves, bright flowers, big seeds, and, in the wild, sizeable colonies. If you are unfamiliar with these plants, conjure up an image of a sunflower, shrink it to 1 to 2 feet in height, and you have a good mental picture of mules ears.

These slow-growing, taprooted plants are long-lived. Their broadly ovate leaves seemingly emerge directly from the ground, but are actually produced in loose rosettes from branching underground stems. The 3- to 5-inch-wide golden yellow flower heads appear from spring to early summer and are typically held erect by short, thick stems. Over time, mules ears can make large showy colonies. Unfortunately, these herbaceous plants go completely deciduous by middle to late summer and are rarely commercially available.

Mountain mules ears growing against a redwood fence, private garden, Swall Meadows. STEPHEN INGRAM

Excellent garden companions for mules ears include California poppy, Ed Gedling whorled lupine, blue-eyed grass, ceanothus, and any of the greener-leaved species of manzanitas. Like sunflowers, mules ears make excellent cut flowers and have edible seeds.

Although mules ears are typically pest free, their tender, emerging shoots require protection from snails and slugs in the spring. Plants may succumb to fungal rots if they receive excess summer watering. Young plants are often difficult, or excruciatingly slow, to establish.

Species: All types of mules ears are beautiful plants, but the following are the most successful choices for gardens: gray mules ears *(Wyethia helenioides)* has green leaves that are covered by soft white hairs; green mules ears *(Wyethia glabra)* has nearly hairless green leaves; and mountain mules ears *(Wyethia mollis)* has gray-felted leaves. All three species have large flowers. Mountain mules ears naturally grows at high elevations and is rarely successfully cultivated outside its mountain habitat. Hall mules ears *(Wyethia elata)* has green leaves and smaller flowers than the others listed here. This species is known to be especially long-lived, with one garden planting exceeding 50 years in age.

Yucca brevifolia
JOSHUA TREE
Agave Family (Agavaceae)

Plant Type: Evergreen tree.
Geographic Zones: Deserts and dry intermediate and interior valleys.
Light: Sun.
Soil: Well-drained.
Water: Drought tolerant.
Natural Habitat and Range: Dry alluvial slopes and plains in desert woodlands to 6000 feet; Mojave Desert to southwestern Utah and western Arizona.

The presence of Joshua trees evokes the spirit and mystery of the Mojave Desert. Although these unconventional trees are not confined to the Mojave, most occur within its boundaries. To the Mormon pioneers who named them, the appearance of these desert trees with upraised branches—which came at the midpoint of their long journey from Salt Lake City to Los Angeles—was a welcome sight that made them think of the prophet Joshua, beckoning them to the promised land.

Joshua tree's branching habit, and hence its distinctive shape, is the result of flower production. A Joshua tree trunk will not branch until it flowers. Every flower cluster terminates the growth of its shoot and typically initiates the growth of two new side branches. Rounded, waxy, greenish white flowers occur in foot-long

Top: Joshua tree, beginning to show its branching habit, private garden, Palm Desert. STEPHEN INGRAM
Bottom: Banana yucca, with showy flower cluster, Santa Barbara Botanic Garden. CAROL BORNSTEIN

clusters and are often mistaken for flower buds. The flowers have an unpleasant smell, but fortunately they are perched high above the ground. The olive green to blue-green dagger-like leaves are densely packed, and each is formidably attired with a sharp, stiff terminal spine. Dried leaves remain firmly attached to branches and trunks for many years before the deeply ridged gray-black bark is revealed.

Joshua trees require hot, dry summers and well-drained soils. They are slow growing, but in gardens they may eventually reach 20 to 30 feet high. Additional irrigation will speed their growth and is necessary to establish small plants in desert gardens. They tolerate freezing temperatures and, in the wild, the sight of Joshua trees dusted with winter snow is not uncommon.

This plant and its pollinator provide an excellent example of symbiosis. In order to produce seeds, Joshua tree flowers must be visited by a particular species of yucca moth *(Tegeticula synthetica)* that can only complete its life cycle on Joshua trees.

Other Species: There are two other long-lived, slow-growing, desirable desert-dwelling *Yucca* species native to California. Both are easy to grow in full sun and well-drained soil. Banana yucca *(Yucca baccata)* is found in the wild in the eastern desert mountains of California and to Utah and Texas. This yucca is named for its sizeable fruits that may be roasted and eaten like plantains. Large, showy, bell-shaped flowers are held in clusters up to 3 feet long. Plants rarely develop woody stems, but in cultivation some have grown to 6 feet high. Its leaves may be steel blue to dark green. Mojave yucca *(Yucca schidigera)* ranges from the Mojave Desert to coastal San Diego County and Baja California. This shrubby to tree-like plant produces few branches and reaches from 3 to 15 feet tall in cultivation. Dark green to yellow-green leaves are clustered toward the tips of the branches. Creamy white flowers are produced in showy terminal clusters up to 4 feet long.

Zauschneria species
CALIFORNIA FUCHSIAS
Evening Primrose Family (Onagraceae)

Plant Type: Semi-evergreen subshrubs and herbaceous perennials.
Geographic Zones: All.
Light: Sun to partial shade.
Soil: Adaptable; well-drained preferred.
Water: Drought tolerant to occasional.
Natural Habitat and Range: Sunny dry slopes and rocky areas in many plant communities below 10,000 feet; California Floristic Province to Oregon, Wyoming, New Mexico, and northern Mexico.

California fuchsias are the exception to our standard format in this book. They are such a complex and variable group that botanists disagree about the taxonomy of the genus (other than *Z. septentrionalis*). Therefore we have chosen to address the majority of these plants

at the generic level rather than assigning them to species or subspecies. Botanists have recently reclassified *Zauschnerias* and have placed them into the genus *Epilobium,* but horticulturally they are so different from that group that the name *Zauschneria* is still commonly seen and used by gardeners.

Summer dormancy, *de rigueur* for much of California's native flora, is turned on its head by California fuchsias. Rather than competing for the attention of pollinators in the heady days of spring, California fuchsias wait until late summer and fall to produce their abundant blooms. The southern migration of hummingbirds coincides with the start of their blooming period, and the tubular- to funnel-shaped flowers are tailor-made for hummingbirds. Carpenter bees and honeybees are too large to slip inside the narrow throat of California fuchsia flowers, but instead of ceding this food source to the hummingbirds, they perch on the base of the floral tube and puncture the blossoms with their sharp mouthparts in order to steal the nectar. Unfortunately for the plant, this theft is accomplished without pollinating the flowers.

Similar to many other plants that are widely distributed over a large geographic region, California fuchsias display remarkable variability in plant size and growth habit, as well as in the color, shape, and size of their flowers and leaves. The smallest California fuchsias may

Above: California fuchsias produce abundant blooms when many natives are dormant, private garden, El Cerrito. SAXON HOLT
Left: Close-up of California fuchsia flowers, Santa Barbara Botanic Garden.
STEPHEN INGRAM

Silver Select California fuchsia has appealing gray foliage, Sierra Azul Nursery and Gardens, Watsonville. SAXON HOLT

reach only 2 inches high, while the tallest grow to 5 feet. Flowers may be short and slender to long and widely flared at the mouth. Colors vary from white, pink, and salmon to myriad tones of orange-red. Leaves may be narrow or up to 1 inch wide, and reach ½ inch to 3 inches in length. Leaf colors cover a wide range: silver, gray, blue-gray, pale green, medium green, and dark green.

California fuchsias are usually recommended for casual or informal gardens, as some tend toward invasiveness. However, many of the cultivars selected for use in gardens are much better behaved and may even be effectively used in formal settings. Plants can spread via underground rhizomes to form broad colonies, or they may generate volunteer seedlings. These seedlings are not hard to differentiate from new sprouts arising from underground stems, and they can be promptly removed or carefully observed to see what kind of flowers, foliage, and growth habit they will produce.

Vigorous and easily grown, California fuchsias are readily used in gardens, but most should be placed with care to avoid overwhelming small or delicate plants. They are stunning when planted on slight slopes among boulders, emerging from stones or gravels in dry streambeds, against rock walls, or in rock gardens. California fuchsias are equally effective as foils to the late-season structure of dried flower stems on Allen Chickering sage and Saint Catherine's lace or the bare branching pattern of California buckeye. Placed with similarly late-blooming natives, such as Silver Carpet California aster, California buckwheat, or California sunflower, these plants provide spirited color and contrast. California fuchsias that remain small are recommended for use at the front of perennial borders or as edging plants to define informal paths.

For best results, California fuchsias need extra attention. In most situations these plants perform much better with some additional summer watering,

though established plants are completely drought tolerant. Do not prune them during their first year; after that, all but the woodiest types greatly benefit from a hard pruning. During the fall and winter months, after they are through flowering, cut them back to inch-long stubs to make way for the lush new spring growth.

Larger California fuchsias have a tendency to flop apart just as their heavy blooms open, revealing dead leaves and naked stems. To counteract this tendency, gardeners have two choices that require early action. In late May or June, pinch or lightly prune the outermost tips to stimulate the production of more side branches that will intertwine and hold the plant together during the blooming season. The other choice is to provide staking or other physical supports to hold the stems upright.

The two primary pests of California fuchsias are leafhoppers and root mealybugs. Infestations of either may be devastating to your plants. Leafhoppers suck juices from the plant's stems and leaves; they frequently go undetected until their populations reach epidemic proportions and their feeding turns stems and leaves partially brown. Horticultural oils may be used to contain small outbreaks. Root mealybugs are more difficult to diagnose and control. Plants infested with these pests may appear stunted for no particular reason. To combat these pests you may need to apply an appropriate insecticide to the soil.

Spittle bugs and white-line sphinx moth caterpillars may also afflict the plants. The former may be washed away with water, and caterpillars are relatively easy to pick off by hand if you use a flashlight to check the plants an hour or two after dusk. An application of the biological control BT *(Bacillus thuringiensis)* will also kill caterpillars.

One distinctive species of California fuchsia that is always separately recognized by botanists is Humboldt County fuchsia *(Zauschneria septentrionalis* or *Epilobium septentrionale).* In the wild it grows in sunny to partially shaded habitats in the outer North Coast Ranges in Humboldt, Trinity, and Mendocino counties. This low-growing perennial forms mats of beautiful silver foliage and produces orange-red flowers. In hotter climates, it is best located in afternoon shade.

Cultivars: Of the nearly 50 named selections, the following offer the most to gardens and landscapes.

Low-growing (less than 1 foot)
'Everett's Choice' produces lanceolate leaves that are covered with long white hairs. This vigorous selection typically reaches 2 to 4 inches tall and spreads from 3 to 5 feet wide. The flared, orange-red flowers appear in profusion. Plants are effective cascading over the edges of containers and raised planters. This selection

Top: Sierra Salmon California fuchsia is named for the color of its blossoms, Rancho Santa Ana Botanic Garden, Claremont. BART O'BRIEN
Bottom: Everett's Choice California fuchsia, Leaning Pine Arboretum, Cal Poly, San Luis Obispo. DAVID FROSS

Medium (1 to 2 feet tall)

'Brilliant Smith' has bright green leaves that are lightly hairy and the largest individual blooms (nearly an inch across) of any California fuchsia. Mature plants are 8 to 18 inches tall and have a slightly wider spread. This clone is not a heavy bloomer, but its scarlet flowers are quite attractive. Of all the California fuchsias, 'Calistoga' may develop the largest individual leaves. Plants growing in fertile soil have enticing, oval-shaped gray leaves that reach 2 to 3 inches long and an inch wide. The small red-orange flowers are never profuse, and the plant generally reaches about 18 inches in height. This clone is particularly recommended as a companion to Bee's Bliss sage, as the foliage of the two plants is nearly identical. 'Hurricane Point' has narrow, linear leaves and an arching growth habit. It grows from 1 to 2 feet tall and from 2 to 4 feet wide. Plants produce long-lasting clusters of orange-red blossoms. This subshrub does not require annual pruning. 'Sierra Salmon' is a winning combination of narrow blue-gray leaves and salmon-colored blooms. Plants have a distinctly upright growth habit from 8 to 24 inches tall and equally wide. This selection also has a tendency to seed in the garden, and the seedlings are seldom as attractive as the parent.

Large (over 2 feet tall)

'Catalina' features narrow, inch-long soft gray leaves and a superabundance of orange-red flowers late in the season. This particularly vigorous selection may reach from 2 to 4 feet tall in a single season. If plants have support from adjacent plantings and are not cut back hard annually, they may easily reach heights of 5 feet. 'Route 66' features bright green, softly hairy leaves and is the heaviest, and often the latest, bloomer. Plants easily reach 2 to 3 feet tall and spread slightly wider. Unlike most California fuchsias, this selection generates branched inflorescences that carry innumerable orange-red flowers. Note that in gardens north of San Francisco, this plant may freeze before it flowers.

produces copious seedlings. 'Select Mattole' produces unique silver leaves and orange flowers. Plants hug the ground and form spreading mats up to 3 feet wide. This spectacular selection is best grown in containers or raised beds, as it tends to have a more delicate constitution—a rarity among California fuchsias. 'Summer Snow' features broadly triangular, pale green to gray-green leaves and large, wide-open, pure white flowers. It is the best white-flowered selection. Plants typically have an arching, low growth habit, reaching heights from 3 to 12 inches and spreading up to 3 feet or more.

ANNUALS

Plant Type: Annual.
Geographic Zones: All.
Light: Sun. Exceptions noted below.
Soil: Adaptable. Exceptions noted below.
Water: Infrequent to moderate. Exceptions noted below.

Elegant clarkia massed in a flower bed, private garden, Sonoma. SAXON HOLT

Gardeners around the globe love to grow California's native annuals. As native plant authority Roger Raiche likes to remind us, "Annuals are the laughter in a garden." There are hundreds of different, delightfully whimsical and colorful California wildflowers to grow in your landscape. In this section, we present you with a selection of the best choices.

Annuals are plants that complete their entire life cycle—from germination to seed production to death —in less than one year. In California, most of our native annuals have adopted this strategy to avoid the long, dry summer months. These plants are perfectly aligned with our Mediterranean climate. Seeds of annuals germinate shortly after the first fall rain. Seedlings often seem to grow slowly through the cold winter months, but this appearance is deceptive. Below ground, annuals are establishing a deep root system that enables them to grow at a frantic rate and put forth a profusion of flowers during the warm, heady days of spring. When the heat of summer arrives, most of our native annuals have already produced a rich cache of seeds for next year's crop, and the plants wither and die. A few of our native annual daisies, including sunflower and tarweed, develop such extensive root systems and are so efficient with their use of water that they are able to flower during the summer months.

To cultivate annuals, you can sow the seeds directly where you want them to grow. You can also plant them in flats or purchase container-grown specimens to transplant to the desired garden location. Seeds and young plants require protection from birds, rabbits, ground squirrels, gophers, mice, snails, slugs, and other pests. Young seedlings are especially vulnerable to both over- and under-watering and require careful monitoring at this stage of development. Nearly all annuals benefit from supplemental watering from winter through spring if rains are infrequent. Most young plants may be pinched to promote branching and additional flowers. If plants are stunted due to poor soils, encourage their growth by applying a weak fertilizer.

You can ensure a crop of new seedlings from your garden annuals each year if you collect their seeds, clean them, store them in a cool dry place, and sow them in fall. If your garden is not watered during the summer months, plants may distribute their seeds naturally, and a fair number of seedlings will germinate in the following year. Seeds exposed to regular summer irrigation will most likely rot.

Adventurous gardeners may wish to push the bloom season of some of our native annuals. You can accomplish this by sowing seeds in mid- to late spring and carefully watering the young plants through the summer until they bloom in late summer and fall. California poppy, punch-bowl godetia, elegant clarkia, tansy leaf phacelia, and desert bluebells are some of the spring-flowering annuals that respond successfully to this treatment.

Annuals work well as fillers between young trees and shrubs, in mixed borders, and in wildflower meadows. Most are also suited to container culture.

Tidy tips, California poppy, and baby blue eyes, Carrizo Plain National Monument. KAREN MUSCHENETZ

Clarkia amoena
FAREWELL TO SPRING
Evening Primrose Family (Onagraceae)

Natural Habitat and Range: Coastal scrub, grasslands, and openings in mixed-evergreen and coniferous forests; British Columbia south along the coast through Marin and Napa counties.

Above: Satin Mixed farewell to spring offers a variety of flower colors, Rancho Santa Ana Botanic Garden, Claremont.
BART O'BRIEN
Left: Elegant clarkia, close-up of flower spike, private garden, Morgan Hill.
STEPHEN INGRAM

True to its common name, farewell to spring blooms, appropriately enough, in late spring and early summer. This plant's large, bowl-shaped flowers crowd together at the top of each stem. There are dozens of named cultivars that have been selected for flower size, color, and plant size. Their flowers are either single or double and may be white, pink, salmon, rose, lavender, or red. Dwarf selections may reach 4 to 8 inches in height, whereas the tallest selections will grow at least 3 feet high. Farewell to spring makes an excellent cut flower; if you remove the stems before any seeds have ripened and continue to water the plant, farewell to spring will often produce a second, but smaller, set of blooms.

Other Species: Punch-bowl godetia *(Clarkia bottae)* grows naturally in coastal scrub and forests from Monterey County south along the coast and into the western Transverse and Peninsular ranges. These slender plants have graceful, 1-foot-long stems with well-spaced pale pink flowers. This species tolerates partial shade and blooms from April to June.

Red ribbons *(Clarkia concinna)* is native to forests and woodlands in the Coast Ranges from Humboldt and Siskiyou counties south to Santa Clara County, and the Sierra Nevada foothills from Butte and Yuba counties. Especially suitable for smaller gardens, red ribbons is usually less than a foot tall and has showy pink flowers with deeply cut petals. This plant prefers partial shade and blooms earlier than most other species of *Clarkia*.

Elegant clarkia *(Clarkia unguiculata)* blooms in late spring and early summer. It grows in grasslands, chaparral, and woodlands of the Coast Ranges from Mendocino and Lake counties south to San Diego County and in Butte and Kern counties in the Sierra Nevada foothills. Plants are often quite large and well branched and may reach over 3 feet in height and width. The blossoms are well spaced along the stems and are produced over a long period of time. Individual petals have a long, stalk-like base and give the flowers a spidery appearance. Blooms are typically dark pink, but may vary between white and rose on different plants. Use elegant clarkia as a background or filler annual; it is vigorous and can easily overwhelm more delicate plants.

Collinsia heterophylla
CHINESE HOUSES
Figwort Family (Scrophulariaceae)

Light: Sun to partial shade.
Natural Habitat and Range: Shaded slopes in many plant communities; California Floristic Province.

Chinese houses were named for their fancied resemblance to pagodas. The two-lipped flowers are produced in dense whorls. Typically, the upper lip is white and the lower lip is purple, but pure white flowers are not uncommon. Vigorous specimens often branch from near the base of the plant and produce several inflorescences. Plants in full bloom reach from 6 to 15 inches in height. Chinese houses combine well with wind poppy and smaller bunchgrasses.

Chinese houses, rural roadside, western San Benito County.
BART O'BRIEN

Eschscholzia californica
CALIFORNIA POPPY
Poppy Family (Papaveraceae)

Natural Habitat and Range: Open areas in grasslands, chaparral, and woodlands; California Floristic Province, western edge of the eastern Sierra Nevada, western portion of the Mojave Desert, and to southern Washington, Nevada, and New Mexico.

California poppy is, without a doubt, the most celebrated of our wildflowers. It is the iconic California wildflower and our official state flower. This poppy is the one native plant that virtually everyone can identify and is the easiest of our native annuals to grow. Sow it and it will come; it may even overstay its welcome.

After the first wave or two of blossoms, California poppy plants may be cut back, or even mowed, to 1-inch-long stubs and then watered. These refreshed poppies then flower for another month or more, blooming nearly year-round in some areas. Like many of our native plants, California poppy is tremendously variable in nature. Plants may be annual or perennial, prostrate or erect in growth form, and the flowers may be single or double. The pure orange poppy is the most commonly encountered, but California poppy blossoms come in a dazzling array of colors, including cream, pink, purple, lavender, yellow, burnt-orange, and red. Gardeners have selected and bred these color forms since the 1800s to create dozens of seed strains. In most gardens it is time-consuming work to keep these strains separate, and if left alone over time, they succumb to the domination of the orange genes. If you want to grow a different color form of California poppy, you must constantly remove all of the orange-flowered seedlings that inevitably spring up before they are able to pollinate the desired blooms.

Top, right: Mahogany Red California poppy, with brightly colored blossoms, private garden, Arroyo Grande. DAVID FROSS
Bottom: California poppy planted throughout a backyard rock garden, private garden, San Luis Obispo. THOMAS ELTZROTH

Sundew frying pans displays open, sunny yellow blooms, Rancho Santa Ana Botanic Garden, Claremont. BART O'BRIEN

Other Species: Frying pans (*Eschscholzia lobbii*) is typically mislabeled for sale as *Eschscholzia caespitosa*, which is the scientific name for an entirely different poppy. Frying pans have pale to golden yellow, slightly cupped flowers that are about 1 inch across. Plants produce dense tufts of thread-like leaves.

Gilia capitata
GLOBE GILIA
Phlox Family (Polemoniaceae)

Light: Sun to partial shade.
Natural Habitat and Range: Slopes in many plant communities; California Floristic Province, north to British Columbia and Idaho.

Globe gilia is one of the easiest annuals to grow. It is also quite variable in size, with flowering specimens ranging from 6 inches to 2 feet tall. The individual small flowers are pale sky blue and are held in tight head-like clusters that look like miniature drumsticks. The dissected bright green leaves are also attractive. It is an excellent companion for California poppy and tidy tips.

Globe gilia, massed hillside planting in partial shade, Santa Barbara Botanic Garden. JOHN EVARTS

Other Species: Bird's eye gilia (*Gilia tricolor*) is also easy to grow. In the wild it is found in grasslands in the Coast Ranges from Humboldt to San Benito counties, in the Central Valley from Tehama to Tulare counties, and in the Sierra Nevada foothills from Kern to Shasta counties. Bird's eye gilia's flowers are much larger than those of globe gilia—up to ½ inch across—and are held loosely atop 4- to 12-inch-long stems. The flowers are quite beautiful; the outer edges are dark violet and grade into white. The throat of each flower has a ring of dark violet and a central yellow eye. The plant's foliage is deeply cut into linear segments. Bird's eye gilia has the same growing requirements as globe gilia.

Helianthus annuus
SUNFLOWER
Sunflower Family (Asteraceae)

Water: Drought tolerant to occasional.
Natural Habitat and Range: Roadsides and waste areas; throughout California, to Canada, eastern United States, and northern Mexico.

The sunflowers native to California are large coarse plants producing dozens of 3- to 5-inch-wide daisy-like flowers. Each flower head has a dark center that is surrounded by a ring of golden "petals," which are actually ray flowers. Unlike many of the annuals listed here, sunflowers typically bloom from June until frost. Bees and other insects are attracted to sunflowers, and their seeds are favored by many species of birds. A rust fungus often defoliates sunflower plants that receive overhead irrigation in the summer; the best technique for watering to enhance flower production is to flood the ground. In areas of California that regularly experience freezing temperatures, sunflowers should be sown in spring as the weather warms. Use these tall plants in backgrounds or mixed among shrubs; they also make good cut flowers.

Sunflowers are a summer-blooming wildflower, private ranchland, Round Valley near Bishop. STEPHEN INGRAM

Layia platyglossa
TIDY TIPS
Sunflower Family (Asteraceae)

Natural Habitat and Range: Grasslands and open areas; Mendocino and Butte counties south to northwestern Baja California.

Tidy tips growing wild in Poly Canyon, Cal Poly, San Luis Obispo. DAVID FROSS

The cheerful, daisy-like flowers of tidy tips have a yellow center that is surrounded by a ring of white-tipped, creamy yellow ray flowers. This slender, spring-blooming plant typically grows 6 to 12 inches tall and has dark-colored stems and narrow, hairy leaves. Tidy tips is most effective in drifts and is especially attractive with globe gilia and blue-flowered lupines.

Limnanthes douglasii
MEADOWFOAM
False Mermaid Family (Limnanthaceae)

Light: Sun to partial shade.
Soil: Adaptable; heavy preferred.
Water: Occasional to regular.
Natural Habitat and Range: Grasslands and vernal pools; southern Oregon to San Luis Obispo and Madera counties.

Top: Meadowfoam carpets the ground beneath quaking aspen, San Francisco Botanical Garden. PHILIP VAN SOELEN
Bottom: Close-up of meadowfoam flowers, Rancho Santa Ana Botanic Garden, Claremont. STEPHEN INGRAM

Meadowfoam is a delightful, low-growing annual that loves water. This spring-blooming plant has shiny green leaves and showy bright yellow flowers that are tipped with white. Grow meadowfoam in masses so its stems knit together and produce a carpet of spring color. It is an excellent choice for planting in a drainage swale, seasonally dry streambed, or in a seasonal retention basin; in these types of locations it often naturalizes. Meadowfoam will also tolerate drier garden situations, and it performs admirably as a spring edging. Try seeding it in a container with native bulbs and let it cascade over the edge.

Linanthus parviflorus
STARDUST
Phlox Family (Polemoniaceae)

Light: Sun to partial shade.
Water: Infrequent to occasional.
Natural Habitat and Range: Grasslands, chaparral, and woodlands; throughout the California Floristic Province.

Annuals from seed packages or seed flats that are labeled "mixed colors" are often disappointing when they flower, since one color tends to dominate all others in the mix. Stardust is a glorious exception. It displays a tremendous range of colors, including white, pink, lavender, yellow, orange, purple, maroon, and gold. Individual plants are typically 3 to 8 inches tall. The small, spring-blooming flowers are produced a few at a time in head-like inflorescences. The hairy leaves are deeply divided into linear segments. Stardust is an excellent choice for edging, containers, and rock gardens.

Other Species: Grand linanthus *(Linanthus grandiflorus)* is found in many plant communities on open slopes and flats in the Coast Ranges from Sonoma to Santa Barbara counties. Plants are often single-stemmed and are normally from 6 inches to 2 feet tall. The showy white to pale lavender flowers are about ½ inch across and are carried in dense heads. The leaves are held opposite from one another and are divided into rigid linear segments. It has the same horticultural preferences as stardust.

Lupinus microcarpus var. *densiflorus*
WHORLED LUPINE
Pea Family (Fabaceae)

Water: Infrequent to occasional.
Natural Habitat and Range: Grasslands and woodlands; most of the California Floristic Province from the vicinity of the Transverse Ranges northward.

Although a single flower color typically dominates each wild population of whorled lupine, this plant may have rose, pink, lavender, purple, white, yellow, or gold blossoms. As its common name indicates, the flowers of whorled lupine are produced at defined intervals along the stem. Plants vary in size from 6 to 30 inches tall. The stems and palmately compound gray-green leaves are lightly covered with short hairs. This wildflower prefers well-drained soils but can be grown in heavier soils if care is taken with watering. The single-named seed strain 'Ed Gedling' has deep golden yellow flowers and is an especially garden-worthy subject.

Lupine has evolved a symbiotic relationship with nitrogen-fixing bacteria that form nodules in the lupine's root systems. These bacteria supply the plant with nitrogen and release this nutrient into the soil after they die. Because of this feature, lupines need no

Stardust blossoms come in multiple hues, Rancho Santa Ana Botanic Garden, Claremont. BART O'BRIEN

Arroyo lupine (foreground) and California sunflower, private garden, Solvang. STEPHEN INGRAM

Sky lupine has a fragrant scent as well as beautiful blossoms, private garden, Arroyo Grande. DAVID FROSS

additional nitrogen and can be used as cover crops to improve soil fertility. Studies have shown that it is usually not necessary to add nitrogen-fixing bacteria when planting lupine seed, as the bacteria are almost invariably present on the seed coat.

All lupine seeds benefit from special treatments, known as scarification, that enable the seeds to absorb water. To follow an easy method of scarification: bring a pot of water to a boil, pour the water into a pyrex bowl, immediately add the lupine seeds, and leave the seeds in the cooling water for several hours or until they swell. Swollen seeds appear quite noticeably different and need to be sown immediately; if they are allowed to dry out, they usually die. Unswollen seeds may be subjected to retreatment. Other ways to scarify seeds involve nicking the seed coat with a file or knife, or gently rubbing them between sheets of sandpaper. Both of these techniques are time consuming and may result in damaged seeds.

Other Species: Arroyo lupine *(Lupinus succulentus)* is one of the most commonly encountered lupines. In the wild, it grows in grasslands and open areas of the Coast Ranges and adjacent valleys from Mendocino County south to northwestern Baja California. The lush green, palmately divided leaves, thick hollow stems, and numerous blue flowers are features that may seem too exuberant in a small garden but are welcome additions to meadow gardens and landscapes. Arroyo lupine varies in size from 1 to 3 feet tall and is equally wide. Lupines and California poppies are a classic planting combination. Sky lupine *(Lupinus nanus)* has the beautiful blue flowers with white spots that are hallmarks of the genus. It grows naturally in grasslands and coastal scrub throughout most of the California Floristic Province north of Los Angeles County. Sky lupine has a delicate appearance that enhances any garden. This fragrant wildflower reaches 6 to 24 inches in height.

Madia elegans
TARWEED
Sunflower Family (Asteraceae)

Light: Sun to partial shade.
Water: Infrequent to occasional.
Natural Habitat and Range: Dry slopes and grasslands; throughout the California Floristic Province to Oregon and the Great Basin.

Tarweeds bloom from late spring through summer when few other native annuals are flowering. They get their common name and their pungent aroma from sticky glands that cover the stems, leaves, and flower buds. Next to the sunflower, tarweed is the tallest of the annuals listed here. It often reaches 4 to 6 feet in height. In winter and spring, the young plants form dense tufts of hairy leaves, but as the weather warms, a central stem emerges and elongates. At its summit, a widely branched inflorescence appears, carrying dozens of golden yellow daisy-like flowers. These 1-inch-wide flowers are often stained a deep chestnut toward the base of the rays. Each flower head opens shortly after dusk and wilts before noon of the following day, though flowers may remain open during foggy or heavily overcast days. Goldfinches are especially fond of tarweed seeds.

Tarweed is a tall annual with a pungent aroma, University of California Botanical Garden, Berkeley. SAXON HOLT

Mentzelia lindleyi
BLAZING STAR
Loasa Family (Loasaceae)

Soil: Well-drained.
Water: Drought tolerant to infrequent.
Natural Habitat and Range: Coastal scrub, chaparral, and woodlands; South Coast Ranges from Alameda to Santa Clara counties; Sierra Nevada foothills from Tuolumne to Tulare counties.

Blazing star and blue-eyed grass in a shopping center landscape, Solvang. JOHN EVARTS

Top: Baby blue eyes, a long-time garden favorite, Larner Seeds, Bolinas. SAXON HOLT
Bottom: Five spot has a purple spot at the tip of each petal, Santa Barbara Botanic Garden. STEVE JUNAK

Blazing star is likely the most difficult to grow of the annuals listed here. Plants need full sun and require excellent drainage to perform well. The silky textured yellow flowers have a dark orange ring at their base and are 2 to 3 inches across. The center of each flower is filled with a starburst of numerous linear stamens. The comb-like leaves and tan stems are covered with short, stiff hairs and feel like sandpaper. Plants may be expected to reach from 6 to 24 inches tall and bloom from mid- to late spring. Try planting blazing stars alone or with other plants, such as desert bluebells and California bells, that share their more exacting growing requirements.

Nemophila menziesii
BABY BLUE EYES
Waterleaf Family (Hydrophyllaceae)

Light: Sun to partial shade.
Natural Habitat and Range: Grasslands, chaparral, and woodlands; California Floristic Province.

Baby blue eyes has been grown in gardens for more than a century. The forms most often seen in cultivation have sky blue, bowl-shaped flowers with a ¾-inch width. Baby blue eyes is a low-growing plant that usually reaches 4 to 6 inches in height and spreads up to 12 inches wide. In the wild, baby blue eyes is quite variable; sometimes the flowers are pure white or dark purple. Leaves of seedlings are frequently spotted white. One of the earliest annuals to bloom, baby blue eyes continues flowering until a few days of hot weather trigger seed production. Grow baby blue eyes at the front of a border or let it cascade from containers filled with spring bulbs. Birds relish its large black seeds.

Other Species: Five spot (*Nemophila maculata*) appears similar to, and has the same growing requirements as, baby blue eyes. Its flowers are slightly larger and are pure white with a large round purple spot at the tip of each of the five petals. It is also an early bloomer and occurs naturally in grasslands and woodlands of the western slope of the Sierra Nevada from Plumas to Kern counties.

Phacelia tanacetifolia
TANSY LEAF PHACELIA
Waterleaf Family (Hydrophyllaceae)

Natural Habitat and Range: Open areas in many plant communities; Mojave Desert, Central Valley, and bordering ranges, from Lake and Butte counties south to northwestern Baja California.

Tansy leaf phacelia showing typical coiled inflorescences, Opal Mountain, northwest of Barstow. STEPHEN INGRAM

Above: Desert bluebells in front of sticky monkeyflower, private garden, Bolinas.
SAXON HOLT
Left: Tropical Surf sticky phacelia, close-up of intricate petal patterns, Rancho Santa Ana Botanic Garden, Claremont.
BART O'BRIEN

Tansy leaf phacelia is particularly vigorous and easy to grow. In recent California history, it was even employed as a cover crop in orchards of deciduous fruit trees. Plants may grow from 1 to 4 feet tall and have many large, divided green leaves. Tansy leaf phacelia's individual lavender blue flowers are rather small—about ¼ inch across—but create quite a show, as they appear in large numbers. Like all *Phacelia* species listed here, they have coiled inflorescences that resemble fiddlenecks, and as the flowers bloom these coils unravel. Some people are allergic to all phacelias, and when they come in contact with the plants they break out in a rash similar in appearance to that caused by poison oak.

Other Species: Desert bluebells *(Phacelia campanularia)* grows naturally in sandy and gravelly washes in the southern Mojave Desert and the northern Colorado Desert and is highly valued for its large bell-shaped to bowl-shaped, rich pure blue flowers. Desert bluebells requires full sun; it prefers well-drained soils but may perform in a variety of soil types as long as it is allowed to dry a bit between irrigations. When well grown, desert bluebells is a showstopper. Combine it with California poppy or sticky monkeyflower for a dazzling display. California bells *(Phacelia minor)* has large, bell-shaped royal purple flowers. It is found in chaparral and coastal sage scrub throughout most of the non-desert regions of southern California, from the Santa Monica Mountains south to northwestern Baja California. This plant is often a fire-follower; it germinates and thrives in the ash-enriched soils left behind by wildfires and may grow 2 to 4 feet tall. If you plant it in your garden expect it to reach half that height, and be prepared for erratic seed germination. California bells prefers full sun and well-drained soils. Sticky phacelia *(Phacelia viscida)* has bowl-shaped azure blue flowers. You may need magnification to fully appreciate the beauty of the intricate blue patterns that detail the white center of each flower with designs worthy of a Persian carpet. This wildflower grows naturally in coastal scrub and chaparral near the coast, from Monterey to San Diego counties. It accepts most soils and prefers full sun.

Platystemon californicus
CREAM CUPS
Poppy Family (Papaveraceae)

Light: Sun to partial shade.
Natural Habitat and Range: Low-elevation grasslands, chaparral, and woodlands; throughout most of the California Floristic Province, western desert edges, and to Oregon, Utah, and Arizona.

Cream cups are one of the earlier annuals to bloom and will continue flowering until the weather warms up. Each plant forms a 3- to 6-inch-wide basal tuft of short, lanceolate leaves. The leaves, flower stems, and buds are covered with long white hairs. A vigorous plant produces 20 or more leafless flower stems that emerge from its base. Each stem carries a single bud that opens into a pale, cream-colored flower up to nearly ¾ inch across. The unusual segmented seed pods are briefly attractive before they shatter. Cream cups are best grown in masses. Plant these diminutive annuals in rock gardens or containers where they may be closely examined.

Cream cups surround a solitary (pink) owl's clover, Carrizo Plain National Monument. KAREN MUSCHENETZ

Stylomecon heterophylla
WIND POPPY
Poppy Family (Papaveraceae)

Light: Partial shade.
Soil: Adaptable; well-drained preferred.
Natural Habitat and Range: Low-elevation grasslands, chaparral, and woodlands; San Joaquin Valley, southern Sierra Nevada foothills; from Coast Ranges in Lake County south to northwestern Baja California.

Wind poppies are the embodiment of refined delicacy. Each plant produces a basal rosette of pale green divided leaves that may reach 3 to 8 inches across. The thin flower stalks rise 8 to 12 inches above the foliage and carry 1- to 2-inch-wide dusky-orange flowers. There is a flush of dark purple at the base of each of the four flat petals. The flowers face outward, perpendicular to the ground.

Wind poppy in a wildland setting, San Martin Island, Baja California.
STEVE JUNAK

BULBS

If annuals are the "laughter" in a garden, then bulbs are the "magic and promise". These specialized storage structures rest during the dry summer months and begin to stir underground when the cool temperatures and first rains of autumn trigger their new growth cycle. If all goes well—and there's no guarantee—the adventurous gardener will be amply rewarded with endearing, beautiful flowers.

Wild hyacinth providing nectar for a swallowtail butterfly, Golden West College Native Garden, Huntington Beach.
DAN SONGSTER

California boasts an impressive array of bulbous species. Many are increasingly rare in the wild due to development pressures and other human disturbances, so be sure to purchase bulbs that are nursery-propagated and not dug from the wild. Native bulbs have a distribution that spans the state, from coastal terraces and bluffs to alpine meadows. They are typically found in grasslands, openings in chaparral, and the dappled shade of woodlands. Flowering is highly dependent upon rainfall; bulbs may produce only foliage in lean years. Some species bloom profusely following wildfires, suggesting an affinity for the potassium released from wood ashes and increased amounts of ground-level sunlight.

A few native bulbs are now mass produced by large mail-order bulb growers, but most remain collector items. Gardeners hooked on these gems should look for them at botanic garden plant sales and specialty nurseries. Once established, several species multiply by producing cormels or bulblets. Others must be propagated from seed; the degree of ease or difficulty for this task is dependent upon species.

When cultivating bulbs, careful attention to watering is essential. Start by determining whether the bulbs you want to grow occur naturally in habitats that become dry in summer. Most California bulbs benefit from regular water during their growth phase (desert species excepted), followed by a dry period after flowering. Yellowing leaves are your visual cue to curtail watering or risk rotting the bulbs. To maximize transfer of nutrients back to the bulb or corm, avoid the temptation to remove the withering leaves.

Be prepared to guard against a host of predators. The juicy new shoots are a delicacy for snails, slugs, rabbits, mice, and birds. Gophers, other rodents, and birds eat the bulb itself, while deer nibble lily buds just when you think you have earned the flowers. Aphids and other sucking insects stress bulbs and simultaneously spread harmful viruses.

Planting native bulbs in containers or raised beds makes pest and water management much easier. As the bulbs come into bloom, tuck the pots into the garden to brighten a border or complement other containers, then whisk them away when flowering ends. When grown in pots, the bulbs described below can be planted throughout California.

Most native bulbs are surprisingly tolerant of heavy soils, as long as water is withheld during the dormant period. It is safer, however, to plant them in well-drained soils, whether in the open ground or pots. A one-time dose of low-nitrogen fertilizer is acceptable within the first month of active growth but is not necessary.

Some native bulbs have exacting cultural requirements; those described in this section are forgiving and relatively easy to procure.

Allium unifolium
SINGLE LEAF ONION
Onion Family (Alliaceae)

Geographic Zones: All except high mountains and deserts.
Light: Sun to partial shade.
Soil: Adaptable.
Water: Infrequent to moderate.
Natural Habitat and Range: Moist, usually heavy soils in chaparral and mixed-evergreen and coniferous forests below 3500 feet; Coast Ranges from Monterey County north to Oregon.

Single leaf onion actually has several leaves, San Francisco Botanical Garden. SAXON HOLT

Single leaf onion is one of the easiest to cultivate of California's 50 or so native onions. Indeed, it borders on weediness and spreads via bulblets or seed. Its common name is a misnomer, as single leaf onion sports two to three bluish green leaves. It produces 2- to 3-inch-wide umbels of light to rose pink flowers on 6- to 18-inch-long stalks. This carefree, spring-blooming native blends well with buckwheats, dudleyas, grasses, and sages. The tiny bulbs are edible, and the leaves have a garlic flavor. Try single leaf onion in a mixed border or at the edge of a tree canopy; it will even tolerate locations with summer irrigation. The parchment-colored umbels are attractive as they ripen, and black seeds are scattered as they disintegrate. Simply remove the umbels if you want to prevent volunteer seedlings.

Brodiaea elegans
HARVEST BRODIAEA
Brodiaea Family (Themidaceae)

Geographic Zones: All except high mountains and deserts.
Light: Sun to partial shade.
Soil: Adaptable.
Water: Infrequent to moderate.
Natural Habitat and Range: Heavy soils in grasslands, woodlands, and forests below 7000 feet; Sierra Nevada to North Coast Ranges and southwestern Oregon.

California brodiaea, close-up of flower umbel, University of California Botanical Garden, Berkeley. KAREN MUSCHENETZ

One can hardly go wrong when choosing a brodiaea. All have erect umbels with pretty flowers of white, pink, blue, or violet. Harvest brodiaea is one of the best in the genus, with large violet flowers that open a few at a time atop 6- to 20-inch-long stalks. The lengthy stems make this late-spring to summer bloomer a good cut flower, but most gardeners prefer to enjoy harvest brodiaea in the garden, especially when it is mixed with other perennials or annual wildflowers.

Other Species: California brodiaea *(Brodiaea californica)* is the tallest of the genus, with stems up to 30 inches high. The late-spring or summer flowers range from white to purple or occasionally pink. On the other end of the spectrum is dwarf brodiaea *(Brodiaea terrestris* ssp. *terrestris),* which is a perfect choice for rock gardens. Its blue-violet flowers bloom on stems barely 3 inches high and appear to float just above the ground.

Calochortus species
MARIPOSA LILIES, FAIRY LANTERNS
Calochortus Family (Calochortaceae)

Fairy lanterns, mariposa lilies, and cat's ears are a few of the common names used to describe the 43 species and several varieties within the genus *Calochortus.* They are the jewels in California's bulb kingdom. Their shapely blossoms come in the softest tints or in saturated hues and some are adorned with elaborate hairs. Often their petals have amazing painterly detail. One never tires of the beauty of these exquisite blooms.

In some years, certain *Calochortus* species produce one broad, strap-shaped leaf. This either precedes flowering or indicates that the bulb is resting and will not flower.

Calochortus albus
WHITE FAIRY LANTERN

Geographic Zones: All except high mountains and deserts.
Light: Sun to partial shade.
Soil: Adaptable; well-drained preferred.
Water: Drought tolerant to moderate.
Natural Habitat and Range: Widespread in shaded sites in open woods or brush in many plant communities below 5000 feet; Sierra Nevada foothills, South Coast Ranges to Peninsular Ranges.

Five species of fairy lanterns, also known as globe lilies, occur in California. White fairy lantern is the most widespread of these species and is also one of the more adaptable members of the genus. The plant sends up 1- to 2-foot-long branched flower stalks bearing rounded,

White fairy lantern lights up shaded garden sites, private garden, Soquel. SUZANNE SCHETTLER

Top: White mariposa lily, with unusual pink-colored blossoms, Antelope Valley, east of Gorman. BART O'BRIEN
Bottom: White mariposa lily flowers with characteristic reddish blotch, San Francisco Botanical Garden. KAREN MUSCHENETZ

1-inch-wide blossoms that are pearly white and occasionally greenish or deep pink. These delicate, nodding orbs brighten shaded sites in woodlands and gardens. Try white fairy lantern beneath the open shade of an upright manzanita with coastal wood fern, coast melic grass, western meadow rue, irises, and shade-tolerant annuals.

Other Species: Golden fairy lantern (*Calochortus amabilis*) is found in shaded woods and brush in the North Coast Ranges. Its 8- to 20-inch-long stalks bear deep yellow flowers in spring. Imagine it paired with California buttercup, blue-eyed grass, yellow- or blue-flowered iris, and an arborescent ceanothus.

Calochortus venustus
WHITE MARIPOSA LILY

Geographic Zones: All except low deserts.
Light: Sun to partial shade.
Soil: Well-drained.
Water: Drought tolerant to moderate.
Natural Habitat and Range: Sandy soils in grasslands, woodlands, and coniferous forests below 8000 feet; Sierra Nevada from El Dorado to Kern counties, South Coast Ranges to Transverse Ranges.

Mariposas, which are also known as tulip lilies, are bulbs of stunning beauty. Intricate detailing reminiscent of fine hand-painted china is revealed within each of their cup-like blooms. White mariposa lily is one of the easiest mariposas to cultivate. An exceedingly variable species, its 2-inch-wide blossoms can be white, yellow, purple, or dark red, but most have petals marked with a reddish blotch. The 8- to 24-inch-long stalks carry one to six buds that open in late spring or early summer. Plant bulbs where the patterns within each flower are easily viewed.

Other Species: Yellow mariposa lily (*Calochortus luteus*)

is a wide-ranging species. In the wild, it grows in heavy clay soils. This easy-to-grow spring bloomer has reddish brown markings within the brilliant yellow petals.

Chlorogalum pomeridianum
SOAP PLANT
Hyacinth Family (Hyacinthaceae)

Geographic Zones: All except high mountains and deserts.
Light: Sun to partial shade.
Soil: Adaptable.
Water: Drought tolerant to occasional.
Natural Habitat and Range: Dry open slopes and plains in many plant communities below 5000 feet; coastal mountains and valleys from southwestern Oregon to San Diego County.

Most native bulbs have unremarkable foliage, but soap plant is an exception. The wavy margins of its long, strap-like leaves add textural interest to the garden from winter to early summer, whereas the towering, 4- to 8-foot-tall flower stalk commands attention in late spring and summer. Scattered along the stalk are

hundreds of evening-blooming, 1-inch-wide white flowers with green or purple midveins; they open over several weeks, each lasting only one night. Widely used by California Indians for food, fiber, soap, glue, and to stupefy fish, this bulb is easy to cultivate. It may even multiply to form a small colony. Try several in a shrubby border or meadow or at the edge of an oak canopy, where the dark background will accentuate its pale-colored flowers.

Dichelostemma capitatum
WILD HYACINTH
Brodiaea Family (Themidaceae)

Geographic Zones: All except high mountains.
Light: Sun to partial shade.
Soil: Adaptable.
Water: Drought tolerant to moderate.
Natural Habitat and Range: Open slopes and plains in many plant communities up to 7000 feet; California to Oregon, Utah, New Mexico, and northern Mexico.

Even during drought years, springtime hikers are almost sure to find wild hyacinth dotting the landscape. The dense, roughly 1-inch-wide ball-like heads of white, lilac, or violet flowers are held on slender, 1- to 3-foot-long stalks. Few gardeners grow this widespread species, perhaps because it resents summer

Above: Soap plant with tall, many-branched flowering stalks, Rancho Santa Ana Botanic Garden, Claremont. BART O'BRIEN
Below: Wild hyacinth growing in a grassland, Happy Camp Canyon Regional Park, Ventura County. BILL EVARTS

Firecracker flower has striking and unusual blossoms, University of California Botanical Garden, Berkeley. RON LUTSKO

water. Weave several through a dry meadow or border, where the blossoms blend agreeably with other colors.

Other Species: The pendulous, 1-inch-long, crimson red and green blossoms of firecracker flower *(Dichelostemma ida-maia)* do not resemble wild hyacinth in the slightest. This late-spring beauty grows on grassy slopes and forest margins in the North Coast Ranges and Klamath Mountains into Oregon. Grow it in either sun or part shade with red-flowered coral bells for a lively combination.

Lilium species
LILIES
Lily Family (Liliaceae)

California boasts a dozen species of true lilies, all breathtakingly beautiful. Often separated into wet-growing and dry-growing categories, most of these late-spring to summer bloomers are vexing in cultivation. The following two species are the most reliable and readily available, and they make outstanding garden specimens.

Lilium humboldtii
HUMBOLDT LILY

Geographic Zones: All except high mountains and deserts.
Light: Sun to partial shade.
Soil: Well-drained.
Water: Drought tolerant to moderate.
Natural Habitat and Range: Dry openings or moist shade in chaparral, woodlands, and forests below 5000 feet; Cascade Range to the Sierra Nevada and South Coast Ranges to the Peninsular Ranges.

Humboldt lily, close-up showing perianth, stamens, and style, private garden, Altadena. RICHARD FISHER

Humboldt lily's tall stems (up to 8 feet) are encircled by several whorls of deep green strap-shaped leaves. Its golden orange perianth is recurved and has maroon spots. Humboldt lily falls into the dry-growing category when it comes to cultivation; it appreciates the dappled shade of oaks and produces numerous blossoms as the soil begins to dry in summer. Resist the tendency to water in summer; excess moisture may cause the bulbs to succumb to rot. Effective companions are western meadow rue, woodland strawberry, coast melic grass, California fescue, coastal wood fern, coffeeberry, and species in the genus *Ribes.*

Lilium pardalinum
LEOPARD LILY

Geographic Zones: All except high mountains and deserts.
Light: Sun to partial shade.
Soil: Adaptable, except poorly drained.
Water: Occasional to moderate.
Natural Habitat and Range: Moist places and streambanks in many plant communities below 6000 feet; California Floristic Province and southern Oregon.

Queen Fabiola Ithuriel's spear has dark blue flowers, Rancho Santa Ana Botanic Garden, Claremont. BART O'BRIEN

Leopard lily with pendent flower and buds at the edge of a patio, San Luis Obispo. SAXON HOLT

Natural Habitat and Range: Widespread in heavy soils in many plant communities below 5000 feet; southwestern Oregon and through the California Floristic Province to the Transverse Ranges.

Triteleias are rewarding, easy-care bulbs for the dry garden that tolerate some summer water. Of the dozen species in this genus, Ithuriel's spear is the most popular. This variable spring bloomer has 1- to 2-inch-long flowers ranging in color from white to purple to blue-violet. The blossoms sit atop 6- to 28-inch-long stalks.

Cultivars: 'Queen Fabiola' has notably large umbels of dark blue flowers.

Other Species: White triteleia *(Triteleia hyacinthina)* has milky white (rarely pale blue) flowers on 1- to 3-foot-long stalks and is especially easy to grow. Golden triteleia *(Triteleia ixioides)* has creamy to dark yellow flowers with contrasting midveins.

An exceedingly variable species, leopard lily is gorgeous in all its forms. Its 3- to 8-foot-long stalks bear up to 30 pendent blossoms in late spring or summer. The recurved perianth segments, typically orange at the base and red at the tips, are speckled with maroon. Over time, the occasionally rhizomatous bulb may form large clumps. Plant it under the high canopy of California sycamore or alders accompanied by giant chain fern, coral bells, and western azaleas, or other moisture-loving shrubs.

Triteleia laxa
ITHURIEL'S SPEAR
Brodiaea Family (Themidaceae)

Geographic Zones: All except high mountains and deserts.
Light: Sun to partial shade.
Soil: Adaptable.
Water: Drought tolerant to moderate.

RECOMMENDED PLANT SELECTIONS

Most gardeners find it useful to have a menu of choices when selecting a plant for a particular function or desirable feature. Consulting a list can make garden planning more manageable, whether you are picking a ground cover, a shrub with aromatic foliage, or a palette of plants for a meadow garden. To help with these kinds of decisions, the following lists provide recommendations of species and cultivars from this book for a variety of common landscape situations or plant attributes. These lists are not exhaustive and other plants may be appropriate. Don't be afraid to experiment, but be sure to consult the Plant Profiles for details about each plant.

The entries in each list are organized by plant type; the plants within each of these categories are alphabetized by scientific name and accompanied by a common name. If an individual species has several forms and/or cultivars, these are not listed separately but are included in the recommendation unless noted otherwise. For example, when *Ceanothus griseus* appears on a list, this infers that var. *horizontalis* and the cultivars 'Louis Edmunds', 'Yankee Point', and 'Diamond Heights' are all suitable choices. If a genus name is followed by the notation "(all)", this means all species within that genus that are described in the book are included in the recommendation. For example, the entry *"Pinus* (all)" means that all seven pine species in the book fit the list's description.

The facing column has a table of contents of list headings and the page number where each appears.

Western redbud and purple sage, found together on several of the above lists. STEPHEN INGRAM

ALLERGENIC PLANTS

Plants with pollen that commonly produces allergic reactions. Those with an * induce symptoms due to contact with plant hairs or oils. The word "both" in parentheses indicates the potential for both pollen-induced and contact allergic reactions.

Allergenic Plants: Coulter pine.
JOHN EVARTS

Trees

Acer (all), maple
Alnus (all), alder
Calocedrus decurrens, incense cedar
Cupressus forbesii, Tecate cypress
Pinus (all), pine
Platanus racemosa (both), California sycamore
Populus (all), cottonwood, aspen
Quercus (all), oak
Sequoia sempervirens, coast redwood
Thuja plicata, western red cedar
Umbellularia californica, California bay

Shrubs and subshrubs

Artemisia (all), sagebrush
Baccharis pilularis, coyote brush
*Fremontodendron** (all), fremontia
Garrya elliptica, coast silk-tassel
Iva hayesiana, poverty weed
Malacothamnus (all), bush mallow
Prunus (all), cherry
Rhamnus (all), coffeeberry, redberry
*Rhus** (all), lemonade berry, sugar bush, etc.
Sphaeralcea ambigua, apricot mallow

Perennials

Achillea millefolium, yarrow
Aster chilensis, coast aster
Carex (all), sedge
Ranunculus californicus, California buttercup

Romneya coulteri, Matilija poppy
Thalictrum fendleri var. *polycarpum,* western meadow rue

Grasses

Aristida purpurea var. *purpurea,* purple three-awn
Bothriochloa barbinodis, silver beardgrass
Bouteloua (all), grama grass
Calamagrostis (all), reedgrass
Festuca (all), fescue
Leymus (all), wild rye
Melica imperfecta, coast melic grass
Muhlenbergia rigens, deer grass
Nassella (all), needlegrass
Sporobolus airoides, alkali sacaton

Ferns

Woodwardia fimbriata, giant chain fern

Annuals

*Phacelia** (all), phacelia

AROMATIC FOLIAGE

Plants with aromatic foliage. In some cases, the leaves need to be crushed or bruised to release their fragrance. Those marked with an * smell bad.

Trees

Calocedrus decurrens, incense cedar
Cupressus forbesii, Tecate cypress
Pinus (all), pine
Sequoia sempervirens, coast redwood
Thuja plicata, western red cedar
Umbellularia californica, California bay

Shrubs and subshrubs

Artemisia californica, California sagebrush
Artemisia tridentata, Great Basin sagebrush
Calycanthus occidentalis, spicebush
Hyptis emoryi, desert lavender

Aromatic Foliage: hummingbird sage. JOHN EVARTS

Isomeris arborea*, bladderpod
Lepechinia (all), pitcher sage
Monardella linoides, flax-leaved monardella
Monardella villosa, coyote mint
Myrica californica, Pacific wax myrtle
Prunus (all), cherry
Ribes malvaceum, chaparral currant
Ribes sanguineum var. *glutinosum,* pink-flowering currant
Ribes viburnifolium, Catalina perfume
Rosa nutkana, Nootka rose
Salvia (all), sage
Trichostema lanatum, woolly blue curls

Perennials
Asarum caudatum, wild ginger
Datura wrightii*, sacred datura
Salvia spathacea, hummingbird sage
Satureja douglasii, yerba buena
Thalictrum fendleri var. *polycarpum**, western meadow rue

Annuals
Madia elegans, tarweed

ATTRACTIVE BARK
Plants that have interesting, colorful, or appealing bark.

Trees
Aesculus californica, California buckeye
Alnus (all), alder
Arbutus menziesii, madrone
Calocedrus decurrens, incense cedar
Cercidium floridum, palo verde
Cupressus forbesii, Tecate cypress
Lyonothamnus floribundus ssp. *aspleniifolius,* Santa Cruz Island ironwood
✕*Parkinsidium* 'Desert Museum', Desert Museum palo verde

Attractive Bark: bigberry manzanita. DAVID FROSS

Platanus racemosa, California sycamore
Populus (all), cottonwood, aspen
Quercus agrifolia, coast live oak
Quercus kelloggii, black oak
Quercus lobata, valley oak
Sequoia sempervirens, coast redwood
Thuja plicata, western red cedar

Shrubs
Adenostoma sparsifolium, redshanks
Arctostaphylos (all), manzanita
Artemisia tridentata, Great Basin sagebrush
Carpenteria californica, bush anemone
Comarostaphylis diversifolia, summer holly
Cornus sericea, creek dogwood
Eriogonum arborescens, Santa Cruz Island buckwheat
Eriogonum giganteum, Saint Catherine's lace
Ornithostaphylos oppositifolia, palo blanco
Ribes malvaceum, chaparral currant

Vines
Vitis (all), wild grape

BANK COVER
Plants up to 6 feet tall that are recommended for use on larger slopes and banks.

Shrubs and subshrubs
Adenostoma fasciculatum var. *prostratum,* prostrate chamise
Arctostaphylos edmundsii, Edmunds manzanita
Arctostaphylos hookeri, Hooker manzanita
Arctostaphylos 'John Dourley', John Dourley manzanita
Arctostaphylos 'Pacific Mist', Pacific Mist manzanita
Arctostaphylos pumila, sandmat manzanita
Artemisia californica 'Canyon Gray', Canyon Gray California sagebrush
Baccharis pilularis, coyote brush
Ceanothus gloriosus, Point Reyes ceanothus

Bank Cover: deer grass. DAVID FROSS

Ceanothus griseus, Carmel ceanothus
Ceanothus 'Joyce Coulter', Joyce Coulter ceanothus
Ceanothus thyrsiflorus var. *repens* 'Taylor's Blue', Taylor's Blue ceanothus
Eriogonum cinereum, ashleaf buckwheat
Eriogonum fasciculatum, California buckwheat
Fremontodendron decumbens, Pine Hill fremontia
Fremontodendron 'Ken Taylor', Ken Taylor fremontia
Fremontodendron 'El Dorado Gold', El Dorado Gold fremontia
Galvezia speciosa, island snapdragon
Iva hayesiana, poverty weed
Lepechinia calycina 'Rocky Point', Rocky Point pitcher sage
Ribes viburnifolium, Catalina perfume
Rosa (all), wild rose
Salvia 'Bee's Bliss', Bee's Bliss sage
Salvia leucophylla 'Point Sal Spreader', Point Sal Spreader sage
Salvia leucophylla 'Point Sal', Point Sal sage
Salvia mellifera 'Terra Seca', Terra Seca sage
Salvia 'Mrs. Beard', Mrs. Beard sage
Salvia munzii 'Emerald Cascade', Emerald Cascade sage
Symphoricarpos mollis, creeping snowberry

Perennials
Zauschneria (all), California fuchsia

Grasses
Aristida purpurea var. *purpurea,* purple three-awn
Festuca californica, California fescue
Leymus condensatus 'Canyon Prince', Canyon Prince wild rye
Leymus triticoides 'Grey Dawn', Grey Dawn creeping wild rye
Muhlenbergia rigens, deer grass

Ferns
Polystichum munitum, western sword fern

Succulents
Agave shawii, Shaw agave

Vines
Aristolochia californica, California Dutchman's pipe

DEER RESISTANT
Plants that, when established, are rarely browsed by deer.

Trees
Brahea (all), fan palm
Calocedrus decurrens, incense cedar
Chilopsis linearis, desert willow

✕*Chitalpa tashkentensis,* chitalpa
Fraxinus dipetala, flowering ash
Pinus (all), pine
Sequoia sempervirens, coast redwood
Washingtonia filifera, California fan palm

Deer Resistant: single leaf onion (foreground) and azalea-flowered monkeyflower.
CAROL BORNSTEIN

Shrubs and subshrubs
Artemisia (all except *douglasiana*), sagebrush
Atriplex lentiformis ssp. *breweri,* quail bush
Baccharis pilularis, coyote brush
Berberis nevinii, Nevin barberry
Eriogonum (all except *grande* var. *rubescens* and *latifolium*), buckwheat
Isomeris arborea, bladderpod
Iva hayesiana, poverty weed
Lepechinia (all), pitcher sage
Mimulus (all), monkeyflower
Monardella villosa, coyote mint
Rhus (all), lemonade berry, sugar bush, etc.
Salvia (all), sage
Symphoricarpos (all), snowberry
Verbena lilacina, lilac verbena

Perennials
Asclepias (all), milkweed
Aster chilensis, coast aster
Carex (all), sedge
Coreopsis maritima, sea dahlia
Datura wrightii, sacred datura
Juncus (all), wire grass
Monardella (all), coyote mint
Mimulus cardinalis, scarlet monkeyflower
Mimulus guttatus, seep monkeyflower
Penstemon (all), penstemon
Satureja douglasii, yerba buena
Sisyrinchium (all), blue-eyed grass, golden-eyed grass
Zauschneria (all), California fuchsia

Grasses

Aristida purpurea var. *purpurea,* purple three-awn
Bothriochloa barbinodis, silver beardgrass
Bouteloua (all), grama grass
Calamagrostis (all), reedgrass
Festuca (all), fescue
Leymus (all), wild rye
Melica imperfecta, coast melic grass
Muhlenbergia rigens, deer grass
Nassella (all), needlegrass
Sporobolus airoides, alkali sacaton

Ferns

Adiantum (all), western five-fingered fern, southern
   maidenhair
Dryopteris arguta, coastal wood fern
Polypodium (all), polypody fern
Polystichum munitum, western sword fern
Woodwardia fimbriata, giant chain fern

Succulents

Agave (all), agave
Dudleya (all), dudleya
Hesperoyucca whipplei, Our Lord's candle
Lewisia (all), cliff maids
Nolina (all), beargrass
Opuntia basilaris, beavertail cactus
Yucca (all), yucca

Vines

Aristolochia californica, California Dutchman's pipe
Clematis (all), clematis

Bulbs

Allium unifolium, single leaf onion

Annuals

Clarkia (all), clarkia
Madia elegans, tarweed
Phacelia (all), phacelia

DRIED ARRANGEMENTS

Plants with flowers, fruits, or foliage that make them
excellent choices for dried arrangements.

Trees

Lyonothamnus floribundus ssp. *aspleniifolius,* Santa Cruz
   Island ironwood

Shrubs, and subshrubs

Calycanthus occidentalis, spicebush
Cercocarpus (all), mountain mahogany
Eriogonum arborescens, Santa Cruz Island buckwheat
Eriogonum fasciculatum, California buckwheat

Eriogonum giganteum, Saint Catherine's lace
Hesperoyucca whipplei, Our Lord's candle
Nolina (all), beargrass
Salvia 'Allen Chickering', Allen Chickering sage
Salvia 'Aromas', Aromas sage
Salvia 'Pozo Blue', Pozo Blue sage
Salvia 'Whirly Blue', Whirly Blue sage
Salvia apiana, white sage
Salvia clevelandii, Cleveland sage
Salvia leucophylla, purple sage
Yucca schidigera, Mojave yucca

Dried Arrangements: Santa Cruz Island buckwheat.
DAVID FROSS

Perennials

Achillea millefolium, yarrow
Asclepias (all), milkweed
Juncus (all), wire grass
Salvia spathacea, hummingbird sage

Grasses

Bothriochloa barbinodis, silver beardgrass
Bouteloua (all), grama grass
Leymus (all), wild rye
Muhlenbergia rigens, deer grass
Sporobolus airoides, alkali sacaton

Succulents

Agave (all), agave

Vines

Clematis (all), clematis

EROSION

Plants that are good choices for erosion control.

Trees

Aesculus californica, California buckeye
Lyonothamnus floribundus ssp. *aspleniifolius,* Santa Cruz
   Island ironwood
Pinus (all), pine
Populus (all), cottonwood, quaking aspen

Erosion: Edmunds manzanita (ground cover), Howard McMinn manzanita, and coast live oak.
JOHN EVARTS

Quercus (all), oak
Sequoia sempervirens, coast redwood
Thuja plicata, western red cedar

Shrubs and subshrubs

Adenostoma (all except *fasciculatum* 'Black Diamond'), chamise, redshanks
Arctostaphylos (all), manzanita
Artemisia (all), sagebrush
Atriplex lentiformis ssp. *breweri,* quail brush
Baccharis pilularis, coyote brush
Calliandra eriophylla, fairy duster
Calycanthus occidentalis, spicebush
Ceanothus (all), ceanothus
Cercis occidentalis, western redbud
Cercocarpus (all), mountain mahogany
Cornus sericea, creek dogwood
Dendromecon (all), bush poppy
Encelia (all), California sunflower, incienso
Eriogonum (all), buckwheat
Eriophyllum nevinii 'Canyon Silver', Canyon Silver island snowflake
Galvezia (all), island snapdragon, Baja bush snapdragon
Hesperoyucca whipplei, Our Lord's candle
Heteromeles arbutifolia, toyon
Isomeris arborea, bladderpod
Iva hayesiana, poverty weed
Malacothamnus (all), bush mallow
Mimulus (all except *cardinalis* and *guttatus*), monkeyflower
Ornithostaphylos oppositifolia, palo blanco
Philadelphus lewisii, western mock orange
Prunus (all), cherry
Rhamnus (all), coffeeberry, redberry
Rhus (all), lemonade berry, sugar bush, etc.
Ribes (all), currant, gooseberry

Rosa (all), wild rose
Salvia (all), sage
Sambucus mexicana, western elderberry
Symphoricarpos (all), snowberry

Perennials

Achillea millefolium, yarrow
Aster chilensis, coast aster
Carex (all), sedge
Iris douglasiana, Douglas iris
Juncus (all), rush, wire grass
Romneya coulteri, Matilija poppy
Solidago (all), goldenrod
Tanacetum (all), dune tansy
Zauschneria (all), California fuchsia

Grasses

Bothriochloa barbinodis, silver beardgrass
Bouteloua (all), grama grass
Festuca (all), fescue
Leymus (all), wild rye
Muhlenbergia rigens, deer grass
Nassella (all), needlegrass
Sporobolus airoides, alkali sacaton

Vines

Calystegia macrostegia ssp. *macrostegia* 'Anacapa Pink', Anacapa Pink California morning glory
Vitis (all), wild grape

ESPALIER

Plants that can be pruned in a formal or informal pattern against a fence or wall.

Espalier: Santa Cruz Island ironwood.
JOHN EVARTS

Trees

Lyonothamnus floribundus ssp. *aspleniifolius,* Santa Cruz
Island ironwood

Shrubs

Arctostaphylos bakeri 'Louis Edmunds', Louis Edmunds
manzanita
Arctostaphylos 'Howard McMinn', Howard McMinn
manzanita
Arctostaphylos 'Sentinel', Sentinel manzanita
Cercis occidentalis, western redbud
Cercocarpus betuloides, mountain mahogany
Cornus sericea, creek dogwood
Fremontodendron (all except *decumbens*), fremontia
Galvezia speciosa, island snapdragon
Garrya elliptica, coast silk-tassel
Heteromeles arbutifolia, toyon
Ornithostaphylos oppositifolia, palo blanco
Rhamnus crocea, redberry
Ribes aureum var. *gracillimum,* golden currant
Ribes malvaceum 'Dancing Tassels', Dancing Tassels currant
Ribes sanguineum var. *glutinosum,* pink-flowering currant
Ribes speciosum, fuchsia-flowered gooseberry
Ribes viburnifolium, Catalina perfume

Vines

Aristolochia californica, California Dutchman's pipe
Vitis (all), wild grape

FALL FOLIAGE COLOR

Plants with colorful fall foliage (degree of color may
vary temporally and geographically).

Fall Foliage Color: western redbud. DAVID FROSS

Trees

Acer (all), maple
Fraxinus dipetala, flowering ash
Platanus racemosa, California sycamore
Populus (all), cottonwood, quaking aspen
Quercus kelloggii, black oak

Shrubs

Berberis (all except *nevinii*), barberry
Calycanthus occidentalis, spicebush
Cercis occidentalis, western redbud
Cornus sericea, creek dogwood
Rhododendron occidentale, western azalea
Rhus trilobata, basket bush

Perennials

Thalictrum fendleri var. *polycarpum,* western
meadow rue

Grasses

Bothriochloa barbinodis, silver beardgrass

Vines

Vitis (all), wild grape

FAST GROWING

Plants that will typically grow to mature size at a rapid
rate.

Trees

Acer macrophyllum, big-leaf maple
Alnus (all), alder
✕*Chitalpa tashkentensis,* chitalpa
Cupressus forbesii, Tecate cypress
Lyonothamnus floribundus ssp. *aspleniifolius,* Santa Cruz
Island ironwood
Pinus radiata, Monterey pine
Pinus sabiniana, foothill pine
Pinus torreyana, Torrey pine
Platanus racemosa, California sycamore
Populus fremontii, Fremont cottonwood
Sequoia sempervirens, coast redwood
Washingtonia filifera, California fan palm

Shrubs and subshrubs

Abutilon palmeri, Indian mallow
Artemisia (all), sagebrush
Atriplex lentiformis ssp. *breweri,* quail bush
Baccharis pilularis, coyote brush
Calycanthus occidentalis, spicebush
Ceanothus arboreus, island ceanothus
Ceanothus 'Concha', Concha ceanothus
Ceanothus 'Dark Star', Dark Star ceanothus
Ceanothus 'Far Horizons', Far Horizons ceanothus
Ceanothus 'Gentian Plume', Gentian Plume ceanothus
Ceanothus griseus (all except 'Diamond Heights'),
Carmel ceanothus
Ceanothus 'Joyce Coulter', Joyce Coulter ceanothus
Ceanothus 'Julia Phelps', Julia Phelps ceanothus
Ceanothus 'Ray Hartman', Ray Hartman ceanothus
Ceanothus 'Sierra Blue', Sierra Blue ceanothus
Ceanothus thyrsiflorus, blue blossom ceanothus

Fast Growing: Ray Hartman ceanothus. JOHN EVARTS

Cercocarpus betuloides, mountain mahogany
Cornus sericea, creek dogwood
Encelia (all), California sunflower, incienso
Eriogonum cinereum, ashyleaf buckwheat
Eriogonum fasciculatum, California buckwheat
Eriogonum giganteum, Saint Catherine's lace
Eriophyllum nevinii 'Canyon Silver', Canyon Silver
    island snowflake
Fremontodendron (all except *decumbens*), fremontia
Galvezia (all), island snapdragon, Baja bush snapdragon
Hesperoyucca whipplei, Our Lord's candle
Iva hayesiana, poverty weed
Lavatera (all), malva rosa, Purisima mallow
Lepechinia (all), pitcher sage
Lupinus (all), bush lupine, grape soda lupine
Malacothamnus (all), bush mallow
Myrica californica, Pacific wax myrtle
Philadelphus (all) mock orange
Ribes aureum var. *gracillimum,* golden currant
Ribes sanguineum var. *glutinosum* 'Claremont',
    Claremont currant
Ribes sanguineum var. *glutinosum* 'Tranquillon Ridge',
    Tranquillon Ridge currant
Salvia (all except 'Betsy Clebsch'), sage
Sambucus mexicana, western elderberry
Venegasia carpesioides, canyon sunflower
Verbena lilacina, lilac verbena

Perennials

Grindelia stricta var. *platyphylla,* spreading gum plant
Lessingia filaginifolia 'Silver Carpet', Silver Carpet
    California aster
Romneya coulteri, Matilija poppy
Zauschneria (all), California fuchsia

Grasses

Muhlenbergia rigens, deer grass

Vines

Calystegia macrostegia ssp. *macrostegia* 'Anacapa Pink',
    Anacapa Pink California morning glory
Vitis (all except *californica* and Walker Ridge),
    wild grape

FROST TENDER

Plants that will not tolerate freezing temperatures on a regular basis, although some will tolerate an occasional freeze if they are well established and healthy. Plants noted with an * are those whose frost tolerance is not yet fully understood. A number of these plants have populations that regularly endure occasional freezing temperatures with no damage, while other populations of the same plant (often more coastal or southern in origin) will not endure any frost.

Frost Tender: malva rosa. BART O'BRIEN

Trees

Brahea (all), fan palm
*Cercidium floridum**, palo verde
✕*Parkinsidium* 'Desert Museum'*, Desert Museum palo
    verde

Shrubs and subshrubs

Abutilon palmeri, Indian mallow
*Calliandra eriophylla**, fairy duster
Coreopsis gigantea, giant coreopsis
Encelia californica, California sunflower
*Encelia farinosa**, incienso
Eriophyllum nevinii 'Canyon Silver', Canyon Silver
    island snowflake
Galvezia juncea, Baja bush snapdragon
*Galvezia speciosa**, island snapdragon
Hyptis emoryi, desert lavender
Justicia californica, chuparosa
Lavatera (all), malva rosa, Purisima mallow
Perityle incana, Guadalupe Island rock daisy

Rhus lentii, pink-flowering sumac
Rosa minutifolia*, Baja littleleaf rose
Salvia munzii, Munz sage
Sphaeralcea ambigua ssp. *rosacea*,* pink mallow
Verbena lilacina*, lilac verbena

Perennials
Coreopsis maritima, sea dahlia
Heuchera maxima*, island alum root

Succulents
Agave deserti*, desert agave
Agave shawii, Shaw agave
Dudleya brittonii, Britton dudleya
Dudleya candelabrum*, candelholder dudleya

Vines
Calystegia macrostegia ssp. *macrostegia* 'Anacapa Pink',
  Anacapa Pink California morning glory

GROUNDCOVERS
Plants usually less than 3 feet high (some are taller
when flowering) that can be used as groundcovers.

Shrubs and subshrubs
Adenostoma fasciculatum var. *prostratum,* prostrate
  chamise
Arctostaphylos edmundsii, Edmunds manzanita
Arctostaphylos 'Emerald Carpet', Emerald Carpet
  manzanita
Arctostaphylos hookeri, Hooker manzanita
Arctostaphylos 'John Dourley', John Dourley manzanita
Arctostaphylos 'Pacific Mist', Pacific Mist manzanita
Arctostaphylos pumila, sandmat manzanita
Arctostaphylos uva-ursi, kinnikinnick
Artemisia californica 'Canyon Gray', Canyon Gray
  California sagebrush

*Groundcovers: Select Mattole California fuchsia and a
kinnikinnick hybrid.* BART O'BRIEN

Artemisia californica 'Montara', Montara California
  sagebrush
Baccharis pilularis cultivars, coyote brush
Berberis aquifolium 'Compacta', Compacta Oregon
  grape
Berberis aquifolium var. *repens,* creeping barberry
Berberis nervosa, longleaf barberry
Ceanothus gloriosus, Point Reyes ceanothus
Ceanothus griseus var. *horizontalis,* Carmel creeper
  ceanothus
Ceanothus hearstiorum, Hearst ceanothus
Ceanothus 'Joyce Coulter', Joyce Coulter ceanothus
Ceanothus maritimus, maritime ceanothus
Ceanothus thyrsiflorus var. *repens* 'Taylor's Blue', Taylor's
  Blue ceanothus
Eriogonum fasciculatum cultivars, California buckwheat
Galvezia speciosa, island snapdragon
Iva hayesiana, poverty weed
Ribes viburnifolium, Catalina perfume
Salvia 'Bee's Bliss', Bee's Bliss sage
Salvia leucophylla 'Point Sal Spreader', Point Sal
  Spreader sage
Salvia leucophylla 'Point Sal', Point Sal sage
Salvia mellifera 'Terra Seca', Terra Seca sage
Salvia 'Mrs. Beard', Mrs. Beard sage
Salvia munzii 'Emerald Cascade', Emerald Cascade sage
Symphoricarpos mollis, creeping snowberry

Perennials
Achillea millefolium, yarrow
Asarum caudatum, wild ginger
Aster chilensis 'Point Saint George', Point Saint George
  coast aster
Carex (all except *spissa*), sedge
Erigeron (all), seaside daisy
Fragaria (all), strawberry
Grindelia stricta var. *platyphylla,* spreading gum plant
Heterotheca sessiliflora ssp. *bolanderi* 'San Bruno
  Mountain', San Bruno Mountain golden aster
Heuchera (all), coral bells
Iris (all), iris
Lessingia filaginifolia 'Silver Carpet', Silver Carpet
  California aster
Oxalis oregana, redwood sorrel
Salvia spathacea, hummingbird sage
Satureja douglasii, yerba buena
Solidago (all), goldenrod
Tanacetum (all), dune tansy
Zauschneria 'Hurricane Point', Hurricane Point
  California fuchsia
Zauschneria 'Select Mattole', Select Mattole California
  fuchsia
Zauschneria septentrionalis, Humboldt County fuchsia
Zauschneria 'Summer Snow', Summer Snow California
  fuchsia

Grasses

Bouteloua curtipendula (rhizomatous forms only), side-oats grama
Bouteloua gracilis, blue grama
Calamagrostis foliosa, Cape Mendocino reedgrass
Festuca (all), fescue
Leymus triticoides 'Grey Dawn', Grey Dawn creeping wild rye
Muhlenbergia rigens, deer grass
Sporobolus airoides, alkali sacaton

Ferns

Dryopteris arguta, coastal wood fern
Polypodium (all) polypody fern

Succulents

Agave shawii, Shaw agave
Dudleya 'Frank Reinelt', Frank Reinelt dudleya
Dudleya virens ssp. *hassei,* Catalina Island dudleya

Vines

Aristolochia californica, California Dutchman's pipe
Calystegia macrostegia ssp. *macrostegia* 'Anacapa Pink', Anacapa Pink California morning glory

HEDGES AND SCREENS

Plants, both large and small, that make good hedges or screens. Those with an * can be sheared as formal hedges.

Trees

Calocedrus decurrens*, incense cedar
Cupressus forbesii*, Tecate cypress
Lyonothamnus floribundus ssp. *aspleniifolius,* Santa Cruz Island ironwood
Pinus contorta ssp. *contorta,* shore pine
Pinus monophylla, singleleaf pinyon
Pinus quadrifolia, Parry pinyon
Quercus agrifolia*, coast live oak
Quercus durata, leather oak
Sequoia sempervirens*, coast redwood
Thuja plicata*, western red cedar
Umbellularia californica*, California bay

Shrubs and subshrubs

Adenostoma fasciculatum*, chamise
Adenostoma fasciculatum 'Black Diamond'*, Black Diamond chamise
Arctostaphylos bakeri 'Louis Edmunds', Louis Edmunds manzanita
Arctostaphylos glauca, big berry manzanita
Arctostaphylos 'Howard McMinn'*, Howard McMinn manzanita
Arctostaphylos manzanita, Parry manzanita

Arctostaphylos pajaroensis, Pajaro manzanita
Arctostaphylos refugioensis, Refugio manzanita
Arctostaphylos 'Sentinel', Sentinel manzanita
Arctostaphylos 'Sunset', Sunset manzanita
Artemisia tridentata, Great Basin sagebrush
Atriplex lentiformis ssp. *breweri**, quail bush
Baccharis pilularis*, coyote brush
Berberis aquifolium, Oregon grape
Berberis 'Golden Abundance', Golden Abundance barberry
Berberis nevinii, Nevin barberry
Berberis pinnata, California barberry
Berberis 'Skylark', Skylark barberry
Calycanthus occidentalis, spicebush
Carpenteria californica, bush anemone
Ceanothus arboreus, island ceanothus
Ceanothus 'Concha', Concha ceanothus
Ceanothus 'Dark Star', Dark Star ceanothus
Ceanothus 'Far Horizons', Far Horizons ceanothus
Ceanothus 'Gentian Plume', Gentian Plume ceanothus
Ceanothus griseus (all except 'Diamond Heights') Carmel ceanothus
Ceanothus 'Julia Phelps', Julia Phelps ceanothus
Ceanothus 'Ray Hartman', Ray Hartman ceanothus
Ceanothus 'Sierra Blue', Sierra Blue ceanothus
Ceanothus thyrsiflorus (all except 'Taylor's Blue'), blue blossom ceanothus
Cercis occidentalis, western redbud
Cercocarpus betuloides*, mountain mahogany
Comarostaphylis diversifolia, summer holly
Cornus sericea, creek dogwood
Dendromecon harfordii, island bush poppy
Eriogonum arborescens, Santa Cruz Island buckwheat
Eriogonum crocatum, saffron buckwheat
Eriogonum giganteum, Saint Catherine's lace
Fremontodendron* (all except *decumbens*), fremontia
Galvezia juncea, Baja bush snapdragon

Hedges and Screens: lemonade berry. DAVID FROSS

*Galvezia speciosa**, island snapdragon
Garrya elliptica, coast silk-tassel
*Heteromeles arbutifolia**, toyon
Isomeris arborea, bladderpod
*Iva hayesiana**, poverty weed
Justicia californica, chuparosa
*Lavatera assurgentiflora**, malva rosa
*Myrica californica**, Pacific wax myrtle
Ornithostaphylos oppositifolia, palo blanco
Philadelphus lewisii, western mock orange
*Prunus** (all), cherry
*Rhamnus** (all), coffeeberry, redberry
*Rhus** (all except *trilobata*), lemonade berry,
   sugar bush, etc.
Ribes malvaceum, chaparral currant
Ribes sanguineum var. *glutinosum,* pink-flowering currant
Salvia leucophylla, purple sage
Sambucus mexicana, western elderberry
*Simmondsia chinensis**, jojoba

HUMMINGBIRDS
Plants recommended for attracting hummingbirds.

Trees
Chilopsis linearis, desert willow
X*Chitalpa tashkentensis,* chitalpa

Shrubs and subshrubs
Arctostaphylos (all), manzanita
Calliandra eriophylla, fairy duster
Comarostaphylis diversifolia, summer holly
Galvezia (all), island snapdragon, Baja bush snapdragon
Justicia californica, chuparosa
Keckiella (all), keckiella

Hummingbirds: scarlet monkeyflower. WILDSCAPING.COM

Mimulus (all), monkeyflower
Monardella (all), coyote mint
Ornithostaphylos oppositifolia, palo blanco
Ribes (all), currant, gooseberry
Salvia (all), sage

Perennials
Heuchera (all), coral bells
Mimulus cardinalis, scarlet monkeyflower
Mimulus guttatus, seep monkeyflower
Penstemon (all), penstemon
Salvia spathacea, hummingbird sage
Satureja mimuloides, monkeyflower savory
Zauschneria (all), California fuchsia

Succulents
Agave (all), agave
Dudleya (all), dudleya

Bulbs
Dichelostemma ida-maia, firecracker flower
Lilium (all), Humboldt lily, leopard lily

MEADOWS
Plants suitable for a meadow garden.

Shrubs and subshrubs
Eriogonum grande var. *rubescens,* red-flowered buckwheat
Eriogonum latifolium, coast buckwheat
Eriophyllum confertiflorum, golden yarrow
Lupinus albifrons var. *collinus,* prostrate silver bush
   lupine
Salvia 'Bee's Bliss', Bee's Bliss sage
Salvia 'Dara's Choice', Dara's Choice sage
Salvia 'Mrs. Beard', Mrs. Beard sage

Perennials
Achillea millefolium, yarrow
Aquilegia formosa, western columbine
Asclepias (all), milkweed
Aster chilensis, coast aster
Carex (all except *spissa*), sedge
Coreopsis maritima, sea dahlia
Datura wrightii, sacred datura
Erigeron (all), seaside daisy
Fragaria (all), strawberry
Grindelia (all), gum plant
Heterotheca sessiliflora ssp. *bolanderi* 'San Bruno
   Mountain', San Bruno Mountain golden aster
Iris (all), iris
Juncus (all except *acutus*), wire grass, rush
Lessingia filaginifolia, California aster
Mimulus cardinalis, scarlet monkeyflower
Mimulus guttatus, seep monkeyflower

Oenothera elata, Hooker evening primrose
Penstemon centranthifolius, scarlet bugler
Penstemon heterophyllus, foothill penstemon
Penstemon spectabilis, royal penstemon
Ranunculus californicus, California buttercup
Salvia spathacea, hummingbird sage
Sidalcea (all), checkerbloom
Sisyrinchium (all), blue-eyed grass, golden-eyed grass
Solidago (all), goldenrod
Tanacetum (all), dune tansy
Wyethia (all), mules ears
Zauschneria (all), California fuchsia

Meadows: tidy tips. BART O'BRIEN

Grasses
Aristida purpurea var. *purpurea,* purple three-awn
Bothriochloa barbinodis, silver beardgrass
Bouteloua (all), grama grass
Calamagrostis (all), reedgrass
Festuca (all), fescue
Leymus (all), wild rye
Melica imperfecta, coast melic grass
Muhlenbergia rigens, deer grass
Nassella (all), needlegrass
Sporobolus airoides, alkali sacaton

Succulents
Dudleya 'Frank Reinelt', Frank Reinelt dudleya
Dudleya virens ssp. *hassei,* Catalina Island dudleya

Annuals
Clarkia (all), clarkia
Collinsia heterophylla, Chinese houses
Eschscholzia (all), California poppy, frying pans

Gilia (all), gilia
Helianthus annuus, sunflower
Layia platyglossa, tidy tips
Limnanthes douglasii, meadowfoam
Linanthus (all), linanthus
Lupinus (all), lupine
Madia elegans, tarweed
Mentzelia lindleyi, blazing star
Nemophila (all), baby blue eyes, five spot
Phacelia (all), phacelia
Platystemon californicus, cream cups

Bulbs
Allium unifolium, single leaf onion
Brodiaea (all), brodiaea
Calochortus (all), Mariposa lily, fairy lantern
Chlorogalum pomeridianum, soap plant
Dichelostemma (all), wild hyacinth, firecracker flower
Triteleia (all), triteleia

MOIST HABITATS
Plants that prefer year-round moisture. Those noted with an * tolerate periodic flooding in winter.

Trees
*Alnus** (all), alder
Platanus racemosa,* California sycamore
*Populus** (all), cottonwood, quaking aspen
Sequoia sempervirens,* coast redwood
Thuja plicata, western red cedar
Umbellularia californica,* California bay
Washingtonia filifera, California fan palm

Shrubs and subshrubs
Calycanthus occidentalis, spicebush
Cornus sericea,* creek dogwood
Iva hayesiana, poverty weed
Myrica californica, Pacific wax myrtle
Philadelphus lewisii, western mock orange
Rhododendron occidentale, western azalea
Ribes aureum var. *gracillimum,* golden currant
Sambucus (all), elderberry

Perennials
Aquilegia formosa, western columbine
Artemisia douglasiana,* mugwort
Asarum caudatum, wild ginger
Carex (all, with an * for *pansa, praegracilis,* and *spissa*), sedge
Epipactis gigantea, stream orchid
*Juncus** (all), wire grass, rush
Mimulus cardinalis, scarlet monkeyflower
Mimulus guttatus, seep monkeyflower
Oenothera elata, Hooker evening primrose

*Oxalis oregana**, redwood sorrel
Satureja mimuloides, monkeyflower savory
Sidalcea calycosa ssp. *rhizomata,* Point Reyes
   checkerbloom
Sisyrinchium californicum, golden-eyed grass
Solidago (all except *californica*), goldenrod

Grasses
Calamagrostis nutkaensis, Pacific reedgrass
*Festuca rubra**, red fescue
Leymus triticoides 'Grey Dawn'*, Grey Dawn creeping
   wild rye
*Muhlenbergia rigens**, deer grass
*Sporobolus airoides**, alkali sacaton

Ferns
Adiantum (all), western five-fingered fern, southern
   maidenhair
Polystichum munitum, western sword fern
*Woodwardia fimbriata**, giant chain fern

Vines
Vitis (all), wild grape

Annuals
*Limnanthes douglasii**, meadowfoam

Bulbs
Lilium pardalinum, leopard lily
Triteleia hyacinthina, white triteleia

NARROW BEDS
Plants suitable for areas less than three feet wide, typically with a wall, fence, or path on one side. All annuals and bulbs are appropriate but are not listed.

Shrubs and subshrubs
Artemisia pycnocephala 'David's Choice', David's Choice
   sandhill sagebrush
Berberis (all except *nevinii*), barberry
Eriogonum grande var. *rubescens,* red-flowered buckwheat
Eriogonum crocatum, saffron buckwheat
Eriogonum latifolium, coast buckwheat
Eriogonum umbellatum var. *polyanthum,* sulfur
   buckwheat
Eriophyllum confertiflorum, golden yarrow
Heterotheca sessiliflora ssp. *bolanderi* 'San Bruno
   Mountain', San Bruno Mountain golden aster
Mimulus (all), monkeyflower
Ribes aureum var. *gracillimum,* golden currant
Ribes malvaceum, chaparral currant
Ribes sanguineum var. *glutinosum,* pink-flowering currant
Symphoricarpos (all), snowberry

Perennials
Achillea millefolium, yarrow
Aquilegia formosa, western columbine
Asarum caudatum, wild ginger
Aster chilensis, coast aster
Carex (all except *spissa*), sedge
Erigeron (all), seaside daisy
Fragaria (all), strawberry
Heuchera (all), coral bells
Iris (all), iris
Juncus (all except *acutus*), wire grass, rush
Oxalis oregana, redwood sorrel

Moist Habitats: seep monkeyflower (foreground) and western columbine. BART O'BRIEN

Narrow Beds: Douglas iris. JOHN EVARTS

Ranunculus californicus, California buttercup
Salvia spathacea, hummingbird sage
Satureja (all), yerba buena, monkeyflower savory
Sidalcea (all), checkerbloom
Sisyrinchium (all), blue-eyed grass, golden-eyed grass
Thalictrum fendleri var. *polycarpum,* western meadow rue
Zauschneria (all), California fuchsia

Grasses
Aristida purpurea var. *purpurea,* purple three-awn
Bouteloua (all), grama grass
Calamagrostis (all), reedgrass
Festuca (all), fescue
Melica imperfecta, coast melic grass
Nassella (all), needlegrass
Sporobolus airoides, alkali sacaton

Ferns
Adiantum (all), western five-fingered fern, southern
    maidenhair
Dryopteris arguta, coastal wood fern
Polystichum munitum, western sword fern

Succulents
Dudleya (all), dudleya
Lewisia (all), cliff-maids

ORNAMENTAL FRUITS
Plants with ornamental fruits or fruiting structures.

Trees
Aesculus californica, California buckeye
Alnus rhombifolia, white alder
Arbutus menziesii, madrone
Brahea (all), fan palm
Calocedrus decurrens, incense cedar
Cercidium floridum, palo verde
Cupressus forbesii, Tecate cypress
Pinus (all), pine
Platanus racemosa, California sycamore
Populus fremontii (females only), Fremont cottonwood
Quercus (all tree species), oak
Sequoia sempervirens, coast redwood
Thuja plicata, western red cedar
Umbellularia californica, California bay
Washingtonia filifera, California fan palm
Yucca brevifolia, Joshua tree

Shrubs and subshrubs
Arctostaphylos (all), manzanita
Berberis (all), barberry
Calliandra eriophylla, fairy duster
Calycanthus occidentalis, spicebush
Cercis occidentalis, western redbud

Ornamental Fruits:
toyon. JOHN EVARTS

Cercocarpus betuloides, mountain mahogany
Comarostaphylis diversifolia, summer holly
Cornus sericea, creek dogwood
Eriogonum arborescens, Santa Cruz Island buckwheat
Eriogonum crocatum, saffron buckwheat
Eriogonum fasciculatum, California buckwheat
Eriogonum giganteum, Saint Catherine's lace
Eriogonum umbellatum var. *polyanthum,* sulfur buckwheat
Garrya elliptica (females only), coast silk-tassel
Hesperoyucca whipplei, Our Lord's candle
Heteromeles arbutifolia, toyon
Isomeris arborea, bladderpod
Nolina (all), beargrass
Prunus (all), cherry
Quercus durata, leather oak
Rhamnus (all), coffeeberry, redberry
Rhus (all), lemonade berry, sugar bush, etc.
Ribes (all except *viburnifolium*), currant, gooseberry
Rosa (all), wild rose
Sambucus (all), elderberry
Simmondsia chinensis (females only), jojoba
Solanum (all), blue witch
Symphoricarpos (all), snowberry
Yucca baccata, banana yucca
Yucca schidigera, Mojave yucca

Perennials
Asclepias (all), milkweed
Fragaria (all except 'Aulon'), strawberry

Grasses
Bothriochloa barbinodis, silver beardgrass

Vines
Aristolochia californica, California Dutchman's pipe
Clematis (all), clematis
Vitis (all), wild grape

Annuals
Stylomecon heterophylla, wind poppy

Bulbs
Allium unifolium, single leaf onion

PARKWAY PLANTS
Plants suitable for landscaping the area between the street and the sidewalk, as well as for use in street medians. Most are relatively low growing and durable.

Trees
Brahea (all), fan palm
Washingtonia filifera, California fan palm

Parkway Plants: Catalina Island dudleya.
DAVID FROSS

Shrubs and subshrubs
Abutilon palmeri, Indian mallow
Baccharis pilularis, coyote brush
Berberis aquifolium 'Compacta', Compacta Oregon grape
Berberis aquifolium var. *repens,* creeping barberry
Calliandra eriophylla, fairy duster
Iva hayesiana, poverty weed
Nolina (all), beargrass
Quercus durata, leather oak
Salvia 'Bee's Bliss', Bee's Bliss sage
Salvia 'Mrs. Beard', Mrs. Beard sage
Verbena lilacina, lilac verbena

Perennials
Achillea millefolium, yarrow
Aster chilensis 'Point Saint George', Point Saint George aster
Carex (all except *spissa*), sedge
Erigeron (all), seaside daisy
Fragaria (all), strawberry
Grindelia stricta var. *platyphylla,* spreading gum plant
Iris douglasiana, Douglas iris

Juncus (all except *acutus*), wiregrass, rush
Lessingia filaginifolia 'Silver Carpet', Silver Carpet California aster
Sisyrinchium (all), blue-eyed grass, golden-eyed grass
Solidago (all), goldenrod
Tanacetum (all), dune tansy
Zauschneria (all), California fuchsia

Grasses
Bouteloua (all), grama grass
Festuca rubra, red fescue
Leymus condensatus 'Canyon Prince', Canyon Prince wild rye
Leymus triticoides 'Grey Dawn', Grey Dawn creeping wild rye
Muhlenbergia rigens, deer grass
Sporobolus airoides, alkali sacaton

Succulents
Agave deserti, desert agave
Agave shawii, Shaw agave
Dudleya virens ssp. *hassei,* Catalina Island dudleya

Annuals
Eschscholzia californica, California poppy

POISONOUS PLANTS
Plants known to cause illness or death when ingested by humans. The plant part(s) that are poisonous appear after the common name.

Trees
Aesculus californica, California buckeye—all parts

Shrubs and subshrubs
Berberis (all), barberry—roots and leaves
Lupinus (all), lupine—seeds, fresh leaves, and stems

Poisonous Plants: arroyo lupine. JOHN EVARTS

Prunus (all), cherry—seeds
Rhamnus (all), coffeeberry, redberry—leaves, berries, and bark
Rhododendron occidentale, western azalea—all parts
Sambucus (all), elderberry—all except ripe berries and flowers
Solanum (all) blue witch—all parts
Symphoricarpos (all), snowberry—berries

Perennials
Datura wrightii, sacred datura—all parts
Ranunculus californicus, California buttercup—juice of plant

Vines
Clematis (all), clematis—leaves

Annuals
Eschscholzia (all), California poppy, frying pans—all parts
Lupinus (all), lupine—seeds, fresh leaves, and stems

RESISTANT TO OAK ROOT FUNGUS
Plants known to tolerate soils infected with oak root fungus.

Resistant to Oak Root Fungus: foothill sedge under valley oak.
CAROL BORNSTEIN

Trees
Acer macrophyllum, big-leaf maple
Aesculus californica, California buckeye
Arbutus menziesii, madrone
Calocedrus decurrens, incense cedar
Fraxinus dipetala, flowering ash
Quercus lobata, valley oak

Shrubs
Baccharis pilularis, coyote brush
Berberis (all), barberry
Calycanthus occidentalis, spicebush
Carpenteria californica, bush anemone

Cercis occidentalis, western redbud
Prunus (all), cherry
Sambucus (all), elderberry

Perennials
Carex (all), sedge

Ferns
Dryopteris arguta, coastal wood fern

Vines
Aristolochia californica, California Dutchman's pipe

SEASHORE CONDITIONS
Plants tolerant of exposed areas adjacent to the ocean where winds and salt spray are the norm. (Many other natives, too many to list, can safely be planted in coastal areas in protected sites beyond the ocean spray.)

Trees
Pinus contorta ssp. *contorta,* shore pine
Pinus radiata, Monterey pine
Pinus torreyana, Torrey pine

Shrubs and subshrubs
Arctostaphylos edmundsii, Edmunds manzanita
Arctostaphylos hookeri, Hooker manzanita
Arctostaphylos pumila, sandmat manzanita
Arctostaphylos uva-ursi, kinnikinnick
Artemisia californica, California sagebrush
Artemisia pycnocephala, sandhill sagebrush
Atriplex lentiformis ssp. *breweri,* quail bush
Baccharis pilularis, coyote brush
Ceanothus gloriosus, Point Reyes ceanothus
Ceanothus griseus (all except 'Diamond Heights'), Carmel ceanothus
Ceanothus hearstiorum, Hearst ceanothus
Ceanothus maritimus, maritime ceanothus
Ceanothus thyrsiflorus, blue blossom ceanothus
Cercocarpus betuloides, mountain mahogany
Coreopsis gigantea, giant coreopsis
Encelia californica, California sunflower
Eriogonum arborescens, Santa Cruz Island buckwheat
Eriogonum cinereum, ashyleaf buckwheat
Eriogonum fasciculatum 'Dana Point', Dana Point buckwheat
Eriogonum giganteum, Saint Catherine's lace
Eriogonum grande var. *rubescens,* red-flowered buckwheat
Eriogonum latifolium, coast buckwheat
Eriophyllum nevinii 'Canyon Silver', Canyon Silver island snowflake
Garrya elliptica, coast silk-tassel
Heteromeles arbutifolia, toyon
Isomeris arborea, bladderpod

Lavatera assurgentiflora, malva rosa
Lepechinia calycina 'Rocky Point', Rocky Point pitcher sage
Lupinus arboreus, yellow bush lupine
Myrica californica, Pacific wax myrtle
Prunus ilicifolia ssp. *ilicifolia,* hollyleaf cherry
Rhamnus californica, coffeeberry
Rhus integrifolia, lemonade berry
Rhus lentii, pink-flowering sumac
Salvia brandegeei, Brandegee sage
Salvia leucophylla, purple sage
Salvia mellifera, black sage
Salvia munzii, Munz sage

Seashore Conditions: seaside daisy. BART O'BRIEN

Perennials

Achillea millefolium, yarrow
Aster chilensis 'Point Saint George', Point Saint George aster
Carex praegracilis, dune sedge
Coreopsis maritima, sea dahlia
Erigeron glaucus, seaside daisy
Fragaria chiloensis, beach strawberry
Grindelia (all except *hirsutula*), gum plant
Iris douglasiana, Douglas iris
Juncus patens, wire grass
Lessingia filaginifolia, California aster
Sidalcea malviflora, checkerbloom
Tanacetum (all), dune tansy

Grasses

Festuca rubra, red fescue
Leymus condensatus, giant wild rye

Ferns

Polypodium scouleri, leather leaf polypody fern

Succulents

Agave shawii, Shaw agave
Dudleya brittonii, Britton dudleya
Dudleya 'Frank Reinelt', Frank Reinelt dudleya
Dudleya virens ssp. *hassei,* Catalina Island dudleya

SHELTERBELTS AND WINDBREAKS

Plants suitable for use in dense thickets and windbreaks.

Trees

Brahea (all), fan palm
Calocedrus decurrens, incense cedar
Chilopsis linearis, desert willow
✕*Chitalpa tashkentensis,* chitalpa
Cupressus forbesii, Tecate cypress
Lyonothamnus floribundus ssp. *aspleniifolius,* Santa Cruz Island ironwood
Pinus contorta ssp. *contorta,* shore pine
Pinus torreyana, Torrey pine
Populus (all), cottonwood, quaking aspen
Quercus agrifolia, coast live oak
Thuja plicata, western red cedar
Umbellularia californica, California bay
Washingtonia filifera, California fan palm
Yucca brevifolia, Joshua tree

Shrubs and subshrubs

Adenostoma (all except 'Black Diamond'), chamise, redshanks
Arctostaphylos 'Howard McMinn', Howard McMinn manzanita
Arctostaphylos 'Sunset', Sunset manzanita
Artemisia tridentata, Great Basin sagebrush
Atriplex lentiformis ssp. *breweri,* quail bush
Baccharis pilularis, coyote brush
Berberis nevinii, Nevin barberry
Berberis pinnata, California barberry
Ceanothus griseus (all except 'Diamond Heights'), Carmel ceanothus
Ceanothus thyrsiflorus, blue blossom ceanothus

Shelterbelts and Windbreaks: Pacific wax myrtle.
JOHN EVARTS

Cercis occidentalis, western redbud
Cercocarpus betuloides, mountain mahogany
Cornus sericea, creek dogwood
Eriogonum fasciculatum 'Dana Point', Dana Point
  buckwheat
Eriogonum giganteum, Saint Catherine's lace
Garrya elliptica, coast silk-tassel
Heteromeles arbutifolia, toyon
Isomeris arborea, bladderpod
Lavatera assurgentiflora, malva rosa
Myrica californica, Pacific wax myrtle
Ornithostaphylos oppositifolia, palo blanco
Prunus (all), cherry
Rhamnus (all), coffeeberry, redberry
Rhus (all), lemonade berry, sugar bush, etc.
Salvia leucophylla, purple sage
Salvia mellifera, black sage
Simmondsia chinensis, jojoba
Yucca baccata, banana yucca
Yucca schidigera, Mojave yucca

Grasses
Leymus cinereus, Great Basin wild rye
Leymus condensatus, giant wild rye
Muhlenbergia rigens, deer grass

SILVER, GRAY, WHITE, OR BLUE FOLIAGE
Plants with silver, gray, white, or blue foliage. Those
with an * have green forms as well. Coloration may
vary by season or geographic area.

Trees
Brahea armata, blue fan palm
Cercocarpus traskiae, Santa Catalina Island mountain
  mahogany
Pinus coulteri, Coulter pine
Pinus monophylla, singleleaf pinyon
Pinus quadrifolia*, Parry pinyon
Pinus sabiniana*, foothill pine
Pinus torreyana, Torrey pine
Quercus douglasii, blue oak
Quercus engelmannii, Engelmann oak
Sequoia sempervirens cultivars*, coast redwood
Yucca brevifolia, Joshua tree

Shrubs and subshrubs
Abutilon palmeri, Indian mallow
Arctostaphylos bakeri 'Louis Edmunds', Louis Edmunds
  manzanita
Arctostaphylos glauca, big berry manzanita
Arctostaphylos 'John Dourley', John Dourley manzanita
Arctostaphylos 'Pacific Mist', Pacific Mist manzanita
Arctostaphylos pajaroensis*, pajaro manzanita
Arctostaphylos pumila*, sandmat manzanita

Artemisia (all except *douglasiana*) sagebrush
Atriplex lentiformis ssp. *breweri,* quail bush
Berberis nevinii, Nevin barberry
Dendromecon (all), bush poppy, island bush poppy
Encelia farinosa, incienso
Eriogonum arborescens, Santa Cruz Island buckwheat
Eriogonum cinereum, ashyleaf buckwheat
Eriogonum crocatum, saffron buckwheat
Eriogonum latifolium*, coast buckwheat
Eriogonum umbellatum var. *polyanthum*,* sulfur buckwheat
Eriophyllum (all), golden yarrow, Canyon Silver island
  snowflake
Galvezia juncea*, Baja bush snapdragon
Hesperoyucca whipplei*, Our Lord's candle
Hyptis emoryi, desert lavendar
Isomeris arborea, bladderpod
Justicia californica*, chuparosa
Lepechinia* (all), pitcher sage
Lupinus albifrons, silver bush lupine
Lupinus excubitus, grape soda lupine
Malacothamnus arcuatus 'Edgewood', Edgewood bush
  mallow
Malacothamnus jonesii, Jones bush mallow
Monardella villosa var. *obispoensis,* San Luis Obispo
  coyote mint
Nolina* (all), beargrass
Perityle incana, Guadalupe Island rock daisy
Rhus lentii*, pink-flowering sumac
Salvia 'Allen Chickering', Allen Chickering sage
Salvia apiana, white sage
Salvia 'Aromas', Aromas sage
Salvia 'Bee's Bliss', Bee's Bliss sage
Salvia clevelandii, Cleveland sage
Salvia leucophylla, purple sage
Salvia 'Mrs. Beard', Mrs. Beard sage
Salvia 'Pozo Blue', Pozo Blue sage

*Silver, Gray, White, or Blue Foliage: island bush poppy and
Canyon Silver island snowflake.* JOHN EVARTS

Salvia 'Whirly Blue', Whirly Blue sage
Simmondsia chinensis*, jojoba
Solanum umbelliferum*, blue witch
Sphaeralcea ambigua*, apricot mallow
Yucca baccata*, banana yucca
Yucca schidigera*, Mojave yucca

Perennials
Achillea millefolium 'Calistoga', Calistoga yarrow
Asclepias speciosa, showy milkweed
Carex spissa, San Diego sedge
Juncus patens*, wire grass
Lessingia filaginifolia, California aster
Oenothera californica, California evening primrose
Penstemon centranthifolius, scarlet bugler
Penstemon grinnellii*, Grinnell penstemon
Penstemon newberryi var. *sonomensis*, Sonoma
    penstemon
Penstemon palmeri, Palmer penstemon
Penstemon × *parishii**, Parish penstemon
Penstemon spectabilis*, royal penstemon
Romneya coulteri, Matilija poppy
Tanacetum camphoratum*, dune tansy
Thalictrum fendleri var. *polycarpum*, western
    meadow rue
Wyethia mollis*, mountain mules ears
Zauschneria 'Calistoga', Calistoga California fuchsia
Zauschneria 'Catalina', Catalina California fuchsia
Zauschneria 'Everett's Choice', Everett's Choice
    California fuchsia
Zauschneria septentrionalis, Humboldt County fuchsia
Zauschneria 'Sierra Salmon', Sierra Salmon California
    fuchsia

Grasses
Calamagrostis foliosa, Cape Mendocino reedgrass
Festuca californica*, California fescue
Festuca idahoensis*, Idaho fescue
Festuca rubra 'Jughandle', Jughandle fescue
Festuca rubra 'Patrick's Point', Patrick's Point fescue
Leymus cinereus, Great Basin wild rye
Leymus condensatus 'Canyon Prince', Canyon Prince
    wild rye
Leymus triticoides 'Grey Dawn', Grey Dawn wild rye

Succulents
Agave deserti, desert agave
Agave utahensis, Utah agave
Dudleya* (all except *candelabrum*), dudleya
Lewisia cotyledon*, cliff-maids
Opuntia basilaris, beavertail cactus

Annuals
Eschscholzia californica*, California poppy
Platystemon californicus, cream cups

SLOW GROWING
Plants typically regarded as slow growing throughout
their lives. Those with an * are often slow growing for
the first few years, but then have a moderate to fast
growth rate.

Slow-Growing Plants: California Dutchman's pipe.
DAVID FROSS

Trees
Arbutus menziesii*, madrone
Brahea armata, blue fan palm
Fraxinus dipetala*, flowering ash
Pinus monophylla, singleleaf pinyon
Pinus quadrifolia, Parry pinyon
Quercus douglasii, blue oak
Quercus kelloggii, black oak
Umbellularia californica*, California bay
Yucca brevifolia*, Joshua tree

Shrubs
Acer circinatum, vine maple
Adenostoma fasciculatum 'Black Diamond', Black
    Diamond chamise
Berberis aquifolium var. *repens*, creeping barberry
Berberis nervosa, longleaf barberry
Comarostaphylis diversifolia, summer holly
Nolina (all), beargrass
Prunus* (all), cherry
Quercus durata, leather oak
Rhus* (all except *trilobata*) lemonade berry, sugar bush,
    pink-flowering sumac
Rosa minutifolia*, Baja littleleaf rose
Simmondsia chinensis*, jojoba
Yucca baccata*, banana yucca
Yucca schidigera*, Mojave yucca

Perennials
Wyethia (all), mules ears

Ferns
Dryopteris arguta*, coastal wood fern
Polypodium scouleri, leather leaf polypody fern

Vines
Aristolochia californica*, California Dutchman's pipe

Bulbs
Lilium humboldtii, Humboldt lily

SMALL TREES AND LARGE SHRUBS
Small trees, and large shrubs that can become treelike, either naturally or with pruning.

Trees
Aesculus californica, California buckeye
Brahea (all), fan palm
Cercidium floridum, palo verde (can be large in native habitat)
Chilopsis linearis, desert willow
Fraxinus dipetala, flowering ash
Pinus contorta ssp. *contorta,* shore pine
Pinus monophylla, singleleaf pinyon

Small Trees and Large Shrubs: Dr. Hurd manzanita, a cultivar of Parry manzanita. JOHN EVARTS

Pinus quadrifolia, Parry pinyon
Quercus douglasii, blue oak (can be large in native habitat)
✕*Chitalpa tashkentensis,* chitalpa
Yucca brevifolia, Joshua tree

Shrubs
Acer circinatum, vine maple
Adenostoma sparsifolium, redshanks
Arctostaphylos glauca, big berry manzanita
Arctostaphylos manzanita, Parry manzanita
Arctostaphylos refugioensis, Refugio manzanita
Ceanothus arboreus, island ceanothus
Ceanothus 'Gentian Plume', Gentian Plume ceanothus
Ceanothus 'Ray Hartman', Ray Hartman ceanothus
Ceanothus 'Sierra Blue', Sierra Blue ceanothus
Ceanothus thyrsiflorus (all except var. *repens*), blue blossom ceanothus
Cercis occidentalis, western redbud
Cercocarpus (all), mountain mahogany
Comarostaphylis diversifolia, summer holly
Cornus sericea, creek dogwood
Garrya elliptica, coast silk-tassel
Heteromeles arbutifolia, toyon
Myrica californica, Pacific wax myrtle
Nolina parryi, beargrass
Ornithostaphylos oppositifolia, palo blanco
Prunus (all), cherry
Rhamnus californica (all except Leatherleaf coffeeberry and Mound San Bruno coffeeberry), coffeeberry
Rhus (all except *trilobata*), lemonade berry, sugar bush, etc.
Sambucus (all), elderberry
Yucca schidigera, Mojave yucca

SPINY BARRIERS
Plants with spines, thorns, or other features that are unpleasant to encounter. They are good choices for security or perimeter plantings, especially when fences, walls, or other constructed barriers are not practical or allowed.

Trees
Cercidium floridum (some forms), palo verde
Yucca brevifolia, Joshua tree

Shrubs and subshrubs
Berberis (all except *aquifolium* var. *repens*), barberry
Fremontodendron (all), fremontia
Hesperoyucca whipplei, Our Lord's candle
Prunus ilicifolia ssp. *ilicifolia,* hollyleaf cherry
Quercus durata, leather oak
Ribes speciosum, fuchsia-flowered gooseberry
Rosa (all), wild rose
Yucca baccata, banana yucca
Yucca schidigera, Mojave yucca

Spiny Barriers: Shaw agave. DAVID FROSS

Perennials
Carex spissa, San Diego sedge
Juncus acutus ssp. *leopoldii,* spiny rush

Succulents
Agave (all), agave
Opuntia basilaris, beavertail cactus

SUCCULENTS AND COMPANIONS
Plants usually considered to be in the "cacti and succulent" group and plants that may be grown with them to create a desert-like effect.

Cacti and succulent group:
Agave (all), agave
Dudleya (all), dudleya
Hesperoyucca whipplei, Our Lord's candle
Lewisia cotyledon, cliff-maids
Nolina (all), beargrass
Opuntia basilaris, beavertail cactus
Yucca (all), yucca

Cacti and succulent companions:

Trees
Brahea (all), fan palm
Cercidium floridum, palo verde
Chilopsis linearis, desert willow
✕*Parkinsidium* 'Desert Museum', Desert Museum palo verde
Pinus monophylla, singleleaf pinyon
Pinus quadrifolia, Parry pinyon
Washingtonia filifera, California fan palm

Shrubs and subshrubs
Abutilon palmeri, Indian mallow
Adenostoma fasciculatum var. *prostratum,* prostrate chamise

Artemisia tridentata, Great Basin sagebrush
Calliandra eriophylla, fairy duster
Encelia farinosa, incienso
Eriogonum arborescens, Santa Cruz Island buckwheat
Eriogonum crocatum, saffron buckwheat
Eriogonum giganteum, Saint Catherine's lace
Galvezia juncea, Baja bush snapdragon
Hyptis emoryi, desert lavender
Justicia californica, chuparosa
Keckiella antirrhinoides, yellow keckiella
Ornithostaphylos oppositifolia, palo blanco
Rosa minutifolia, Baja littleleaf rose
Salvia apiana, white sage
Salvia clevelandii, Cleveland sage
Salvia munzii, Munz sage
Simmondsia chinensis, jojoba
Sphaeralcea ambigua, apricot mallow

Perennials
Datura wrightii, sacred datura
Heterotheca sessiliflora ssp. *bolanderi* 'San Bruno Mountain', San Bruno Mountain golden aster
Juncus patens, wire grass
Oenothera californica, California evening primrose
Penstemon (all except mountain species), penstemon

Grasses
Aristida purpurea var. *purpurea,* purple three-awn
Bothriochloa barbinodis, silver beardgrass
Bouteloua (all), grama grass
Leymus cinereus, Great Basin wild rye
Leymus condensatus 'Canyon Prince', Canyon Prince wild rye
Sporobolus airoides, alkali sacaton

Annuals
Phacelia campanularia, desert bluebells
Phacelia minor, California bells

Succulents and Companions: Britton dudleya. JOHN EVARTS

UNDER OAK TREES

Plants that have the ability to compete with the root system of a mature oak and need little or no irrigation in summer. (With the exception of black and valley oak, supplemental summer irrigation can injure California's native tree oaks.) Plants on this list may be grown under deciduous oaks. Those with an * can also be used under evergreen oaks.

Shrubs and subshrubs

Acer circinatum, vine maple
Arctostaphylos edmundsii, Edmunds manzanita
Arctostaphylos hookeri, Hooker manzanita
Arctostaphylos 'Howard McMinn', Howard McMinn manzanita
Arctostaphylos 'Pacific Mist', Pacific Mist manzanita
Arctostaphylos pumila, sandmat manzanita
Arctostaphylos 'Sentinel', Sentinel manzanita
Arctostaphylos 'Sunset', Sunset manzanita
Arctostaphylos uva-ursi, kinnikinnick
*Berberis** (all), barberry
Calycanthus occidentalis, spicebush
*Carpenteria californica**, bush anemone
Ceanothus arboreus, island ceanothus
Ceanothus 'Centennial'*, Centennial ceanothus
Ceanothus 'Far Horizons', Far Horizons ceanothus
Ceanothus gloriosus, Point Reyes ceanothus
*Ceanothus griseus**, Carmel ceanothus
Ceanothus 'Joyce Coulter', Joyce Coulter ceanothus
Ceanothus 'Ray Hartman', Ray Hartman ceanothus
Ceanothus 'Skylark', Skylark ceanothus
Ceanothus thyrsiflorus, blue blossom ceanothus
*Cercis occidentalis**, western redbud
Cercocarpus betuloides, mountain mahogany
Eriogonum latifolium, coast buckwheat
Eriogonum umbellatum var. *polyanthum,* sulfur buckwheat
*Galvezia speciosa**, island snapdragon
*Garrya elliptica**, coast silk-tassel
*Heteromeles arbutifolia**, toyon
*Keckiella cordifolia**, heartleaf keckiella
Lavatera assurgentiflora, malva rosa
Lepechinia (all), pitcher sage
Mimulus (all except *cardinalis* and *guttatus*), monkeyflower
Monardella villosa, coyote mint
Philadelphus lewisii, western mock orange
Prunus ilicifolia ssp. *ilicifolia,* hollyleaf cherry
*Rhamnus** (all), coffeeberry, redberry
Rhododendron occidentale, western azalea
*Rhus integrifolia**, lemonade berry
Rhus trilobata, basket bush
Ribes (all, with an * for *sanguineum* var. *glutinosum, speciosum,* and *viburnifolium*), currant, gooseberry
Rosa (all except *minutifolia*), wild rose
Salvia mellifera 'Terra Seca', Terra Seca sage
Salvia 'Mrs. Beard', Mrs. Beard sage

Under Oak Trees: Yankee Point ceanothus under coast live oak. JOHN EVARTS

*Symphoricarpos** (all), snowberry
*Venegasia carpesioides**, canyon sunflower

Perennials

Achillea millefolium, yarrow
*Aquilegia formosa**, western columbine
Artemisia douglasiana, mugwort
*Carex** (all except *spissa*), sedge
Erigeron (all), seaside daisy
Fragaria (all with an * for *vesca*), strawberry
Heuchera (all, with an * for *maxima*), coral bells
*Iris** (all), iris
*Juncus patens**, wire grass
*Ranunculus californicus**, California buttercup
*Salvia spathacea**, hummingbird sage
*Satureja** (all), yerba buena, monkeyflower savory
Sidalcea (all except *calycosa* ssp. *rhizomata*), checkerbloom
Sisyrinchium bellum, blue-eyed grass
*Solidago californica**, California goldenrod
Tanacetum camphoratum, dune tansy
Thalictrum fendleri var. *polycarpum**, western meadow rue
Zauschneria 'Summer Snow', Summer Snow California fuchsia

Grasses

Calamagrostis (all), reedgrass
*Festuca californica**, California fescue
*Leymus condensatus**, giant wild rye
Leymus triticoides 'Grey Dawn', Grey Dawn wild rye
*Melica imperfecta**, coast melic grass
Nassella (all), needlegrass

Ferns

*Dryopteris arguta**, coastal wood fern
*Polypodium californicum**, California polypody fern
*Woodwardia fimbriata**, giant chain fern

Succulents

Dudleya (all except *brittonii* and *pulverulenta*), dudleya

Vines

Aristolochia californica*, California Dutchman's pipe
Calystegia macrostegia ssp. *macrostegia* 'Anacapa Pink', Anacapa Pink California morning glory
Clematis* (all), clematis
Vitis (all), wild grape

Annuals

Clarkia concinna, red ribbons
Collinsia heterophylla*, Chinese houses
Nemophila (all), baby blue eyes, five spot
Phacelia tanacetifolia, tansy leaf phacelia
Platystemon californicus, cream cups
Stylomecon heterophylla, wind poppy

Bulbs

Calochortus albus*, white fairy lantern
Calochortus amabilis, golden fairy lantern
Dichelostemma ida-maia, firecracker flower
Lilium* (all), Humboldt lily, leopard lily
Triteleia (all), triteleia

WOODLAND GARDEN

Plants recommended for creating a woodland environment or for sites that already have mature trees.

Trees

Acer macrophyllum, big-leaf maple
Aesculus californica, California buckeye
Alnus (all), alder
Arbutus menziesii, madrone
Cupressus forbesii, Tecate cypress
Lyonothamnus floribundus ssp. *aspleniifolius*, Santa Cruz Island ironwood
Pinus (all), pine
Platanus racemosa, California sycamore
Populus (all), cottonwood, quaking aspen
Quercus (all) oak
Sequoia sempervirens, coast redwood
Thuja plicata, western red cedar
Umbellularia californica, California bay

Shrubs and subshrubs

Acer circinatum, vine maple
Berberis (all), barberry
Calycanthus occidentalis, spicebush
Carpenteria californica, bush anemone
Ceanothus arboreus, island ceanothus
Ceanothus 'Centennial', Centennial ceanothus
Ceanothus griseus, Carmel ceanothus
Ceanothus 'Ray Hartman', Ray Hartman ceanothus
Ceanothus thyrsiflorus, blue blossom ceanothus
Comarostaphylis diversifolia, summer holly
Cornus sericea, creek dogwood
Galvezia speciosa, island snapdragon
Garrya elliptica, coast silk-tassel
Heteromeles arbutifolia, toyon
Keckiella (all), keckiella
Lavatera (all), malva rosa, Purisima mallow
Lepechinia (all), pitcher sage
Mimulus (all), monkeyflower
Monardella villosa, coyote mint
Myrica californica, Pacific wax myrtle
Philadelphus (all), mock orange
Prunus (all), cherry
Quercus durata, leather oak
Rhamnus (all), coffeeberry, redberry
Rhododendron occidentale, western azalea
Rhus integrifolia, lemonade berry
Rhus trilobata, basket bush
Ribes (all), currant, gooseberry
Rosa (all except *minutifolia*), wild rose
Salvia 'Dara's Choice', Dara's Choice sage
Sambucus (all), elderberry
Solanum xanti, blue witch
Symphoricarpos (all), snowberry
Venegasia carpesioides, canyon sunflower

Perennials

Aquilegia formosa, western columbine
Artemisia douglasiana, mugwort
Asarum caudatum, wild ginger
Carex (all), sedge
Epipactis gigantea, stream orchid
Fragaria (all), strawberry
Heuchera (all), coral bells
Iris (all), iris

Woodland Garden: coral bells and currant under valley oak.
CAROL BORNSTEIN

Woodland Garden: canyon sunflower.
BART O'BRIEN

Juncus (all except *acutus*), wire grass, rush
Monardella macrantha 'Marian Sampson', Marian Sampson scarlet coyote mint
Oxalis oregana, redwood sorrel
Ranunculus californicus, California buttercup
Salvia spathacea, hummingbird sage
Satureja (all), yerba buena, monkeyflower savory
Sidalcea malviflora, checkerbloom
Solidago californica, California goldenrod
Thalictrum fendleri var. *polycarpum,* western meadow rue

Grasses
Calamagrostis nutkaensis, Pacific reedgrass

Festuca californica, California fescue
Festuca rubra, red fescue
Leymus condensatus, giant wild rye
Melica imperfecta, coast melic grass

Ferns
Adiantum (all), western five-fingered fern, southern maidenhair
Dryopteris arguta, coastal wood fern
Polypodium (all), polypody fern
Polystichum munitum, western sword fern
Woodwardia fimbriata, giant chain fern

Succulents
Dudleya cymosa, canyon dudleya

Vines
Aristolochia californica, California Dutchman's pipe
Clematis (all), clematis
Vitis (all), wild grape

Annuals
Clarkia concinna, red ribbons
Collinsia heterophylla, Chinese houses
Nemophila (all), five spot, baby blue eyes
Stylomecon heterophylla, wind poppy

Bulbs
Calochortus albus, white fairy lantern
Calochortus amabilis, golden fairy lantern
Lilium (all), Humboldt lily, leopard lily

Carmel Sur manzanita grown as a groundcover beneath oaks. STEPHEN INGRAM

APPENDIX A: PLACES TO SEE CALIFORNIA NATIVE PLANTS

Visiting gardens that feature California native plants is an excellent way to gather inspiration and ideas for your own native garden. The following list includes our recommendations of public gardens that exhibit native plants in a designed setting. Those with an * are particularly noteworthy for the wide diversity of natives in their displays. Your local chapter of the California Native Plant Society, botanic gardens, garden clubs, or native plant nurseries may also be able to direct you to private gardens in your area. For inspiration from the wild, consult *California's Wild Gardens* (see Bibliography), which describes some of California's most spectacular natural landscapes.

Bio Trek Rain Bird Ethnobotany Learning Center
Biological Sciences Department
California State Polytechnic University
3801 West Temple Avenue
Pomona, CA 91768
(909) 869-6701
www.csupomona.edu/~biotrek

CSUN Botanic Garden
California State University, Northridge
Biology Department
18111 Nordhoff Street
Northridge, CA 91330-8303
(818) 677-3496
www.csun.edu/botanicgarden

Descanso Gardens
1418 Descanso Drive
La Cañada Flintridge, CA 91011
(818) 949-4200
www.descanso.org

Foothill College Native Garden
southeast of the Horticulture Dept. greenhouses
12345 El Monte Road
Los Altos Hills, CA 94022
(650) 949-7777
www.foothill.fhda.edu/index.php

Fullerton Arboretum
1900 Associated Road
Fullerton, CA 92831
(714) 278-3579
www.arboretum.fullerton.edu

Gavilan College
5055 Santa Teresa Boulevard
Gilroy, CA 95020
(408) 848-4800
www.gavilan.edu

Golden West College Native Garden
Golden West College
15744 Golden West Street
Huntington Beach, CA 92647-2748
(714) 892-7711
www.gwc.info/index4.html

Huntington Botanical Gardens
1151 Oxford Road
San Marino, CA 91108
(626) 405-3500
www.huntington.org

Leaning Pine Arboretum*
Horticulture and Crop Science Department
California Polytechnic State University
San Luis Obispo, CA 93407
(805) 756-2888
www.dir.gardenweb.com/directory/calpoly

Lester Rowntree Native Plant Garden
25600 Hatton Road
Carmel, CA 93921

Lindsay Wildlife Museum
1931 First Avenue
Walnut Creek, CA 94597
(925) 935-1978
www.wildlife-museum.org

Living Desert Zoo and Gardens, The
47-900 Portola Avenue
Palm Desert, CA 92260
(760) 346-5694
www.livingdesert.org

Madrona Marsh Nature Center & Preserve
3201 Plaza del Amo
Torrance, CA 90503
(310) 782-3989
www.tprd.torrnet.com/marsh.htm

Mary DeDecker Native Plant Garden
Eastern California Museum
155 N. Grant Street
Independence, CA 93526
(760) 878-0258
www.bristleconecnps.org/dedecker.htm
www.countyofinyo.org/ecmuseum (museum info. only)

Mendocino Coast Botanical Gardens
18220 North Highway One
Fort Bragg, CA 95437
(707) 964-4352
www.gardenbythesea.org

Mourning Cloak Ranch and Botanical Gardens
22101 Old Town Road
Tehachapi, CA 93561
(661) 822-1661
www.mourningcloakranch.com

Nipomo Native Garden
Corner of El Camino Caballo and Pomeroy Streets,
    across from Nipomo Regional Park
Nipomo, CA 93444
(805) 929-6710
www.nipomonativegarden.org

Old Mill Foundation, The
1120 Old Mill Road
San Marino, CA 91108
(626) 449-5458
www.oldmill.info

Quail Botanical Gardens
230 Quail Gardens Drive
Encinitas, CA 92024
(760) 436-3036
www.qbgardens.com

Rancho Santa Ana Botanic Garden*
1500 North College Avenue
Claremont, CA 91711
(909) 625-8767
www.rsabg.org

Regional Parks Botanic Garden*
Wildcat Canyon Road (at the foot of South Park)
c/o Tilden Regional Park
Berkeley, CA 94708-2396
(510) 841-8732
www.nativeplants.org
www.ebparks.org/parks/bot.htm

San Diego Zoo's Wild Animal Park
15500 San Pasqual Valley Road
Escondido, CA 92027-7017
(760) 747-8702
www.sandiegozoo.org/CF/plants/index.cfm

San Francisco Botanical Garden at Strybing Arboretum*
Golden Gate Park
Ninth Avenue at Lincoln Way
San Francisco, CA 94122

(415) 661-1316
www.strybing.org

San Luis Obispo Botanical Garden
El Chorro Regional Park
Highway 1 between San Luis Obispo and Morro Bay
P.O. Box 4957
San Luis Obispo, CA 93403
(805) 546-3501
www.slobg.org

Santa Barbara Botanic Garden*
1212 Mission Canyon Road
Santa Barbara, CA 93105
(805) 682-4726
www.sbbg.org

SOKA University Botanical Center
26800 West Mulholland Highway
Calabasas, CA 91302-1950
(818) 880-6400
www.soka.edu/

Susanna Bixby Bryant Ranch House and Museum
5700 Susanna Bryant Drive
Yorba Linda, CA 92887
(714) 694-0235
www.ylpl.lib.ca.us/sbb.php

**Theodore Payne Foundation for Wild Flowers and
    Native Plants**
10459 Tuxford Street
Sun Valley, CA 91352-2116
(818) 768-1802
www.theodorepayne.org

University of California Botanical Garden*
200 Centennial Drive, #5045
Berkeley, CA 94720-5045
(510) 643-2755
www.botanicalgarden.berkeley.edu

University of California Davis Arboretum
One Shields Avenue
Davis, CA 95616-8526
(530) 752-4880
www.arboretum.ucdavis.edu

University of California Irvine Arboretum
Building 96
Irvine, CA 92697
(949) 824-5833
www.darwin.bio.uci.edu/arboretum

University of California Riverside Botanic Gardens
Riverside, CA 92521-0124
(951) 827-4650
www.gardens.ucr.edu

University of California Santa Cruz Arboretum
1156 High Street
Santa Cruz, CA 95064
(831) 427-2998
www2.ucsc.edu/arboretum

Wrigley Memorial and Botanical Garden
  (Catalina Island)
1400 Avalon Canyon Road
Avalon, CA 90704
(310) 510-2897
www.catalinaconservancy.org
www.catalina.com/memorial.html

Yerba Buena Nursery
19500 Skyline Boulevard
Woodside, CA 94062
(650) 851-1668
www.yerbabuenanursery.com

APPENDIX B: ADDITIONAL RESOURCES FOR NATIVE PLANT HORTICULTURE

A number of the botanic gardens that are listed in Appendix A, "Places to See California Native Plants," offer educational programs about native plant horticulture and actively support conservation of the state's flora through classes, field trips, symposiums, and publications. In addition, the following four organizations are valuable horticultural and botanical resources and promote the knowledge, preservation, and restoration of California's native flora.

California Invasive Plant Council
1442-A Walnut Street #462
Berkeley, CA 94709
(510) 843-3902
www.caleppc.org

California Native Grasslands Association
P.O. Box 72405
Davis, CA 95617
(530) 759-8458
(866) 456-2642
www.cnga.org

California Native Plant Society
2707 K Street, Suite 1
Sacramento, CA 95816-5113
(916) 447-2677
www.cnps.org

California Society for Ecological Restoration
2701 20th Street
Bakersfield, CA 93301-3334
Tel. (661) 634-9228
www.sercal.org

APPENDIX C: SOURCES OF CALIFORNIA NATIVE PLANTS

Aitkens's Salmon Creek Gardens
608 NW 119th Street
Vancouver, WA 98685
(360) 573-4472
www.flowerfantasy.net
mail order
irises

Bay View Gardens
1201 Bay Street
Santa Cruz, CA 95060
(831) 423-3656
mail order

irises

California Flora Nursery
P.O. Box 3
Fulton, CA 95439
(707) 528-8813
www.calfloranursery.com
retail, wholesale
perennials, shrubs, trees

Central Coast Wilds
114 Liberty Street
Santa Cruz, CA 95060

(831) 459-0655
www.centralcoastwilds.com
retail, wholesale, mail order
perennials, shrubs, trees

C.H. Baccus
900 Boynton Avenue
San Jose, CA 95117
(408) 244-2923
retail
bulbs

Circuit Rider Productions
9619 Old Redwood Highway
Windsor, CA 95492
(707) 838-6641
www.crpinc.org
retail, wholesale
annuals, perennials, shrubs, trees

Clyde Robin Seed Co, Inc.
P.O. Box 2366
Castro Valley, CA 94546
(510) 785-0425
www.clyderobin.com
retail, wholesale, mail order
seeds

ConservaSeed
P.O. Box 1069
Walnut Grove, CA 95690
(916) 776-1200
www.conservaseed.com
retail, wholesale, mail order
seeds

Cornflower Farms
P.O. Box 896
Elk Grove, CA 95759
(916) 689-1015
www.cornflowerfarms.com
retail, wholesale, mail order, contract growing
annuals, perennials, shrubs, trees

Elkhorn Native Plant Nursery
Moss Landing location
1957B Highway 1
Moss Landing, CA 95039
(831) 763-1207
Soquel location
3621 North Main Street
Soquel, CA 95073
(831) 476-4564
www.elkhornnursery.com
retail, wholesale, contract growing

perennials, shrubs, grasses, trees

El Nativo Growers, Inc.
200 South Peckham Road
Azusa, CA 91702
(626) 969-8449
www.elnativogrowers.com
wholesale, contract growing
perennials, shrubs, trees

Environmental Seed Producers, Inc.
P.O. Box 2709
Lompoc, CA 93438-2709
(805) 735-8888
www.espseeds.com
wholesale
seeds

Far West Bulb Farm
14499 Lower Colfax Road
Grass Valley, CA 95945
(530) 272-4775
www.californianativebulbs.com
mail order
bulbs

Floral Native Nursery
2511 Floral Avenue
Chico, CA 95973-2511
(530) 892-2511
floralnativenursery.com
retail, wholesale
perennials, shrubs, trees

Forestfarm
990 Tetherow Road
Williams, OR 97544-9599
(541) 846-7269
www.forestfarm.com
mail order
perennials, shrubs, trees

Freshwater Farms
5851 Myrtle Avenue
Eureka, CA 95503-9510
(800) 200-8969
(707) 444- 8261
www.freshwaterfarms.com
retail, wholesale, mail order, contract growing
seeds, perennials, shrubs, trees

Greenlee Nursery, Inc.
257 East Franklin Avenue
Pomona, CA 91766
(909) 629-9045

www.greenleenursery.com
retail by appointment only, wholesale
grasses

Greer Gardens
1280 Goodpasture Island Road
Eugene, OR 97401
(541) 686-8266
(800) 548-0111
www.greergardens.com
retail
rhododendrons, shrubs, trees

Growing Solutions
P.O. Box 30081
Santa Barbara, CA 93130
(805) 452-7561
www.solutions.org
wholesale, contract growing
perennials, shrubs, trees

Hedgerow Farms
21740 County Road 88
Winters, CA 95694
(530) 662-6847
www.hedgerowfarms.com
retail, wholesale, mail order, contract growing
grasses, seeds

High Country Gardens
2902 Rufina Street
Santa Fe, NM 87507
(800) 925-9387
www.highcountrygardens.com
mail order
seeds, annuals, perennials, shrubs, trees

Intermountain Nursery
30443 North Auberry Road
Prather, CA 93651-9600
(559) 855-3113
www.intermountainnursery.com
retail, wholesale
perennials, shrubs, trees

Iris Gallery, The
33450 Little Valley Road
Fort Bragg, CA 95437
(707) 964-7971
(800) 757-4747
www.allthingsiris.com
retail
irises

Jim Duggan Flower Nursery
638 Seabright Lane
Solana Beach, CA 92075
www.thebulbman.com
mail order
bulbs

J.L. Hudson, Seedsman
Star Route 2
Box 337
La Honda, CA 94020-9733
www.jlhudsonseeds.net
mail order
seed

Larner Seeds
235 Grove Road,
P.O. Box 407
Bolinas, CA 94924
(415) 868-9407
www.larnerseeds.com
retail, mail order
seeds, perennials, shrubs, trees

Las Pilitas Nursery
Escondido location
8331 Nelson Way
Escondido, CA 92026
(760) 749-5930
Santa Margarita location
3232 Las Pilitas Road
Santa Margarita, CA 93453
(805) 438-5992
www.laspilitas.com
retail, wholesale, mail order, contract growing
perennials, shrubs, trees

Living Desert Zoo and Gardens, The
47-900 Portola Avenue
Palm Desert, CA 92260
(760) 346-5694
www.livingdesert.org
retail
seeds, perennials, shrubs, trees

Manzanita Nursery
880 Chalk Hill Road
Solvang, CA 93463
(805) 688-9692
www.manzanitanursery.com
retail
perennials, shrubs, trees

Matilija Nursery
8225 Waters Road

Moorpark, CA 93021
(805) 523-8604
www.matilijanursery.com
retail, wholesale, mail order
perennials, shrubs, trees

Mockingbird Nursery
1670 Jackson Street
Riverside, CA 92506
(951) 780-3571
retail, wholesale, contract growing
perennials, shrubs, trees

Mostly Natives Nursery
27235 Highway 1
Tomales, CA 94971
(707) 878-2009
www.mostlynatives.com
retail
perennials, shrubs, trees

Mountain States Wholesale Nursery
10020 West Glendale Avenue
Glendale, AZ 85307
(800) 840-8509
(623) 247-8509
www.mswn.com
wholesale
perennials, shrubs, trees

Native Here Nursery
101 Golf Course Road
Tilden Park
Berkeley, CA 94708
(510) 549-0211
www.ebcnps.org/NativeHereHome.htm
retail
perennials, shrubs, trees

Native Revival Nursery
2600 Mar Vista Drive
Aptos, CA 95003
(831) 684-1811
www.nativerevival.com
retail, wholesale
perennials, shrubs, trees

Native Sons, Inc.
379 West El Campo Road
Arroyo Grande, CA 93420
(805) 481-5996
www.nativeson.com
wholesale
perennials, shrubs, trees

North Coast Native Nursery
2710 Chileno Valley Road
P.O. Box 660
Petaluma, CA 94953
(707) 769-1213
www.northcoastnativenursery.com
retail by appointment, wholesale, contract growing
perennials, shrubs, trees

Plants of the Southwest
3095 Agua Fria Road
Santa Fe, NM 87507
(505) 438-8888
(800) 788-7333
6680 4th Street NW
Albuquerque, NM 87107
(505)344-8830
www.plantsofthesouthwest.com
retail, wholesale, mail order
seeds, perennials, shrubs, trees

Rana Creek Habitat Restoration
35351 East Carmel Valley Road
Carmel, CA 93924
(831) 659-3820
www.ranacreek.com
wholesale, mail order, contract growing
seeds, perennials, shrubs, trees

Rancho Santa Ana Botanic Garden
1500 North College Avenue
Claremont, CA 91711
(909) 625-8767
www.rsabg.org
retail
seeds, perennials, shrubs, trees

Reveg Edge, The
P.O. Box 609
Redwood City, CA 94064
(650) 325-7333
www.ecoseeds.com/nature.html
mail order, contract growing
grasses, seeds

Rosendale Nursery
2660 East Lake Avenue
Watsonville, CA 95076.1420
(831) 728-2599
wholesale
perennials, shrubs, trees

Russell Graham Nursery
4030 Eagle Crest Road
Salem, OR 97304

(503) 362-1135
retail, wholesale
perennials

S&S Seeds
P.O. Box 1275
Carpinteria, CA 93014-1275
(805) 684-0436
www.ssseeds.com
mail order, wholesale, contract growing
seeds

San Marcos Growers
125 South San Marcos Road
Santa Barbara, CA 93111
P.O. Box 6827 (mail)
Santa Barbara, CA 93160
(805) 683-1561
www.smgrowers.com
wholesale
perennials, shrubs, trees

Santa Barbara Botanic Garden
Garden Growers Nursery
1212 Mission Canyon Road
Santa Barbara, CA 93105
(805) 682-4726 ext. 127
www.sbbg.org
retail
seeds, perennials, shrubs, trees

Santa Barbara Natives
16000-A Calle Real
Gaviota, CA 93117
(805) 698-4994
alac@sbnatives.com
retail, wholesale, contract growing
perennials

Seedhunt
P.O. Box 96
Freedom, CA 95019-0096
(831) 728-5131
www.seedhunt.com
mail order
seeds

Sierra Azul Nursery and Gardens
2660 East Lake Avenue
Watsonville, CA 95076
(831) 763-0939
www.sierraazul.com
retail
perennials, shrubs, trees

Siskiyou Rare Plant Nursery
2825 Cummings Road
Medford, OR 97501
(541) 772-6846
www.srpn.net
retail, mail order
perennials, shrubs, trees

slo starts
1858 Los Osos Valley Road
Los Osos, CA 93402
(805) 528-7533
wholesale
perennials, shrubs, trees

Specialty Oaks, Inc.
12552 Highway 29
Lower Lake, CA 95457
(707) 995-2275
www.specialtyoaks.com
wholesale
large oak trees

Stover Seed Company
1415 East 6th Street
P.O. Box 21488
Los Angeles, CA 90021
(800) 621-0315
(213) 626-9668
www.stoverseed.com
wholesale
seeds

Suncrest Nurseries, Inc.
400 Casserly Road
Watsonville, CA 95076
(800) 949-5064
(831) 728-2595
www.suncrestnurseries.com
wholesale
perennials, shrubs, trees

Sunset Coast Nursery
2745 Tierra Way
Aromas, CA 95004
(831) 726-1672
retail by appointment, wholesale, contract growing
perennials, shrubs, trees

Tarweed Native Plants
4520 Dundee Drive
Los Angeles, CA 90027-1214
(323) 663-0113
www.tarweednativeplants.com
retail, wholesale (both by appointment only)

perennials, shrubs, trees

Theodore Payne Foundation for Wild Flowers and Native Plants
10459 Tuxford Street
Sun Valley, CA 91352-2116
(818) 768-1802
www.theodorepayne.org
retail, mail order (seed only)
seeds, perennials, shrubs, trees

Tree of Life Nursery
33201 Ortega Highway
P.O. Box 635
San Juan Capistrano, CA 92693
(949) 728-0685
www.treeoflifenursery.com
retail on Fridays, wholesale, contract growing
perennials, shrubs, trees

Trillium Gardens
P.O. Box 803

Pleasant Hill, OR 97455
(541) 937-3073
retail by appointment, wholesale, mail order, contract growing
perennials, shrubs, trees

Wildwood Garden
P.O. Box 250
Mollalla, OR 97038
(503) 829-3102
irises
mail order

Yerba Buena Nursery
19500 Skyline Boulevard
Woodside, CA 94062
(650) 851-1668
www.yerbabuenanursery.com
retail
perennials, shrubs, trees

APPENDIX D: SCIENTIFIC NAMES FOR NON-FEATURED PLANTS

This list contains the names of plants that are not featured in the Plant Profiles section but are mentioned in the text or captions by common name only (with a few exceptions). They are presented here alphabetically by common name and followed by their scientific name. Entries with an * are California native plants. All of the featured plants in the Plant Profiles section are listed in the Index to Common and Scientific Plant Names beginning on page 260.

acacia, *Acacia* species
agapanthus, *Agapanthus* species
Aleppo pine, *Pinus halepensis*
aloe, *Aloe* species
alstroemeria, *Alstroemeria* species
Atrorubens currant, *Ribes sanguineum* 'Atrorubens'*
Australian tea tree, *Leptospermum laevigatum*
baboon flower, *Babiana* species
bermuda grass, *Cynodon dactylon*
bindweed, *Convolvulus arvensis*
bitterroot, *Lewisia rediviva**
blue fescue, *Festuca ovina* var. *glauca*
blue hibiscus, *Alyogyne huegelii*
blue marguerite, *Felicia amelloides*
bottlebrush, *Callistemon* species
bougainvillea, *Bougainvillea* species
boxwood, *Buxus* species

bristlecone pine, *Pinus longaeva**
brome grass, *Bromus* species
broom, *Cytisus* species
broom, *Genista* species
broom, *Spartium junceum*
cabbage rose, *Rosa centifolia*
cactus, Cactaceae family
California rose bay, *Rhododendron macrophyllum**
calla lily, *Zantedeschia* species
camellia, *Camellia* species
Cape ivy, *Delairea odorata* (formerly *Senecio mikanioides*)
castor bean, *Ricinus communis*
catalpa, *Catalpa bignonioides*
cherry, *Prunus* species
Chilean wine palm, *Jubaea chilensis*
citrus, *Citrus* species
clivia, *Clivia* species
cork oak, *Quercus suber*
creosote bush, *Larrea tridentata**
crocus, *Crocus* species
culinary sage, *Salvia officinalis*
daffodil, *Narcissus* species
eucalyptus, *Eucalyptus* species
eugenia, *Syzygium paniculatum* (formerly *Eugenia myrtifolia* and *Eugenia paniculata*)
Fastigiata Monterey cypress, *Cupressus macrocarpa* 'Fastigiata'*

fig, *Ficus carica*
filaree, *Erodium* species
freesia, *Freesia* species
freeway daisy, *Osteospermum fruticosum*
gazania, *Gazania* species
geranium, *Geranium* species
giant reedgrass, *Arundo donax*
giant sequoia, *Sequoiadendron giganteum**
gladiolus, *Gladiolus* species
goldenrod, *Solidago* species*
gray sedge, *Carex divulsa*
grevillea, *Grevillea* species
hellebore, *Helleborus* species
hen and chicks, *Echeveria* species
holly, *Ilex aquifolium*
Huachuca agave, *Agave parryi* var. *huachucensis*
ice plant, *Aptenia* species
ice plant, *Carpobrotus* species
ice plant, *Delosperma* species
ice plant, *Lampranthus* species
Indian hawthorn, *Rhaphiolepis indica*
interior live oak, *Quercus wislizeni**
    (formerly *Quercus wislizenii*)
Italian stone pine, *Pinus pinea*
jacaranda, *Jacaranda mimosifolia*
jade plant, *Crassula ovata* (formerly *Crassula argentea*)
Japanese maple, *Acer palmatum*
Japanese silver grass, *Miscanthus sinensis*
Jeffrey pine, *Pinus jeffreyi**
kangaroo paw, *Anigozanthos* species
lavender, *Lavandula* species
lilac, *Syringa* species
lilac vine, *Hardenbergia* species
lily, *Lilium* species
littleleaf palo verde, *Cercidium microphyllum**
London plane tree, *Platanus* × *acerifolia*
Mahogany Red California poppy, *Eschscholzia californica* 'Mahogany Red'*
maple, *Acer* species
marijuana, *Cannabis sativa*
Mendocino fritillary, *Fritillaria roderickii**
Mexican palo verde, *Parkinsonia aculeata*
mistletoe, *Arceuthobium* species*
mistletoe, *Phoradendron* species*
mustard, *Brassica* species
nasturtium, *Tropaeolum majus*
New Zealand flax, *Phormium* species
oleander, *Nerium oleander*
olive, *Olea europaea*
oregano, *Origanum* species
owl's clover, *Castilleja* species* (formerly *Orthocarpus*)
oxalis, *Oxalis* species
pachysandra, *Pachysandra terminalis*
pampas grass, *Cortaderia jubata*
pampas grass, *Cortaderia selloana*

panic veldt grass, *Ehrharta erecta*
Payne's lupine, *Lupinus paynei**
Payne's seacliff buckwheat, *Eriogonum parvifolium* var. *paynei**
pincushions, *Leucospermum* species
Pine Hill ceanothus, *Ceanothus roderickii**
Pitkin Marsh lily, *Lilium pardalinum* ssp. *pitkinense**
pittosporum, *Pittosporum* species
poison oak, *Toxicodendron diversilobum**
pomegranate, *Punica granatum*
pop weed, *Cardamine oligosperma**
protea, *Protea* species
puya, *Puya* species
ragweed, *Ambrosia* species*
restio, Restionaceae family
rockrose, *Cistus* species
rosemary, *Rosmarinus officinalis*
sand verbena, *Abronia umbellata**
Satin Mixed farewell to spring, *Clarkia amoena* 'Satin Mixed'*
Scott Mountains fawn lily, *Erythronium citrinum* var. *roderickii**
Shreve oak, *Quercus parvula* var. *shrevei**
Schoener's Nutkana rose, *Rosa* 'Schoener's Nutkana'*
silver shield, *Plectranthus argentatus*
snapdragon, *Antirrhinum majus*
strawberry tree, *Arbutus unedo*
sugar pine, *Pinus lambertiana**
Sundew frying pans, *Eschscholzia lobbii* 'Sundew'*
sweet bay laurel, *Laurus nobilis*
table grape, *Vitis vinifera*
tanbark oak, *Lithocarpus densiflora**
tansy, *Tanacetum vulgare*
Theodore Payne ceanothus, *Ceanothus* 'Theodore Payne'*
thyme, *Thymus* species
Tropical Surf sticky phacelia, *Phacelia viscida* 'Tropical Surf'*
trumpet vine, *Clytostoma callistegioides*
trumpet vine, *Distictis* species
tufted poppy, *Eschscholzia caespitosa**
tule, *Scirpus acutus* var. *occidentalis**
tulip, *Tulipa* species
Valentine shrubby monkeyflower, *Mimulus* 'Valentine'
watsonia, *Watsonia* species
western white pine, *Pinus monticola**
Wayne's Dwarf blue-eyed grass, *Sisyrinchium bellum* 'Wayne's Dwarf'*
Wheeler Canyon ceanothus, *Ceanothus* 'Wheeler Canyon'*
White Cloud Matilija poppy, *Romneya* 'White Cloud'*
wild oats, *Avena fatua*

CALIFORNIA TOPOGRAPHY MAP

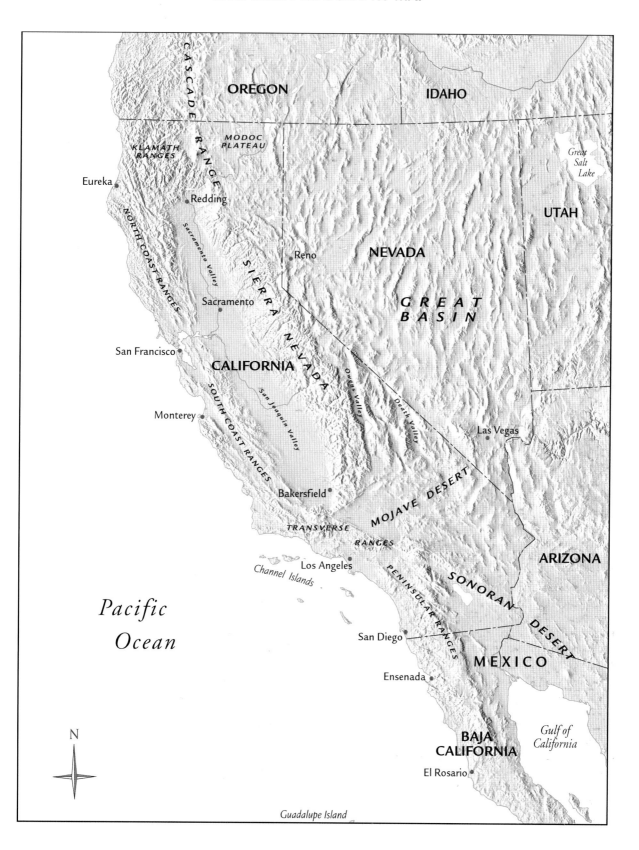

GLOSSARY

alternate. Leaves, buds, flowers, or branches arranged singly at different levels along a stem or axis, not opposite or whorled.

anther. The pollen-bearing part of a flower.

awn. A slender, usually terminal bristle.

axillary. Located in the upper angle between the stem and a leaf, branch, or flower.

bifacial leaves. Leaves with distinctly different upper and lower surfaces, usually in reference to color or hairiness.

bract. Reduced, modified leaf at the base of a flower, inflorescence, or cone.

BT *(Bacillus thuringiensis).* Bacteria that paralyze the gut of caterpillars, causing starvation and death.

burl. The dense, woody, often bulbous growth—usually located at or slightly below ground level—of some woody plants. Composed of densely packed dormant buds that typically grow after the aboveground portion of the plant has been damaged or destroyed.

California Floristic Province. That portion of the state of California— along with northwestern Baja California, Mexico and southwestern-most Oregon— that has a Mediterranean climate and a unique assemblage of plants. See also map on page 12.

calyx. The collective name for the sepals at the base of a flower.

catkin. A dense, narrow, scaly spike of flowers, often drooping or nodding.

caudex. The thickened woody, often succulent, base of a plant.

chlorosis. A condition typified by yellowish leaves with dark green veins and often caused by iron deficiency.

cool-season grass. A grass that usually grows and flowers during the cool months of the year.

coppice. A pruning practice traditionally applied to woody species that involves cutting the entire plant back to, or near, ground level.

corm. The fleshy bulb-like base of an underground stem.

cormel. A new corm arising from the original corm.

crown. The base of a plant where the aboveground portion meets the ground. Also the leaves and living branches of a tree.

culm. A hollow or pithy stem, typically of grasses, rushes, and sedges.

cultivar. Literally any "cultivated variety" that has been given a unique non-Latin name to differentiate it from other cultivars. Such names are always enclosed in single quotation marks: *Arctostaphylos* 'Sunset', *Ceanothus griseus* var. *horizontalis* 'Diamond Heights', etc. except when used as common names: Sunset manzanita, Diamond Heights ceanothus, etc.

deadheading. The pruning practice of removing individual flowers or inflorescences as they die, generally before they set seed. This action may promote further flower production and gives a clean look to the plant.

deciduous. Falling off, as with leaves or petals. At the onset of seasonal dormancy, some species naturally shed their leaves, such as maples and dogwood. Other species have vegetative growth that dies completely back to the ground when dormant, such as mules ears and California polypody. Grasses that are considered deciduous have foliage that persists but does not remain evergreen.

drift. An informal mass planting of a single plant. Drifts may be composed of as few as three to thousands of individual plants.

endemic. Native and restricted to a distinct geographic area, for example, endemic to Santa Cruz Island or the Big Sur coast. Also used for plants restricted to certain soil substrates, such as serpentine.

extirpation. Elimination of a species from part of its natural range.

fireblight. A bacterial pathogen *(Erwinia amylovora)* that affects plants in the rose family. The most obvious symptoms are young shoots and blossoms that appear wilted and blackened, as if scorched by fire.

fire-follower. A plant that typically grows most abundantly in the first few years immediately after a wildfire.

floriferous. Bearing many flowers.

geophyte. A perennial plant that grows from an underground storage organ. Examples include bulbs, corms, tubers, and rhizomes.

glabrous. Lacking hairs.

glaucous. Having a whitish or bluish coating, usually on leaves and stems, which may rub off when touched.

herbaceous. Lacking woody tissue.

inflorescence. The arrangement of flowers on a plant.

knot garden. An intricate planting of low-growing, usually meticulously clipped evergreen plants arranged in a geometric pattern.

lanceolate. Lance-shaped, much longer than broad.

lax. Loose.

monotypic. The only one of its kind. For example, Garryaceae is a monotypic family with only one genus, *Garrya. Simmondsia* is a monotypic genus with only one species, *S. chinensis.*

nectar guide. Markings on the petals or sepals of a flower that lead pollinators to the nectar.

node. Location where a leaf is connected to a stem.

opposite. Leaves, buds, flowers, or branches arranged directly across from each other along a stem or axis, not alternate or whorled.

palmate. Lobes, divisions, or veins arranged in a radiating pattern from a central point, as in the leaflets of California buckeye and lupines.

panicle. A many-branched inflorescence whose flowers open from the bottom upward.

perennial. A plant that lives for more than two years or growing seasons.

perianth. The collective petals (corolla) and sepals (calyx) of a flower.

petiole. The stalk of a leaf, which joins the leaf to a stem.

plumose. Feathery, with fine hairs or bristles on either side of an axis or in tufts.

pollen. The microspores produced in the anthers that fertilize the egg cells in the ovary; the equivalent of sperm in the animal kingdom.

pubescent. Covered with short, downy hairs.

raceme. An unbranched inflorescence with stalked flowers that open from the bottom upward.

ray. In the sunflower family (Asteraceae), the flat, strap-shaped "petal" of the ray floret. Ray florets usually surround a center formed of tubular disk flowers.

reflexed. Bent backward or downward.

rhizome. An underground stem growing horizontally at or just beneath the soil surface. A rhizome will often produce roots from its lower surface and shoots from its upper surface.

rockery. A natural or artificial assemblage of rocks, stones, and soil where rock garden species, such as cliff-maids, dudleyas, and other small plants, are grown.

rosette. A radiating cluster of leaves, often at or near the surface of the soil.

rust. A fungal disease characterized by the presence of powdery orange, yellow, or rust-colored pustules of spores.

samara. A winged, one-seeded fruit (achene).

selection. A plant collected or bred for a desirable feature.

senescent. Aging, growing old.

sepal. Individual part of the calyx, usually green. Sepals generally enclose the inner parts of a flower in bud.

spray. When used in a horticultural context, refers to a branch or stem with its leaves, flowers, or fruit; or to the flattened branchlets of some conifers.

stamen. The male portion of a flower, typically consisting of anther and filament, where pollen is produced.

stellate. Describes plant hairs that branch from the base and resemble diminutive stars.

stigma. The female portion of a flower on which the pollen germinates.

stolon. A horizontal stem that roots at a node, giving rise to a new plant.

string trimmer. A gasoline- or electric-powered tool with a blade or nylon string used to prune low-growing herbaceous plants or to control weeds. Also known as a weedeater or weedwhip.

subshrub. An herbaceous plant that develops a woody base, typically dying back seasonally.

succulent. Refers to thickened and fleshy water-storing stems, roots, and/or leaves. Also used to describe plants that possess these features.

thatch. In grasses, the tightly intermingled layer of dead and decaying tissue derived from stems, roots, and leaves.

tuft. A tight, dense clump.

umbel. An inflorescence with pedicels (stalks of individual flowers) arising from a common central point of attachment, usually with a flattened top.

Verticillium wilt. Disease caused by fungi in the genus *Verticillium;* affected plants often wilt and have yellowing leaves.

warm-season grass. A grass that typically grows and flowers during the warm months of the year.

water sprout. A rapid-growing vegetative shoot that develops from the root, crown, or stem of a plant, sometimes in response to a wound or pruning cut.

Western X disease. Caused by a phytoplasma (a unique type of bacteria), which is transmitted by leafhoppers. Affects hollyleaf cherry by causing constricted internodes and tiny leaves.

whorl. A ring of three or more similar structures, such as buds, shoots, flowers or leaves, arranged around the stem at a node.

whorled. Buds, shoots, flowers, or leaves arranged in a ring around the stem at a node; not opposite or alternate.

witches' broom. A tuft or cluster of congested, often thin stems found occasionally on shrubs and trees.

BIBLIOGRAPHY

Books, Bulletins, Interviews, and Reports

Bakker, Elna S. 1971. *An Island Called California: An Ecological Introduction to its Natural Communities.* Berkeley and Los Angeles: University of California Press.

Balls, Edward K. 1962. *Early Uses of California Plants.* Berkeley and Los Angeles: University of California Press.

Barbour, Michael G., and Jack Major, eds. 1977. *Terrestrial Vegetation of California.* New York: Wiley-Interscience, John Wiley & Sons. Expanded edition, Sacramento: California Native Plant Society, 1988.

Barbour, Michael G., Bruce Pavlik, Frank Drysdale, and Susan Lindstrom. 1993. *California's Changing Landscapes: Diversity and Conservation of California Vegetation.* Sacramento: California Native Plant Society.

Beck, Beatrice M. 1990. Drought Tolerant Planting Bibliography. Rancho Santa Ana Botanic Garden Technical Report No. 6. Claremont, CA: Rancho Santa Ana Botanic Garden.

Beck, Beatrice M. 1994. *Ethnobotany of the California Indians: Vol. 1, A Bibliography and Index.* Champaign, IL: Koeltz Scientific Books USA.

Blackburn, Thomas C., and Kat Anderson, eds. 1993. *Before the Wilderness: Environmental Management by Native Californians.* Menlo Park, CA: Ballena Press.

Brenzel, Kathleen Norris, ed. 2001. *Sunset Western Garden Book.* Menlo Park, CA: Sunset Publishing Corporation.

Busco, Janice, and Nancy R. Morin. 2003. *Native Plants for High-Elevation Western Gardens.* Golden, CO: Fulcrum Publishing, in partnership with The Arboretum at Flagstaff.

California Native Plant Society. 1977. *Native Plants – A Viable Option.* Special Publication #3. Sacramento: California Native Plant Society.

Chickering, Allen L. 1938. *Growing Calochortus. Monographs, Horticultural Series #1.* Santa Ana, CA: Rancho Santa Ana Botanic Garden.

Citron, Joan, ed. 2000. *Selected Plants for Southern California Gardens.* Los Angeles: Southern California Horticultural Society.

Coate, Barrie D., ed. 1980. *Selected Native Plants in Color.* Saratoga, CA: Saratoga Horticultural Foundation.

Coate, Barrie D. et al. 1986. *Water-Conserving Plants & Landscapes for the Bay Area.* Alamo, CA: East Bay Municipal Utility District.

Connelly, Kevin. 1991. *Gardener's Guide to California Wildflowers.* Sun Valley, CA: Theodore Payne Foundation.

Cornell, Ralph D. 1938. *Conspicuous California Plants, With Notes On Their Garden Uses.* Pasadena: San Pasqual Press.

Costello, Laurence R., Nelda P. Matheny, J. R. Clark, and Katherine S. Jones. 2000. A Guide to Estimating Irrigation Water Needs of Landscape Plantings in California: The Landscape Coefficient Method and WUCOLS III. University of California Cooperative Extension, California Department of Water Resources, United States Bureau of Reclamation.

Crampton, Beecher. 1974. *Grasses in California.* Berkeley and Los Angeles: University of California Press.

Dallman, Peter R. 1998. *Plant Life in the World's Mediterranean Climates.* Sacramento: California Native Plant Society; Berkeley and Los Angeles: University of California Press.

Darke, Rick. 1999. *The Color Encyclopedia of Ornamental Grasses.* Portland, OR: Timber Press.

De Hart, Jeanine. 1994. *Propagation Secrets for California Native Plants.* Encinitas, CA: J. De Hart.

Dreistadt, Steve H., Jack Kelly Clark, and Mary Louise Flint. 2004. *Pests of Landscape Trees and Shrubs An Integrated Pest Management Guide.* 2nd ed., Berkeley and Los Angeles: University of California Press.

Dobyns, Winifred Starr. 1931. *California Gardens.* New York: Macmillan Publishing Company.

Ehrlich, Paul R, David S. Dobkin, and Darryl Wheye. 1988. *The Birder's Handbook: A Field Guide to the Natural History of North American Birds.* New York: Simon and Schuster.

Ellstrand, Norman C. 2003. *Dangerous Liaisons? When Cultivated Plants Mate with Their Wild Relatives.* Baltimore and London: Johns Hopkins University Press.

Emery, Dara E. 1985. "Dara E. Emery Oral History. September 21, 1984 to June 24, 1985." Interview by Nancy Hawver. Tape recordings: fully indexed, partially transcribed. Santa Barbara: Santa Barbara Botanic Garden.

Emery, Dara E. 1988. *Seed Propagation of Native California Plants.* Santa Barbara: Santa Barbara Botanic Garden.

Everett, Percy C. 1957. *A Summary of the Culture of California Plants at the Rancho Santa Ana Botanic Garden 1927-1950.* Claremont, CA: Rancho Santa Ana Botanic Garden.

Faber, Phyllis M., ed. 1997. *California's Wild Gardens.* Sacramento: California Native Plant Society.

Flint, Mary Louise. 1998. *Pests of the Garden and Small*

Farm: A Grower's Guide to Using Less Pesticide. Berkeley and Los Angeles: University of California Press.

Flint, Mary Louise, and Steve H. Dreistadt. 1998. *Natural Enemies Handbook: The Illustrated Guide to Biological Pest Control.* Berkeley and Los Angeles: University of California Press.

Francis, Mark, and Andreas Reimann. 1999. *The California Landscape Garden.* Berkeley and Los Angeles: University of California Press.

French, Jere S. 1993. *The California Garden and the Landscape Architects Who Shaped It.* Washington, D. C.: Landscape Architecture Foundation.

Gabrielson, Ira N. 1932. *Western American Alpines.* New York: Macmillan Publishing Company.

Gildemeister, Heidi. 1995. *Mediterranean Gardening: A Waterwise Approach.* Palma de Mallorca, Spain: Editorial Moll.

Gildemeister, Heidi. 2004. *Gardening the Mediterranean Way: How to Create a Waterwise, Drought Tolerant Garden.* New York: Harry N. Abrams.

Gilmer, Maureen. 1994. *California Wildfire Landscaping.* Dallas: Taylor Publishing Company.

Glassberg, Jeffrey. 2001. *Butterflies Through Binoculars: The West. A Field Guide to the Butterflies of Western North America.* New York: Oxford University Press.

Greenlee, John. 1992. *The Encyclopedia of Ornamental Grasses.* Emmaus, PA: Rodale Press.

Grissell, Eric. 2001. *Insects and Gardens.* Portland, OR: Timber Press.

Hagen, Bruce W., Barrie D. Coate, and Keith Oldham. 1991. *Compatible Plants Under and Around Oaks.* Sacramento: California Oak Foundation.

Hardesty, Nancy M., and Associates. 1984. *Oak Woodland Preservation and Land Planning: Portola Valley Ranch.* Rev. ed., Menlo Park, CA: Hardesty Associates Landscape Architects.

Harlow, Nora, ed. 2004. *Plants and Landscapes for Summer-dry Climates of the San Francisco Bay Region.* Oakland: East Bay Municipal Utility District.

Harlow, Nora, and Kristin Jakob, eds. 2004. *Wild Lilies, Irises, and Grasses: Gardening with California Monocots.* Berkeley and Los Angeles: University of California Press.

Heath, Fred, and Herbert Clarke. 2004. *Introduction to Southern California Butterflies.* Missoula, MT: Mountain Press Publishing Company.

Heims, Dan, and Grahame Ware. 2005. *Heuchera and Heucherellas: Coral Bells and Foamy Bells.* Portland, OR: Timber Press.

Heritage Oak Committee. 1976. *Native Oaks, Our Valley Heritage.* Sacramento: Sacramento County Office of Education.

Hickman, James C., ed. 1993. *The Jepson Manual: Higher Plants of California.* Berkeley and Los Angeles: University of California Press.

Hogue, Charles L. 1993. *Insects of the Los Angeles Basin.* 2nd ed., Los Angeles: Natural History Museum of Los Angeles County.

Holland, V. L., and David J. Keil. 1995. *California Vegetation.* Dubuque, IA: Kendall/Hunt Publishing Company.

Hoover, Robert F. and Betty Hoover. 1972. *Native Plants in Our Garden.* San Luis Obispo, CA.

Isenberg, Gerda. 1991. "Gerda Isenberg: California Native Plants Nurserywoman, Civil Rights Activist, and Humanitarian." Interview by Suzanne B Riess. California Horticulture Oral History Series, Regional Oral History Office, The Bancroft Library, University of California, Berkeley.

Johnson, Eric A. 1997. *Pruning, Planting & Care: Johnson's Guide to Gardening – Plants for the Arid West.* Tucson: Ironwood Press.

Jones, Warren D., and Charles M. Sacamano. 2000. *Landscape Plants for Dry Regions.* Tucson: Fisher Books.

Junak, Steve, Tina Ayers, Randy Scott, Dieter Wilken, and David Young. 1995. *A Flora of Santa Cruz Island.* Santa Barbara: Santa Barbara Botanic Garden; Sacramento: California Native Plant Society.

Keator, Glenn. 1990. *Complete Garden Guide to the Native Perennials of California.* San Francisco: Chronicle Books.

Keator, Glenn. 1994. *Complete Garden Guide to the Native Shrubs of California.* San Francisco: Chronicle Books.

Keator, Glenn, Linda Yamane, and Ann Lewis. 1995. *In Full View: Three Ways of Seeing California Plants.* Berkeley: Heyday Books.

Keator, Glenn, and Susan Bazell. 1998. *The Life of an Oak: An Intimate Portrait.* Berkeley: Heyday Books; Oakland: California Oak Foundation.

Kruckeberg, Arthur R. 1982. *Gardening With Native Plants of the Pacific Northwest.* Seattle: University of Washington Press.

Labadie, Emile L. 1978. *Native Plants for Use in the California Landscape.* Sierra City, CA: Sierra City Press.

Landis, Betsey. 1999. *Southern California Native Plants for School Gardens.* Sacramento: California Native Plant Society.

Lanner, Ronald M. 1999. *Conifers of California.* Los Olivos, CA: Cachuma Press.

Lenz, Lee W. 1956. *Native Plants for California Gardens.* Claremont, CA: Rancho Santa Ana Botanic Garden.

Lenz, Lee W., and John Dourley. 1981. *California*

Native Trees and Shrubs For Garden & Environmental Use in Southern California And Adjacent Areas. Claremont, CA: Rancho Santa Ana Botanic Garden,

Lowry, Judith Larner. 1999. *Gardening with a Wild Heart: Restoring California's Native Landscapes at Home.* Berkeley and Los Angeles: University of California Press.

McMinn, Howard E. 1939. *An Illustrated Manual of California Shrubs.* San Francisco: J. W. Stacey.

Mielke, Judy. 1993. *Native Plants for Southwestern Landscapes.* Austin: University of Texas Press.

Munz, Philip A., and David D. Keck. 1973. *A California Flora with Supplement.* Berkeley and Los Angeles: University of California Press.

Munz, Philip A. 1974. *A Flora of Southern California.* Berkeley and Los Angeles: University of California Press.

Newman, Sarah R., Barbara Meacham, and A. L. Riley. 1981. Plants for California Landscapes: A Catalog of Drought Tolerant Plants. Bulletin 209. rev. ed., Sacramento: Resources Agency, Department of Water Resources, State of California.

Newton, Gail, and Laura Laidet. 1990. Nursery Sources for California Native Plants. Division of Mines and Geology Open-File Report 90-04. Sacramento: California Department of Conservation, Office of Mine Reclamation, Division of Mines and Geology.

O'Brien, Bart C., Lorrae C. Fuentes, and Lydia F. Newcombe, eds. 1997. *Out of the Wild and Into the Garden I.* California's Horticulturally Significant Plants. Rancho Santa Ana Botanic Garden Occasional Publications. Number 1. Claremont, CA: Rancho Santa Ana Botanic Garden.

O'Brien, Bart C., Lorrae C. Fuentes and Lydia F. Newcombe, eds. 1997. *Out of the Wild and Into the Garden II.* California's Horticulturally Significant Plants. Rancho Santa Ana Botanic Garden Occasional Publications. Number 2. Claremont, CA: Rancho Santa Ana Botanic Garden.

O'Brien, Bart C., Lorrae C. Fuentes, and Lydia F. Newcombe, eds. 1999. *Out of the Wild and Into the Garden III.* California's Horticulturally Significant Plants. Rancho Santa Ana Botanic Garden Occasional Publications. Number 3. Claremont, CA: Rancho Santa Ana Botanic Garden.

O'Brien, Bart C. 2000. *California Native Plant Gardens Care and Maintenance.* Claremont, CA: Rancho Santa Ana Botanic Garden.

Ogren, Thomas L. 2000. *Allergy-Free Gardening: A Revolutionary Approach to Healthy Landscaping.* Berkeley: Ten Speed Press.

Olkowski, William, Sheila Daar, and Helga Olkowski. 1991. *Common Sense Pest Control: Least-toxic Solutions for Your Home, Garden, Pets and Community.* Newtown, CT: Taunton Press.

Ornduff, Robert, Phyllis M. Faber, and Todd Keeler-Wolf. 2003. *Introduction to California Plant Life.* Berkeley and Los Angeles: University of California Press.

Padilla, Victoria. 1961. *Southern California Gardens: An Illustrated History.* Berkeley and Los Angeles: University of California Press.

Pavlik, Bruce M., Pamela C. Muick, Sharon Johnson, and Marjorie Popper. 1991. *Oaks of California.* Los Olivos, CA: Cachuma Press; Oakland: California Oak Foundation.

Payne, Theodore. 2004. *Theodore Payne In His Own Words: A Voice For California Native Plants.* Pasadena: Theodore Payne Foundation, and Many Moons Press.

Peattie, Donald Culross. 1953. *A Natural History of Western Trees.* Boston: Houghton Mifflin Co.

Perry, Robert C. 1980. *Trees and Shrubs for Dry California Landscapes.* San Dimas, CA: Land Design Publishing.

Perry, Robert C. 1992. *Landscape Plants for Western Regions.* Claremont, CA: Land Design Publishing.

Peterson, Roger Tory. 1990. *Western Birds.* 3rd ed., Boston: Houghton Mifflin Co.

Pittenger, Dennis R., ed. 2002. California Master Gardener Handbook. University of California, Agriculture and Natural Resources, Publication #3382.

Phillips, Steven J., and Patricia Wentworth Comus, eds. 2000. *A Natural History of the Sonoran Desert.* Tucson: Arizona-Sonora Desert Museum Press; Berkeley and Los Angeles: University of California Press.

Powell, Jerry A., and Charles L. Hogue. 1979. *California Insects.* Berkeley and Los Angeles: University of California Press.

Power, Nancy G. 1995. *The Gardens of California: Four Centuries of Design from Mission to Modern.* New York: Clarkson N. Potter.

Raven, Peter H., and Daniel Axelrod. 1995. *Origins and Relationships of the California Flora.* Sacramento: California Native Plant Society.

Roderick, Wayne. 1991. "Wayne Roderick: California Native Plantsman: UC Berkeley Botanical Garden, Tilden Botanic Garden." Interview by Suzanne B. Riess. California Horticulture Oral History Series, Regional Oral History Office, The Bancroft Library, University of California, Berkeley.

Roof, James B. 1959. *Guide to the Plant Species of the Regional Parks Botanic Garden.* Oakland: East Bay Regional Park District.

Rowntree, Lester. 1936. *Hardy Californians.* New York: Macmillan Publishing Company.

Rowntree, Lester. 1939. *Flowering Shrubs of California.*

Stanford: Stanford University Press.

Rowntree, Lester. 1979. "Lester Rowntree: California Native Plant Woman." Interview by Rosemary Levenson. Regional Oral History Office, The Bancroft Library, University of California, Berkeley.

Rundell, Phillip W., and Robert Gustafson. 2005. *Introduction to the Plant Life of Southern California.* Berkeley and Los Angeles: University of California Press.

Sawyer, John O., and Todd Keeler-Wolf. 1995. *A Manual of California Vegetation.* Sacramento: California Native Plant Society.

Schmidt, Marjorie G. 1980. *Growing California Native Plants.* Berkeley and Los Angeles: University of California Press.

Schoenherr, Allan A. 1992. *A Natural History of California.* Berkeley and Los Angeles: University of California Press.

Shepherd, Matthew, Stephen L. Buchman, Mace Vaughan, and Scott Hoffman Black. 2003. *Pollinator Conservation Handbook.* Portland, OR: Xerces Society, in association with The Bee Works.

Showers, Mary Ann. 1999. Nursery Sources for California Native Plants 1999. Division of Mines and Geology Open-File Report 90-04. 4th ed., California Department of Conservation, Office of Mine Reclamation; in cooperation with the Division of Mines and Geology, Sacramento, California.

Sibley, David Allen. 2000. *The Sibley Guide to Birds.* New York: Alfred A. Knopf.

Sibley, David Allen, Chris Elphick, and John B. Dunning, Jr. 2001. *The Sibley Guide to Bird Life and Behavior.* New York: Alfred A. Knopf.

Smith, Genny, ed 2000. *Sierra East: Edge of the Great Basin.* Berkeley and Los Angeles: University of California Press.

Streatfield, David C. 1994. *California Gardens: Creating a New Eden.* New York: Abbeville Press Publishers.

Stevens, Barbara, and Nancy Connor. 1997. *Where on Earth: A Guide to Specialty Nurseries and Other Resources for California Gardeners.* 3rd ed., Berkeley: Heyday Books.

Strike, Sandra. 1994. *Ethnobotany of the California Indians, Vol. 2: Aboriginal Uses of California's Indigenous Plants.* Champaign, IL: Koeltz Scientific Books USA.

Sutton, Sharon F., ed. 1976. Alpines of the Americas: the Report of the First Interim International Rock Garden Plant Conference, 1976. Northwestern Chapter of the American Rock Garden Society and the Alpine Garden Club of British Columbia.

Troetschler, Ruth, Alison Woodworth, Sonja Wilcomer, Janet Hoffmann, and Mary Allen. 1996. *Rebugging Your Home & Garden: a Step by Step Guide to Modern Pest Control.* Los Altos, CA: PTF Press.

University of California Agricultural Extension Service. 1966. Native California Plants for Ornamental Use. Leaflet 2831.

University of California Agricultural Extension Service. 1976. Growing Coast and Sierra Redwoods — Outside Their Natural Ranges. Leaflet 2706.

University of California Agricultural Extension Service. 1979. Oaks on Home Grounds. Leaflet 2783.

Urquhart, Peter. 1999. *The New Native Garden: Designing with Australian Plants.* Sydney: New Holland Publishers.

Van Rensselaer, Maunsell, and Howard E. McMinn. 1942. *Ceanothus.* Santa Barbara: Santa Barbara Botanic Garden.

Wasowski, Sally, with Andy Wasowski. 1995. *Native Gardens for Dry Climates.* New York: Clarkson Potter Publishers.

Wells, Philip V. 2000. *The Manzanitas of California: also of Mexico and the World.* Lawrence, KS: P. V. Wells.

Whitson, Tom D., ed. 1992. *Weeds of the West.* Revised ed. Newark, CA: The Western Society of Weed Science in cooperation with the Western United States Land Grant Universities Cooperative Extension Services and the University of Wyoming.

Wiggins, Ira L. 1980. *Flora of Baja California.* Stanford: Stanford University Press.

Wolf, Carl B. 1945. *California Wild Tree Crops.* Santa Ana, CA: Rancho Santa Ana Botanic Garden.

Wood, David L., Thomas W. Koerber, Robert F. Scharpf, and Andrew J. Storer. 2003. *Pests of the Native California Conifers.* Berkeley and Los Angeles: University of California Press.

Journals, Serials, and Web Sites
(Listed alphabetically by publisher.)

American Conifer Society. *Conifer Quarterly:* 2002 to date (and its predecessor, *American Conifer Society Bulletin:* 1983-2001). The Western Section of this society covers California. (www.conifersociety.org)

American Penstemon Society. *Bulletin of the American Penstemon Society:* 1946 to date.

Audubon Society. *Audubon:* 1961 to date (and its predecessors, *Audubon Magazine:* 1941-1961 and *Bird Lore:* 1899-1940). There are 51 California chapters of this national organization. (www.audubon.org)

Cactus and Succulent Society of America. *Cactus and Succulent Journal:* 1929 to date. There are 25 affiliate groups in California. (www.cssainc.org)

Calflora Database. A web site of California native plant habitat and distribution information, photographs, and more. (www.calflora.org)

California Invasive Plant Council. *Cal-IPC News:* 2003 to date (and its predecessor, *CalEPPC News:* 1993-2003). (www.caleppc.org)

California Native Grass Association. *Grasslands:* 1991 to date. (www.cnga.org)

California Native Plant Society. *Fremontia:* 1973 to date (and its predecessor, *The Bulletin:* 1965-1973). There are 33 chapters of this statewide organization. (www.cnps.org)

California Society for Ecological Restoration. *Ecesis:* 1991 to date. (www.sercal.org)

Calochortus Society. *Mariposa:* 1989 to date.

Regional Parks Botanic Garden. Berkeley, CA. *The Four Seasons:* 1964 to date and *Manzanita:* 1997 to date. (www.ebparks.org/parks/bot.htm)

Garden Media Incorporated. Van Nuys, CA. *The Southern California Gardener:* 1991-1999.

Growing Native Research Institute. *Growing Native:* #1 (1990) to #59 (2001). (www.growingnative.com)

International Bulb Society. *Herbertia:* 1934 to date (and its cohort, *Plant Life:* 1945-1948; combined editions titled *Plant Life* ran from 1949-1952). *Bulbs:* 1999 to date (and its predecessor, *The Underground:* 1995-1998). (www.bulbsociety.com)

James B. Roof. Orinda, CA. *The Changing Seasons:* 1979-1982.

LZS & Associates. Van Nuys, CA. *The Gardener's Companion:* 2000-2003.

Mediterranean Garden Society. *The Mediterranean Garden:* 1995 to date. There are three California branches of this international organization. (www.mediterraneangardensociety.org)

National Wildlife Federation. Backyard Wildlife Habitat program. *National Wildlife:* 1962 to date. (www.nwf.org/backyardwildlifehabitat)

North American Butterfly Association. *American Butterflies:* 1993 to date. *Butterfly Gardener:* 2001 to date (and its predecessor, *Butterfly Garden News:* 1996 to 2000) (www.naba.org)

North American Lily Society, Inc. *The Lily Yearbook:* 1947 to date (and its predecessor, *American Lily Year Book* for 1939, 1940, 1942, and 1946 by the American Horticultural Society). *The North American Lily Society Quarterly Bulletin:* 1947 to date. (www.lilies.org)

North American Rock Garden Society. *Rock Garden Quarterly:* 1995 to date (and its predecessor, *Bulletin of the American Rock Garden Society:* 1943-1994). There are three chapters based in California. (www.nargs.org)

Pacific Horticulture Foundation. *Pacific Horticulture:* 1976 to date (and its predecessor, *California Horticultural Society Journal:* 1940-1975). (www.pacifichorticulture.org)

Rancho Santa Ana Botanic Garden. Santa Ana, CA. *Leaflets of Popular Information:* #1 (1938) to #73 (1944). *Occasional Papers:* #1 (1935) and #2 (1938). *El Aliso:* A technical journal, though gardeners will find the following issue of interest: 1(1). 1948. Issue on cypresses including "Diseases of American Cypresses" and "Horticulture of New World Cypresses". (www.rsabg.org)

Rancho Santa Ana Botanic Garden. Claremont, CA. *Aliso:* A technical journal, though gardeners will find the following issues of interest: 2(2). 1950. The horticultural issue; and 9(1). 1977. "Rancho Santa Ana Botanic Garden. The First Fifty Years 1927-1977". *Newsletter:* 1985 to date. (www.rsabg.org)

Santa Barbara Botanic Garden. *Leaflets of the Santa Barbara Botanic Garden:* #1 (1944) to #13 (1977). *Newsletter:* 1975 to date. *Santa Barbara Botanic Garden Informational Bulletin:* #1 (1989) to date. (www.sbbg.org)

Society for Pacific Coast Native Iris. *Almanac:* 1973 to date. (www.pacificcoastiris.org)

Theodore Payne Foundation for Wild Flowers and Native Plants. *Poppy Print:* 1975 to date. (www.theodorepayne.org)

Xerces Society. *Wings:* 1974 to date. *Atala:* 1973-1990. (www.xerces.org)

INDEX TO SUBJECT MATTER

coffeeberry, 164-166
    Eve Case, 165
    Leatherleaf, 165
    Mound San Bruno, 165
Collinsia heterophylla, 201
Comarostaphylis diversifolia, 89-90
Compacta Oregon grape, 66
Constancea nevinii, see *Eriophyllum nevinii*
coral bells, 116-120
    Bella Blanca, 118
    Canyon Belle, 118
    Canyon Chimes, 118
    Canyon Delight, 118
    Canyon Duet, 118
    Canyon Melody, 118
    Canyon Pink, 118
    Chiqui, 119
    Chiquita, 119
    elegant, 117
    Genevieve, 119
    Lillian's Pink, 119
    mountain, 118
    Old La Rochette, 119
    Opal, 119
    Pink Wave, 118
    Rosada, 119
    Santa Ana Cardinal, 119
    Santa Rosa Mountains, 118
    Susanna, 119
    Wendy, 119
Coreopsis
    gigantea, 90-91
    maritima, 91
Cornus
    sericea, 91-92
    sericea 'Stinson Beach', 92
cottonwood
    black, 155
    Fremont, 154-155
    Nevada Fremont, 155
coyote brush, 64-65
    Pigeon Point, 65
    Twin Peaks #2, 65
coyote mint, 136-137
    Marian Sampson scarlet, 136
    San Luis Obispo, 137
cream cups, 209
creek dogwood, 91-92
    Stinson Beach, 92
Cupressus forbesii, 92
currant, 168-172
    chaparral, 169-170
    Claremont, 170
    Dancing Tassels, 170
    golden, 168-169

Inverness White, 170
Montara Rose, 170
Ortega Beauty, 170
Ortega Ruby, 170
pink-flowering, 170
southern chaparral, 170
Spring Showers, 170
Tranquillon Ridge, 170

Datura wrightii, 93
deer grass, 137-138
Dendromecon, 94
    harfordii, 94
    rigida, 94
desert bluebells, 208
desert lavender, 120
desert willow, 87-88
    Bubba, 88
    Burgundy Lace, 88
    Lois Adams, 88
    Mesquite Valley Pink, 88
    Regal, 88
    Warren Jones, 88
Dichelostemma
    capitatum, 213-214
    ida-maia, 214
Diplacus, see *Mimulus*
Douglas iris, 121-122
    Canyon Snow, 122
Dryopteris arguta, 94-95
dudleya, 95-97
    Britton, 96
    candleholder, 96
    canyon, 96
    Catalina Island, 97
    chalk, 96
    Frank Reinelt, 97
Dudleya, 95-97
    brittonii, 96
    candelabrum, 96
    cymosa, 96
    'Frank Reinelt', 97
    pulverulenta, 96
    virens ssp. *hassei,* 97
dune tansy, 187

elderberry
    red, 179
    western, 178-179
elegant clarkia, 201
Encelia
    californica, 97
    californica 'El Dorado', 97
    farinosa, 97
Epilobium, see *Zauschneria*

blue, 69-70
side-oats, 69
grand linanthus, 205
Grindelia
camporum, 113
hirsutula, 113
stricta var. *platyphylla*, 113
Guadalupe Island rock daisy, 146-147
gum plant
Great Valley, 113
hairy, 113
spreading, 113

Helianthus annuus, 203
Hesperoyucca whipplei, 113-114
Heteromeles
arbutifolia, 114-116
arbutifolia var. *cerina*, 116
arbutifolia var. *cerina* 'Davis Gold', 116
Heterotheca sessiliflora ssp. *bolanderi* 'San Bruno
Mountain', 116
Heuchera, 116-120
'Canyon Belle', 118
'Canyon Chimes', 118
'Canyon Delight', 118
'Canyon Duet', 118
'Canyon Melody', 118
'Canyon Pink', 118
'Chiqui', 119
elegans, 117
elegans 'Bella Blanca', 118
'Genevieve', 119
hirsutissima, 118
'Lillian's Pink', 119
maxima, 119
micrantha, 118
micrantha 'Martha Roderick', 118
'Old La Rochette', 119
'Opal', 119
parishii 'Chiquita', 119
'Pink Wave', 118
'Rosada', 119
rubescens, 118
'Santa Ana Cardinal', 119
'Susanna', 119
'Wendy', 119
hollyleaf cherry, 155-156
Humboldt County fuchsia, 197, 198
Hyptis emoryi, 120

incense cedar, 72
incienso, 97
Indian mallow, 42
iris, 120-122
Canyon Snow Douglas, 122

Douglas, 121-122
Oregon, 121
Pacific Coast hybrid, 122
Iris, 120-122
douglasiana, 121-122
douglasiana 'Canyon Snow', 122
innominata, 121
island snapdragon, 111-112
Bocarosa, 112
Firecracker, 112
island snowflake, 105
Canyon Silver, 105-106
Isomeris arborea, 122-123
Ithuriel's spear, 215
Queen Fabiola, 215
Iva hayesiana, 123

jojoba, 181-182
Joshua tree, 196-197
Juncus
acutus ssp. *leopoldii*, 124
effusus, 124
patens, 124
patens 'Carman's Gray', 124
patens 'Elk Blue', 124
patens 'Occidental Blue', 124
Justicia
californica, 124-125
californica 'Dick Tilforth', 125
californica 'Tecate Gold', 125

keckiella
heartleaf, 125-126
yellow, 126
Keckiella
antirrhinoides, 126
cordifolia, 125-126
kinnikinnick
Point Reyes, 57
Radiant, 57

Lavatera
assurgentiflora, 126
'Purisima', 126
Layia platyglossa, 204
lemonade berry, 166-167
Lepechinia, 127-128
calycina 'Rocky Point', 127
fragrans, 127-128
fragrans 'El Tigre', 128
Lessingia
filaginifolia, 128
filaginifolia 'Silver Carpet', 128
Lewisia
cotyledon, 128-129

pink mallow, 185
pink-flowering sumac, 168
Pinus, 148-151
    contorta ssp. *contorta,* 151
    coulteri, 148-149
    monophylla, 149
    quadrifolia, 151
    radiata, 151
    sabiniana, 150
    torreyana, 150-151
pinyon
    Parry, 151
    singleleaf, 149
pitcher sage, 127-128
    El Tigre, 128
    fragrant, 127-128
    Rocky Point, 127
Platanus racemosa, 152
Platystemon californicus, 209
Plena California wild rose, 173
Polypodium
    californicum, 153
    californicum 'Sarah Lyman', 153
    scouleri, 153
polypody
    California, 153
    leather leaf, 153
    Sarah Lyman California, 153
Polystichum munitum, 153-154
poppy
    California, 202
    Matilija, 172
    wind, 209
Populus
    balsamifera ssp. *trichocarpa,* 155
    fremontii, 154-155
    fremontii 'Nevada', 155
    tremuloides, 155
poverty weed, 123
Prunus
    ilicifolia ssp. *ilicifolia,* 155-156
    ilicifolia ssp. *lyonii,* 156
punch-bowl godetia, 201
Purisima mallow, 126
purple three-awn, 58

quail bush, 63-64
quaking aspen, 155
Quercus, 156-163
    agrifolia, 159-160
    douglasii, 160
    durata, 160-161
    engelmannii, 161
    kelloggii, 162
    lobata, 162-163

    tomentella, 163

Ranunculus californicus, 164
red ribbons, 201
redberry, 165-166
redshanks, 45
redwood sorrel, 143-144
reedgrass
    Cape Mendocino, 70-71
    Pacific, 71
Rhamnus
    californica, 164-165
    californica 'Eve Case', 165
    californica 'Leatherleaf', 165
    californica 'Mound San Bruno', 165
    crocea, 165-166
Rhododendron
    occidentale, 166
    occidentale 'Irene Koster', 166
Rhus
    integrifolia, 166-167
    lentii, 168
    ovata, 166-167
    trilobata, 168
Ribes, 168-172
    aureum var. *gracillimum,* 168-169
    malvaceum, 169-170
    malvaceum 'Dancing Tassels', 170
    malvaceum 'Montara Rose', 170
    malvaceum var. *viridifolium,* 170
    malvaceum var. *viridifolium* 'Ortega Beauty', 170
    malvaceum var. *viridifolium* 'Ortega Ruby', 170
    sanguineum var. *glutinosum,* 170
    sanguineum var. *glutinosum* 'Claremont', 170
    sanguineum var. *glutinosum* 'Inverness White', 170
    sanguineum var. *glutinosum* 'Spring Showers', 170
    sanguineum var. *glutinosum* 'Tranquillon Ridge', 170
    speciosum, 170-171
    viburnifolium, 171-172
Romneya coulteri, 172
Rosa
    californica, 172-173
    californica 'Plena', 173
    gymnocarpa, 173
    minutifolia, 173
    nutkana, 173
rose
    Baja littleleaf, 173
    California wild, 172-173
    Nootka, 173
    Plena California wild, 173
    wood, 173
rush
    soft, 124
    spiny, 124